Crete

RETIRÉ DE LA COLLECTION UNIVERSELLE

Bibliothèque et Archives nationales du Québec

Victoria Kyriakopoulos

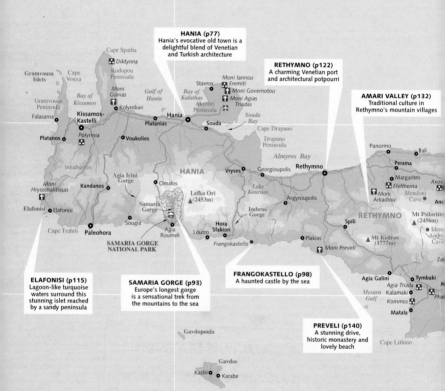

ELEVATION

	2000m
	1500m
	1000m
	500m
	0

LEGEND

	Freeway
	Primary Road
	Secondary Road
	Tertiary Road
	Unsealed Road

0 — 20 km
0 — 12 miles

SEA OF CRETE

HANIA (p77)
Hania's evocative old town is a delightful blend of Venetian and Turkish architecture

RETHYMNO (p122)
A charming Venetian port and architectural potpourri

AMARI VALLEY (p132)
Traditional culture in Rethymno's mountain villages

ELAFONISI (p115)
Lagoon-like turquoise waters surround this stunning islet reached by a sandy peninsula

SAMARIA GORGE (p93)
Europe's longest gorge is a sensational trek from the mountains to the sea

FRANGOKASTELLO (p98)
A haunted castle by the sea

PREVELI (p140)
A stunning drive, historic monastery and lovely beach

Cape Spatha
Diktynna
Gramvousa Islets
Cape Vouxa
Rodopou Peninsula
Moni Gonias
Gulf of Hania
Stavros
Moni Iannou Eremiti
Moni Governotou
Bay of Kalathas
Gramvousa Peninsula
Bay of Kissamos
Kolymbari
Akrotiri Peninsula
Moni Agias Triadas
Falasarna
Kissamos-Kastelli
Hania
Souda
Souda Bay
Cape Drapano
Platanias
Platanos
Polyrria
Voukolies
Drapano Peninsula
Almyros Bay
Panormo
Bali
Innahorion
Agia Irini Gorge
HANIA
Vryses
Georgioupolis
Rethymno
Perama
Margarites
Eleftherna
Axos
Moni Hrysoskalitissas
Kandanos
Omalos
Lefka Ori (2453m)
Lake Kournas
Argyroupolis
Moni Arkadiou
Sfendoni Cave
Anc
Elafonisi
Elafonisi
Samaria Gorge
Imbros Gorge
Spili
RETHYMNO
Mt Psiloritis (2456m)
Ideo Andro Cave
Cape Trahili
Paleohora
Sougia
Agia Roumeli
Hora Sfakion
Loutro
Plakias
Mt Kedros (1777m)
Moni Preveli
SAMARIA GORGE NATIONAL PARK
Frangokastello
Agia Galini
Tymbaki
Gavdopoula
Mesara Gulf
Agia Triada
Kalamaki
Kommos
Pha
Matala
Gavdos
Kastri
Karabe
Cape Lithino
24° E

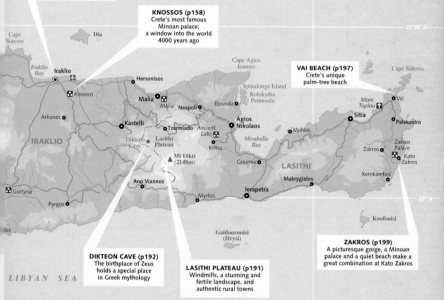

IRAKLIO (p147)
The treasures of Minoan
civilisation in the exceptional
Archaeological Museum

KNOSSOS (p158)
Crete's most famous
Minoan palace;
a window into the world
4000 years ago

VAI BEACH (p197)
Crete's unique
palm-tree beach

DIKTEON CAVE (p192)
The birthplace of Zeus
holds a special place
in Greek mythology

LASITHI PLATEAU (p191)
Windmills, a stunning and
fertile landscape, and
authentic rural towns

ZAKROS (p199)
A picturesque gorge, a Minoan
palace and a quiet beach make a
great combination at Kato Zakros

On the Road

VICTORIA KYRIAKOPOULOS

My last days on the road, I drove south through the mountains to Sougia. Something about this laid-back place draws you back. It's refreshingly undeveloped, the sea is clear, the long pebble beach isn't overrun by umbrellas and loungers, and there are a couple of friendly tavernas and relaxed open-air clubs if you ever tire of staring at the stars.

MY FAVOURITE TRIP

The best trips are those where one great experience follows another. From the historic Moni Odigitrias (p174) in southern Iraklio, I walked the stunning Agiofarango gorge (p174), passing climbers and goats and little cave chapels, to emerge at a spectacular beach for a swim. On the way back, I stopped for great traditional food at a village *kafeneio* run by friendly environmentalists.

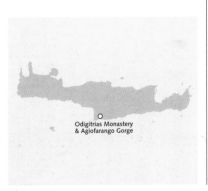

Odigitrias Monastery
& Agiofarango Gorge

AUTHOR

Victoria Kyriakopoulos is a freelance writer based in Melbourne. She has travelled widely throughout Greece since first visiting her parents' homeland in 1988. She may not have descended from Crete, but it feels like a second home after she spent several months exploring the hospitable island for the last two editions of Lonely Planet's *Crete*. Victoria is also the author of Lonely Planet's *Best of Athens*.

She lived in Athens between 2000 and 2004 where she covered the city's Olympics preparations and other events, edited the Greek diaspora magazine *Odyssey* and worked as a researcher for several TV programs about Greece. She has written about Greek cuisine for *Greek Gourmet Traveller* and other publications and is a restaurant reviewer for the *Age Good Food Guide*. She is regular contributor to the *Age* and other Australian and international publications, a former staff writer with the *Bulletin* and a media-relations consultant.

CRETE

People love Crete for very different reasons. This vast and hospitable island offers a unique and alluring combination of history and culture, beautiful beaches, dramatic mountains and gorges, sophisticated and historic towns, bustling resorts and traditional bucolic villages. You can start the day exploring ancient sites, visit historic monasteries, drive through spectacular mountains, stop for coffee at a traditional village *kafeneio* and end up swimming at a quiet cove and eating fish by the sea. It's impossible to experience all that Crete offers in one visit, but the island has a way of leaving you with enough to draw you back again.

Minoan & Ancient Crete

The glory of the Minoan civilisation that thrived in Crete more than 4000 years ago is present in the ruins of grand palaces and Minoan sites. The exquisite collections gracing museums around the island are also a window into the myths, legends and intrigue of Crete's ancient past.

❶ Iraklio Archaeological Museum

The most important Minoan treasures, including the famous frescoes from Knossos, are on show at the superb Archaeological Museum of Iraklio (p149).

❷ Knossos

Crete's most-visited site and former capital of the Minoan world, the palace of Knossos (p158) is the most significant and controversial Minoan site. The partly reconstructed palace gives you a real insight into the lifestyle of the Minoans.

❸ Phaestos

The impressive citadel of Phaestos (p169), the second most important Minoan site in Crete, is vast and intriguing. It's set in a stunning location overlooking the Mesara Plain and Mt Psiloritis.

❹ Zakros

The last of the Minoan palaces to be discovered, the isolated and evocative Zakros (p199) in the extreme east of the island allows visitors to combine the best of Crete. Reach the site by walking through the picturesque Gorge of the Dead and cool off afterwards at lovely Kato Zakros beach (p199).

❺ Malia

The palace at Malia (p178) revealed many exquisite artefacts from Minoan society. Malia is one of the better preserved and best presented Minoan sites, making it easy to envisage its original layout and splendour.

❻ Gortyna

Crete's largest archaeological site is the impressive Roman site at Gortyna (p168), from where the Dorians ruled the island. Stone tablets engraved with the 6th-century-BC Laws of Gortyna are the earliest law code in the Greek world.

Nature Trails

Crete's vast coastline offers endless beaches, while the hinterlands are dominated by soaring mountains, isolated plateaus, fertile valleys and picturesque gorges spilling out to the rugged south coast. Abundant wild flowers and diverse natural habitats make Crete a magnet for walkers, a botanist's and bird-watcher's paradise and a haven for those wanting to enjoy water sports and more extreme outdoor activities.

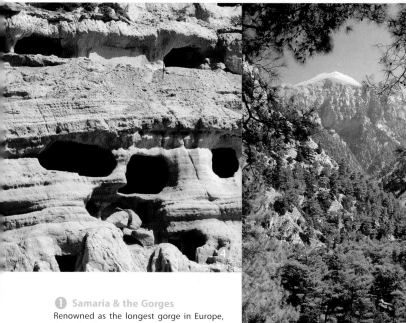

① Samaria & the Gorges

Renowned as the longest gorge in Europe, the 16km Samaria Gorge (p93) is one of the most stunning and must-do walks on Crete. Less taxing, but nonetheless impressive, gorges include the Imbros (p95), Agia Irini (p100) and Agiofarango (p174) gorges.

② Lasithi Plateau

The windmills of the fertile Lasithi Plateau (p191) are now almost outnumbered by cyclists, but it's a great place to get a glimpse of pastoral Crete and you can visit the Dikteon Cave (p192) where Zeus was allegedly born.

③ Outdoor Adventures

Thrillseekers can go paragliding over the hills of Avdou (p166), bungee jumping off the Aradena bridge (p97), canyoning through the Ha Gorge (p205) and climbing up the rockface of Mt Kofinas (p175).

④ Historic Caves

Crete has endless caves to explore, from the stalagmites and stalactites of Rethymno's impressive Sfendoni to the historic Melidoni cave (p135), with its moving memorial to martyrs who died there, and the famous hippie caves in the cliffs of Matala (p173).

⑤ Palm Beach

Palm-fringed Vai Beach (p197) in eastern Crete is Europe's only date-palm beach forest, with the trees reaching all the way to the sandy shore.

⑥ Isolated Beaches

The stunning lagoon-like white sandy beach of Balos (p111) is on the wild and remote Gramvousa Peninsula, while Rethymno's best beaches are the rugged south-coast beaches of Agios Pavlos and Triopetra (p141).

⑦ Mountain High

The striking Lefka Ori (p92) stay snow-capped well into the start of summer, while Crete's highest peak, the imposing Mt Psiloritis (p137) is entrenched in the island's folklore and mentioned in many songs. Both are part of the E4 European walking trail.

Legacies & Traditions

Crete's long and turbulent history is evident in the mix of Eastern and Western influences found across the island, from Venetian ports and fortresses to Ottoman minarets. Crete is dotted with Byzantine monasteries and chapels, while traditional handicrafts can still be found in local villages.

1 Venetian Fortresses

The remains of massive fortifications abound all over Crete. The impressive Frangokastello (p98) stands isolated on the southern coast; Iraklio's Koules Venetian fortress (p153) dominates the capital's harbour.

2 Spinalonga

Members of Spinalonga's infamous leper colony were the last inhabitants of this fascinatingly eerie island (p190), originally an (almost) impregnable Venetian fortress that eventually succumbed to Turkish sieges.

3 Monasteries

Moni Arkadiou (p134), with its impressive ornate façade and history, has become a symbol of the island's resistance and survival. The historic monasteries of Toplou (p196) and Agia Triada (p171) produce some of the best olive oil and wine on Crete.

4 Hania

Crete's most enchanting city, Hania (p78), has a delightful Venetian harbour and the cobbled streets of the evocative old town are full of atmospheric boutique hotels, romantic restaurants and artisans workshops.

5 Byzantine Art

The most outstanding frescoes are in the domed church of Panagia Kera (p187) near the village of Kritsa, while Iraklio's Museum of Religious Art (p153) has superb icons.

6 Rethymno

A massive *fortezza* stands sentinel above the pretty Venetian port of Rethymno (p121). The old town is a charming maze of narrow streets scattered with Venetian, Ottoman and Byzantine architecture.

7 Traditional Crafts

The pottery villages of Margarites (p134) and Thrapsano (p165) are thriving ceramic centres, where you can see potters at work and also buy some of their handiwork.

Inside Crete

Get out of the cities and coastal resorts if you want to see the heart and soul of Crete. The hinterland has a wealth of traditional mountain villages where you'll find old fashioned tavernas serving authentic Cretan fare. It's here where you'll best get a sense of Cretan provincial life.

❶ Traditional Villages

Anogia (p135) is arguably Crete's most emblematic village where many men still wear traditional dress and continue the region's strong musical tradition. But there are more remote mountain villages scattered throughout Crete, from the less-visited Innahorion (p113) villages in Hania, to the pretty Amari Valley (p132).

❷ Argyroupolis

The springs of Argyroupolis (p130) are a delightful watery oasis, with tavernas tucked among the waterfalls and spouting streams of the old water mills.

❸ Restored Settlements

The remote hamlet of Milia (p115) is an exemplary eco-lodge with rustic stone cottages, an organic farming operation and a taverna where you can have some of the best Cretan food on offer. Other traditional-style settlements include the village of Vamos (p119) and the unique settlement at Aspros Potamos (p206).

Contents

Regional Map Contents

Hania
p79

Rethymno
p122

Iraklio
p148

Lasithi p182

Destination Crete

Crete is a vast and fascinating island whose diversity and stature are unrivalled by any other Greek isle. The birthplace of Zeus evokes a wealth of myths, legends and history. Its sun-blessed and dramatic landscape is dominated by soaring mountains and stunning beaches. Its proud and hospitable people uphold their unique culture and traditions and, despite the onslaught of mass tourism, rural life remains a dynamic and enduring part of the island's soul.

Crete's rich mosaic presents visitors with an abundance of choices and experiences. The island's rugged interior is sliced by dramatic gorges and interspersed with fertile plains and hillsides blanketed in olive groves, vineyards, wildflowers and aromatic herbs. In the west thousands of people trek through the Samaria Gorge, reputedly Europe's longest, while the far east has Europe's only palm-tree-lined forest beach.

FAST FACTS:

Population 601,131

Area: 8336 sq km

GDP: €9 billion (5.3% of Greece's GDP)

Unemployment: 6.1%

Number of olive trees: 30 million

Percentage employed in tourism: 40

Annual number of visitors to Crete: 2.5 million

Number of visitors to Knossos in 2006: 705,305

Number of people who walked the Samaria Gorge in 2006: 176,747

Estimated number of guns: 1 million

Crete's natural beauty is equalled only by the richness of a history that spans millennia. The palace of Knossos is the most famous vestige of the glorious Minoan civilisation that once ruled the Aegean, and Minoan palaces and treasures can be found across the island. At the crossroads of three continents, Crete has been coveted and occupied by consecutive invaders. A profusion of evocative ruins reveals its turbulent past, from Roman settlements, Venetian fortresses, Ottoman mosques and Byzantine monasteries, while history comes alive in the charming old towns of Hania and Rethymno.

Crete has the dubious honour of hosting nearly a quarter of Greece's tourists but it's big enough for independent travellers to venture off and find their own style of travel, from world-class luxury resorts and spas and historic boutique hotels to restored stone cottages in mountain villages. Free spirits and naturists gravitate to the remote southern beaches and island of Gavdos; intrepid hikers explore the final leg of the E4 European walking trail; cyclists whizz around the Lasithi Plateau; while nature-lovers arrive en masse in spring to walk among the stunning wildflowers. Crete's terrain provides an exciting challenge for climbing, canyoning and all manner of extreme sports.

This is an ideal road-trip destination, with picturesque (and often harrowing) drives through the spectacular mountains leading to remote beaches, traditional mountain villages and isolated agricultural settlements.

While the renowned Cretan hospitality has been somewhat lost in the tourist-ridden resort towns, you can still find glimpses of the old Crete if you head off the beaten track. The 4WDs might outnumber the mules, but you'll inevitably stop to let a flock of goats cross the road and occasionally come across men in traditional dress at the village *kafeneio* (coffee house).

Cretans fiercely protect their culture and maintain a profound attachment to the traditions, music and dances that have forged their identity. Crete's distinctive cuisine and its abundance of fresh produce provide the elements for a developing gourmet trail.

A lively destination year-round, Greece's largest and wealthiest island may feel more like a small country, with its sprawling cosmopolitan capital, big cities and towns filled with sophisticated cafés, bars, restaurants, universities and commercial activity. Above all, Crete maintains its distinctive island identity and enduring allure.

Getting Started

Crete is an exciting destination but, unlike other Greek islands, it's not just a matter of hopping off the boat and taking it from there. Crete is a massive and extraordinarily diverse island open to endless exploration and experiences. Most people only ever scratch the surface of what it has to offer. You can pack a lot in with careful planning, especially if you base yourself in central Crete.

You will probably need to choose between the east and west, even between north and south, and take the time to explore one region thoroughly – it's a good excuse to come back and see the rest. In peak season, it is best to have booked accommodation, but most of the time you can find somewhere to stay.

Bear in mind that navigating the mountainous interior means zigzagging across the island, though the upside is that you see some spectacular territory and pass traditional villages on your way to that remote southern beach you're after. The distances aren't always huge, but winding through mountains can be hard going, so be realistic about how far you can drive in one day.

The best way to see Crete is by car or motorbike, but an extensive part of the island is accessible by bus.

WHEN TO GO

Crete's sunny disposition and long summers mean you can swim from mid-April to November, particularly off the southern coast. The best times to visit are in late spring/early summer and in autumn when the weather is not too hot for hiking and other outdoor activities. Conditions are perfect between Easter and late June, when the weather is pleasantly warm in most places, the sea warm enough for a swim, the wildflowers are in bloom, beaches and ancient sites are relatively uncrowded, public transport operates on close to full schedules, and accommodation is cheaper and easy to find.

The high season kicks in around late June and lasts until the end of August. Accommodation can be booked solid in August and is significantly more expensive. July and August are the hottest months and the most crowded, and while this is a great time for hanging out at the beach and enjoying balmy nights, it's tough-going traipsing around archaeological sites or walking in the heat. In July and August, the *meltemi* (strong northeasterly winds) can play havoc with ferry schedules and make sandy beaches unpleasant. There's usually no rain at all during summer. In winter, most beach resorts close down and tourist services and attractions are scaled right back, especially outside major cities.

See Climate Chart (p211) for more information on rainfall and temperature ranges throughout the year.

COSTS & MONEY

Crete is cheap by northern European standards, but not as cheap as it used to be, especially in the high season (July and August) when prices rise dramatically. The following budgets are for individuals; couples sharing a room and meals can get by on less. Add €25 to €30 per day for car hire.

A rock-bottom daily budget would require €30 to €40. This would mean taking buses, staying in hostels or camping, and only occasionally eating in tavernas and visiting sites and museums.

Allow at least €60 per day in the summertime for a simple room, meals in local tavernas, drinks at night and some sightseeing.

If you want more-comfortable hotels, good wine, and visits to restaurants, bars, museums and sites, you will need more than €100 per day.

An average taverna meal works out to about €10 to €15 per person including house wine; you can virtually double that for a fancier restaurant.

DON'T LEAVE HOME WITHOUT...

■ Sturdy walking shoes for clambering around ancient sites and hiking gorges.

■ Sunglasses, hat, sunscreen and mosquito repellent.

■ Swimming gear, shorts and light cotton clothing (a light sweater or jacket for evenings and when in the mountains).

■ A healthy appetite, adventurous palate and a stomach for raki.

■ Room enough in your bag to bring home some fabulous olive oil and bags of herbs.

■ Valid travel insurance, ID card or passport and driving licence.

■ A camera...Pic opportunities abound.

■ A compass, whistle and good maps if you are going to hike in remote areas.

■ A torch (flashlight) for occasional blackouts and for exploring caves.

■ Binoculars for checking out the birds.

■ A mobile phone so you don't feel left out (even the shepherds have one).

■ A Swiss Army knife for all eventualities (no Cretan would be without a knife).

BOOKS ABOUT CRETE

HOW MUCH?

Packet of 20 cigarettes €2.80

An iced cappuccino €3.50

A Greek salad €3.50

Double room at a 3-star hotel €70

Mixed drink at a bar €6

Crete is the subject of numerous travelogues and novels.

Essential reading includes Nikos Kazantzakis' classic *Zorba the Greek* (1946) and *Freedom and Death* (1950), both of which give a thoroughly engaging account of Cretan life, struggles and characters.

Falling for Icarus is a humorous and well-written memoir of English writer Rory MacLean's bizarre attempt to build a plane in Crete, helped by a colourful cast of Cretans.

The Island, by Victoria Hislop, is a compelling novel uncovering dark family secrets and delving into life on the Spinalonga leper colony.

Christopher Somerville writes a delightful and witty account of his midlife crisis walk across Crete's E4 trail in *The Golden Step: A Walk Through the Heart of Crete*, weaving in history and characters.

George Psychoundakis' *The Cretan Runner* is an exciting and personal account of the Cretan resistance. The author was a runner delivering messages to the Allies. It was translated into English by author and fellow Resistance fighter Patrick Leigh Fermor, who also wrote the introduction.

Across Crete, edited by Johan de Bakker, is the first of a three-part series that takes the reader from Hania to Iraklio as seen through the eyes of 18th- and 19th-century British travellers such as Richard Pokocke, Robert Pashley, Captain Spratt and Edward Lear.

Memory of Tides, by Angelo Loukakis is a moving novel about the parallel lives of a Greek-Australian soldier and a Cretan woman who meet during WWII, set in both Crete and Australia.

Winds of Crete, by David MacNeill Doren, is an amusing account of island life as experienced by an American and his Swedish wife.

INTERNET RESOURCES

Explore Crete (www.explorecrete.com) Good general travel site for Crete.

InfoCrete (www.infocrete.com) A site with about 100 Crete tourist-site web links.

Interkriti (www.interkriti.gr) Links to hotels, apartments, shops and restaurants, as well as an active bulletin board.

Greek National Tourism Organisation (www.visitgreece.gr) Has some information about Crete and links to the useful culture ministry site.

TOP PICKS

FESTIVALS & EVENTS

The Cretans take their festive occasions very seriously and use any excuse to get together for a big meal, good company, music and free-flowing raki. There are festivals dedicated to snails, chestnuts and potatoes, as well as religious and cultural events. For a comprehensive list of festivals, see p213.

- Carnival, Rethymno (three weeks before Lent)
- Feast of Agios Yiorgos (St George), Asi Gonia (23 April)
- Easter Festivities, mountain villages (March–April)
- Renaissance Festival, Rethymno (July–September)
- Iraklio Festival (July–August)
- Yakinthia Festival, Anogia (July)
- Sultana Festival, Sitia (August)
- Traditional Cretan Wedding (Kritsa; August)
- Raki distilling season, everywhere (October)

BEACHES

Crete has stunning beaches. The best are normally the hardest to get to, but the following are all accessible, some with a bit of a walk. Crowds can detract from many of the more popular beaches, but they are gorgeous nonetheless.

- Balos, Gramvousa Peninsula, Hania (p111)
- Agios Pavlos & Triopetra, Rethymno (141)
- Vai, Lasithi (p197)
- Elafonisi, Hania (p115)
- Falasarna, Hania (p112)
- Preveli Beach, Rethymno (p140)
- Agiofarango, Iraklio (p174)
- Kommos, Iraklio (p174)
- Hrysi Island, Lasithi(p204)

CRETAN VILAGES

Crete's mountains are dotted with authentic little villages that are a world away from the coastal tourist resorts. While some have become tourist attractions in themselves, you can still gain an insight into rural village life, especially after the last tour buses leave. Venturing off the beaten track leads to remote and unspoilt villages. These are some of the ones worth seeing:

- Argyroupolis (p130)
- Anogia (p135)
- Spili (p133)
- Margarites (p134)
- Kritsa (p186)
- Askyfou (p94)
- Maroulas (p132)
- Arhanes (p163)

Lonely Planet (www.lonelyplanet.com) Has information on Crete, as well as travel news, updates to our guidebooks and links to other travel resources.
Stigmes (www.forthnet.gr/stigmes/destcret.htm) Insightful Crete magazine.
West Crete (www.west-crete.com) Comprehensive guide to western Crete.

Itineraries
CLASSIC ROUTES

If you only have a week, this route takes in the island's major archaeological sites, a couple of stunning beaches and mountain villages, the Samaria Gorge and Crete's most picturesque towns. It's a jam-packed schedule covering about 320km.

CRETE HIGHLIGHTS
Seven days / 320km

Starting in **Iraklio** (p146), check out the superb archaeological museum and make the obligatory pilgrimage to the palace of **Knossos** (p158). On day two head south to explore the Roman **Gortyna** (p168) and the Minoan Palace of **Phaestos** (p169), stopping for a swim by the hippie caves at **Matala** (p172) or at nearby **Kommos** (p174). A visit to the excellent folk museum at **Vori** (p172) is a worthwhile detour. Spend the night by the beach or head inland to the village of **Zaros** (p166). Travelling west, stop in the village of **Spili** (p133) on the way to **Moni Preveli** (p140) and **Preveli Beach** (p141) and spend the night in **Plakias** (p138). Go north to **Rethymno** (p122) and spend a day exploring the old town. Heading west, stop at **Vryses** (p120) for lunch before driving to **Hania** (p78) for the evening. Take the early bus to the start of the **Samaria Gorge** (p93) and trek to Agia Roumeli, where you can take the boat west to **Loutro** (p98). The next morning take the boat to **Hora Sfakion** (p96) and bus it back to Hania.

SEA OF CRETE

LIBYAN SEA

CENTRAL-WEST CRETE
12 to 14 Days / 500km

This itinerary covers some of Crete's most stunning natural attractions, the unspoilt southern villages and its two most attractive towns. Starting in **Iraklio** (p146), head inland to **Anogia** (p136) and the villages and caves at the foothills of **Mt Psiloritis** (p137). Stop by the pottery village of **Margarites** (p134) and the historic **Moni Arkadiou** (p134) before spending some time in the Venetian port of **Rethymno** (p122) with its 16th-century fortress. Heading south, the fountains at **Spili** (p133) make a good coffee stop before a visit to **Moni Preveli** (p140) and **Preveli Beach** (p141). From here you could continue east to the stunning southern beaches of **Agios Pavlos & Triopetra** (p141) or head west to the traveller hang-out of **Plakias** (p138) and the beachfront fortress of **Frangokastello** (p98).

This covers a pretty thorough wish list of Crete's high-lights and involves lots of winding mountain drives. You should allow for plenty of stops and distractions. Total distance covered would be more than 500km.

Heading west through the Kourtoulioti Gorge you come to the coastal port of **Hora Sfakion** (p96). You can either take a boat trip along the southern coast to **Loutro** (p98) or **Sougia** (p100) and double back, or take the steep road north to the Lefka Ori along the **Imbros Gorge** (p95) to the mountain village of **Askyfou** (p94). Spend at least a day in alluring **Hania** (p78).

To the north, the **Akrotiri Peninsula** (p89) has some lovely monasteries and the famous beach at **Stavros** (p89) where *Zorba the Greek* was filmed. Take the circular route southwest via **Kolymbari** (p108) and the villages of **Innahorion** (p113), to the westernmost tip of the island at **Elafonisi** (p115).

Return to Hania via the coastal road, detouring to **Falasarna** (p112) and north to the **Gramvousa Peninsula** (p111) to the spectacular beach at **Balos** (p111). Returning east it's worth stopping at the springs of **Argyroupolis** (p130), southwest of Rethymno, and the lovely resort town of **Panormo** (p143), on the eastern coast heading to Iraklio.

TAILORED TRIPS

IN THE FOOTSTEPS OF THE MINOANS   Six to Seven Days / 400km

The Minoans knew how to choose their real estate so this is not a bad way to see some of the best spots on the island. Allow at least half a day at the museum in **Iraklio** (p146) to appreciate the richness of Minoan civilisation through the treasures found at the major sites. After exploring the palace at **Knossos** (p158), take a short detour to the sanctuary of **Anemospilia** (p164). At **Arhanes** (p163), you can stop at the excellent small museum and the **Vathypetro Villa** (p164) nearby, which was probably the house of a Minoan noble.

Head east inland or along the coast to the palace of **Malia** (p178), and then to the important site of **Gournia** (p192), about 19km southeast of Agios Nikolaos. Continuing east veer off the highway to the seaside village of **Mohlos** (p193), where there are tombs near the cliffs and an islet opposite with the ruins of Minoan houses. Continue east past Sitia to **Palekastro** (p197), where ongoing excavations are expected to uncover a major palace. The palace of **Zakros** (p199) is ideally located next to the lovely beach of **Kato Zakros** (see p200) and the Zakros Gorge. It is a long drive west cutting inland to the major palace at **Phaestos** (p169) and the summer villa at **Agia Triada** (p171). The minor sites at **Kamilari** (p174) and **Kommos** (p103) are next to good beaches.

GORGES & SOUTH COAST TOWNS   Three to Five Days / 120km

This itinerary combines a trek through two stunning gorges, including the famous Samaria Gorge, and a boat trip to a couple of great beaches. It is best done by bus and you need to be travelling very light or organise to have your luggage delivered ahead in a few places. From **Hania** (p78) take the early bus

to **Omalos** (p92) and walk through the **Samaria Gorge** (p93), leaving early to ensure you get to **Agia Roumeli** (p95) in time to cool off with a swim and catch the afternoon boat to **Sougia** (p100). Rest your weary body at this laid-back beach community in preparation for a 7km walk down the smaller **Agia Irini Gorge** (p101) the next day. A bus or taxi from Sougia takes you to the start of the gorge and it is a reasonable walk back. The next day you can take the boat to **Paleohora** (p102). You can also take the stunning **coastal walk** (p106) from Sougia to Paleohora, which is one of the most popular parts of the E4 trail, stopping at the ruins of ancient **Lissos** (p102). Relax in Paleohora before taking the bus back to Hania.

History

Crete's colourful history goes back 5000 years and is evident across the island, from ancient palaces and Roman cities to spectacular Byzantine churches, Venetian fortresses and Ottoman buildings. Crete's prominent place in world history is a legacy of the illustrious Minoan civilisation that was living in grand palaces when the rest of Europe was still in primitive huts. Crete has also left an indelible mark in the popular imagination because of its prominent place in ancient Greek mythology. It was where Rhea gave birth to Zeus and hid him from his child-gobbling father, and it was Zeus' son Minos who became the legendary King of Minoan Crete. Icarus and Daedalus launched their ill-fated flight in Crete, while Theseus made the voyage from Athens to Crete to slay the Minotaur in the famous labyrinth.

Crete's more recent history has been characterised by war and struggle, as the island was a strategic pawn in the battles for control of the Mediterranean. Crete has been invaded numerous times and ruled by eight different foreign powers since Minoan times – by the Mycenaeans, Dorians, Romans, Venetians, Byzantines, Arabs, Ottomans and Germans. That Crete only united with Greece in 1913 explains its enduring independent spirit.

The mythical Talos, a bronze giant, is believed to be the first robot invented. Hephaestus offered him as a servant to King Minos. He had one vein from neck to ankle, where a bronze nail retained the blood.

THE MINOANS

The Minoans were the first advanced civilisation to emerge in Europe in the Bronze Age, predating the great Mycenaean civilisation on the Greek mainland. Minoan civilisation drew its inspiration from two great Middle Eastern civilisations: the Mesopotamian and Egyptian. Immigrants arriving from Anatolia around 3000 BC brought with them the skills necessary for making bronze, a technological quantum leap that enabled the emerging Minoans to flourish almost uninterrupted for over one-and-a-half millennia.

While many aspects of Neolithic life endured during the Early Minoan period, the advent of bronze allowed the Minoans to build better boats and thus expand their trade opportunities. Pottery and goldsmithing became more sophisticated, foreshadowing the subsequent great achievements of Minoan art, and the island prospered from trade.

Controversy still shrouds the mysterious Minoans. Evidence uncovered in the grand palaces on Crete indicates they were a peaceful, sophisticated, well-organised and prosperous civilisation with robust international trade, splendid architecture and art and seemingly equal status for women. They had highly developed agriculture, an extensive irrigation system as well as advanced hydraulic sewerage systems. They may have spoken an early Indo-Iranian

TIMELINE

6500 BC	3000 BC	2000 BC
Crete's early inhabitants hunt and fish and engage in ancestor worship. Neolithic people live in caves or wooden houses, worship female fertility goddesses, farm, raise livestock and make primitive pottery.	Immigrants from the North African or Levantine mainland arrive with the skills for making bronze, heralding the Bronze Age in Crete. In this Pre-Palatial period, society changes; the inhabitants begin to trade; pottery and jewellery making develops.	The first palaces are built in Knossos, Phaestos, Malia and Zakros. Minoan civilisation reaches its peak. Architectural advances are accompanied by great strides in pottery production techniques. The first Cretan script emerges.

KING MINOS: MAN OR MYTH?

The legend of King Minos has captured the imagination of generations of scholars intent on finding evidence of the events described by Homer in *The Odyssey*: 'Out on the dark blue sea there lies a rich and lovely land called Crete that is densely populated and boasts 90 cities… One of the 90 cities is called Knossos and there for nine years, King Minos ruled and enjoyed the friendship of the mighty.'

The legendary ruler of Crete was the son of Zeus and Europa and attained the Cretan throne with the help of Poseidon. With Knossos as his base, Minos gained control over the whole Aegean basin, colonising many of the islands and ridding the seas of pirates. He married Pasiphae, the daughter of Helios, who bore him a number of children, including the infamous half-bull, half-human Minotaur.

How long King Minos actually reigned, however, is open to debate. The Homeric reference *enneaoros* used to describe Minos could mean 'for nine years' or 'from the age of nine years'. Was Minos able to create an empire in nine short years, or was he a long-reigning monarch who started his kingly career as a boy? He eventually came to a nasty end in Sicily when the daughters of King Kokalios poured boiling water over him as he was taking a bath.

---

language, and the accounts and records left behind suggest their society was organised as an efficient and bureaucratic commercial enterprise.

Although the evidence for a matriarchal society is scant, women apparently enjoyed a great degree of freedom and autonomy. Minoan art shows women participating in games, hunting and all public and religious festivals. They also served as priestesses, administrators and participated in the trades.

Not everyone buys into this rosy account of life in Minoan times; one radical archaeologist claims it was more likely a sinister society based on a death cult, with sacrificial orgies, and even argues that the distinctive giant *pithoi* were used as burial urns, not storage.

Even the chronology on the Minoan age is still debated. But most archaeologists generally split the Minoan period into three phases: Protopalatial (3400–2100 BC), Neopalatial (2100–1450 BC) and Postpalatial (1450–1200 BC). These periods roughly correspond, with some overlap, to the older divisions of Early Minoan (some parts also called Pre-Palatial), Middle Minoan and Late Minoan (the terms are used interchangeably throughout this book).

The Minoan civilisation reached its peak during the Protopalatial period, also called the Old Palace or Middle Minoan period. Around 2000 BC, the large palace complexes of Knossos, Phaestos, Malia and Zakros were built, marking a sharp break with Neolithic village life.

During this period, Crete is believed to have been governed by local rulers, with the island's power and wealth concentrated at Knossos. Society was organised on hierarchical lines, with a large population of slaves, and there were great architectural advances.

> For photos and descriptions of more than 50 Minoan sites around Crete, see archaeology buff Ian Swindle's comprehensive website at www.uk.digiserve.com/mentor/minoan/index.htm.

1700 BC	1450 BC	1400 BC
Minoan palaces are destroyed, most likely by an earthquake. The Minoans rebuild the palaces to a more complex and lavish design with multiple storeys, storerooms, workshops, living quarters for staff and an advanced drainage system.	Minoan culture comes to an abrupt and unexplained halt. The palaces (except Knossos) are destroyed in what archaeologists now believe was a massive tsunami following the earthquake in Thira (Santorini).	The Mycenaeans colonise Crete, building new cities such as Lappa (Argyroupolis), Kydonia (Hania) and Polyrrinia. The manufacture of weapons flourishes, the fine arts fall into decline. Greek gods replace worship of the Mother Goddess.

The first Cretan script also emerged during this period. At first highly pictorial, the writing gradually changed from the representations of natural objects to more abstract figures that resembled Egyptian hieroglyphics.

In 1700 BC the palaces were suddenly destroyed by what most archaeologists believe was an earthquake. In what is considered the Minoan golden age, the Minoans then rebuilt the palaces at Knossos, Phaestos, Malia and Zakros to a more complex design centuries ahead of its time. There were multiple storeys, sumptuous royal apartments, grand reception halls, storerooms, workshops, living quarters for staff and an advanced drainage system. The design later gave rise to the myth of the Cretan labyrinth (see the boxed text, p160).

During the Neopalatial period, the Minoan state developed into a powerful thalassocracy, purportedly ruled by King Minos with the capital based at Knossos. Trade with the eastern Mediterranean, Asia Minor and Egypt continued to boom and was helped by Minoan colonies in the Aegean. Minoan pottery, textiles and agricultural produce such as olive oil and livestock subsequently found ready markets throughout the Aegean, Egypt, Syria and possibly Sicily.

Minoan civilisation came to an abrupt and mysterious halt beginning around 1450 BC after the palaces (except for Knossos) and numerous smaller settlements were smashed to bits. New scientific evidence suggests the Minoans were weakened by a massive tsunami and ash fallout from a cataclysmic volcano that erupted on nearby Santorini (see boxed text, p26). But there is much debate about both the timing and explanation for the ultimate demise of the Minoans. Some argue it was caused by a second, powerful earthquake a century later. Other archaeologists blame the invading Mycenaeans. Whether the Mycenaeans caused the catastrophe or merely profited from it, it is clear that their presence on the island closely coincided with the destruction of the palaces and Minoan civilisation.

MYCENAEAN CRETE

The Mycenaean civilisation, which reached its peak between 1500 and 1200 BC, was the first great civilisation on the Greek mainland. Named after the ancient city of Mycenae, it is also known as the Achaean civilisation after the Indo-European branch of migrants who had settled on mainland Greece.

Unlike Minoan society, where the lack of city walls seems to indicate relative peace under some form of central authority, Mycenaean civilisation was characterised by independent city-states, the most powerful of them all being Mycenae, ruled by kings who inhabited palaces enclosed within massive walls on easily defensible hilltops.

The Mycenaeans wrote in Linear B script (see the boxed text, p27). Clay tablets inscribed with the script found at the palace of Knossos is evidence of Mycenaean occupation of the island. Their colonisation of Crete lasted

Beyond the rich artistic and cultural legacy, the Minoans also invented the earliest 'flushing' toilet and advanced sewerage systems, described in detail on www.theplumber.com.

The Minoans knew how to enjoy themselves – playing board games, boxing, wrestling and performing bold acrobatic feats including the sport of bull-leaping, while Minoan dancing was famous throughout ancient Greece.

1100 BC	431–386 BC	67 BC
The Dorians overrun the Mycenaean cities and become Crete's new masters. They reorganise the political system, divide society into classes. A rudimentary democracy replaces monarchical government.	While Greece is embroiled in the Peloponnesian War, Crete is busy with its own internal battles, Knossos against Lyttos, Phaestos against Gortyna, Kydonia against Apollonia, Itanos against Ierapitna. An earthquake wreaks havoc in 386.	The Romans finally conquer Crete after starting their invasion two years earlier in Kydonia. Gortyna becomes the new capital and the island's most powerful city. A new era of peace follows as internal wars end.

from 1400 to 1100 BC. Knossos probably retained its position as capital of the island, but its rulers were subject to the mainland Mycenaeans. The Minoan Cretans either left the island or hid in its interior while the Mycenaeans founded new cities such as Lappa (Argyroupolis), Kydonia (Hania) and Polyrrinia.

The economy of the island stayed more or less the same, still based upon the export of local products, but the fine arts fell into decline. Only the manu-

---

CRETAN TSUNAMI

The sudden demise of the Minoans has been one of archaeology's biggest mysteries, but new scientific evidence confirms that they were wiped out by a cataclysmic tsunami more powerful than the 2004 Asian Tsunami.

In deposits found at key sites up to 7m above sea level, scientists discovered Minoan pottery, cups and building materials mixed up with pebbles, sea shells and tiny marine life that experts say could only have been scooped up from the seabed by something as strong as a tsunami.

Archaeologist Joseph Alexander MacGillivray, who has spent more than 25 years in Crete studying the Minoans, says tsunami science has been able to explain the scale of the disaster and answer many questions baffling archaeologists.

'When that wave hit the north coast, it was 23m high and 15km long. Three waves came ashore and the Minoan cities on the coast were wiped out,' says MacGillivray, who is in charge of the British School of Archaeology's excavations at Palekastro (see the boxed text, p198).

Radiocarbon dates for the deposits on Crete coincide with the massive volcanic eruption 70km north on Santorini around 1500 BC.

MacGillivray says 7cm of undisturbed Thira ash was found as far as Zakros, on the eastern coast. While the waves would not have reached Knossos, the damage to crops, their ports and fleets would have decimated the society.

The timing also explains what the Minoans were doing in Egypt soon after 1500 BC, requesting the breath of life from Pharaoh Hatshepsut.

'We've known for a century that the Minoans only went for that one period and now we think they went specifically to ask for help from the Pharaoh, who was the most powerful person on earth at that time.'

DNA science and the human genome have also provided some clues to the origins of the Minoans, including a new theory that the Bronze Age migration may have come from Troy, in northwest Anatolia.

French accountant Hubert la Marle's decipherment of Linear A script showed the Minoans spoke a language that came from Persia (Iran), but MacGillivray says it may not necessarily have travelled with the major population. 'There is an Iranian DNA in Crete but it does not seem as strong as the Trojan one. But this is just the beginning of the study,' he says.

As for the controversial theory that it could be Plato's lost continent of Atlantis, MacGillivray says Plato was 'no idiot…The classical Greeks had a very good idea of Minoan history because it was part of Greek history…they knew where Crete was.'

---

27 BC	AD 63	250
Crete united with Libya to form the Roman province of Cyrene.	Christianity emerges after St Paul visits Crete and leaves his disciple, Titus, to convert the island.	The first Christian martyrs, the so-called Agii Deka (Ten Saints) are killed in the village of the same name, as Christian persecutions begin in earnest.

facture of weapons flourished, reflecting the new militaristic spirit that the Mycenaeans brought to Crete. The Mycenaeans also replaced worship of the Mother Goddess with new Greek gods such as Zeus, Hera and Athena.

Mycenaean influence stretched far and wide, but eventually weakened by internal strife; they were no match for the warlike Dorians.

DORIAN CRETE & THE CLASSICAL AGE

Despite fierce resistance, the Dorians conquered Crete around 1100 BC, causing many of the inhabitants to flee to Asia Minor. Those who remained, known as Eteo-Cretans or true Cretans, retreated to the hills and thus preserved their culture.

The Dorians heralded a traumatic break with the past. The next 400 years are often referred to as Greece's 'dark age', although it would be unfair to dismiss the Dorians completely: they brought iron with them and developed a new style of pottery, decorated with striking geometrical designs. They also worshipped male gods instead of fertility goddesses and adopted the Mycenaean gods of Poseidon, Zeus and Apollo, paving the way for the later Greek religious pantheon.

The Dorians reorganised the political system of Crete and divided the society into three classes: free citizens who owned property and enjoyed political liberty (which included land-holding peasants); merchants and seamen; and slaves. The monarchical system of government was replaced by a rudimentary democracy. Ruling committees were elected by free citizens and set policy. They were guided by a council of elders and answered to an assembly of free citizens. Unlike Minoan times, women were condemned to a subordinate role.

The Man Who Deciphered Linear B, by Andrew Robinson, tells the fascinating story of Michael Ventris, the young genius who cracked the code in 1952, solving one of archaeology's greatest linguistic mysteries and establishing Linear B as the oldest European writing system.

DECIPHERING THE MYSTERIES OF LINEAR B

The methodical decipherment of the Linear B script by English architect and part-time linguist Michael Ventris in 1952 gave the first tangible evidence that the Greek language had a recorded history longer than any scholar had previously believed. The language was an archaic form of Greek 500 years older than the Ionic Greek used by Homer.

Linear B was written on clay tablets that lay undisturbed for centuries until they were unearthed at Knossos in Crete. Further tablets were unearthed later on the mainland at Mycenae, Tiryns and Pylos in the Peloponnese and at Thebes in Boeotia in Central Greece.

The clay tablets, found to be mainly inventories and records of commercial transactions, consist of about 90 different signs, and date from the 14th to the 13th centuries BC. Little of the social and political life of these times can be deduced from the tablets, although there is enough to give a glimpse of a fairly complex and well-organised commercial structure.

Importantly, what is clear is that the language is undeniably Greek, thus giving the modern-day Greek language the second-longest recorded written history, after Chinese.

395	727	824
The Roman Empire splits and Crete is ruled by Byzantium. Crete becomes a self-governing province with Gortyna as its administrative and religious centre. Piracy decreases, trade flourishes and many churches are built.	Crete's icon worship provokes a revolt after Emperor Leo III bans their worship as part of the iconoclastic movement. The uprising is smashed and the Byzantine emperors unleash a fierce wave of retribution.	The Arabs conquer Crete and establish a fortress called Chandax (Iraklio) to store their pirated treasure. As the island's criminal reputation grows, its economy dwindles and cultural life grinds to a halt.

Minotaur: Sir Arthur Evans and the Archaeology of the Minoan Myth, by Joseph Alexander MacGillivray, is a fascinating portrait of the British archaeologist who revealed the palace of Knossos to the world, and a study in relative archaeology.

By about 800 BC, local agriculture and animal husbandry had become sufficiently productive to trigger a resumption of maritime trading. As new Greek colonies were established throughout the Mediterranean basin, Crete took on a prominent trade role.

The people of the various city-states were unified by the development of a Greek alphabet, the verses of Homer and the founding of the Olympic Games. The establishment of central sanctuaries, such as Delphi, for the first time gave Cretans a sense of national identity as Greeks.

Rethymno, Polyrrinia, Falasarna, Gortyna, Phaestos and Lato were built according to the new defensive style of Dorian city-states, with a fortified acropolis at the highest point, above an agora (marketplace), a bustling commercial quarter, and beyond it residential areas.

The 6th-century-BC *Laws of Gortyna,* discovered at the end of the 19th century AD at Gortyna, open a window onto the societal structure of Dorian Crete. Inscribed on 12 large stone tablets, the laws covered civil and criminal matters, with clear distinctions drawn among the classes of free citizens and between citizens and slaves. They are still in situ at the site.

As the rest of Greece entered its golden age from the 6th to 4th centuries BC, Crete remained a backwater. Constant warfare between large commercial centres and smaller traditional communities left the island increasingly impoverished. Although Crete did not participate in the Persian wars or the Peloponnesian War, economic circumstances forced many Cretans to sign up as mercenaries in foreign armies or turn to piracy.

During this time, Crete's role as the birthplace of Greek culture drew the attention of philosophers such as Plato and Aristotle, who wrote extensively about Crete's political institutions.

Knossos, Gortyna, Lyttos and Kydonia (Hania) continued to vie for supremacy, causing ongoing turmoil. Egypt, Rhodes and Sparta got involved in the Cretan squabbles and piracy flourished.

ROMAN RULE

While Alexander the Great was forging his vast empire in the East, the Romans expanded theirs to the west and began making inroads into Greece. Their various interests in Crete included reducing piracy and exerting control over important sea routes. The Roman presence in Crete dates back to the 3rd century BC, but it wasn't until the second Mithridatic War (74–64 BC) that they used piracy as an excuse for intervention. Marcus Antonius, father of Mark Antony, undertook an unsuccessful naval campaign against Crete. The Cretans tried to negotiate and send envoys to Rome, but they were rebuffed. Expecting a Roman invasion, the island united and assembled an army of 26,000 men. The Roman campaign began in 69 BC under the Roman consul Metellus near Kydonia, and spread throughout the island. Although the Cretans fought valiantly, the Romans succeeded in subjugating the island two years later.

960	1204	1363
Byzantine general Nikiforos Fokas attacks Chandax in a bitter siege, retaking Crete. The Byzantines fortify the Cretan coast. Chandax becomes the island's capital and seat of the Cretan archdiocese. A powerful land-holding class emerges.	After the sacking of Constantinople by Crusaders, Boniface of Montferrat sells Crete to Venice. Venice rapidly colonises Crete and starts building towns and defences in Rethymno, Hania, Iraklio and across the island.	Venetians swiftly quell an uprising by Crete's feudal leaders (Venetians and Cretans) attempting to establish an independent state under the name of St Titus.

Although Crete lost power and influence under the Romans, a new era of peace was ushered in, ending Crete's internal wars. Crete did not mount a major challenge to Roman rule, although it became embroiled in the later rivalry between Antony and Octavian, both of whom punished the cities that supported their rival.

In the early years of Roman rule, parts of Crete were given as favours to various Roman allies. In 27 BC Crete was united with Libya to form the Roman province of Cyrene. The Romans built the first new cities since Minoan times, with Gortyna becoming the capital and most powerful city in Crete. The Romans built an amphitheatre, temples and public baths, and the population increased. Knossos appeared to fall into disuse, but Kydonia (Hania) in the west became an important centre. Roman towns were linked by a network of roads, bridges and aqueducts, parts of which can still be seen today. Under the Romans, the Cretans continued to worship Zeus in the Dikteon and Ideon Caves, and also incorporated Roman and Egyptian deities into their religious rituals.

CHRISTIANITY & BYZANTINE CRETE

Christianity arrived early in Crete with St Paul's visit in AD 63. He left it to his disciple, Titus, to convert the island. Titus became the first bishop of Crete. Little is known about the early years of Christianity in Crete, but by the 3rd century persecution of Christians began in earnest. The first Christian martyrs were the so-called Agii Deka (Ten Saints) killed in the village of the same name in AD 250.

In 324 Emperor Constantine I (also known as Constantine the Great), a Christian convert, transferred the capital of the empire from Rome to Byzantium, which was renamed Constantinople (now İstanbul). By the end of the 4th century, the Roman Empire was formally divided into western and eastern sections; Crete, along with the rest of Greece, found itself in the eastern half. While Rome went into terminal decline, the eastern capital grew, long outliving its western counterpart (the Byzantine Empire lasted until the capture of Constantinople by the Turks in 1453).

Crete was a self-governing province in the Byzantine Empire with Gortyna as its administrative and religious centre. Piracy decreased and trade flourished, leaving the island wealthy enough to build many churches. Crete's attachment to the worship of icons provoked a revolt in 727 when Emperor Leo III banned their worship as part of the iconoclastic movement. The uprising was smashed and the Byzantine emperors unleashed a fierce wave of retribution.

Byzantine rule was interrupted around 824 when the Arabs conquered Crete. The Arabs established a fortress called Chandax in what is now Iraklio, essentially to store their pirated treasure. As the island's criminal reputation grew its economy dwindled and its cultural life ground to a halt.

The Byzantines were in no position to help Crete despite its strategic importance. They had enough problems defending territories closer to home.

You can take a virtual step-by-step video tour of Knossos on the British Archaeological School at Athens website, www .bsa.ac.uk.

1453	1645	1669
Constantinople falls to the Turks. Byzantine scholars and intellectuals flee to Crete, sparking a renaissance of Byzantine art. The Cretan School of icon painting emerges, combining Byzantine and Venetian elements.	A huge Turkish force lands in Hania, provoked by a pirate attack on a Turkish ship off the Cretan coast. The Turks establish their first foothold on the island. After Rethymno is defeated, the Turks secure the western part of the island.	After keeping the enemy at bay for 21 years, Iraklio (Candia) finally falls to the Turks. Crete falls under Ottoman rule, except for Spinalonga and Souda (which fall in 1715). Mosques and Turkish monuments are built.

History of Crete, by Theoharis E Detorakis, is an extraordinarily complete guide to Cretan history from the Minoan times up to (but not including) the Battle of Crete.

Not until the Byzantine general Nikiforos Fokas attacked Chandax in a bitter siege in 960 did the Arabs finally yield.

The Byzantines then lost no time in fortifying the Cretan coast and consolidating their power. Chandax emerged as the island's new capital and the seat of the Cretan archdiocese.

The Orthodox Church has played a pivotal role in Crete's history and preserving the culture and religion under successive invaders. Under Venetian rule, the Orthodox Church was dismantled and replaced with the Catholic Church and, ironically, it was the Ottomans who allowed the Cretans to resurrect the Orthodox religion. Attempts to convert the local population to Catholicism or Islam proved largely futile. Despite relentless persecution, Orthodox monasteries remained hotbeds of resistance and kept the spirit of national unity alive.

VENETIAN CRETE

The Genoese first moved in on Crete, but it was the Venetians who prevailed in 1217. Crete was pivotal to Venetian control of the Mediterranean and remained under Venetian rule until 1669, long after most of Greece had become part of the Ottoman empire. The Venetian influence is evident throughout the island, most notably in Hania, Iraklio, Rethymno, Sitia and Ierapetra, where they built mansions and massive fortresses to guard the developing port towns and harbours.

Venice colonised Crete with noble and military families, many of which settled in Iraklio (Candia). During the first century of Venetian rule about 10,000 settlers came to Crete, induced by the seizure of the island's best and most fertile land. The Cretan owners now worked as serfs for their new Venetian masters, who were not only the major land-holders but also held political control.

Cretan peasants were ruthlessly exploited under Venetian rule, and oppressive taxation added to their woes. Religious life also suffered, as the Venetians viewed the church as a symbol of national identity and supplanted the Orthodox Church with the Catholic Church.

Cretans rebelled regularly against Venetian rule and met with brutal Venetian reprisals. Eventually the rebellions forced concessions from Venice. By the 15th century the Cretan and Venetian communities reached an uneasy compromise that allowed Cretan cultural and economic life to flourish.

After the fall of Constantinople in 1453, Crete became the last remaining bastion of Hellenism. Byzantine scholars and intellectuals fled the dying empire and settled in Crete, establishing schools, libraries and printing presses. The cross-pollination between Byzantine traditions and the flourishing Italian Renaissance sparked a major cultural revival, often called the Cretan Renaissance. Poetry and drama flourished and a Cretan School of icon painting (see p48) developed in the 16th and 17th centuries,

1770	1821	1828
Under their leader Daskalogiannis, 2000 Sfakians mount an assault on the Turks in western Crete but the rebellion is viciously suppressed. Daskalogiannis is skinned alive in the central square of Iraklio.	Greek War of Independence is declared. The insurgence spreads to Crete but Turkish-Egyptian forces outnumber the rebellion. Continued resistance provokes fearsome massacres of Cretan civilians.	Resistance leader Michalis Dalianis and 385 rebels made an heroic last stand at Frangokastello in one of the bloodiest battles in the war for independence. About 800 Turks are killed along with the rebels.

combining Byzantine and Venetian elements. In the midst of this artistic ferment, the painter Dominikos Theotokopoulos emerged, studying in Italy before moving to Spain where he became known as El Greco (see the boxed text, p49).

TURKISH CRETE

By the middle of the 17th century, resource-rich and strategically located Crete became attractive to the expanding Ottoman empire and Venice was too slow in rearranging their defences in the face of the looming threat.

Turkish forces landed in Hania in 1645, and although the fortress was bravely defended it fell within two months. Rethymno was next, giving control of the west to the Turks. Candia's massive walls kept the enemy at bay for 21 years, but the city finally fell in 1669, leaving the entire island in Turkish hands (except for Spinalonga and Souda, which did not fall until 1715).

Life was not easy under the Ottomans, although they did allow the Orthodox Church to reestablish itself and survive essentially intact during more than 200 years of occupation. Nevertheless, there were tremendous political and economic advantages to embracing Islam. Mass conversions were common; sometimes entire villages changed their faith.

Economically, the Cretans were initially no better off under the Ottomans than they were under the Venetians. The Ottomans devised ingenious taxes to wring every drop of wealth out of the island, and the economy degenerated to a subsistence level. Trade picked up, however, around the start of the 18th century, and living standards improved. Crete exported grain, and its abundance of olive oil launched a soap industry.

Rebellion was brewing, though, as many Cretans fled to the mountains, harassing the Turks with sporadic attacks, particularly in the Sfakia region. In 1770 under their leader Daskalogiannis, 2000 Sfakians mounted an assault upon the Turks in western Crete. Promised Russian aid never materialised and the rebellion was viciously suppressed. Daskalogiannis was skinned alive in the central square of Iraklio.

When the Greek War of Independence spread to Crete in 1821, Sfakia was once again the nucleus of rebellion, but the revolutionaries were hampered by poor organisation and constant infighting. The Turks swiftly retaliated with a wave of massacres primarily directed at the clergy.

Bogged down with fighting rebels in the Peloponnese and mainland Greece, the Turks were forced to turn to Egypt for help in dealing with the Cretans. Chronically short of arms and undisciplined, the Cretans fought furiously but were outnumbered by the Turkish-Egyptian forces.

With the rest of Greece torn by war, Crete was left on its own and the revolutionary movement largely flickered out, with sporadic outbreaks of fighting provoking fearsome massacres of Cretan civilians. When an independent Greek state was finally established in 1830, Crete was given to Egypt.

'Rebellion was brewing, though, as many Cretans fled to the mountains, harassing the Turks with sporadic attacks, particularly in the Sfakia region. '

1830	1831	1832
The Great Powers give Crete to Egypt. Egyptian rule brings some improvements, with Muslims and Christians treated equally, schools organised and infrastructure rebuilt, but taxes remain high and new protests emerge.	Ioannis Kapodistrias, the first elected governor of independent Greece is assassinated by political rivals.	The Treaty of London declares an independent Kingdom of Greece and appoints Bavarian teenage Prince Otto as King of Greece.

Egyptian rule initially brought improvements. An amnesty asked Cretans to lay down their arms, Muslims and Christians were to be treated equally, schools were organised and the authorities began rebuilding the island's infrastructure, though taxes remained high and new protests emerged. After Egypt was defeated by the Turks in Syria, the Great Powers gave Crete back to the Ottomans in 1840.

Under restored Ottoman rule, Cretans won important privileges allowing more religious freedom, civil and property rights. But the Sultan's repeated violations of the new laws sparked yet another uprising and demand for *enosis,* or union, with free Greece. Although Russia was partial to the Cretan position, Great Britain and France preferred the status quo and refused any help. Rallying around the slogan 'Union or Death', fighting broke out in western Crete. Once again the Turks joined forces with the Egyptians and attacked the civilian population. In 1866 about 900 rebels and their families took refuge in Moni Arkadiou. When 2000 Turkish soldiers attacked the building, rather than surrender, the Cretans set light to a store of gunpowder. The explosion killed almost everyone, Turks included.

The event shocked the world and the heroic stand gained the Cretan cause worldwide sympathy. Despite demonstrations erupting throughout Europe, Great Britain and France maintained a pro-Turkish stance. The Great Powers forbade Greece from aiding the Cretan rebels and the revolution petered out.

The 1877 Russo-Turkish War prompted another uprising in Crete. Sensing that Turkey might be defeated, the Greek government decided to support Crete. Although the rebels seized major north-coast cities, the Berlin conference of 1878 resolving the Russo-Turkish War rejected Cretan union with Greece. Turkey made new concessions, turning Crete into a semi-autonomous province, sanctioning Greek as the official language and granting a general amnesty.

In 1889 fierce political infighting within the Cretan parliament led to a new rebellion against Turkish rule, prompting Turkey to return to the iron-fisted policies of the past. In Sfakia, Manousos Koundouros formed a secret fraternity to secure autonomy and eventual unification for Crete. They laid siege on the Turkish garrison at Vamos, leading to violent reprisals and eventual intervention by the Great Powers. The Turks were forced to agree to a new constitution.

When violence erupted again in 1896, the Greek government sent a small force to the island and declared unification between Crete and Greece. The Great Powers rejected the idea and blockaded the coast, refusing to allow either the Turks or the Greeks to reinforce their position. Greece became embroiled in a war with Turkey and recalled its forces. The Great Powers appointed Prince George, son of King George of Greece, as high commissioner of Crete.

In 1898 a detachment of British soldiers was implementing the transfer of power in Iraklio when an enraged mob of Turks stormed through the city slaughtering hundreds of Christian civilians – along with 17 British soldiers

Mary Renault's novels *The King Must Die* and *The Bull from the Sea* are vivid tales of Minoan times that provide an excellent feel for ancient Crete.

1840	1866	1877
The Turks defeat Egypt and the Great Powers give Crete back to the Ottomans. Crete wins important new privileges but repeated violations spark another uprising and demand for union. Great Britain and France refuse to help.	About 2000 Turkish soldiers attack the Arkadi monastery, where more than 900 rebels and their families shelter. Refusing to surrender, the Cretans light a store of gunpowder, setting off an explosion that kills almost everyone.	The Russo-Turkish War prompts another uprising in Crete. Greece supports Crete and rebels seize major north-coast cities but the Great Powers reject Cretan union with Greece. Turkey turns Crete into a semi-autonomous province.

and the British consul. The British swiftly rounded up 17 Turkish trouble-makers, hanged them and sent a squadron of ships steaming into Iraklio harbour. The Turks were ordered out, finally ending Ottoman rule over Crete.

After the disastrous Greek invasion of Smyrna, the 1923 Treaty of Lausanne called for a population exchange between Greece and Turkey to prevent future disputes. Crete's remaining Muslim population of about 30,000 people was ordered off the island, abandoning their homes to the incoming Greek refugees. Ironically, many of them were Christians who had converted.

Few legacies of Turkish rule survive in Crete. The most prominent are the old mosque in Hania harbour and the minarets and mosques in Rethymno, as well as remnants of Ottoman architecture in the cities' old Turkish quarters.

UNION WITH GREECE

With the Ottomans gone, Crete was placed under international administration, but union with Greece remained an insatiable desire and would take some years to achieve. A new movement coalesced around the charismatic Hania-born Eleftherios Venizelos, one of the most important figures in Greek and Cretan politics. Venizelos was Prince George's minister of justice and a member of the Cretan Assembly. In the face of Prince George's stubborn refusal to consider unification, Venizelos convened a revolutionary assembly in Theriso, near Hania, in 1905, raising the Greek flag and declaring unity with Greece.

Venizelos then set up a rival government to administer the island. The rebellion spread, forcing the Great Powers to concede that Prince George had lost all support. King George appointed a new governor but the populace continued to agitate for unification.

In 1908 the Cretan assembly declared unity with Greece, but the Greek government refused to allow Cretan deputies to sit in the Greek parliament. Even though Venizelos had become prime minister, Greece remained fearful of antagonising Turkey and the Great Powers who were adamantly opposed to the plan. Not until Greece, Serbia and Bulgaria declared war on the Ottoman Empire over Macedonia in the first Balkan War (1912) were Cretans finally allowed into the Greek Parliament. When the war ended, the 1913 Treaty of Bucharest formally recognised Crete as part of the Greek state.

WWII & THE BATTLE OF CRETE

When German troops marched through Yugoslavia and invaded Greece on 6 April 1941, the country was rapidly overrun. Greek leader Emmanouil Tsouderos set up a government in exile in his native Crete.

With all available Greek troops fighting the Italians in Albania, Greece asked Britain to help defend Crete. Churchill obliged, as he was determined to make a stand and block Germany's advance through southeastern Europe.

For all things ancient and Greek, try the great web portal www.ancient greece.com.

1889	1896	1898
Fierce political infighting within the Cretan parliament sparks a new rebellion and the Great Powers eventually force the Turks to agree to a new constitution.	Violence erupts again. The Greek government sends a force and declares unification with Crete. The Great Powers reject the idea. Greece recalls its forces and the Great Powers appoint Prince George as high commissioner of Crete.	Turks storm through Iraklio slaughtering hundreds of Christian civilians, 17 British soldiers and the British consul. The British order the Turks out and Crete is placed under international administration. Hania becomes the capital.

More than 30,000 British, Australian and New Zealand troops poured into the last remaining part of free Greece, two thirds of them evacuated from mainland Greece.

The Allies were in a poor position to defend the island, since commitments in the Middle East were already draining military resources. The island's defences had been seriously neglected. There were few fighter planes and military preparation was hampered by six changes of command in the first six months of 1941. Crete's difficult terrain also meant the only viable ports were on the exposed northern coast, while inadequate roads precluded resupplying the army from the more protected southern ports.

Hitler was determined to seize Crete and use it as an air base to attack British forces in the eastern Mediterranean. In a stunning disregard for Crete's rebellious history, Hitler actually believed that German forces would be welcomed by the native population. They were not.

After a week-long aerial bombardment, Hitler launched the world's first airborne invasion on 20 May, starting what became known as the Battle of Crete, one of the decisive battles of the war. Aiming to capture the airport at Maleme 17km west of Hania, thousands of parachutists floated down over Hania, as well as Rethymno and Iraklio.

Elderly men, women and children grabbed rifles, old shotguns, sickles and whatever else they could find to defend their homeland. German casualties were appalling, but they managed to capture the Maleme airfield on the first day and, despite the valiant defence, the Allies lost the battle within 10 days.

POSTWAR CRETE

When the external threat of war and foreign occupation finally ended, Greece and the Allies were left to deal with the fraught internal politics of the nation. The mainland resistance had been dominated by communists. Winston Churchill wanted the king back and was afraid of a communist takeover. The 1946 election, which was boycotted by the communists, was won by the royalists with British backing. A rigged plebiscite put George II back on the throne and a brutal and divisive civil war broke out, lasting until 1949.

Crete was largely spared the bloodshed and bitterness that left Greece a political and economic basket case in the 1950s. The close cooperation between the Cretans and British soldiers left the islanders with strong pro-British sentiments, leaving little room for communist infiltration.

In 1967 Greece was thrown into turmoil again when a group of army colonels staged a coup d'état, which established a military junta that imposed martial law, abolished all political parties, banned trade unions, imposed censorship, and imprisoned, tortured and exiled thousands of Greeks who opposed it. Cretan resentment towards the colonels intensified when the colonels muscled through major tourist development projects on the island that were rife with favouritism.

Prince Philip, the Duke of Edinburgh, was part of the Greek royal family – born in Corfu as Prince Philip of Greece and Denmark in 1921. Former King of Greece Constantine is Prince William's godfather and Prince Charles' third cousin.

Distinguished British archaeologist John Pendlebury, who took over Arthur Evans' work at Knossos, was executed by the Germans in 1941 while fighting with the Cretan Resistance. He is buried at the Allied war cemetery in Souda.

Crete: The Battle and the Resistance, by Antony Beevor, is a short and readable analysis of the Allied defeat.

1900	**1905**	**1908**
Arthur Evans begins excavations at Knossos, quickly unearthing the palace and stunning the archaeological world with the discovery of the advanced Minoan civilisation.	A revolutionary assembly in Theriso declares unity with Greece. Venizelos sets up a rival government to administer the island. The Great Powers concede Prince George's loss of support and appoint a new governor of Crete.	The Cretan assembly declares unity with Greece, but Cretan deputies are not allowed to sit in the Greek parliament until 1912.

Suspicions that the coup had been aided by the CIA remain conjectural, but the US silence on the coup and the ensuing regime did not alter the perception of US involvement, which has left a residue of anti-American feeling.

In 1974 Turkish forces invaded Cyprus following a botched junta-sponsored attempt to depose Cyprus' president, Archbishop Makarios. Discredited by the invasion, the junta was quickly dismantled.

The ban on communist parties was lifted and Kostas Karamanlis' right-wing New Democracy (ND) party won the 1974 elections. A national plebiscite voted 69% against restoration of the monarchy. Greece became a pluralist democratic republic and entered an unprecedented era of stability, peace and growth. That same year, the former Greek king and royal family fled to London where they live amongst the aristocracy, although they were stripped of most of their Greek assets in a long-running property dispute.

> Apart from the fatal tsunami that wiped out the Minoans, Crete was hit by a far smaller tsunami in 1956 at Palekastro. Locals recall the massive wave coming in and dumping tonnes of fish in their vineyards.

DEMOCRACY & MODERN GREECE

While it is positively dull in comparison to the past, contemporary Greek politics remains robust and colourful, with plenty of personal and financial scandals and regular accusations of graft, corruption and nepotism.

Since the mid-1970s, Crete's fortunes have been inextricably linked with the political, social and economic developments of mainland Greece, riding both the booms and the economic downturns.

FIGHTING SPIRIT

The rebellious spirit of the Cretans has been a feature of Crete's long history of resistance to foreign occupation, particularly the heroic stances taken against the Venetians and the Turks. Nikos Kazantzakis vividly portrays the fighting Cretan spirit in his book based on a 19th-century Cretan Resistance fighter during the Turkish occupation in *Freedom and Death*.

More recently, the valiant Cretan spirit won them the endearing admiration of British, Australian and New Zealand troops who fought in Crete during WWII. After the battle of Crete, the Cretans risked German reprisals by hiding thousands of Allied soldiers and helping them get to the south to escape across the Libyan Sea. Allied undercover agents supplied from North Africa coordinated the guerrilla warfare waged by the Cretan fighters, known as *andartes*. Allied soldiers and Cretans alike were under constant threat from the Nazis while they lived in caves, sheltered in monasteries such as Preveli, trekked across peaks or unloaded cargo on the southern coast. Among them was celebrated author Patrick Leigh Fermor, who lived in the mountains for two years with the Cretan Resistance and was involved in the daring kidnapping of German commander General Kreipe in 1944.

German reprisals against the civilian population were fierce. Cities were bombed, villages burnt down and men, women and children lined up and shot. When the Germans finally surrendered in 1945 they insisted on surrendering to the British, fearing that the Cretans would inflict upon them some of the same punishment they had suffered for four years.

1913	1921	1941
Greece and Crete are officially united under the Treaty of Bucharest.	Greek troops in Smyrna attack the Turks, but are routed and many Greek inhabitants are massacred. In the ensuing population exchange, Crete's 30,000 Turks are ordered off the island, while Greeks from Smyrna arrive in Crete.	Germany invades Greece and Allied troops arrive to defend Crete. Germany launches an airborne invasion to capture the airport at Maleme, west of Hania, in the famous Battle of Crete. Allied soldiers are evacuated from Hora Sfakion.

WAR MEMORIALS

The Battle of Crete had a monumental impact on the outcome of the WWII, and the massive casualties on all sides make it a significant war memorial pilgrimage. Every May, war veterans from Great Britain, Australia, New Zealand and Greece attend commemoration celebrations held throughout Crete.

Major anniversaries include a reenactment of the airborne invasion at Maleme, west of Hania. Participation of those who served on Crete has dwindled with time, but the anniversaries remain important memorials for Greeks and Allied ex-servicemen and there are regular battlefield tours of Crete. More than 1500 Allied soldiers are buried at the immaculate Souda Bay War Cemetery near Hania. Ironically, one of the long-term caretakers of the German war cemetery at Maleme, where 4500 soldiers are buried, was the late George Psychoundakis, the former shepherd boy whose story about being a runner during the German occupation is told in *The Cretan Runner*. There are also war memorials across the island, including a striking monument overlooking the cliffs at Moni Preveli and at Stravromenos on the north coast of Rethymno.

Andreas Papandreou's PASOK party – which formed Greece's first socialist government – dominated Greek politics for two decades after it was elected in 1981. Papandreou's populist pledge to remove US bases and withdraw from NATO was especially popular in Crete, given the islanders' strong antipathy to the presence of foreign troops. US presence on the island was reduced, though there are still American and NATO bases operating in Crete and the US naval base at Souda Bay is a regular target for protests.

After Greece joined the EU in 1981 (then the EEC), Crete's farmers benefited from EU subsidies, and the island's cultural and tourism infrastructure development was also bolstered. Tourism boomed with direct charter flights to Crete, almost tripling tourist arrivals between 1981 and 1991.

The charismatic Papandreou's significant reforms were marred by numerous scandals, including his public affair with a younger air hostess (whom he later married) and a financial scandal in the late '80s involving the Bank of Crete, in which Papandreou and four ministers were charged with embezzlement (all were later acquitted).

The ND party enjoyed a brief stint in government from 1990 when Konstantinos Mitsotakis, a Cretan, was elected prime minister, but corruption allegations and internal divisions returned PASOK to power three years later.

In 1996 Papandreou's ailing health finally forced him to step down as PASOK leader, ending a colourful era in Greek politics. His successor Costas Simitis, a straight-laced technocrat and economic reformer, led PASOK in a dramatic change of direction that included privatisation and reform of Greece's notorious public sector. Securing the 2004 Olympic Games brought a flood of money into Greece for infrastructure improvements, but Simitis'

1944	1946–49	1951
The Cretan guerrilla resistance kidnaps German commander General Kreipe and, aided by the Allies, sends him to Egypt, sparking fierce German reprisals. Cities are bombed, villages annihilated and civilians, including children, lined up and shot.	Greek civil war breaks out between communists and right-wing royalists. The communists fail to infiltrate Crete, which is largely spared the bloodshed and bitterness that engulfs Greece.	Greece joins NATO. Military bases are established on Crete.

austerity packages – designed to whip Greece into fiscal shape in preparation for full membership of the European Monetary Union in 2002 – caused much discontent, as did major post-euro rises in the cost of living after the introduction of the euro. Simitis handed the reins to Foreign Minister George Papandreou, son of Andreas, in January 2004 but despite Papandreou's political pedigree and personal popularity – particularly in Crete – he was unable to save PASOK from a thumping defeat in two months later.

Kostas Karamanlis' ND party got the glory of presiding over the successful Athens 2004 Olympic Games, which became less about the sport and more about Greece proving it was a modern, developed nation, rather than the European backwater it had been seen. In the post-Olympics chapter of Greek history, ND did not make much headway in its efforts to get the Greek economy into shape in the face of the Olympics cost blow-outs, Greece's premature (and rigged) entry into the euro zone, rising unemployment and inflation as well as attempts to reforms labour laws, social security, education and push through privatisation.

In the summer of 2007, Greece plunged into an environmental and political crisis brought on by the massive fires that destroyed vast tracts of the country and killed 65 people. Yet, the ND government scraped back into power in the September national elections, with voters abandoning the major parties. The communist (KKE) party numbers were boosted and the nationalist LAOS party gained 10 seats, the first far-right party to enter the Greek Parliament since the end of military rule more than 30 years ago. PASOK leader George Papandreou's was left fighting a leadership challenge by party veteran Evangelos Venizelos (remarkably not apparently related to the famous Greek statesman).

> Crete has produced two of independent Greece's prime ministers, Eleftherios Venizelos (several times between 1910 and 1933) and Konstantinos Mitsotakis (1990–93).

CRETE TODAY

In this unprecedented era of peace and stability, Crete has become one of Greece's most dynamic and prosperous islands and a major economic powerhouse. The annual tourist invasion – more than two million visitors, the majority from Germany and the UK – has overtaken agriculture as the dominant industry.

Crete has been a major beneficiary of EU infrastructure programmes and agricultural subsidies and more recently, grants to promote green tourism and preserve cultural heritage through restoration of historic buildings and traditional settlements. With increased urbanisation, its towns have prospered, while the island has also evolved into a major research centre, with several university campuses and research institutes, and a large student population.

Island development has been haphazard however, partly because Crete has no centralised government and the island's four prefectures operate virtually independently, and often competitively. It remains resentful of

1967	1971	1974
Army colonels stage a coup and impose martial law across Greece. Cretan resentment towards the junta intensifies when the colonels muscle through major tourist development projects on the island that are rife with favouritism.	Iraklio resumes its position as the island's capital.	Turkish forces invade Cyprus following a botched junta-sponsored attempt to depose Archbishop Makarios, the president of Cyprus. The junta falls and democracy is restored to Crete. The monarchy is abolished and the royal family exiled.

outside control from Athens, while complex regional politics is based on family and patronage as much as party affiliation, as well as who looks after local interests best. Crete remains a key PASOK stronghold, significantly outpolling ND at national elections.

Crete's often conflicting interests and divisions are now between the north coast tourist zone and the less developed south, between fertile and wealthy agricultural regions such as central Iraklio region and the southeast Lasithi greenhouse zone, and between poorer remote rural communities and increasingly sophisticated towns.

Crete's tourism doubled again between 1990 and 2000, largely due to the cheap package tourism boom, but the trend is causing much dismay among the rest of the industry who see few benefits and the impact on the island's environment and resources. The need for sustainable tourism is becoming increasingly critical.

'Crete's tourism doubled again between 1990 and 2000...'

The lack of planning and regulation is most evident in the overdeveloped north coast tourist zones, which have reached saturation point, while on the schizophrenic southeast coast you'll see hotels built next to ugly greenhouses right on the coast. (Crete has 50% of Greece's greenhouses but along with prosperity, anecdotal evidence suggests health problems and cancer rates in the Lasithi region have risen due to pesticide use.)

The extension of the national highway to Sitia is considered pivotal to regional development of the east, but controversial tourism projects planned around Vai have locals divided, while major growth in the expanding beach resorts around Platanias in Hania suggest lessons have not been learnt.

An alternative push for more sustainable green tourism – the potential of which has not been tapped – as well as agrotourism and more upmarket holidays has led to an increase in special-interest activities such as extreme sports, spas, golf, cultural tourism and culinary and winery tours. Overall the industry has had to shape up and become more professional than the sideline build-it-and-they-will-come approach of the past.

In recent years there has been an increased focus on preserving Crete's cultural identity and traditions in the face of globalisation. While environmental issues are gaining more prominence, consciousness is still very low.

Agriculture remains a major force and way of life. While Crete has one of Greece's highest levels of organic farming, it represents only a tiny percentage of the industry.

Easier access to the mainland, better work and education opportunities and lifestyles have made Crete a more attractive place to live. The tide of young people moving away from the island has started to stem, while small but steady stream of people are abandoning Athens for life on Crete. A boom in holiday and retirement homes for Europeans has seen real estate prices skyrocket.

1981	1990	1993
Greece becomes the 10th member of the EEC. Greeks elect the first PASOK socialist government, led by Andreas Papandreou.	Cretan Konstantinos Mitsotakis is elected prime minister when New Democracy (ND) narrowly wins government. His economic reforms are unpopular in Crete. A breakaway party is formed after corruption allegations, ending ND's capacity to govern.	PASOK returns to power. Andreas Papandreou resigns in 1996 due to ill health, ending an era in Greek politics. Costas Simitis takes over and introduces austerity measures and reforms continuing PASOK 's long reign.

FAMILY AFFAIRS

The Greek political landscape has been characterised as a hereditary democracy, with two families dominating the modern leadership of the country. (Earlier political dynasties included Venizelos and the Rallis clan).

Current New Democracy (ND) leader and prime minister Kostas Karamanlis is the nephew and namesake of former prime minister and president, who dominated Greek politics in the later 20th century.

Enigmatic PASOK founder Andreas Papandreou, whose colourful reign as prime minister spanned more than 12 years, was the son of George Papandreou, prime minister in 1944 and 1963–65. Andreas's son George, a former foreign minister, is the current PASOK leader.

Cretan-born former ND prime minister Konstantinos Mitsotakis' son Kyriakos is an ND MP; his charismatic daughter Dora is foreign minister (and former mayor of Athens) and widely tipped as a future leader. She entered politics after her husband Pavlos Bakoyiannis, also an ND MP, was assassinated by the 17 November (N17) terrorist organisation.

The biggest population shift, however, has been the economic migrants who now do much of the agricultural and building work, while seasonal workers in the tourism sector means your waiter is just as likely to be from Poland than Sfakia.

Preserving Crete's unique character and environment in the face of rapid social and economic changes sweeping the island will be the island's greatest challenge as it enters the next era of its colourful history.

2002	2004	2007
Greece becomes a full member of the European Monetary Union and the drachma is replaced by the euro.	ND, under Kostas Karamanlis, wins power. Greece wins the European Soccer championship. Athens hosts a successful Olympic Games.	Weeks after fires ravage Greece, Kostas Karamanlis's ND is reelected. PASOK is routed and the minor parties gain more seats, including the communist party (KKE) and the right-wing nationalist LAOS party.

The Culture

REGIONAL IDENTITY

The Cretans are a very distinctive clan of Greeks, with their own spirited music and dances, distinct cuisine and traditions. Proud, patriotic yet famously hospitable, Cretans uphold an undeniable connection to their culture. They will always identify as Cretans before they say they are Greek, and even within different parts of Crete people maintain strong regional identities. This becomes particularly apparent when you leave the commercialised major tourist centres. In rural areas, many Cretans still speak a local dialect or have a distinct accent.

Centuries of battling foreign occupiers have left the island with a stubbornly independent streak that sometimes leads to clashes with Athens. National laws that conflict with local customs are often disregarded. Guns, for example, are strictly regulated in Greece, yet the evidence suggests Cretans are stashing an astounding arsenal (see the boxed text, p43).

Nevertheless, the Cretan people have a well-justified reputation for hospitality and for treating strangers as honoured guests, a gesture of pride (and a hangover of historical territorialism) rather than subservience.

Obviously Cretans are no longer offering free food and lodging to millions of tourists a year, but if you wander off the beaten track into mountain villages you may well be invited into someone's home for a coffee or even a meal. In a café or taverna it is customary for people to treat another group of friends or strangers to a round of drinks (however, be mindful that it is not the done thing to treat them straight back – in theory you do the honours another time).

Cretan society is deeply influenced by the Greek Orthodox Church and its rituals and celebrations (see p213 for a list of festivals and events). It maintains strong family ties and a sense of family honour. Crete's infamous vendettas, while increasingly rare, have not entirely ended (see the boxed text, p97).

Cretan weddings and baptisms are still huge affairs, and while shooting pistols in the air is becoming more politically incorrect (and dangerous – people have been accidentally hit and killed), it is still common in some areas, where bullet-riddled road signs are a characteristic part of the landscape.

Rivalries between the prefectures are strong. As the island's capital until 1971, Hania considers itself the historical heart of the island, while Rethymno claims to be its cultural centre.

The dominant political ideology is left-of-centre with the socialist PASOK party repeatedly outdrawing the conservative New Democracy (ND) party in local and national elections.

Cretans remain very ethnocentric, while anti-Americanism is another interesting undercurrent. Apart from general resistance to American hegemony, it originates from what many regard as undue US interference in Greek affairs during the civil war, suspected CIA involvement in the colonels' coup of 1967, US indifference over Cyprus, and its interventions in the Middle East and the Balkans. In Crete this sentiment often culminates in protests over the US military base at Souda or is demonstrated in more subtle ways such as refusing to serve Coke. While there is often heated and forthright objection to American foreign policy, the ire is ideological and not extended to American tourists.

Cretans who migrated to Athens or overseas (far fewer than in other regions of Greece) maintain strong cultural and family links, returning

Harvard anthropologist Michael Herzfeld makes interesting anthropological observations of Cretans in *The Poetics of Manhood: Contest and Manhood in a Cretan Village*, while *A Place in History* looks at life in and around Rethymno, including issues such as the Cretan vendetta.

CULTURAL TIES: IOANNA KARYSTIANI

Hania-born author Ioanna Karystiani has lived in Athens since she was 18, but her heart has never left Crete. She regularly returns to Hania to spend time with her family, who moved to Crete from Turkey in the 1920s population exchange. 'I sit in a room with my parents who are in their 90s now and hold them in my arms, my mother on the right, my father on the left, talking and telling *mandinades* (traditional rhyming couplets),' she says.

Karystiani, one of the Polytechnic generation who revolted against the colonels in 1973, is a former political cartoonist who turned to writing later in life. She is author of the 2004 movie *Brides*; her novel *Koustoumi sto Homa* is based on a family vendetta in Sfakia, the harsh mountain stronghold of the Cretan Resistance.

Karystiani, 55, believes a land and its history and language feeds the next generation and shapes its character.

'Cretans are fiery characters. The diversity and ruggedness of the land and the history of all the revolutions and wars has played a role in that. The Minoan civilisation was peaceful. In later years the hardship of life and the constant invaders have made the Cretans harsh and unique. They have a great pride in their land, which is often demonstrated positively; sometimes it can be expressed in a narrow, parochial way, with a sense of superiority, but most people are not like that.'

While in many other parts of Greece, traditional songs and music have been lost in the quest to become contemporary Europeans or not to be seen as retrograde, the Cretans, she says, have by and large maintained their culture.

'In Crete there are thousands of children who learn how to play lyra and learn Cretan dances and are not embarrassed at all. They may also love rock, but they still tell and compose *mandinades*, and sing and dance and celebrate in the old way. They have brought that part of their culture into the present because it warms their hearts; it still speaks to them.'

---

regularly. Even the island's most remote villages are bustling during holidays, elections and other excuses for family reunions and homecomings.

LIFESTYLE

The Cretan lifestyle has changed dramatically in the past 30 years, the most obvious change being that life has got a lot easier. Cretan society has become increasingly urbanised, living standards have improved significantly, Cretans are conspicuously wealthier and the towns are full of sophisticated restaurants, bars and clubs.

Cretans pride themselves on their capacity to enjoy life. You will see them dressed up and going out en masse for their evening *volta* (stroll), and filling cafés and restaurants.

Like most households in Greece, the Cretans have felt the brunt of higher living costs since the introduction of the euro. Eating out has become much more expensive, although there are still many reasonably priced tavernas in Crete, particularly in the villages.

Cretans often deal with the seasonal invasion of foreign tourists by largely operating in a different time-space continuum from their guests. They will often tell you a particular place is 'only for tourists', and that's normally your cue to avoid it.

From April to around October, many live in the hurly-burly of the coastal resorts – running shops, *pensions* or tavernas – and then return to their traditional life in the hills for the autumn olive and grape harvests.

While tourists eat early in the evening in restaurants along a harbour or beach, Cretans drive out to a village taverna for a dinner that begins around 11pm. Often these tavernas produce their own meat and vegetables, saving on business costs and at the same time providing better food.

Greece has the highest number of smokers in the EU and they smoke anywhere at any time. While smoking restrictions have been introduced with some success in public areas, nonsmoking areas in restaurants are still a rarity.

DOS & DON'TS

Crete is a pretty laid-back destination but there are some cultural sensitivities to respect, particularly outside the main tourist resorts.

Always dress appropriately when visiting a church or monastery. Women should wear skirts that reach below the knees, men should wear long trousers and arms, shoulders and cleavage should be covered (it is always handy to carry a sarong).

Topless sunbathing is allowed in most places in Crete and nudism is tolerated at some remote beaches, though you should take the cue from people around you or check for signs asking you to keep your gear on (p103), especially if you are near a church or monastery or in a family area. Just because it's hot, doesn't mean men should walk around towns and villages without their shirts, just like you wouldn't at home.

If you are wondering why some villages and towns seem like ghost towns in the middle of the day, it's because things shut down for *mesimeri*, the post-lunch siesta time (3pm to 5pm). Try to be quiet during these times and never call on anyone at home.

While Cretans can probably drink you under the table, public drunkenness is frowned upon. Cretans take their hospitality seriously so if you are treated to a drink or meal, accept it graciously as rejecting it can cause offence.

Do try to learn a few words of Greek, it's always appreciated.

Generational and rural-city divides are another feature of modern Crete. In rural areas you will see shepherds with their flock in the mountains and men congregating in the *kafeneia* (coffee house) after their siesta. Mountain villages are repositories of traditional culture and you'll find that many older women and many men are still clad in black garb (a symbol of mourning).

But even pastoral life has changed. While people still live off the land – and provide for their families in the cities – subsistence farming has mostly given way to commercial production. Though you will still see the odd donkey, it has been replaced by the monstrous 4WD pick-up trucks and foreign workers do most of the grunt work.

The younger generation of Cretans is highly educated and most speak English and often German as well.

In the shift from living a largely poor, agrarian existence to becoming increasingly sophisticated urban dwellers, Cretans are also delicately balancing cultural and religious mores.

Cretan society is still relatively conservative and it is uncommon for Greeks to move out of home until they are married, apart from leaving temporarily to study or work. The reasons for this are practical as well as cultural – most will get a house when they get married and who wants to do their own washing and cooking anyway?

ECONOMY

Crete has ridden the wave of Greece's economic growth in the past five years, and the increased availability of credit, has sparked a frenzied, if ultimately unsustainable, consumer spending boom. On the other hand, most households have felt the brunt of higher living costs since Greece joined the Euro Zone in 2001.

Indeed, Crete's per capita GDP and investment levels have been higher than the national average. Crete also has the highest rate of self-employed people in Greece (and amongst the highest in the EU). Crete's farmers have reaped the benefits of EU membership, but tourism has replaced agriculture as the island's dominant economic activity. Crete is nonetheless one of Greece's biggest producers of olives and olive oil, vegetables (potatoes and

---

TRIGGER-HAPPY

Sitting in a café in Askyfou one afternoon, a man at the next table pulls out a semi-automatic pistol and fires a few rounds, just for fun. Late one night after a festival near Lissos, gunshots ring out every time the group of merry Cretans on the beach finishes a song. At Cretan weddings and celebrations, volleys of gunshots – and accidents from stray bullets – have become so common that many musicians refuse to play in certain areas unless they get an assurance that there won't be any guns.

In 2004 acclaimed composer Mikis Theodorakis led a campaign trying to change the island's gun culture, but Cretans have not laid down their arms. Conservative estimates indicate one in two Cretans owns a gun, while others suggest there could be over one million weapons on Crete – more than the island's population.

Road signs riddled with bullet holes are the first inkling that you are entering the somewhat lawless mountain country that was historically a stronghold for Crete's Resistance fighters, particularly around Sfakia and Mylopotamos province in Rethymno. A history of turmoil and invaders has made Cretans determined not to give up their guns, even though in theory the same restrictions apply in Crete as the rest of Greece.

The endemic, machismo gun-ownership – and the act of shooting off a few rounds – is traditionally seen as an act of independence and pride (these days it's also a reckless show of excess and an expensive habit).

But gun mania is not just a cultural or historic hangover. Feuding and raiding is rife in the 'devil's triangle' of Anogia, Zoniana and Livadia, a notorious centre for illegal arms and drugs, the deep ravines being a haven for concealing cannabis crops.

---

tomatoes), oranges and wine, largely produced in fertile areas such as Iraklio's Mesara plain. The massive spread of greenhouses in southern Lasithi have made the region prosperous. Stock breeding of sheep and goats is the other major sector.

Crete has reaped the benefits of EU membership, while tourism has more than doubled since 1990, accounting for 40 per cent of jobs in the region and overtaking agriculture is some areas as the dominant industry.

POPULATION

Crete is Greece's most populous island with more than 600,000 residents. About 42% of the population live in Crete's main cities and urban centres, with about 45% living in rural regions. Close to 49% of the population live in the Iraklio prefecture, which is double the size of the next biggest town, Hania.

MULTICULTURALISM

After the exodus of Crete's Turkish community in the population exchange of 1923, Crete became essentially homogenous, and its population virtually all Greek Orthodox. More recently Crete has become home to a significant population of migrants from the Balkans and Eastern Europe, who have become an economic necessity in the agriculture, construction and tourism sectors. The majority are from Albania.

Economic migrants are a relatively new phenomenon for Crete which, like most of Greece, is struggling to come to terms with the new reality and concepts of multiculturalism. While there are tensions and mistrust, migrants appear to have fared better in Crete than in many other parts of Greece.

A small group of English, Germans and northern European refugees have also settled and bought property on Crete, though they live on the more affluent fringes. Foreign women married to Cretan men, a particularly

> With an estimated 34 million olive trees in Crete, it works out to 62 olive trees for every man, woman and child.

common occurrence in the 1980s, are another characteristic minority group in Cretan society.

SPORT

Football (soccer) is the most popular sport in Crete, followed by basketball. Cretan men are avid sports fans and Crete fields two teams in the Greek national league. If you happen to be eating in a taverna on a night when a big match is being televised, expect indifferent service. Crete hosted the 2004 Olympic soccer preliminaries at Iraklio's massive Pankritio stadium.

RELIGION

The Orthodox faith is the official and prevailing religion of Crete and a key element of Greek identity, ethnicity and culture. There is a prevailing view that to be Greek is to be Orthodox. While the younger generation isn't necessarily devout, nor attends church regularly, most observe the rituals and consider the faith integral to their identity. Between 94% and 97% of the Greek population belongs at least nominally to the Greek Orthodox Church.

After Constantine the Great officially recognised Christianity in AD 313 (converted by a vision of the Cross), he transferred the capital of the Roman Empire to Byzantium (today's İstanbul) in AD 330. By the 8th century, differences of opinion and increasing rivalry emerged between the pope in Rome and the patriarch of the Hellenised Eastern Roman Empire. One dispute was over the wording of the Creed, which stated that the Holy Spirit proceeds 'from the Father', but Rome added 'and the Son'. Other points of difference included Rome decreeing priests had to be celibate, while Orthodox priests could marry before becoming ordained, and the Orthodox Church forbidding wine and oil during Lent.

Their differences became irreconcilable, and in the great schism of 1054 the pope and the patriarch went their separate ways as the Orthodox Church (orthodoxy means 'right belief') and Roman Catholic Church.

The Greek Orthodox Church is closely related to the Russian Orthodox Church; together they form the third-largest branch of Christianity.

During Ottoman times membership of the Orthodox Church was one of the most important criteria in defining a Greek. The Orthodox religion held Cretan culture together during the many dark centuries of repression, despite numerous, largely futile efforts by the Venetians and Turks to turn the Cretans towards Catholicism and Islam.

The year is centred on the saint's days and festivals of the church calendar. Name days (celebrating your namesake saint) are celebrated more than birthdays, and baptisms are an important rite. Most people are named after a saint, as are boats, suburbs and train stations.

There are hundreds of tiny churches dotted around the countryside, predominantly built by individual families, dedicated to particular saints. The tiny roadside iconostases or chapels you see everywhere are either shrines to people who died in road accidents or similar dedications to saints.

The Orthodox Church of Crete is independent from the Greek Orthodox Church and answers directly to the Patriarch of Constantinople.

Regrettably, many small churches and chapels are kept locked nowadays but it's usually easy enough to locate the caretakers, who will be happy to open them for you.

GENDER ROLES

The role of women in Cretan society is complex and shifting, and throws up some interesting paradoxes. While traditional gender roles are prevalent in rural areas and among the older generation, things have become much more

Personal questions are not considered rude in Crete, so don't be surprised if you are grilled about your age, salary, marital status etc, and given sympathy if you are over 25 and not married.

For a useful but by no means exhaustive listing of books about Crete with reviews, visit www.hellenicbookservice.co.uk.

EASTER IN CRETE

Easter is the year's most important religious event and a good time to be in Crete. Many age-old ceremonies and rituals take place throughout Holy Week, culminating in the Resurrection of Christ on the eve of Easter Sunday.

This is a week of strict fasting and many tavernas will only serve special Lenten fare, particularly on Good Friday (though in Crete there is a tradition of seafood suppers after Friday's church service). Eggs are dyed red (symbolising the blood of Christ) in preparation for the post-Resurrection celebrations.

On Good Friday an *epitafio* (bier) representing the body of Christ is decorated with flowers and carried through the streets in a sombre but moving candle-lit procession. In larger towns such as Iraklio, several churches will time their procession so that the biers meet at a central point.

The climax of the week is the Saturday evening resurrection service, when crowds spill out of church into streets and squares. Just before midnight the lights are extinguished until the priest appears with the holy light, which is spread through the candles of the congregation. At midnight the priest announces *Hristos Anesti* (Christ has risen) and fireworks and gunshots herald the start of feasting that lasts through Easter Sunday. The poignant and beautiful ceremony is the most significant moment in the Orthodox year, for it symbolises the Resurrection. Worshippers make their way home, trying to keep their candle lit so they can bless their house with the holy light.

The Lenten fast ends immediately after church, with a traditional supper of *mayiritsa* (tripe soup), served in tavernas and homes. On Easter Sunday you will see spit-roast lambs cooking everywhere – even on the side of the road in villages – which is a key part of the festivities.

liberal for younger women in cities and large towns. Old attitudes towards the 'proper role' for women are changing fast as more women are educated and entering the workforce.

Despite the machismo, Cretan society is essentially matriarchal. Men love to give the impression that they rule the roost and take a front seat in public life, but it's often the women who run the show, both at home and in family businesses.

In villages, men and women still tend to occupy different spheres. When not tending livestock or olive trees, Cretan men can usually be found in a *kafeneio* playing cards and drinking coffee or raki. Although exceptions are made for foreign women, *kafeneia* are off-limits to Cretan women. The older generation of Cretan women are house-proud and spend much time cultivating their culinary skills. Most men rarely participate in domestic duties (or certainly don't own up to it). While it's becoming rarer these days, women busy themselves in their free hours with sewing, crocheting or embroidery, often in a circle of other women. But young Cretan women are more likely to be found in a café than behind a loom.

Rural areas remain relatively conservative and girls who do not pursue an education tend to marry young.

ARTS
Minoan Art & Culture

The rich legacy of Minoan civilisation uncovered in the palaces, settlements and tombs around Crete reflect the glory and brilliance of perhaps the most peaceful and prosperous era in the island's history. The Minoans surrounded themselves in art and heavily decorated their palaces. The surviving painting, small-scale sculptures, carved seals, mosaics, pottery and jewellery on display at archaeological sites and museums around Crete provide a priceless insight into the Minoan world as well as demonstrate their extraordinary artistry. Minoan painting is virtually the only form of Greek painting to have survived, because large-scale sculptures did not make it through the disasters (natural or otherwise) that befell the island. Minoan art inspired the invading Mycenaeans and its influence spread to Santorini and beyond.

POTTERY

Pottery techniques advanced in the early Minoan years. Spirals and curvilinear motifs in white were painted on dark vases and several distinct styles emerged. Pyrgos pottery was characterised by black, grey or brown colours, while the later Vasiliki pottery (made near Ierapetra) was polychrome. In the Middle to Late Minoan period, the style shifted to a dark-on-light colour technique.

Highly advanced levels of artisanship developed in the workshops of the first palaces at Knossos and Phaestos. Kamares pottery, named after the cave where the pottery was first found, was colourful, elegant and beautifully crafted and decorated with geometric, floral, plant and animal motifs. Human forms were rarely depicted. During the entire Middle Minoan period, Kamares vases were used for barter and were exported to Cyprus, Egypt and the Levant.

With the invention of the potter's wheel, cups, spouted jars and *pithoi* (large Minoan storage jars) could be produced quickly and there was a new crispness to the designs. The most striking were the 'eggshell' vases with their extremely thin walls.

In the late Neopalatial era, marine and floral themes in darker colours reigned. After 1500 BC, vases sprouted three handles and were frequently shaped as animal heads, such as the bull's-head stone rhyton (libation vessel) in the Iraklio Archaeological Museum. The decline of Minoan culture saw the lively pottery of previous centuries degenerate into dull rigidity.

'Minoan frescoes are renowned for their vibrant colours and the vivid naturalism...'

JEWELLERY & SCULPTURE

Jewellery making and sculpture in various media reached an exceptional degree of artisanship in the Protopalatial period. The exquisite bee pendant found at Malia displays extraordinary delicacy and imagination. Another Minoan masterpiece is a 15th-century-BC gold signet ring found in a tomb at Isopata, near Knossos, which shows women in an ecstatic ritual dance in a meadow with lilies, while a goddess descends from the sky.

Minoan sculptors created fine miniatures, including idols in faïence (quartz-glazed earthenware), gold, ivory, bronze and stone. One of the most outstanding examples is the bare-breasted serpent goddess with raised arms wielding writhing snakes above an elaborately carved skirt. Another incredible piece is the small rock-crystal rhyton from the Palace of Zakros. All of the above can be seen in the Archaeological Museum of Iraklio.

The art of seal-stone carving also advanced in the palace workshops. Using semiprecious stones and clay, artisans made miniature masterpieces that sometimes contained hieroglyphic letters. Goats, lions and griffins and dance scenes were rendered in minute detail. Arthur Evans spent much of his first trip to Crete collecting these seals.

In the Postpalatial period, the production of jewellery and seal-stones was replaced by the production of weaponry, reflecting the influence of the warlike Mycenaeans.

THE FAMOUS FRESCOES

Minoan frescoes are renowned for their vibrant colours and the vivid naturalism in which they portray landscapes rich with animals and birds; marine scenes teeming with fish and octopuses; and banquets, games and rituals. Although fresco painting probably existed before 1700 BC, all remnants vanished in the cataclysm that destroyed Minoan palaces around that time.

Knossos yielded the richest trove of frescoes from the Neopalatial period, most of which are on display in the Archaeological Museum of Iraklio.

Only fragments of the frescoes survive but they have been very carefully (and controversially) restored and the technique of using plant and mineral dyes has kept the colours relatively fresh. Minoan fresco painters borrowed heavily from certain Egyptian conventions but the figures are far less rigid than most Egyptian wall paintings.

The Knossos frescoes suggest Minoan women were white-skinned with elaborately coiffured glossy black locks. Proud, graceful and uninhibited, these women had hourglass figures and were dressed in stylish gowns that exposed perfectly shaped breasts. The bronze-skinned men were tall, with tiny waists, narrow hips, broad shoulders and muscular thighs and biceps; the children were slim and lithe.

Many of the frescoes show action scenes, from boxing and wrestling to solemn processions, saffron gathering to bull-leaping (see box on p48).

RELIGIOUS SYMBOLS
The Minoans were not given to building colossal temples or religious statuary. Caves and peak sanctuaries appear to have been used for cult or religious activity. Minoan spiritual life was organised around the worship of a Mother Goddess. Often represented with snakes or lions, the Mother Goddess was the deity-in-chief and the male gods were clearly subordinate.

The double-axe symbol that appears in frescoes and on the palace walls of Knossos was a sacred symbol for the Minoans. Other religious symbols that frequently appear in Minoan art include the mythical griffin bird and figures with a human body and an animal head. The Minoans appear to have worshipped the dead and believed in some form of afterlife, while evidence uncovered in Anemospilia, suggests human sacrifice may also have taken place (see p165).

MINOAN WRITING
The Cretan hieroglyphic was the system of writing used in the Protopalatial period that later evolved into Linear A and B script. The most significant example of this writing is on the inscrutable 3600-year-old terracotta tablet known as the Phaestos disk, which has been the object of much speculation since it was discovered at Phaestos in 1908. The disk, about 16cm in diameter, consists of an early Minoan pictographic script made up of 242 'words' written in a continuous spiral from the outside of the disk to the inside (or the other way round). The repetition of sequences of words or sentences has led to speculation it may be a prayer. It has never been deciphered.

Fine Arts
The artistry of the Minoans has still not been surpassed. During a brief artistic renaissance on the island that lasted from the 8th to the 7th centuries BC, a group of sculptors called the Daedalids perfected a new technique of making sculptures in hammered bronze, working in a style that combined Eastern and Greek aesthetics. Their influence spread to mainland Greece. Cretan culture went into decline at the end of the 7th century BC, though there was a brief revival under the Romans, a period notable for richly decorated mosaic floors and marble sculptures.

BYZANTINE ART
Although Byzantine icons and frescoes were created from the earliest years of Byzantine rule, most were destroyed in popular rebellions during the 13th and 14th centuries. In the 11th century, émigrés from Constantinople

'The artistry of the Minoans has still not been surpassed.'

NO BULL

The bull was a potent symbol in Minoan times, featuring prominently in Minoan art. The peculiar Minoan sport of bull-leaping, where acrobatic thrill-seekers seize the charging bull's horns and leap over its back is depicted in several frescoes, pottery and sculptures. Scantily clad men and women are shown participating in the sport, which may have had religious significance. One of the most stunning examples is the Middle Minoan bull-leaping fresco found at the palace of Knossos, which shows a man leaping over the back of a bull with a female figure on each side. Another prized bull is the carved stone rhyton (libation vessel) in the shape of a bull's head, with rock crystal eyes and gilded wooden horns.

brought portable icons to Crete, but the only surviving example from this period is the icon of the Virgin at Mesopantitissa, now in Venice. From the 13th to the early 16th centuries, churches around Crete were decorated with frescoes – many of which can still be seen today. Byzantine art flowered under the Paleologan emperors who ruled from 1258 to 1453, and its influence spread to Crete. The great icon painter of the 14th century was Ioannis Pagomenos, who worked in western Crete.

THE CRETAN SCHOOL

With the fall of Constantinople in 1453, many Byzantine artists fled to Crete. At the same time, the Italian Renaissance was in full bloom and many Cretan artists studied in Italy. The result was the 'Cretan School' of icon painting that combined technical brilliance and dramatic richness. In Iraklio alone there were more than 200 painters working from the mid-16th to mid-17th centuries who were equally at ease in Venetian and Byzantine styles. The Cretan Theophanes Sterlitzas painted monasteries throughout Greece, and spread the techniques of the Cretan School.

Too few examples of the Cretan School are on display in Crete. In Iraklio you can see some fine examples at the Museum of Religious Art (p153) – the centrepiece of the collection being six portable icons from the great Michael Damaskinos, the finest exponent of the Cretan school. Damaskinos' long sojourn in Venice introduced him to new techniques of rendering perspective, which he brought to the Byzantine style of icon painting.

CONTEMPORARY ARTS

The fine arts have a relatively low profile in Crete today, though there are many contemporary artists and artisans working and exhibiting on the island. Many Cretan-born artists live and work in Athens and abroad. Rethymno's Contemporary Arts Centre Rethymno (p126) is one of the island's leading galleries for local and international artists and has a permanent collection of the work of local painter Lefteris Kanakakis. The Centre for Byzantine Art in Rethymno (p125) continues the tradition of the Cretan School of icon painting and exhibits the work of Manolis Koudourakis. Apart from exhibitions of local artists held by municipal art galleries around Crete, new private galleries are starting to appear in Hania and Iraklio. Hania also hosts an annual International Art Festival (check out Omma Centre of Contemporary Art's website, www.omma.us, and click on the links for information).

Dance

Fresco scenes of dancing Minoans suggest that dancing in Crete began in the ancient Greek temples. Dancing is depicted on ancient Greek vases and

EL GRECO THE CRETAN

One of the geniuses of the Renaissance, El Greco ('The Greek' in Spanish), was in fact a Cretan named Dominikos Theotokopoulos. He was born in the Cretan capital of Candia (present-day Iraklio) in 1541, during a time of great artistic activity, following the arrival of painters fleeing Ottoman-held Constantinople. These painters had a formative influence upon the young El Greco, giving him early grounding in the traditions of late-Byzantine fresco painting that was to give such a powerful spiritual element to his later paintings.

El Greco went to Venice in his early 20s, joining the studio of Titian, but he came into his own as a painter after he moved to Spain in 1577, where his highly emotional style struck a chord with the Spanish. He lived in Toledo until his death in 1614. The most famous of his works, such as his masterpiece *The Burial of Count Orgaz* (1586), are in Toledo but his paintings are in museums around the world. *View of Mt Sinai and the Monastery of St Catherine* (1570), painted during his time in Venice, hangs in Iraklio's Historical Museum of Crete (p152), next to the tiny *Baptism of Christ* acquired by the City of Iraklio in 2004. You can see *Concert of Angels* (1608) at the National Gallery in Athens.

A white marble bust of the painter stands in Iraklio's Plateia El Greco, and there are streets taverns and hotels named after him throughout the island. A small museum dedicated to El Greco has been established in the village of Fodele, in the house he allegedly spent time in as a child (see p161).

And it was only a matter of time before we had the movie: *El Greco* (2007), an epic €7 million production was shot in Iraklio, Venice, Spain and Athens. It was directed by Yannis Smaragdis and stars British unknown Nick Ashdon.

there are references to dances in Homer's works, who commented on the ability of Cretan dancers in particular.

Cretan dances are dynamic, fast and warlike, and many of them are danced by groups of men. Dances for women are traditionally related to wedding or courtship, and more delicate and graceful. Like most Greek dances they are normally performed in a circle – in ancient times, dancers formed a circle to seal themselves off from evil influences. In later times of occupation, dancing was a way for men to keep fit under the noses of the enemy.

The most popular Cretan dances are the graceful and slow *syrto* and the *pendozali*. The latter was originally danced by armed warriors and has a slow version and faster one that builds into a frenzy, with the leader doing kicks, variations and fancy moves while the others follow with more mild steps. Another popular dance is the *sousta*, a bouncy courtship dance with small precise steps that is performed by couples. The *maleviziotiko* (also known as *kastrino* or *pidikto*) is a fast triumphant dance.

Dancing well is a matter of great personal pride, and most dancers will take their turn at the front to demonstrate their prowess. Be aware that cutting in on somebody's dance is absolutely bad form, as families have usually paid for the dance (this is how Cretan musicians often make their living).

The best place to see Cretan dancing is at festivals, weddings and baptisms. Folkloric shows are also put on for tourists in many areas. Although these are more contrived, they still put on a decent show.

In addition to Crete's own traditional music and dances, you will also come across mainstream Greek music and dance.

Music

Cretan music is the most dynamic and enduring form of traditional music in Greece today. It remains the most popular music in Crete, staving off mainstream Greek and western pop, and accompanies weddings, births, holidays, harvesting and any other celebration.

Anthony Quinn (Mexican, not Greek) injured his foot while filming *Zorba the Greek*, so the scripted energetic dance became a slow shuffle he falsely claimed was traditional.

Crete's thriving local music scene continues to spawn a new generation of folk performers, who play regularly and produce new recordings of traditional songs as well as a contemporary style of music based on Cretan tradition. Cretan music also has a presence in the world-music scene as a genre in its own right.

The most prominent Cretan musician today is the legendary Psarantonis; he's known for his unique style of playing and is instantly recognisable from his wild beard and straggly mane of hair. Psarantonis performs regularly – everywhere from the smallest Cretan village to the clubs of Athens and the international festival circuit.

The icon of Cretan music, however, is the late Nikos Xylouris, whose career was cut short when he died in 1980 at the age of 43. With his superb voice and talent on the lyra, he remains the biggest selling and most revered Cretan musician.

Cretan music has been influenced by many musical traditions over the centuries and resembles eastern modal music. The lead instruments are the lyra, a three-stringed instrument similar to a violin that is played resting on the knee; the eight-stringed *laouto* (lute); and the *mandolino* (mandolin). Other traditional instruments include the *askomandoura* (bagpipe), *habioli* (whistle) and *daoulaki* (drum). The *bouzouki*, so associated with Greek music, is not part of Cretan music, though popular Greek music is also heard and performed in Crete.

One of Crete's favourite forms of musical expression are *mandinades*, rhyming couplets of 15 syllables that express the age-old concerns of love, death and the vagaries of fate. Probably originating as love songs in 15th-century Venice, thousands of *mandinades* helped forge a sense of national identity during the long centuries of occupation. The best 'rhymers' at Cretan festivals will tailor their songs to the people present and try to outdo each other in skill and composition. These days young Cretans continue the tradition, and *mandinades* are still part of the modern courtship ritual, albeit often via mobile phone text messages.

Another popular form of music is *rizitika*, which are centuries-old songs from the Lefka Ori thought to have derived from the songs of the border guards of the Byzantine Empire, though it is believed they may date back further. Many of the *rizitika* songs deal with historical or heroic themes. One of the most popular is the song of Daskalogiannis, the Sfakian hero who led the rebellion against the Turks in 1770 – the song has 1034 verses.

With more than 10,000 lines, the 17th-century romance *Erotokritos*, written by Vitsentzos Kornaros, has provided ample material for performers, and continues to inspire Crete's musicians. It has been put to music countless times, with each artist presenting their own interpretation of the great work.

Traditional folk music was shunned by the Greek bourgeoisie during the period after independence; however, a new wave of *entehno* (artistic) music that emerged in Athens in the 1960s drew on urban folk instruments such as the *bouzouki* and created popular hits from the works of Greek poets.

Acclaimed composer Yiannis Markopoulos (from Ierapetra) upped the ante by introducing rural folk music into the mainstream and was responsible for bringing Nikos Xylouris to the fore. During the junta years, Xylouris' music became a leading voice of the resistance. Markopoulos himself is best known internationally for his composition for *Who Pays the Ferryman?*

Xylouris was one of a swathe of artists who have emerged from the village of Anogia and part of an extraordinary musical family (see the boxed text, opposite).

For an insight into Cretan music, go to www.cretan-music.com (in English and Greek).

The oldest surviving folk songs in Greece, dating from the 17th century, were found at Mt Athos and were revealed to be *rizitika* (patriotic songs) from western Crete.

MUSICAL FAMILIES

The village of Anogia (p136), in the foothills of Mt Psiloritis in Rethymno, has produced a dispro-portionate number of musically talented sons. The much-loved and now long-lamented singer and lyrist Nikos Xylouris was from Anogia, and his ancestral house is maintained as a kind of musical shrine in the lower village. His idiosyncratic brother Psarantonis has since taken up the reins and is wildly popular nationwide. Brother Giannis Xylouris (Psaroyiannis) is Greece's most accomplished lute player. His heir apparent is Psarantonis' charismatic son, Giorgos Xylouris (Psarayiorgis), whose musical career has blossomed since returning to Crete after a stint living in Australia. Yiorgi's sister, Niki, is one of the few female Cretan singers, and the finest, while their brother Lambis is not surprisingly also in the music game.

Other notable musicians from Anogia include the lyra player Manolis Manouras, Nikiforos Aerakis, Vasilis Skoulas and Giorgos Kalomiris.

The talented but capricious Georgos Tramoundanis, alias Loudovikos ton Anogion (Ludwig from Anogia), sells his brand of folksy, ballad-style Cretan compositions to audiences all over Greece.

Xylouris, Thanasis Skordalos and Kostas Mountakis are considered the great masters of Cretan music, and most musicians today follow one of their styles.

One of the most respected and intriguing figures of Crete's music scene is Ross Daly (of Irish descent), a master of the lyra who has established a musical workshop in Houdetsi (see p164).

The excellent sextet Haïnides is one of the more popular bands to emerge from Crete in recent years, playing their own brand of music and giving memorable live performances around Greece. Other leading figures include Mitsos and Vasilis Stavrakakis and contemporary musicians such as the band Palaïna, Stelios Petrakis from Sitia, Papa Stefanis Nikas and Yiannis Haroulis. Australian-born Sifis Tsourdalakis is another rising young talent.

Popular artists of Cretan origin playing mainstream Greek music include the talented Manos Pirovolakis with his rock-lyra sound.

Literature

Crete has a rich literary tradition that sprang from the Cretan love of songs, verses and word play. In the late 16th and early 17th centuries, Crete had a tremendous literary flowering under Venetian rule.

The era's greatest masterpiece was undoubtedly the epic *Erotokritos* written by Vitsentzos Kornaros of Sitia. More than 10,000 lines long, this poem of courtly love is full of nostalgia for the dying Venetian regime that was threatened by the rise in Turkish power. The poem was recited for centuries by illiterate peasants and professional singers alike, embodying the dreams of freedom that enabled Cretans to endure their many privations. Many of the verses were incorporated into Crete's beloved *mandinades*. It is considered the most important work of early modern Greek literature.

Greece's best-known and most widely read author since Homer is Nikos Kazantzakis, born in Crete in 1883 amid the last spasms of the island's struggle for independence from the Turks. His novels are full of drama and larger-than-life characters. His most famous works are *The Last Temptation*, *Zorba the Greek*, *Christ Recrucified* and *Freedom or Death*. The first two have been made into films. *Zorba the Greek* takes place on Crete and provides a fascinating glimpse of the harsher side of Cretan culture.

Kazantzakis had a chequered and at times troubled literary career, clash-ing frequently with the Orthodox Church for his professed atheism (see the boxed text, p53).

The first complete English prose translation of Crete's 10,000-line epic *Erotokritos*, was published by Byzantina Austral-iensia in 2004, with a scholarly introduction and notes, translated by Gavan Betts, Stathis Gauntlett and Thanasis Spilias.

Literature and Society in Renaissance Crete, by David Holton, is a comprehensive study of the literature of the Cretan Renaissance in its historical, social and cultural context, with chapters on the poetic and dramatic genres contributed by leading experts in the field.

Iraklio may have Kazantzakis, but Rethymno can lay claim to Pandelis Prevelakis. Born in Rethymno in 1900, Prevelakis also studied in Athens and at the Sorbonne. Primarily known as a poet, Prevelakis also wrote plays and novels, and his best-known work is *The Tale of a Town,* which is about his home town.

Contemporary Cretan writers include Rhea Galanaki, whose prize-winning *The Life of Ismail Ferik Pasha* (1989) has been translated into six languages; it's a story about the clash of Christianity and Ottoman Islam in Crete. It is listed in Unesco's Collection of Representative Works.

Ioanna Karystiani (see the boxed text, p41), who wrote the screenplay for *Brides,* has been published in several languages, but only her novel *Little England* has been translated into English

Film

Crete has no local film industry but has been the location for several films, including 1960s classic *Zorba the Greek,* which was shot in Stavros on the Akrotiri Peninsula as well as on other locations around the island. In 1956 the American director Jules Dassin *(Never On Sunday)* chose the village of Kritsa as the backdrop for *He Who Must Die,* the film version of Katzantzakis' novel *Christ Recrucified* starring Dassin's wife, Melina Mercouri. The film lovingly captured the worn faces of the villagers, many of whom acted in the film.

CRETAN MUSIC TOP 10

The following broad selection of recordings provides an introduction to Cretan music past and present.

■ *Tis Kritis Ta Politima* – this 2006 double CD compilation is a good overall introduction to Cretan music, featuring a broad selection of traditional songs by leading Cretan musicians and Greek artists.

■ *Dimotiki Anthologia-Nikos Xylouris* – an early 1976 album that shot Crete's legendary musical son, Nikos Xylouris, to stardom. It's also available in a good-value twin-CD set (*I Kriti Tou Nikos Xylouris*) with another classic album, *Ta Pou Thimoume Tragoudo* (1975).

■ *Ta Oraiotera Tragoudia Tou* – a fine anthology paying tribute to the postwar master of Cretan music, Kostas Mountakis, known as 'the teacher'.

■ *Thanasis Skordalos* – part of the *To Elliniko Tragoudi* series documenting the greats of Greek music, this is a taste one of Crete's lyra legends.

■ *Anastorimata* – a landmark album from 1982 heralding the idiosyncratic Psarantonis' unique musical style. It also features *mandinades* by Vasilis Stavrakakis, and Ross Daly makes his first appearance.

■ *Beyond the Horizon* – Ross Daly's 2002 album presents his exceptional orchestration of traditional Cretan music, continuing the Irishman's influence on Cretan music.

■ *Embolo* – a 2004 double-disc set featuring Yiannis and Giorgos Xylouris, two of the greats of Cretan music, with the best Cretan lute you can hear.

■ *Xatheri* – a stellar collaboration from 2003 featuring Crete's top vocalist Vasilis Stavrakakis, Giorgos Xylouris on lute, Niki Xylouris and other leading musicians playing Cretan classics with a fresh sound.

■ *Palaiina Seferia* – the excellent 1997 self-titled first album of this contemporary Cretan ensemble led by Zacharias Spyridakis, a student of the lyra master Mountakis.

■ *Hainides* – the self-titled first album of this popular Cretan band gives you a good feel for its unique style based on Cretan music.

NIKOS KAZANTZAKIS – CRETE'S PRODIGAL SON

Crete's most famous contemporary literary son is Nikos Kazantzakis. Born in 1883 in Iraklio, the then Turkish-dominated capital, Kazantzakis spent his early childhood in the ferment of revolution and change that was creeping upon his homeland. In 1897 the revolution that finally broke out against Turkish rule forced him to leave Crete for studies in Naxos, Athens and later Paris. It wasn't until he was 31 that he finally turned his hand to writing by translating philosophical books into Greek. For a number of years he travelled throughout Europe – Switzerland, Germany, Austria, Russia and Britain – thus laying the groundwork for a series of travelogues in his later literary career.

Nikos Kazantzakis was a complex writer and his early work was heavily influenced by the prevailing philosophical ideas of the time, including the nihilistic philosophies of Nietzsche. In his writings, Kazantzakis is tormented by a tangible metaphysical and existentialist anguish. His relationship with religion was always troubling – his official stance being that of a nonbeliever, yet he always seemed to toy with the idea that perhaps God did exist. His self-professed greatest work is his *Odyssey*, a modern-day epic loosely based on the trials and travels of the ancient hero Odysseus (Ulysses). A weighty and complex opus of 33,333 iambic verses, *Odyssey* never fully realised Kazantzakis' aspirations to be held in the same league as Homer, Virgil or the Renaissance Italian, Tasso.

Ironically it was only much later in his career, after Kazantzakis belatedly turned to novel writing, that his star finally shone. It was through works such as *Christ Recrucified* (1948), *Kapetan Mihalis* (1950; now known as *Freedom and Death*) and *The Life and Manners of Alexis Zorbas* (1946) that he became internationally known. This last work gave rise to the image of the ultimate, free-spirited Greek male, 'Zorba the Greek', which was immortalised by Anthony Quinn in the movie of the same name.

Kazantzakis died while travelling in Freiburg, Germany, on 26 October 1957. Despite resistance from the Orthodox Church, he was given a religious funeral and buried in the southern Martinenga Bastion of the old walls of Iraklio.

More recently, Crete was the setting for the rather lacklustre 2000 romantic comedy, *Beware of Greeks Bearing Guns*, an old-fashioned tale of mistaken identity and a Cretan vendetta starring Greek satirist Lakis Lazopoulos and Greek-Australian actress Zoe Carides. The Greek-Australian co-production was shot in Crete and Melbourne.

The 2007 epic *El Greco*, a film about the life of Crete's famous painter (see the boxed text, p49), directed by Yiannis Smaragdis, was shot in Crete. Meanwhile, please stay tuned for two movies shot in Crete in 2007. Olga Malea's *First-Time Godfather* was shot in the village of Fres, while Greek-Australian actor Alex Dimitriades plays the lead role in the romantic comedy *Reception Will Follow*, produced by Greek-American Christine Crokos.

While Crete has no local TV production, one of the most popular recent TV series was *Tis Agapis Mahairia* (The Knives of Love), a drama based on a Cretan vendetta.

Greece's film industry overall is going through a period of flux. For many years it was in the doldrums, due largely to inadequate government funding and a tendency to produce slow-moving esoteric films loaded with symbolism and too avant-garde to have mass appeal, despite being well made with some outstanding cinematography.

The leader of this style is Greece's most acclaimed film director, Theodoros Angelopoulos, who won the 1988 Golden Palm award at the Cannes Film Festival for *Eternity and a Day*. His other well-known films include *Ulysses Gaze*, starring Harvey Keitel, *The Beekeeper*, *Alexander the Great* and *Landscapes in the Mist*.

More recently Greek filmmakers have begun producing commercially successful films, a trend started by the 2000 box-office hit *Safe Sex,* a light-hearted look at Greek sexuality by Thanasis Reppas and Mihalis Papathanasiou.

But Greece has not has a major international hit since *Zorba,* and beyond the festival circuit, few have made an impact outside Greece. Two major mainstream films that gained international cinematic releases – the first in many years – were Tassos Boulmetis' *A Touch of Spice* (2003) and Pantelis Voulgaris' 2004 hit *Brides,* which was executive-produced by Martin Scorcese.

The latest wave of filmmakers is attracting international attention with films that present a grittier, up-close and candid look at contemporary Greek life, a shift from idealised and romanticised views from the past. Directors to watch include Konstantinos Giannaris, whose provocative documentary-style films such as *From the Edge of the City* and his most recent release *Hostage* seem to split audiences and critics alike. Yannis Economidis, whose punishing second film *Soul Kicking* (2006) was screened at Cannes, has been likened to a younger Mike Leigh on speed.

Food & Drink

Cretan cuisine has its own distinct identity within Greek cooking. Regional specialities found across Crete and the quality and range of produce grown on the island by various small-scale producers present a diverse gourmet trail. One of the delights of travelling through Crete is coming across a family-run taverna where authentic Cretan dishes are made with fresh, home-grown produce, where the wild aromatic greens were picked in the mountains, the oil and cheese is homemade, tender lamb is from a local shepherd or the fish was caught by the owner.

Unfortunately, since the advent of mass tourism, the food dished up to visitors at many of the island's bland tourist tavernas has hardly done the cuisine justice. This is changing, however, as pride in promoting Cretan cuisine increases and more traditional home-style dishes are appearing on restaurant menus. Even in popular areas, many tavernas have stopped pandering to foreign predilections, trading schnitzel for *stifado* (braised meat with onions), while a new generation of professional chefs is experimenting with variations on traditional dishes and flavours to create nouveau-Cretan cuisine.

Crete may be a potential gourmet travel destination, but the essence of its rustic cuisine remains its simple seasonal and balanced approach, which reflects the bounty of a sun-blessed fertile land and a history of resourcefulness that comes from subsistence living during hard times.

Cretan cuisine gained legendary status for its health benefits following scientific studies of the Mediterranean diet in the 1960s that showed Cretans had the lowest levels of heart disease and other chronic illnesses (see the boxed text, p57). This was largely attributed to a greater reliance on pulses, fresh vegetables and fruit than on meats and processed foodstuffs, and copious use of virgin olive oil.

Food and the ritual of dining together play an integral role in Cretan life, whether at home or eating out with family and friends. Cretans will travel far to get to a great restaurant or eat specific food, heading to the mountains for local meat and the sea for fresh fish. Some of the best tavernas are tucked away in unexpected places.

'...Cretans had the lowest levels of heart disease and other chronic illnesses...'

THE CRETAN KITCHEN

Greek and Cretan dishes often overlap, but there are Cretan specialities, as well as regional variations across the island. Cretan cuisine has its roots in antiquity and has been influenced by various cultures over time but it essentially relies on fresh, unadulterated seasonal produce, aromatic herbs and ingredients that speak for themselves. The olive oil, produced in vast quantities across the island, is among the world's best and is an integral part of meals. Apart from its beneficial qualities, olive oil also makes vegetables and salads taste better.

The island's diet evolved from subsistence and what could be grown or made locally. For centuries Cretans have been gathering *horta* (wild greens) from the hills and boiling them for warm salads or cooking them in pies and stews. *Hohlii* (snails) are collected after rainfall and prepared in dozens of interesting ways: try *hohlii boubouristi*, simmered in vinegar and rosemary, or snails stewed with *hondros* (cracked wheat). Cretan *paximadia* (rusks), a hangover from times of famine, are made from barley flour or whole wheat and double-baked to produce a hard loaf that can keep, literally, for years. They are moistened with water and topped with

---

THE GOOD OIL

The Minoans were among the first to grow wealthy on the olive, and Crete remains an important olive-growing area, producing the largest quantity of extra virgin olive oil in Greece. More and more organic oil is being produced and at least nine olive regions have gained the EU's Protected Appellation of Origin status.

The best Cretan olive oil is from Kolymbari, west of Hania, and Sitia in the east. Biolea, near Hania, makes superb organic olive oil, as do monasteries – particularly the award-winning olive oil produced at Moni Agia Triada near Hania and Moni Toplou in the East.

The oil that is prized above all others is *agoureleo* (meaning unripe), a thick green oil pressed from unripe olives.

Greeks are the world's biggest per-capita consumers of olive oil; in Crete annual per-person consumption averages 31L.

---

tomato, olive oil and feta or *myzithra* (sheep's-milk cheese) in the popular dish called *dakos* (or *koukouvagia*).

Meat features more regularly than it did in the past. Cretans eat a lot of locally reared lamb and goat and are also fond of rabbit, which is stewed with rosemary and *rizmarato* (vinegar). While grills dominate taverna menus, Cretans have their own way of barbecuing called *ofto*, in which big chunks of meat are grilled upright around hot coals. In parts of Crete meat is cooked *tsigariasto* (sautéed), while in traditional mountain village tavernas you will find surprisingly tasty boiled mutton or goat. Meat is also cooked with vegetables, often lamb stewed with *stamnagathi* (wild greens) or artichokes, or chicken with okra.

The resourceful Cretans use almost every part of the animal – including delicacies such as *ameletita* ('unspeakables'– fried sheep's testicles), and *gardhoumia* (stomach and offal wrapped in intestines).

Psari (fish) has long been a staple (except in mountain areas) cooked with minimum fuss – usually grilled whole and drizzled with *ladholemono* (a lemon-and-oil dressing). Smaller fish like red mullet and tiny whitebait are usually lightly fried.

Kalitsounia, lightly fried pastries filled with *myzithra* cheese or *horta*. Cheese versions are also served with honey.

Where Cretan cuisine shines is in vegetable dishes such as artichokes and broad beans or tasty zucchini flowers (*anthoi*) stuffed with rice and herbs.

Crete produces wonderful cheeses from goat and sheep's milk, or a combination. *Graviera*, a nutty, mild gruyere-like sheep's-milk cheese, is often aged in special mountain caves and stone huts called *mitata*. It is delicious eaten with thyme honey. Other local cheeses include *myzithra* (a soft, mild ricotta-like cheese that can be eaten soft or hardened for grating), the hardened sour *Xynomyzithra*, *anthotyro* (a similar soft whey cheese) and *galomyzithra* (a creamy speciality of Hania). *Staka* is a rich, soft buttery cheese, often added to rice *pilafi* (pilaf) to make it creamier.

Thick, tangy sheep's-milk yogurt is something to savour, best eaten with honey, walnuts or fruit, especially in areas like Vryses (see p120).

DRINKS
Beverages

A legacy of Ottoman rule, Greek coffee is traditionally brewed on hot sand in a special copper *briki* (pot) and served in a small cup, where the grounds sink to the bottom (don't drink them). It is drunk *glyko* (sweet), *metrio* (medium) and *sketo* (without sugar). Greek coffee is, however, struggling to maintain its place as the national drink against the ubiquitous frappé,

Cretans probably eat more snails than the French – Cretan snails are even exported to France.

the iced instant-coffee concoction that you see everyone drinking. Alternatives are espresso and cappuccino chilled – *freddo*. Herbal teas are popular, especially camomile or aromatic Cretan *tsai tou vounou* (mountain tea), which is both nutritious and delicious. The endemic Diktamo (dittany) tea is known for its medicinal qualities, while Crete's reputedly medicinal warm tipple is *rakomelo* – raki, honey and cloves.

Beer & Spirits

Greek beers are making their mark in a market dominated by big European breweries such as Amstel and Heineken. The major Greek brands are Mythos and Alfa, while boutique beers include the Vergina and Hillas lagers from Northern Greece, organic Piraiki made in Piraeus and Craft, which is widely available in draught form. Crete also has its own beer produced at the Rethymniaki brewery (p132). Greeks are not big beer drinkers, however: they only consume about half the EU per capita average.

Supermarkets are the cheapest place to buy beer, which is also available in kiosks.

Ouzo, the famous Greek spirit, has a more limited following in Crete, where it is drunk mostly by mainlanders or foreigners. It is served neat, with ice and a separate glass of water for dilution (which makes it turn milky white).

Wine

Wine has been produced in Crete since Minoan times and Crete's farmers have long grown small vineyards and made wine for their own consumption. It wasn't until industrialisation (and the resulting rapid urban growth and onset of tourism) that bottled wine was mass produced commercially – and retsina was introduced to the world.

In the past 20 years, a renaissance in the Greek wine industry has seen a new generation of progressive internationally-trained winemakers reinventing Greek wine using local and international varieties. About 20% of Greek wine is produced in Crete and while, on the whole, Cretan wine may not make connoisseurs tremble with delight, the island produces many

---

THE CRETAN DIET

The health benefits of the Cretan diet first gained attention after an influential international study, begun in the 1960s, found that Cretan men had the lowest rate of heart disease and cancer. Thirty years later, half the Cretan participants were still alive, compared to no survivors in Finland. The mystery is attributed to a balanced diet high in fruits, vegetables, pulses, whole grains, olive oil and wine. Another important factor may be the *horta* (wild greens) that Cretans gathered in the hills and survived on during war, which may have protective properties that are not yet fully understood. Regular fasting may also play a role, along with the use of sheep and goat's milk instead of cow's, and many will swear by the medicinal properties of raki and wine and their role in ensuring longevity. Unfortunately the Cretan diet and lifestyle is changing as the island has prospered and become urbanised. Meat and cheese feature more in the diet, few Cretans still work in the fields and obesity, heart disease and cancer rates are rising.

Apart from the health benefits, Cretan cuisine is also finally being recognised as a key part of the cultural heritage. A resurgence of interest and pride in Cretan cuisine has started to change the island's gastronomic map. In recent years more emphasis is being placed on promoting Cretan cuisine through programmes such as **Concred** (www.concred.gr), a restaurant certification programme established in 2004, which has about 30 restaurants on board. Many are in large hotels, which once served only international food, but the list includes a range of classy restaurants and simple tavernas, in the cities, in mountains villages and by the sea, who serve Cretan food. But there are plenty of authentic places to discover in your travels.

CRETAN FIRE WATER

Raki – *tsikoudia* – is an integral part of Cretan culture. A shot of the fiery brew is offered as a welcome, at the end of a meal and pretty much at any time and on all occasions. Distilled from grape stems and pips left over from the grapes pressed for wine, it is similar to the Middle Eastern *arak,* Italian grappa, Irish poteen or Turkish raki. Each October, the raki distilling season starts, with distilleries around the island (including many private stills) producing massive quantities of raki. The season is usually accompanied by a lots of drinking and feasting. If you pass a village distilling raki, you may well get an invitation. Good raki has a smooth mellow taste with no noticeable after-burn. As long as you eat food with it, don't mix it with other alcohol and drink plenty of water, you can drink considerable amounts without serious after-effects or hangovers.

distinguished wines. Wine tourism is slowly picking up as wineries are becoming more visitor-friendly (see p166).

About 70% of Cretan wine comes from the Peza area, Crete's main Appellation of Origin region. Much of it is blended and produced in bulk by cooperatives and the quality can be uneven. Other key wine regions are Dafnes, Arhanes and Sitia, which has a significant industry (p194) producing some crisp whites, while there are also fine wineries in Hania (see p95). The most popular Cretan white grape varieties are *vilana* and *thrapsathiri.* The oldest variety, *liatiko,* has been used to make red wine for the last 4000 years, while reds include *kotsifali* and *mandilari.*

For comprehensive information on the country's wine regions and producers, visit www .greekwine.gr or www .greekwinemakers.com.

House wines served in restaurants are usually very presentable and much cheaper than bottled wine. Some Cretan house reds have a light port taste. Ask for *kokkino* (red), *roze* (rose) or *lefko* (white).

Nowadays retsina, white wine flavoured with the resin of pine trees, has taken on an almost folkloric significance with foreigners, some of whom confuse it with barrel wine (which is non-resinated). It goes well with strongly flavoured food, especially seafood, but it is an acquired taste.

FEASTS & CELEBRATIONS

Food plays an integral part in Cretan religious and cultural celebrations, which are inevitably accompanied by a feast. Festivities invariably involve spit-roasting (and/or boiling) lamb or kid goat, accompanied by a delicious rice *pilafi* made from the stock.

Easter is preceded by the Lenten fast, which involves special dishes without meat or dairy products – or even oil if you go strictly by the book. Come the resurrection, though, the celebrations begin with a bowl of *mayiritsa* (an offal soup), and an Easter Sunday lunch of lamb and *kreatotourta* (meat pies).

Red-dyed boiled eggs are part of the Easter festivities and also used to decorate the *tsoureki,* a brioche-style bread flavoured with *mahlepi* (mahaleb cherry kernels).

Easter sweets include *koulourakia* (biscuits), *melomakarona* (honey biscuits) and *kourambiedhes* (almond biscuits).

A *kouloura* – an intricately decorated loaf of bread that takes hours to make – is a traditional wedding gift. Honey and walnuts, considered an aphrodisiac or fertility-booster, are given to the bridal couple.

The *Vasilopita,* a New Year's cake, has a coin inserted into the mix, giving the recipient good luck for the year.

Throughout the year, there are many celebrations centred on various harvest festivals – from chestnuts to sultanas (see p213 for a full list).

DINING OUT

In most places there is usually a distinction between 'tourist' tavernas and places aimed at more discerning locals, and the key is to find the latter. Friendly touts and big illuminated signs in English with unappealing photos of dishes is a big giveaway, though admittedly there are rare exceptions. Given the later dining times, you may find that a restaurant that was empty at 7pm is heaving with locals when you leave the taverna you chose, so try to adapt to local eating times (see Habits & Customs, p62).

By law, every eating establishment must display a written menu including prices. Restaurant staff will automatically put bread on your table and this comes at a nominal extra charge. Tipping is not mandatory but the bill is usually rounded up or around 10% is added for good service.

As a general rule of thumb, the further you move from the north-coast tourist resorts the better the food becomes, especially in the villages where they are likely to use fresh local produce. Beware of small tavernas with over-extensive menus, as they could not realistically produce all the dishes fresh to order.

Where To Eat & Drink

Other types of eateries include the following:

Estiatorio A restaurant where you once paid more for essentially the same dishes you got in a taverna, but with a nicer setting and formal service. These days *estiatorio* often refers to an upmarket restaurant serving more international cuisine.

Kafeneio One of the oldest institutions, *kafeneio* normally only serve Greek coffee and spirits but in many Cretan villages they will always have meals. They are still largely the domain of men.

Mayireio A restaurant specialising in big trays of the day's cooked dishes, including both traditional baked dishes and one-pot favourites.

Mezedopoleio The key here is lots of different mezedes, small dishes that are shared.

Psarotaverna A taverna specialising in fish and seafood dishes.

Psistaria A taverna specialising in char-grilled or spit-roasted meat.

Rakadiko The Cretan equivalent of an *ouzerie* serves increasingly sophisticated mezes with each round of raki. Particularly popular in Sitia, Ierapetra and Rethymno.

Taverna The classic Greek eateries are casual, family-run (and child-friendly) places where the waiter arrives with bread and cutlery in a basket, and water. They have barrel wine and paper tablecloths and fairly standard menus. Trendy modern tavernas offer creative takes on Greek classics in fancier surrounds, with higher prices and good wine lists but not necessarily better food.

Zaharoplasteio A cross between a patisserie and a café (though some only do take-away).

Mezedes & Starters

Mezedes (appetisers) are normally shared before the main meal, though it is quite acceptable to make a full meal of them. You can also order a *pikilia* (mixed mezedes plate).

Common mezedes are dips such as taramasalata (fish roe), tzatziki (yogurt, cucumber and garlic), *melidzanosalata* (aubergine or eggplant) and

---

GOURMET DELIGHTS

You can pick up a range of delicious souvenirs on your travels, such as excellent Cretan honey, aromatic herbs and teas, spoon sweets (traditional syrupy fruit preserves) pickles, raki and, of course, olive oil. Some of the best places for local produce are women's cooperatives such as **Krousonas** (p163) where you can see women at work and buy some excellent traditional products, including rusks, spoon sweets, pastries, biscuits and pastas. In Hania, **Miden Agan** (p88) has a delectable range of deli foods, olive oils and an extensive wine selection, as does **Avli Raw Materials** (p129) in Rethymno.

DOS & DON'TS

- Do ask to look in the pots in the kitchen or select your own fish.
- Do ask for specific local specialities in every region.
- Don't insist on paying if you are invited out – it insults your host.
- Don't refuse a coffee or glass of raki – it's offered as a gesture of hospitality and good will.

fava (split-pea puree). Hot mezedes include *keftedes* (meatballs), *loukanika* (village sausages), *bourekaki* (tiny meat pies), *saganaki* (fried cheese) and *apaki* (vinegar-cured pork). Vegetarian mezedes include rice-filled *dolmades*, deep-fried zucchini or aubergine slices, *gigantes* (lima beans in tomato and herb sauce), and vegetable fritters, most commonly *kolokythokeftedes* (with zucchini) or *domatokeftedhes* (with tomato).

Typical seafood mezedes are pickled or grilled *Ohtapodi* (octopus), cured *lakerda* (fish), mussel or prawn saganaki (cooked with tomato sauce and cheese), crispy fried calamari, fried *maridha* (whitebait) and *gavros* (mild anchovy) either marinated or grilled.

Soup is not normally eaten as a starter, but can be an economical and hearty meal in itself with bread and a salad. *Psarosoupa* is a fish soup with vegetables; *kakavia* (Greek bouillabaisse) is made to order and laden with seafood. If you're into offal, don't miss *mayiritsa*, the traditional Easter tripe soup.

The ubiquitous Greek or village salad, *horiatiki salata*, accompanies most meals and is made with tomatoes, cucumber, onions, olives and feta cheese, sprinkled with oregano and dressed with olive oil, occasionally garnished with fresh *glistrida* (purslane or capers). Hand-cut potatoes fried in olive oil are also a favourite.

Mains

In tavernas, main dishes normally include a combination of one-pot and oven-baked dishes *(mayirefta)* and food cooked to order *(tis oras)* such as grills. Fancier and more international-style restaurants have more conventional menus. The most common *mayirefta* are *boureki* (a cheese, zucchini and potato bake), mousakas (layers of aubergine, minced meat and potatoes topped with cheese sauce and baked), *pastitsio* (baked cheese-topped pasta with minced meat), *yemista* (stuffed tomatoes or green peppers), *yuvetsi* (casserole of lamb or veal and pasta), *stifado* (braised meat with onions), *soutzoukakia* (spicy meatballs in tomato sauce) and *hohlii* (snails). *Ladhera* are largely vegetable dishes stewed or baked with plenty of olive oil.

Mayirefta are usually prepared early in the day and left to cool, which enhances the flavour (they are better served lukewarm than microwaved).

Meat is commonly baked with potatoes, with lemon and oregano, or cooked in tomato-based stews or casseroles (*kokkinisto*).

Most places will make tasty charcoal-grilled meats such as *brizoles* (pork chops) or *païdakia* (lamb cutlets).

Seafood mains may include octopus with macaroni, and squid stuffed with cheese and herbs or rice. Cuttlefish (*soupies*) is excellent grilled or stewed with wild fennel. Fried salted cod served with *skordalia* (a lethal garlic and potato dip) is another tasty dish.

Fish is usually sold by weight in restaurants and it is customary to pick your victim from the selection on display or in the kitchen. Make sure it's weighed (raw) so you don't get a shock when the bill arrives, as fresh fish is not cheap.

While Crete's fishing industry ensures a lot of fresh fish, there is certainly not enough local fish to cater for the millions of tourists who descend each

Feasting and Fasting in Crete, by Diana Farr Louis, is a hard-back portrait of the island and its culinary history traditions. It includes 140 recipes gathered during her travels and chapters on the island's wine, cheeses and herbs as well as special recipes for weddings and religious festivities.

summer. Most places will state if the fish and seafood is frozen, though sometimes only on the Greek menu (indicated by the abbreviated 'kat' or an asterisk). Smaller fish are often a safer bet – the odder the sizes, the more chance that they are local.

The choice fish for grilling are *tsipoura* (gilthead sea bream), *lavraki* (sea bass) and *fangri* (bream), while smaller fish such as *barbunya* (red mullet) are delicious fried. See the Food Glossary (p64) for other common fish names.

For updates, information and articles on Greek and Mediterranean food, check out www .gourmed.gr.

Sweet Treats

Fruit, rather than sweets, is traditionally served after a meal – but that's not to say that you won't find some delectable local sweets and cakes. Women pride themselves on their baking and confectionary skills.

As well as traditional Greek sweets such as *baklava, loukoumades* (fritters with honey or syrup), *kataïfi* (chopped nuts inside shredded pastry soaked in honey), *rizogalo* (rice pudding), and *galaktoboureko* (custard-filled pastry with syrup), Cretans have their own sweet specialities.

Sfakianes pite, from the Sfakia region of Hania, are fine pancake-like sweets with a light *myzithra* filling, served with honey. *Xerotigana* are deep-fried pastry twirls with honey and nuts.

Traditional syrupy fruit preserves (known as spoon sweets) are served on tiny plates but are also delicious as a topping on yogurt or ice cream. Some tavernas serve halva (made from semolina) after a meal.

Quick Eats

Souvlaki is the favourite fast food of Crete. *Gyros,* skewered or kebab versions are wrapped in pitta bread, with tomato, onion and lashings of tzatziki. There are plenty of western-style *fastfoudadika,* as fast-food joints are known, in major cities and towns. A range of *pittes* including *kalitsounia* and the classic *tyropita* (cheese pie) and *spanakopita* (spinach pie) – can be found in bakeries. If you are in a hurry but want a real meal, tavernas with *mayirefta* are the best bet.

VEGETARIANS & VEGANS

Crete has very few vegetarian restaurants per se, but a combination of lean times and the Orthodox faith's fasting traditions has made Cretans accidental vegans, so there are normally plenty of vegetarian options. *Ladhera* are the mainstay of religious fasts. Beans and pulses were the foundation of the winter diet, so you will find dishes such as delicious *gigantes* (lima beans in tomato and herb sauce).

Look for dishes such *fasolakia yiahni* (green bean stew), *gemista* (stuffed tomatoes) and *bamies* (okra). Aubergines are also widely used, particularly in dishes such as *briam* (mixed vegetables).

Horta (wild greens) are extremely nutritious. The *vlita* variety are the sweetest, while *stamnagathi,* found in the mountains, is considered a delicacy and served boiled as a salad or stewed with meat. Other common *horta* include wild radish, dandelion, stinging nettles and sorrel.

There are more than 100 edible *horta* (wild greens) on Crete, although even the most knowledgeable would not recognise more than a dozen.

Fruit

Crete grows many varieties of beautiful fruit, which are tastier than supermarket offerings back home. A delicious fruit that grows wild on the opunctia cactus is the *frangosyko* (prickly pear, also known as the Barbary fig), though they need to be approached with extreme caution because of the thousands of tiny prickles (invisible to the naked eye) that cover their skin. Never pick one up with your bare hands. Peel them by trimming the ends off with a knife and slit the skin from end to end.

Another unusual fruit you may see are *mousmoula* (loquats), small orange fruit with juicy flesh that are pleasantly acidic.

EATING WITH KIDS

Crete is very child-friendly and families will feel comfortable at informal tavernas and *psistarias*, where children are welcome and treated well and no-one is too fussed if they play between the tables. You will often see families dining out late at night and packs of children playing outside tavernas while their parents indulge in a long dinner. Kids' menus are not common, but most places will make up special plates or accommodate requests.

HABITS & CUSTOMS

Hospitality is a key element of Cretan culture, from the glass of water on arrival to the customary complimentary fruit and raki at the end of a meal. People prefer to share lots of dishes, which makes for more social and relaxed dining and allows you to taste everything. Cretans rarely eat alone.

Cretans aren't big on breakfast. Budget hotels usually provide continental-style breakfasts (rolls or bread with jam, and tea or coffee) and more up-market hotels serve full buffets including Cretan-style pastries.

Athough changes in working hours are affecting traditional meal patterns, lunch is still usually the big meal of the day and does not start until after 2pm. Most Greeks wouldn't think of eating dinner before dark, which coincides with shop closing hours, so restaurants don't fill up until after 10pm. In between, cafés do a roaring trade, particularly after the mid-afternoon siesta (when many places become ghost towns).

Dining is a drawn-out ritual so, if you are eating with locals, pace yourself and don't gorge on mezedes, because there will be plenty more to come. The service can be slow by western standards, but staff are not in a rush to get you out of there either. Once you have your meals they are likely to leave you alone and will often not clear the table until you ask for the bill. Cretans order plenty of dishes and have food left over at the end of the meal. Many places will oblige if you want to take leftovers with you, though when locals do so, it really is a doggie bag.

Ordering a Greek salad or tzatziki as a meal – a common practice among young and budget tourists – is often quietly sneered at by the restaurant staff.

PRESERVING TRADITION

Since making Crete her second home, Greek American chef Nikki Rose has become a quiet ambassador for preserving Cretan culture with sustainable agrotourism through her programme, Crete's Culinary Sanctuaries.

As well as cooking demonstrations in local homes, Rose takes small groups to visit people who still take the time to still make cheese, honey or bake bread in an old wood oven the traditional way. 'It's a lifestyle that's fast disappearing,' she explains.

By slowly establishing an informal islandwide network of organic farms and small producers using traditional methods, she hopes to help preserve Crete's culinary heritage.

'Sustainable tourism and agriculture work together to create better quality tourism and protect the environment and at the same time protect the communities.'

Rose is concerned about the increasing number of 'agro-Disney' ventures, which she fears are alienating and squeezing out the real thing.

'It's very dangerous for real cultural heritage preservation. The tourists don't venture to a real village but they go to these re-creations of traditional Cretan life. If these traditional villages still exist, people should at least go to those places and leave their tourist dollars there.'

Greeks don't traditionally drink coffee after a meal and many tavernas don't offer it.

COOKING COURSES

Culinary tours and cooking courses are becoming more popular on Crete. General courses start from €50.

Rodialos (☎ 28340 51310, www.rodialos.gr) regularly hosts one- to seven-day cooking seminars in a lovely villa in Panormo near Rethymno. Mary Frangaki takes participants through the principles of Cretan cooking and cooks several courses. Rodialos also hosts holistic programmes incorporating yoga and t'ai chi. Workshops cost €50 per day and include eating what you cook. Participants can stay at the villa. Check the website for more details.

Enagron (☎ 28340 61611; www.enagron.gr) outside the village of Axos runs cooking workshops and also organises seasonal events around the production of cheese, wine and raki. The farm setting is lovely and there is accommodation on site (see p136).

Crete's Culinary Sanctuaries (www.cookingincrete.com) focuses on organic agriculture and traditional approaches to Cretan cuisine with hands-on classes and demonstrations in people's homes, visits to local farmers and producers. Headed by Greek-American chef and writer Nikki Rose, the custom-made courses are conducted around Crete (see boxed text, opposite).

Tastes of Crete (☎ 28210 41458; www.diktynna-travel.gr) is an informal hands-on one-day cooking seminar held in an impressive 18th-century farmhouse about 10 minutes from Hania. Classes are limited to eight people and are held twice weekly from May to October. Classes cost €95, which includes transfers, visits to markets, lessons and lunch.

Logari (☎ 2810 752 808; www.logari.gr) was founded by Katerina Hamilaki who runs regular cooking seminars and food-related holidays at her farm and taverna in Katalagari, near Iraklio, which also has a raki still.

EAT YOUR WORDS

Get behind the cuisine scene by getting to know the language. For pronunciation guidelines see p234.

Useful Phrases

**I want to make a reservation
for this evening.**
   the·lo na *kli*·so e·na tra·*pe*·zi ya a·po·pse

Θέλω να κλείσω ένα τραπέζι
για απόψε.

A table for ... please.
   e·na tra·*pe*·zi ya ..., pa·ra·ka·*lo*

Ένα τραπέζι για ... παρακαλώ.

I'd like the menu, please.
   to me·*nu*, pa·ra·ka·*lo*

Το μενού, παρακαλώ.

Do you have a menu in English?
   e·hye·te to me·*nu* sta ang·li·ka?

Έχετε το μενού στα αγγλικά;

I'd like ...
   tha *i*·the·la ...

Θα ήθελα ...

Please bring the bill.
   to lo·ghar·ya·*zmo*, pa·ra·ka·*lo*

Το λογαριασμό, παρακαλώ.

I'm a vegetarian.
   i·me hor·to·*fa*·ghos

Είμαι χορτοφάγος.

**I don't eat meat or
dairy products.**
   dhen *tro*·o *kre*·as i gha·la·kto·ko·mi·*ka* pro·i·*on*·da

Δε τρώω κρέας ή γαλακτοκομικά
προϊόντα.

Cretan Cooking, by Maria and Nikos Psilakis, is a well-translated version of their popular guide to Cretan cooking. It contains 265 mouth-watering recipes, some fascinating asides on the history of the dishes and background to the Cretan dietary phenomenon.

The Glorious Foods of Greece, by award-winning Greek-American food writer Diane Kochilas, is a 'must have' for any serious cook, with a regional exploration of Greek food and a 60-page chapter on Crete.

Food Glossary

STAPLES

pso·*mi*	ψωμί	bread
vu·ti·ro	βούτυρο	butter
ti·*ri*	τυρί	cheese
a·*vgha*	αυγά	eggs
me·li	μέλι	honey
gha·la	γάλα	milk
e·le·*o*·la·dho	ελαιόλαδο	olive oil
e·*lyes*	ελιές	olives
pi·*pe*·ri	πιπέρι	pepper
a·*la*·ti	αλάτι	salt
za·ha·ri	ζάχαρη	sugar
ksi·dhi	ξύδι	vinegar

MEAT, FISH & SEAFOOD

vo dhi *no*	βοδινό	beef
ro·*fos*	ροφός	blackfish
ko·*to*·pu·lo	κοτόπουλο	chicken
sou·*pia*	σουπιά	cuttlefish
ke·*fa*·los	κέφαλος	grey mullet
sfi·ri·da	σφυρίδα	grouper, white
zam·*bon*	ζαμπόν	ham
la·*ghos*	λαγός	hare
ka·tsi·*ka*·ki	κατσικάκι	kid (goat)
ar·*ni*	αρνί	lamb
a·sta·*kos*	αστακός	lobster
ko·li·*os*	κολιός	mackerel
mi·di·a	μύδια	mussels
ohta·*po*·dhi	χταπόδι	octopus
hyi·ri·*no*	χοιρινό	pork
gha·*ri*·dhes	γαρίδες	prawns
kou·*ne*·li	κουνέλι	rabbit
bar·*bou*·nia	μπαρμπούνια	red mullet
sar·*dhe*·les	σαρδέλες	sardines
la·*vra*·ki	λαβράκι	sea bass
fa·*ghri*/li·*thri*·ni/me·la·*nou*·ri	φαγρί/λιθρίνι/μελανούρι	sea bream
ka·la·*ma*·ri	καλαμάρι	squid
ksi·*fi*·as	ξιφίας	swordfish
ma·*ri*·dha	μαρίδα	whitebait
mos·ha·ri ga·lak·tos	μοσχάρι γαλάκτος	veal

FRUIT & VEGETABLES

mi·lo	μήλο	apple
ang·gi·na·ra	αγγινάρα	artichoke
spa·*rang*·gi	σπαράγγι	asparagus
me·li·*dza*·na	μελιτζάνα	aubergine
la·ha·no	λάχανο	cabbage
ka·*ro*·to	καρότο	carrot
ke·*ra*·si	κεράσι	cherry
sy·*ka*	σύκα	figs
skor·dho	σκόρδο	garlic
sta·*fi*·li·a	σταφύλια	grapes
(a·ghri·a) hor·ta	(άγρια) χόρτα	greens, wild
le·*mo*·ni	λεμόνι	lemon

kre·*mi*·dhi·a	κρεμμύδια	onions
por·to·*ka*·li	πορτοκάλι	orange
ro·*dha*·ki·no	ροδάκινο	peach
a·ra·*kas*	αρακάς	peas
pi·per·*yes*	πιπεριές	peppers
pa·*ta*·tes	πατάτες	potatoes
spa·*na*·ki	σπανάκι	spinach
fra·u·la	φράουλα	strawberry
do·*ma*·ta	ντομάτα	tomato
kar·*pou*·zi	καρπούζι	watermelon
gli·*stri*·da	γλυστρίδα	purslane

DRINKS

bi·ra	μπύρα	beer
ka·*fes*	καφές	coffee
καφές	ρακί	raki
tsa·i	τσάι	tea
ne·ro	νερό	water
kra·*si* (*ko*·ki·no/*a*·spro)	κρασί (κόκκινο/άσπρο)	wine (red/white)

Environment

THE LAND

Crete is the largest island in the Greek archipelago with an area of 8335 sq km. It's 250km long, about 60km at its widest point and 12km at its narrowest. The island has an extraordinary geographical and ecological diversity, with mountainous ranges, dramatic gorges, a vast coastline and a plethora of caves. Crete's biodiversity also provides a broad range of habitats for wildlife in a relatively small geographic area, including a few interior wetlands. The island is renowned for its flora and in spring there is an abundance of wildflowers, including many endemic and rare species.

Three major mountain groups – the Lefka Ori (White Mountains) in the west, Mt Psiloritis (also known as Mt Idi) in the centre and the Lasithi Mountains in the east – define the island's rugged interior. The Lefka Ori are known for their spectacular gorges, such as Samaria, plus the snow that lingers on the mountains well into spring. The Omalos Plateau is in the Lefka Ori at an altitude of 1000m. The highest mountain peak is Psiloritis (p137), at 2456m. It has hundreds of caves, including the Ideon Andron Cave where Zeus allegedly grew up, and the Rouvas Forest on its southern slopes.

The Lasithi Mountains harbour the famous Lasithi Plateau (p191) and Mt Dikti (2148m) whose southern slopes preserve an example of the magnificent forests that once blanketed the island. Far-eastern Crete is the driest part of the island and its highest mountain is the wild Mt Thripti at 1476m.

Western Crete is the most mountainous and greenest part of the island, while eastern Crete tends to be barren and rocky. Most of the interior is mountainous and marked by olive trees, scrub and wild herbs. High upland plateaus are either cultivated or used for pasturing goats (like the Omalos Plateau). The largest cultivable area in the south is the fertile Mesara Plain. Lake Kournas (p117), near Hania, is the only natural freshwater lake on the island. Gavdos island (p106), the most southerly point in Europe, just 300km from Africa, is also part of Crete.

WILDLIFE
Animals

While Crete is known for its massive population of sheep and goats, the island is also home to some endemic fauna, including the indigenous large and big-eared Cretan spiny mouse, and a large population of bats, insects, snails and invertebrates.

Fossils discovered in an underwater cave in Hania in 2000 were revealed to be a new species of dwarf elephant that existed only in Crete 50,000 to 60,000 years ago – the creature now known as the Cretan Elephant (or Elephas Chaniensis).

One of the more intriguing rare animals on Crete is the *fourokattos* (wild cat), about which shepherds have been telling tales for centuries. Scientists assumed it only existed in legend, until a British scientist bought two strange pelts at a market in Hania in 1905. The only other proof ever found was in 1996 when Italian scientists studying Cretan fauna discovered a 5.5kg cat in a trap. It remains unclear whether the cat was indigenous to the island or whether it was a domesticated animal that ran wild.

Other local species include the tiny Cretan tree frog and the Cretan marsh frog. The southern coastline and its steep underwater cliffs are home to the Mediterranean Sea's most significant population of sperm whales, who gather, feed, breed and possibly mate in the area year-round. The southern coast is also inhabited by large groups of striped dolphins, Risso's dolphins and Cuvier's beaked whales. Bottlenose dolphins are often spotted in the shallow waters between Gavdos and Gavdopoula, as well as off the southern coast.

The Cretan Sperm Whale Project, run by the Pelagos Cetacean Research Institute, monitors the whale population and has an eco-volunteer programme. Private dolphin-spotting trips are run from Paleohora (p103).

BIRD LIFE

Crete is a superb destination for bird-watchers as the island is on the main flying routes from East Africa. The island's large and diverse variety of bird life includes many resident and migratory species, as well as some rare predatory birds. Along the coast you'll find birds of passage such as egrets and herons during spring and autumn migrations. Various species of gull nest on coastal cliffs and offshore islets. Rare hawks migrate up from Africa during the summer to nest on the offshore islets. Wood pigeons still nest in cliffs along the coast, but have been hunted to near extinction.

The mountains host a wealth of interesting birds. Look for blue rock thrushes, buzzards and the huge griffon vulture. Other birds in the mountains include Alpine swifts, stonechats, blackbirds and Sardinian warblers. The fields around Malia host tawny and red-throated pipits, stone-curlews, fan-tailed warblers and short-toed larks. On the hillsides below the Moni Preveli (p140) you may find ruppells and subalpine warblers. The Akrotiri Peninsula (p89) is good for bird-watching – around the monasteries of Agias Triadas and Gouvernetou you'll find collared and pied flycatchers, wrynecks, tawny pipits, black-eared wheatears, blue rock thrushes, stonechats, chukars and northern wheatears. Migrating species such as waders, egrets and gulls are found on Souda Bay.

There are small natural wetlands around Crete, while a number of new dams and reservoirs created in the last decade have also become significant wetland habitats for migratory birds. Lookouts and observation decks have been built in key bird-watching areas.

ENDANGERED SPECIES

Crete's most famous animal is the *agrimi* or kri-kri, a distinctive wild goat with large horns often depicted in Minoan art. Only a few survive in the wild in and around the Samaria Gorge (p93) and on the islands of Agioi Theodori off Hania and Dia off Iraklio.

You may spot a *lammergeier* (bearded vulture) – one of the rarest raptors in Europe, with a wing span of nearly three metres – in the Samaria Gorge or hovering above the Lasithi Plateau. The species is now threatened with extinction. Crete has the only four birds known to be in Greece

Crete is battling to protect its population of loggerhead turtles, which have been nesting on Crete since the days of the dinosaurs (see boxed text, p69). The island also has a small population of the rare and endangered Mediterranean monk seals breeding in caves on the south coast.

Plants

Crete has one of the world's most amazing variety of plants and wild flowers and is a mecca for botanical enthusiasts. One Japanese fanatic on a specialist tour came just to see one particular rare tulip. It has been estimated that there are about 2000 plant species on the island and about 160 of those are endemic to Crete. The island's gorges are mini-botanical gardens and their isolation helped preserve many endemic species.

As a rule, a visit in March or April is the surest way to see the island in full flower, but mountain plants and flowers often bloom later in the year and late rains can also extend the growing season.

Along the coast, sea daffodils flower in August and September. In April and May knapweeds are in flower on the west coast and the purple or violet petals of stocks provide pretty splashes of colour on sandy beaches. At the

Hard-core bird-watchers should come equipped with *A Birdwatching Guide to Crete* by Stephanie Coghlan or, for a comprehensive reference on Greece's birdlife, try *The Birds of Greece* by Christopher Helm.

Crete is one of the most significant refuel stopovers for birds migrating between Africa and Europe in spring and autumn, while many migratory birds choose to spend the winter in Crete.

Walks with Crete's Spring Flowers, by Jeff Coleman, is based on walks around the southwestern corner of Crete, particularly Loutro, Paleohora and the Samaria Gorge.

same time of year in eastern Crete, especially around Sitia, watch for crimson poppies on the borders of the beach. At the edge of sandy beaches that are not yet lined with a strip of hotels you'll find delicate pink bindweeds and jujube trees that flower from May to June and bear fruit in September and October. In the same habitat is the tamarisk tree, which flowers in the spring.

Further away from the beach in the lowlands are junipers and holm oak trees, as well as spring-flowering poppies and purple lupins. If you come in the summer, you won't be deprived of colour since milky white and magenta oleanders bloom from June through to August.

On the hillsides look for cistus and brooms in early summer, and yellow chrysanthemums in the fields from March to May. The rare endemic blue carpet blooms called Blavees are only found in the high peaks of the Lefka Ori.

Many varieties of orchid (including 14 endemic species) and ophrys bloom in the spring on the lower slopes of the mountains, turning the hills and meadows pink, purple and violet. The area around the mountain village of Spili is renowned for its abundance of wild orchid species and tulips. Dense-flowering orchids, pink-flowered butterfly orchids and Cretan cyclamens grow on the Lasithi Plateau. Purple and crimson anemones are seen in the same habitat in early spring, followed by yellow buttercups and crowfoots in late spring.

Crete has one of the richest varieties of indigenous herbs in the world, collected for both medicinal and cooking uses. The native dittany *(diktamo)* tea, is renowned for its healing effects and pungent Cretan wild oregano is among the best in Greece. Aromatic sage, rosemary, thyme and oregano grow wild in the mountains and countryside, while you can find all sorts of Cretan herbal remedies at Marianna's Workshop in Maroulas (p132).

NATIONAL PARKS

The only national park in Crete is the Samaria Gorge (p93), the largest and most impressive gorge in Europe (and also on the tentative list for Unesco's World Heritage sites). It is 16km long and has a visitor centre. No-one lives in the gorge; it is an important sanctuary for birds and animals, particular the kri kri. Vast sections of Crete are also part of the special conservation area network of the European NATURA 2000 programme.

ENVIRONMENTAL ISSUES

The level of environmental awareness in Crete is very slowly increasing, although environmental regulation is still lacking. While the concept of eco-tourism is being paid lip-service, too few legitimately eco-friendly developments have emerged. Indeed, a number of alarming development proposals have caused major protests in recent times. The most controversial is a plan to by a British consortium to build a massive €1.6 billion 'eco-friendly' luxury development on virgin coastline in far eastern Crete on land belonging to the Toplou monastery. Objections to the plans – for three golf courses and several hotels and six villages in an area with no water or infrastructure, requiring desalination and wastewater treatment plans – were taken to Greece's highest court. Environmental groups have also been mobilised over contentious plans for a major shipping container port in Tymbaki, which would spoil a huge section of the south coast.

There are no recycling programmes on Crete even though the huge influx of summer visitors produces tonnes of rubbish. Most tourist areas are kept relatively rubbish-free, but in the interior you will often be treated to the pungent odour of garbage decomposing in an illegal dump. There have been moves for the country to clean up its act, however, after the EU fined Greece more than €5 million for not acting on its toxic waste dump at Kouroupitos in western Crete, the problem has not gone away.

The Flowers of Greece & the Aegean, by William Taylor and Anthony Huxley, is the most comprehensive field guide to flowers in Greece and Crete.

There are more than 200 species of wild orchid on Crete, including 14 endemic varieties and Crete's famous Ophrys Cretica, which uses its insect-like appearance as a disguise to attract male insects.

Plants of Crete (Mystis Publication) is a comprehensive glossy botanical guide by Antonis Alibertis outlining the healing, aromatic and edible plants and herbs of Crete.

LOGGERHEAD TURTLES

Since 1990 **Archelon** (Sea Turtle Protection Society of Greece; www.archelon.gr) has worked with state agencies, local authorities, hotel groups, tour operators, fishing operators and local residents to reverse the decline of Crete's population of loggerhead turtles *(Caretta caretta)*.

The north-coast beaches around Rethymno and Hania as well as the south coast along the Mesara Gulf host more than 550 nests each summer – the turtles lay their eggs in the middle of the sandy beaches. Sadly, the ribbons of hotels and tavernas on the northern beaches have seriously disturbed their nesting habits. Because they are so vulnerable on land, the females are frightened by objects on the beach at night and can refuse to lay eggs, while hatchlings emerging at night are disoriented by tavern and hotel lights.

Archelon patrols about 33km of beach through the nesting and hatching season, mostly around Rethymno, Matala and Hania. Signposted metal cages are put around nests to protect them from sun-beds and tourists, many hatcheries are fenced off and the problem of lights on the beach is gradually being addressed by hotels, with the Grecotel group leading the way in implementing Archelon's directives on lighting.

Volunteers are always welcome to assist in their patrol and monitoring work and help to staff information booths, with a minimum stay of one month (contact the Archelon main office in Athens via the website).

The society has the following advice for visitors:

- Leave the beaches clear at night during the May to October nesting season.
- Remove umbrellas and sun-loungers at night.
- Don't touch baby turtles on the way to the sea; they must orient themselves and the walk strengthens them.
- Urge hotel and taverna owners to cooperate with the society and shade their lights when necessary.
- Dispose of rubbish properly; plastic bags, which the turtles mistake for jellyfish, are lethal.

Outside the major cities Crete's air and water is clean, but the flora and fauna are under pressure from deforestation. Centuries of olive cultivation, firewood gathering, shipbuilding, uncontrolled livestock breeding, overgrazing and arson have laid waste to the forests that had carpeted the island at one time. There is no tree-replanting programme, possibly because the 90,000 goats living on the island would chew through the saplings. The use of pesticides and herbicides in farming has eliminated many bird and plant species, and hunting has decimated the animal population.

It is along Crete's shoreline that environmental damage is most acute. Marine life has suffered from overfishing and the local habit of fishing with dynamite and overdevelopment of the northern coast is chasing away migratory birds. Worldwide concern has been roused for the plight of the loggerhead turtles, which nest on the same sandy beaches that tourists prize (see below).

As tourism on Crete has ballooned over the last two decades, the island has had to cope with increasing demands for electricity and renewable energy sources. Solar power is widely used domestically and by hotels and there were plans to build a large solar plant. More than a dozen wind farms around the island also inject much-needed power into the island's electricity grid.

On the plus side, organic farming is taking off, along with a move towards sustainable tourism. Several big hotel groups have introduced eco-friendly practices in their resorts. Green organisations, such as WWF Greece and Greenpeace, have become increasingly active in Greece over the past 10 years, and many local environmental groups have been formed in Crete, most of whom are part of the island-wide Ecocrete network.

Almost a quarter of Greece's cleanest beaches are on Crete. In 2007, 96 beaches in Crete were awarded the European Blue Flag Beach rating. Of those, 39 beaches were in Lasithi prefecture (for the full list see www .blueflag.org).

For the latest information on environmental issues and organisations in Crete, as well as petitions against eco-unfriendly projects, go to www .ecocrete.gr.

Crete Outdoors

Crete's rugged terrain, soaring mountains, dramatic gorges and cobalt-blue seas are a nature-lover's dream. While the heat in summer can make you just want to hit the beach, Crete is a year-round destination for travellers interested in more active experiences and adventure travel. You can climb its high peaks in spring or cycle around the Lasithi Plateau in summer. Spring and autumn are the best time for great walks and serious hikes through beautiful gorges or along scenic coastal paths and alpine trails.

In recent years opportunities for active and challenging holidays have increased, with several specialist operators running activities on the island. There are excellent horse-riding trails and more extreme pursuits such as paragliding, bungee jumping, caving, canyoning or sea kayaking along the south coast. Crete's warm, clear waters offer excellent opportunities for diving and snorkelling. Windsurfers head to Kouremenos on the east coast, and all around the island you will find every imaginable water sport.

The three-volume GPS-compatible 1:100.000 scale touring maps by Anavasi (☎ 210 321 8104; www.anavasi .gr) show the E4 across Crete but its walking maps cover sections in greater detail (at a scale of 1:25,000) for the Lefka Ori (Sfakia and Pahnes), Samaria/Sougia, Mt Psiloritis and Zakros-Vai.

HIKING & TREKKING

Crete offers an enormous variety of options for keen hikers and trekkers that take you through remote villages, across plains and into gorges. Unfortunately, excellent hiking opportunities are poorly documented – there are few detailed English-language guides in publication – and the trails themselves are generally inadequately marked.

The exception to this is the E4 trail, which runs the length of Crete (see boxed text, opposite), though some parts of that are also tricky to find. Add to this the generally rugged and arid nature of Crete's terrain and you'll soon see why hiking and trekking here can be both a blessing and a bane. Nonetheless, the island's generally untrodden interior is probably its attraction and, while the majority of visitors may opt for a guided hike, experienced walkers will find plenty to challenge and stimulate them.

For maps, photos and detailed information and advice on sections of the E4 trail, check out the website www.crete .tournet.gr.

Some of the most popular hikes, including the Samaria Gorge (p93), are detailed throughout this book, and there are newly marked trails at Zakros (p200).

While Crete is a veritable paradise for hikers, walking is not much fun between July and August, when the temperatures can reach 40°C. Spring is when walkers descend en masse.

Crete's numerous gorges attract hikers from all over the world. The walks can be a breathtaking (and hard-going) experience. Along the way you can enjoy the aroma of wild herbs and flowers, stop at shaded picnic spots and wade through streams (in spring and autumn).

Gorge walking will involve a bit of planning if you have your own transport. You will either have to walk back the same way to pick up your vehicle, or arrange for someone to collect you at the other end. Buses can normally get you to within striking distance of a gorge entrance. Most gorge walks are doable by anyone with a reasonable level of fitness. Here is a select list of some of the more accessible gorges:

More than 160,000 people hike the Samaria gorge each year, making it Crete's second most popular tourist attraction after Knossos.

Agia Irini Gorge (p101) A full-day walk best tackled from the village of Agia Irini north of Sougia. This is a challenging hike with dramatic landscape varying from alpine to coastal. It ends at Sougia.

Agiofarango (p174) A popular hike in south-central Crete running from Moni Odigitrias, 24km southwest of Mires, it ends at a lovely beach.

Hohlakies Gorge Not as well known as its near neighbour at Zakros, this short (3km) walk runs from Hohlakies village to the coast. Hikers can walk a further 7km northwards to Palekastro.

Imbros Gorge (p95) Perhaps the second most-popular gorge walk after Samaria, it runs from the village of Imbros for 8km to Komitades, near Hora Sfakion.

Rouvas Gorge (p167) This short link hike runs from the village of Zaros on the southern slopes of Psiloritis to meet up with the alpine route of the E4 trail. It's a convenient way to get to and from the trans-Crete hike.

THE E4 ROUTE

The trans-European E4 walking trail starts in Portugal and ends in Crete. In Crete the trail picks up at the port of Kissamos-Kastelli in the west and ends – after 320km – on the pebbly shore of Kato Zakros in eastern Crete. Enthusiasts planning to tackle the Cretan leg can do it in a minimum of three weeks, allowing for 15km per day, or more comfortably in four weeks allowing for stops and/or shorter hiking trips. You can, of course, tackle only sections of it if your time is limited or if you just want to walk the most interesting parts. However, you will need to make important decisions early on as the trail splits into two distinct sections through western Crete: the coastal route and the alpine route.

The E4 trail is marked throughout its length with black and yellow posts and signs, but is not always well maintained: paths are overgrown and in many sections signs are hard to find. The E4 can be a lonely trail and there is no food (and little water) along most of the route, so it is always wise to get local advice before setting off.

From Kissamos-Kastelli the route first takes a long dip south, following the western coast via Elafonisi to Paleohora. From Paleohora there is a pleasant hike to Sougia (see the boxed text, p106). The first big decision must be made at Sougia. A little east of here, the E4 alpine route shoots north and upwards and heads across the high alpine tracts of the barren Lefka Ori, while the E4 coastal route hugs the rugged coastline as far as Kato Rodakino, between Frangokastello and Plakias. The alpine route is for serious hikers and will involve overnighting in one of three refuges along the way (see p74 for information on Crete's refuges). The E4 coastal route, while not a picnic stroll, is easier but can be quite rough in parts, and the section between Sougia and Agia Roumeli is quite difficult to find and potentially dangerous to follow.

Neither trail actually incorporates the Samaria Gorge as part of its route, but you can easily include it. At Sougia take the first leg of the E4 alpine route towards Omalos and hike south down the Samaria Gorge to the coast (and the E4 coastal route) at Agia Roumeli. Alpine hikers can, of course, head north up the gorge from Agia Roumeli and pick up the E4 alpine route near Omalos. The alpine route from Omalos is perhaps the toughest section of the trail and should not be attempted in the heat and aridity of summer. It is high and exposed and there is no water other than the odd snow bank that may have lingered from winter.

From Argyroupolis, near where the two trails cross each other, the E4 alpine route now runs south of the E4 coastal route, which itself loops northwards along the escarpment of the Psiloritis massif. The E4 alpine route runs through the Amari Valley for some way, via Spili and Fourfouras, before veering west and up to the summit of Mt Psiloritis (2456m). Both trails meet once more at the Nida Plateau on the eastern side of Crete's highest mountain (see the boxed text, p138, for hikes in this area).

Heading eastward the now-unified trail meanders through the more populated Iraklio prefecture via the villages of Profitis Ilias, Arhanes and Kastelli before climbing once more to the Lasithi Plateau.

From Lasithi the route becomes alpine with a crossing of the Mt Dikti (2148m) range to the south, then turning eastwards for the remote passage down to the narrow 'neck' of Crete between Ierapetra and the Bay of Mirabello. Mountains take over as the trail threads its way between Mt Thripti (1476m) to the south and Mt Orno (1238m) to the north. Settlements are fewer at this end of the island, so each day's hiking leg should be planned carefully.

The final leg from Papagiannades and through the villages of Handras and Ziros is less taxing and the last village, Zakros, marks the start of the hike through the 'Valley of the Dead' to the sea at Kato Zakros (see the boxed text, p200). This is the final leg on the long walk from Portugal (if you have come all the way!).

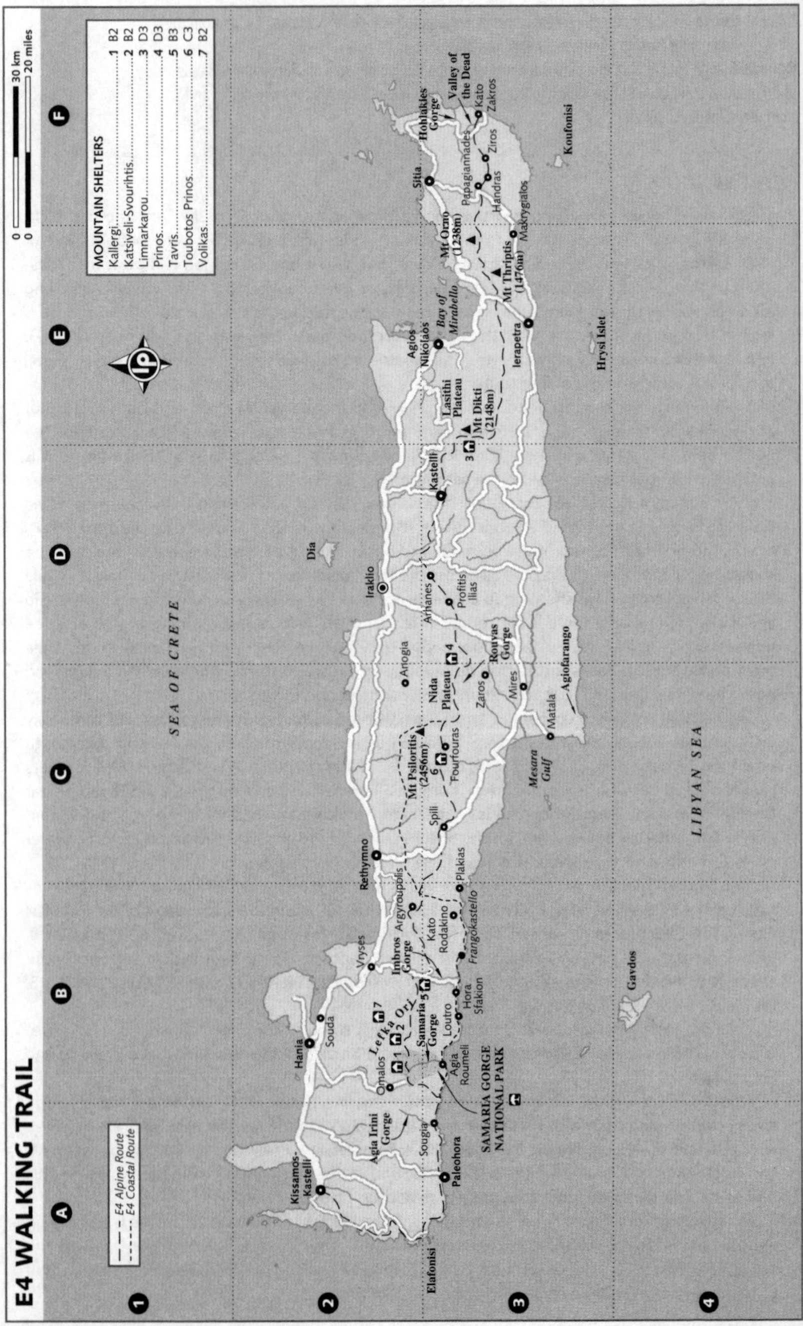

E4 WALKING TRAIL
E4 Alpine Route
E4 Coastal Route
MOUNTAIN SHELTERS
Kallergi 1 B2
Katsiveli-Svourihtis 2 B2
Limnarkarou 3 D3
Prinos 4 D3
Tavris 5 B3
Toubotos Prinos 6 C3
Volikas 7 B2
0 30 km
0 20 miles
SEA OF CRETE
LIBYAN SEA
Kissamos-Kastelli
Elafonisi
Paleohora
Sougia
Agia Irini Gorge
Omalos
Hania
Souda
Lefka Ori
Samaria Gorge
Agia Roumeli
SAMARIA GORGE NATIONAL PARK
Loutro
Hora Sfakion
Vryses
Imbros Gorge
Frangokastello
Kato Rodakino
Argyroupolis
Plakias
Rethymno
Spili
Mt Psiloritis (2456m)
Fourfouras
Nida Plateau
Anogia
Zaros
Rouvas Gorge
Mires
Matala
Mesara Gulf
Agiofarango
Iraklio
Arhanes
Profitis Ilias
Dia
Kastelli
Lasithi Plateau
Mt Dikti (2148m)
Agios Nikolaos
Bay of Mirabello
Ierapetra
Mt Thriptis (1476m)
Mt Orno (1238m)
Makrygialos
Sitia
Papagiannades
Handras
Ziros
Hohlakies Gorge
Valley of the Dead
Kato Zakros
Koufonisi
Hrysi Islet
Gavdos

OUTDOOR ADVENTURES IN CRETE

The following companies run a range of organised hikes, biking and other outdoor activities in Crete. Guide walks start from €44 per day and €500 per week including accommodation, transfers and meals.

Axas Outdoor Activities (☎ 2810 871 239; axas@yahoo.gr) Run by walking and nature enthusiast Dimitris Kornaros, it specialises in custom tours in off-the-beaten-track locations. It's based in Profitis Ilias near Iraklio.

Cretan Adventures (☎ 2810 332 772; www.cretanadventures.gr; Evans 10, Iraklio) Organises hiking and trekking tours, mountain biking and other specialist and extreme activities.

Happy Walker (☎ /fax 28310 52920; www.happywalker.com; Tobazi 56, Rethymno) Runs a range of walks from March to November, including summer walks in the Omalos Plateau and Lefka Ori.

International Centre of Natural Activities (☎ 6977 466900; www.icna.gr) Paragliding, caving, off-road mountain-bike tours, hiking and climbing tours around the island. It's based in Avdou.

Korifi Tours (☎ 28220 41440; www.korifi.de) Hiking and climbing tours around Kapetaniana, in southern Iraklio. It's based in Kapetaniana.

Strata Walking Tours (☎ 28220 24336; www.stratatours.com) In Kissamos-Kastelli, offering anything from leisurely day trips to seven- to 15-day walking tours to the south coast.

Trekking Hellas (☎ 28210 58952; www.greeceoutdoors.com; crete@trekkinhg.gr) One of the biggest mainland operators running out of Athens, it runs extensive activities in Crete.

Trekking Plan (☎ /fax 28210 60861; www.cycling.gr) This outfit at Agia Marina, 10km west of Hania, will take you hiking, rock climbing, mountaining, biking and rapelling in western Crete.

The Valley of the Dead (p199) A two-hour hike in far-eastern Crete. The valley is the last section of the E4 hiking route and runs from Zakros to the palace of Kato Zakros.

Samaria (p93) Crete's longest and most famous walk.

Sirikari Gorge (p111) One of western Crete's most scenic and popular walks, taking about two hours to ancient Polyrrinia and as much again to Kissamos.

Several companies run walking and hiking tours across Crete (see boxed text, above), including specialists Happy Walker and Strata Walking Tours.

CYCLING & MOUNTAIN BIKING

Cycling has caught on in a big way in Crete, despite the mountainous terrain. While it is possible to cycle from one end of Crete to the other and barely raise a sweat, north–south routes and the southern coast are likely to test your stamina and fortitude. However, the escarpment villages and valleys of the north coast and the Mesara Plain of the south do allow for some relatively flat cycling experiences. Crete is a mountain-biker's dream.

Many do it the easy way. Tour companies now transport you and your machine to the top of the mountains so you can cycle down. Plateau tours (especially around the Lasithi Plateau) are big business. There are also more extreme biking options and eight-day tours covering more than 650km (see above)

Independent cyclists coming to Crete with their own bikes are advised to bring sturdy touring bikes with multiple gears. You can hire mountain bikes for €8 to €20 per day from a range of places around the island. Mountain bike tours start from €50 per day.

There are no dedicated biking guides to Crete, so you may be better off joining a tour.

Several companies offer tours (see boxed text, above) for all levels of experience and fitness, including specialist small operators such as **Odysseas the Cyclist** (☎ 28310 58178; odysseasthecyclist@hotmail.com) in Rethymno, who takes organised and custom tours.

British nature lover and Crete fan Peter Thomson has created an online *Walking and Cycling Guide to Crete* at www.peter-thomson.co.uk/crete/contents.html.

CANYONING, CLIMBING & BUNGEE JUMPING

While Crete doesn't offer the kind of stunning alpine terrain that's found in Austria or Switzerland, the island does have a large number of mountains and established mountaineering clubs. Each prefecture has its own club, which maintain the E4 trail and mountain refuges. They are all members of the association of Greek Mountaineering Clubs (EOS) and organise regular climbing, walking, speleology and skiing excursions around Crete, which visitors are welcome to join.

Mountaineering Club of Hania (EOS; ☎ 28210 74560; www.interkriti.org/orivatikos/hania1 .htm; Tzanakaki 90, Hania)

Mountaineering Club of Iraklio (EOS; ☎ 2810 227 609; www.interkriti.org/orivatikos/orivat .html; Dikeosynis 53, Iraklio; ☎ 8.30pm-10.30pm)

Mountaineering Club of Lasithi (EOS; ☎ 28970 23230)

Mountaineering Club of Rethymno (EOS; ☎ 28310 57766; www.eos.rethymnon.com; Dimokratias 12, Rethymno) Lists excursions on its website.

Huts maintained by the clubs are listed in the boxed text, below.

> There are more than 3000 caves recorded in Crete, of which about only 850 have been explored. The 1208m-deep Gourgouthakas cave, in the Lefka Ori, is one the 30 deepest caves in the world (and the deepest in Greece). Its entrance is about a metre wide.

MOUNTAINEERING CLUB REFUGES

Name	Location	Altitude (m)	Capacity (beds)	EOS
Kallergi	Near the Samaria Gorge	1680	50	Hania
Katsiveli-Svourihtis	Svourihtis foothills	1970	25	Hania
Limnarkarou	Lasithi Plateau	1350	15	Lasithi
Prinos	Asites, East Psiloritis	1100	45	Iraklio
Tavris	Plateau of Askyfou	1200	42	Hania
Toubotos Prinos	Mt Psiloritis	1500	28	Rethymno
Volikas	Volikas Keramion	1400	40	Hania

Hikers tackling the E4 trail need to do some planning. While there is nearly always accommodation within the range of a six- to seven-hour daily hike, some of it will need to be arranged beforehand – particularly the mountain refuges, where you might need to pick up keys.

> The multilingual *Canyoning in Crete*, by Yiannis Bromirakis (Road Editions 2007), covers many of Crete's newly accessible gorges in fine detail with maps and drawings.

Canyoning

Canyoning is becoming increasingly popular in Crete, where there is no shortage of wild and beautiful canyons. The newly formed **Cretan Canyoning Association** (☎ 6997 090307; www.canyon.gr) has secured more than 50 gorges in southern Crete since 2005. Among them is the challenging Ha gorge (p205), near Mt Thripti in eastern Crete, which until recently had been traversed by less than a dozen people (and still numbered less than 100 in 2007). The Association's website has useful information and a published guide to Crete's canyons. It organises regular excursions and also runs beginners courses. A four-day, four-canyon course inclusive of equipment costs €155. Guided canyoning trips range from €45 to €70 depending on location.

> Climb in Crete (www .climbincrete.com) has some excellent information on climbing and mountaineering on the island, including articles, photos and hiking guides.

Climbing

Apart from peak climbing up Crete's numerous summits, scaling up the cliff face of mountains and gorges is another increasingly popular sport. Southern Iraklio is one of the most popular areas for climbing, particularly the stunning cliffs around Kapetaniana and Mt Kofinas on the southern flanks of the Asteroussia mountains (p175). The Agiofarango gorge (p174) is another popular climbing spot, while new sites are being opened up around Crete, including sites at Matala and in Theriso, near Hania.

Unless you are experienced, you are advised to contact local organisations before attempting climbs. French climbing enthusiast Philippe Bugada has published a multilingual comprehensive guide *Crete* (Kapetaniana/

Kofinas, €18) to about 150 climbs around Kapetaniana and Agiofarango. It is available on Crete (or through www.lacordi telle.com).

Bungee Jumping

High above the Aradhena Gorge, on the south coast, is a spectacular bungee jumping location, the highest bungee jumping bridge in Greece and the second highest in Europe. Thrill seekers can jump 138m into the narrow gorge from the bridge that crosses over the canyon. Jumps are held every weekend from June to September by **Liquid Bungy** (☎ 6937 615191; www.bungy.gr; €100 per jump).

WATER SPORTS

Crete is a paradise for water sports. Parasailing, water-skiing, jet-skiing, pedal boating and canoeing are available on most of the major beaches. On the northern coast, you'll find a water-sport centre attached to most luxury hotels and you don't need to stay there to use the facilities. Elsewhere, specialist operators run snorkelling and diving courses as well as windsurfing and sea kayaking. There are few waves to catch in Crete so leave the board at home.

Sea Kayaking

Crete's south coast has become increasingly popular for sea kayaking trips. The dramatic cliffs and remote beaches make it a spectacular experience. Sea kayaking can be experienced as a day trip (from €60) or week-long trips including accommodation and pick up. Some can also be combined with hiking.
Alpine Travel (☎ 28210 50939; 6932 252 890; www.alpine.gr; Boniali 11-19) Based in Hania.
Nature Maniacs (☎ 28250 91017; www.naturemaniacs.com) Runs sea kayaking along the south coast from its base in Loutro.

> For detailed descriptions of a range of walks around Crete, check out an intrepid walker's site at www.peter-thomson .co.uk/crete/contents .html

Diving & Snorkelling

Crete's warm, clear and inviting waters make snorkelling and diving a pleasure. With the liberalisation of laws relating to diving, the Greek seas have been opened, except for areas declared archaeological sites. Like much of the Mediterranean, marine life, especially big fish, has been fished out, but Crete has stunning caverns, dramatic cliffs and interesting locations for divers. Some of the more interesting snorkelling is around the sunken city of Olous near Elounda (p188), while Bali (p144), Plakias (p138)and Paleohora (p102) are popular diving sites.

Several diving centres offers courses from beginners to PADI-certification and advanced dive courses. Under Greek law, you must dive as part of a licensed diving operation and you are forbidden to disturb any antiquities you may come across. It's wise to call at least a day in advance to book a dive.

Snorkelling trips are also widely available.

Check out these companies in the following towns:
Agios Nikolaos Cretas Happy Divers (☎ 28410 82546; www.cretashappydivers.com) On the beach of the Coral Hotel and at Plaka and Elounda.
Bali Hippocampos (☎ 28340 94193 www.hippocampos.com) Near the port.
Hania Blue Adventures Diving (☎ 28210 40608; www.blueadventuresdiving.gr; Arholeon 11)
Iraklio Diver's Club (☎ 2810 811 755; www.diversclub-crete.gr; Agia Pelagia); Stay Wet
(☎ 28970 42683; www.staywet.gr; Mononaftis)
Plakias Kalypso Rock's Palace Dive Centre (☎ 28310 20990; www.kalypsodivingcenter.com; Eleftheriou Venizelou 42); Phoenix Diving Club (☎ 28320 31206; www.scu bacrete.com)
Rethymno Paradise Dive Centre (☎ 28310 26317; www.diving-center.gr; Eleftheriou Venizelou 57)
Paleohora Aqua Creta Diving & Adventures (☎ 28230 41393; www.aquacreta.gr)

Windsurfing

The best windsurfing in Crete is at **Kouremenos Beach** (p198), north of Palekastro in Sitia. Windsurfing is also good in Almyrida (p118), near Hania.

The **Hellenic Windsurfing Association** (☎ 210 323 0330) in Athens can provide general information.

Key water-sport centres:

Driros Beach (☎ 6944 932 760; www.spinalonga-windsurf.com) At Plaka, near Elounda.
Freak Windsurf (☎ 28430 61116, 6979 254967; www.freak-surf.com) At Kouremenos.
UCPA Sports (☎ 28250 31443; www.ucpa.com; board hire €8 per hr) In Almyrida.

Yachting

Yachting is a great way to experience Crete, but the winds make it unreliable and its distance from other islands means it is not on the Greek island yachting loop. Some companies, however, do offer daily sailing excursions. Sailing along the southern coast allows you to see some of Crete's finest and most isolated beaches.

'Yachting is a great way to experience Crete…'

Nautilos Yacht Rentals (☎ 28420 89986; www.ierapetra.net/nautilos) in Ierapetra take private yacht tours around the south coast islands of Hrysi and Koufonisi, and can take you around the coast as far as Sitia.

Yachties can get the lowdown on sailing around Crete and Greece at www .sailing.gr or www.yach ting.gr.

OTHER ACTIVITIES
Golf

Crete has a few nine-hole golf courses, but the island's only 18-hole pro course is the **Crete Golf Club** (☎ 28920 26000; www.crete-golf.com) in Hersonisos. This desert-style, par 72 course has been designed to blend in with the environment. The course is quite tough and also has a double-ended driving range, a golf academy and club house. It's not for hackers, though. An 18-hole round in summer will set you back €67 (excluding clubs or buggies).

Horse Riding

Several places on Crete offer horse riding and guided trail rides through the countryside.

The most impressive operation is **Odysseia Stables** (☎ 28970 51080; www.horseriding .gr) above Avdou, at the foot of Mt Dikti (p166). These new stables have excellent facilities (including accommodation) and run anything from two-hour beginners rides to three-days rides through the Lasithi Plateau and week-long trails through the Dikti mountains to the south coast. Typical prices range from €18 for a one hour beach ride, €35 for a two-hour hack, €55 for a day trip and from €474 for 8-day courses including accommodation and meals.

Zoraida's Horseriding (☎ 28250 61745; www.zoraidas-horseriding.com), in Georgoupolis, offers beach and nature trails, including day safaris and a six-day course for advanced riders.

Melanouri Horse Farm (☎ 28920 45040; www.melanouri.com) in Pitsidia near Matala runs rides through the surrounding region.

Paragliding

Crete's climate and terrain make it an ideal location for paragliding (known as *parapente*) and it is a sensational way to see the island if you are game to fly with the birds. There are about 45 excellent paragliding take-off sites around Crete, mostly surrounding the three highest mountains, as well as coastal sites such as Falasarna and Paleohora.

Certified instructor and paragliding enthusiast Grigoris Thomakakis and his team at the **International Centre of Natural Activities** (☎ 6977 466900; www.icna.gr) run flights across the island and near their base in Avdou, south of Malia. Day flights for experienced pilots accompanied by an instructor cost €30. Tandem flights cost €70.

Hania Χανια

The Hania region offers visitors a wealth of activities and experiences, from mountain climbing, gorge hiking and scuba diving to lazing on the beach and dining on the day's catch in small fishing hamlets along the coast. Despite having one of the island's top tourist attractions – the Samaria Gorge – Hania for the most part maintains an authentic feel. It is renowned for its rugged natural beauty, and for its many stunning gorges and spectacular mountain ranges, such as the Lefka Ori and Mt Gingilos in the rugged interior. Its capital, the port town of Hania, is the island's most romantic and alluring town, with a rich mosaic of Venetian and Ottoman architecture.

The northern coastline is becoming highly developed, especially the string of beach resorts along the Gulf of Hania, but it's possible to find more isolated spots on the Akrotiri Peninsula, which has two interesting monasteries, and to the west around Kissamos and the barely inhabited Rodopou and Gramvousa peninsulas. Hania's rocky southern coast is dotted with laid-back beach communities such as Paleohora and Sougia. The nearly deserted west coast has two of Crete's finest beaches – Falasarna in the north and Elafonisi in the far south.

In the hinterland are traditional mountain villages where you'll still see shepherds tending their flocks and find family tavernas that use their own produce. In the province of Sfakia, road signs riddled with bullet holes remind you that this is the Wild West of Crete. Eastern Hania boasts the island's only natural lake, Lake Kournas, and the stunning Imbros Gorge, the underrated rival to Samaria. Gavdos island, off the southern coast in the Libyan sea, is Greece's southernmost island – the ultimate escape from it all.

HIGHLIGHTS

- Hiking the spectacular **Samaria Gorge** (p93) and **Imbros Gorge** (p95)
- Wandering through the narrow streets of the Venetian and Turkish quarters of **Hania** (p82)
- Relaxing on the remote **southern beaches** (p95)
- Chilling out on the island of **Gavdos** (p106)
- Exploring mountain villages such as **Theriso** (p93) and indulging in the region's excellent cuisine.

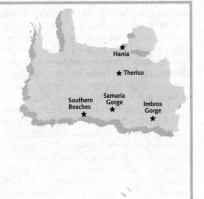

HANIA XANIA

pop 55,838

Hania is unreservedly Crete's most evocative city. Remnants of Venetian walls still border a web of atmospheric streets in the old town that tumble onto a picturesque harbour. Restored Venetian townhouses have been converted into restaurants, cafés, boutique hotels and attractive *pensions*. The prominent former mosque on the harbour front and Ottoman-style timber buildings scattered through the old town are remnants of Turkish rule.

Hania's war-torn history has left it with only a few impressive monuments, but the city wears its scars proudly. Along Zambeliou, Theotokopoulou and Angelou streets in the old quarter you will come across roofless Venetian buildings that have been turned into gracious outdoor restaurants. Even during the height of the tourist season when many of the buildings are festooned with tourist merchandise, Hania retains the exoticism of a city caught between East and West.

Hania has some of the islands finest restaurants. The town also has a tradition of artisanship making it a great shopping city, while the cafés along the harbour are ideal for relaxing and watching passers-by promenade.

HISTORY

Hania is the site of the Minoan settlement of Kydonia, which was centred on the hill to the east of the harbour, between Akti Tombazi and Karaoli Dimitriou. Excavation work has been restricted because the ruins lie under the modern city, but the finding of clay tablets with Linear B script (see boxed text, p27) has led archaeologists to believe that Kydonia was both a palace site and an important town. Fifty late-Minoan graves were found in 2004 in the Agios Ioannis area, part of the cemetery of ancient Kydonia, and excavations are continuing.

Kydonia met the same fiery fate as most other Minoan settlements in 1450 BC, but soon re-emerged as a force. It was a flourishing city-state during Hellenistic times and continued to prosper under Roman and Byzantine rule.

The city came under the control of the Venetians around the beginning of the 13th century, and the name was changed to La Canea. The Venetians lost control of the city to the Genoese in 1266, but they finally wrested it back in 1290. The Venetians con-structed massive fortifications to protect the city from marauding pirates and invading Turks. They did not prove very effective against the latter, who took Hania in 1645 after a two-month siege.

The Turks made Hania the seat of the Turkish Pasha until the end of Turkish rule in 1898. During this time the churches were converted into mosques and the architectural style of the town changed, becoming more Oriental, with wooden walls and latticed windows.

The Great Powers made Hania the island capital in 1898 and it remained so until 1971, when the administration was transferred to Iraklio.

The WWII Battle of Crete largely took place along the coast to the west of Hania. The town itself was heavily bombed during WWII, particularly around Ancient Kydonia, but enough of the old town survives for it to be regarded as Crete's most beautiful city.

ORIENTATION

Hania's bus station is on Kydonias, two blocks southwest of Plateia 1866. From Plateia 1866, the Venetian port is a short walk north up Halidon. Zambeliou, once Hania's main thoroughfare, is lined with craft shops, small hotels and tavernas. The headland near the lighthouse separates the Venetian port from the crowded town beach in the modern Nea Hora quarter. In the other direction, Koum Kapi, a rejuvenated waterfront precinct is where younger Haniots hang out. Boats to Hania dock at Souda, about 7km southeast of town.

INFORMATION
Bookshops

Mediterraneo Bookstore (☎ 28210 86904; Akti Koundourioti 57) An extensive range of English language novels and books on Crete, as well international press.

Newsstand (☎ 28210 95888; Skalidi 8) A wide range of international press and magazines, books, Crete guides and maps.

Pelekanakis (☎ 28210 92512; Halidon 98) Has maps, guidebooks and books in 11 languages.

Emergency

Tourist police (☎ 28210 73333; Kydonias 29; ☯ 8am-2.30pm) At the Town Hall.

Internet Access

Triple W (☎ 28210 93478; Valadinon & Halidon; per hr €2; ☯ 24hr) Extensive facilities & high speed access.

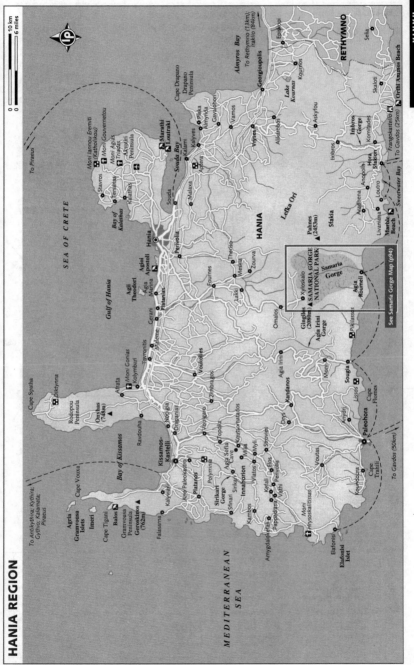

HANIA

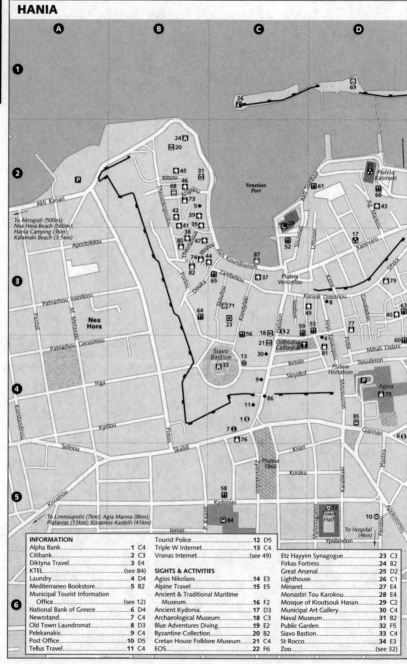

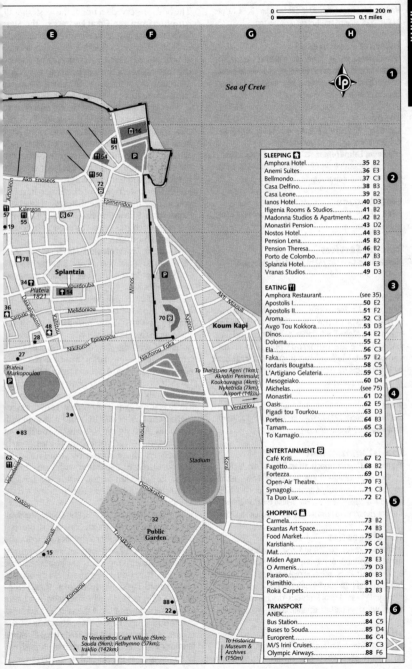

Sea of Crete

Splantzia

Plateia 1821

Vourdouba

Koum Kapi

Plateia Markopoulou

El Venizelou

Stadium

Public Garden

To Thalassino Ageri (1km);
Akrotiri Peninsula;
Koukouvagia (4km);
Nyketrida (7km);
Airport (14km)

To Verekinthos Craft Village (5km);
Souda (9km); Rethymno (57km);
Iraklio (142km)

To Historical
Museum &
Archives
(150m)

| 0 | | 200 m |
| 0 | | 0.1 miles |

SLEEPING

Amphora Hotel	35	B2
Anemi Suites	36	E3
Bellmondo	37	C3
Casa Delfino	38	B3
Casa Leone	39	B2
Ianos Hotel	40	D3
Ifigenia Rooms & Studios	41	B2
Madonna Studios & Apartments	42	B2
Monastiri Pension	43	D2
Nostos Hotel	44	B3
Pension Lena	45	B2
Pension Theresa	46	B2
Porto de Colombo	47	B3
Splanzia Hotel	48	E3
Vranas Studios	49	D3

EATING

Amphora Restaurant	(see 35)	
Apostolis I	50	E2
Apostolis II	51	F2
Aroma	52	C3
Avgo Tou Kokkora	53	D3
Dinos	54	E2
Doloma	55	E2
Ela	56	C3
Faka	57	E2
Iordanis Bougatsa	58	C5
L'Artigiano Gelateria	59	C3
Mesogeiako	60	D4
Michelas	(see 75)	
Monastiri	61	D2
Oasis	62	E5
Pigadi tou Tourkou	63	D3
Portes	64	B3
Tamam	65	C3
To Karnagio	66	D2

ENTERTAINMENT

Café Kriti	67	E2
Fagotto	68	B2
Fortezza	69	D1
Open-Air Theatre	70	F3
Synagogi	71	C3
Ta Duo Lux	72	E2

SHOPPING

Carmela	73	B2
Exantas Art Space	74	B3
Food Market	75	D4
Karistianis	76	C4
Mat	77	D3
Miden Agan	78	E3
O Armenis	79	D3
Paraoro	80	B3
Psimithio	81	D4
Roka Carpets	82	B3

TRANSPORT

ANEK	83	E4
Bus Station	84	C5
Buses to Souda	85	D4
Europrent	86	C4
M/S Irini Cruises	87	C3
Olympic Airways	88	F6

Vranas Internet (☎ 28210 58618; Agion Deka 10; per hr €2; ☒ 9.30am-1am) Full set up & air-con.

Internet Resources

www.chania.gr The Municipality of Hania's website is worth a look for information on the city and cultural events.
www.chania-guide.gr Good information on the Hania city and prefecture.

Laundry

Laundry (☎ 28210 57602; Agion Deka 18; wash & dry €6) Self service or drop off available.
Old Town Laundromat ☎ 28210 59414; Karaoli & Dimitriou 38; wash & dry €7; ☒ 9am-2pm & 6-9pm Mon-Sat) Also does dry cleaning.

Left Luggage

KTEL (☎ 28210 93052; Kydonias 73-77; per day €1.50) At the bus station.

Medical Services

Hania Hospital (☎ 28210 22000; Mournies) Located south of town.

Money

Most banks are in the new city, but there are a few ATMs in the Old Town on Halidon, including **Alpha Bank** (cnr Halidon & Skalidi) and Citibank. There are numerous places to change money outside banking hours. **National Bank of Greece** (cnr Tzanakaki & Giannari) has a 24-hour exchange machine.

Post

Post Office (☎ 28210 28445; Peridou 10; ☒ 7.30am-8pm Mon-Fri, 7.30am-2pm Sat)

Tourist Information

Municipal Tourist Information Office (☎ 28210 36155; tourism@chania.gr; Kydonias 29; ☒ 8am-2.30pm) Located at the Town Hall, it provides helpful practical information and maps. The info booth behind the mosque in Old Harbour also tends to be manned between noon and 2pm.

Travel Agencies

Diktynna Travel (☎ 28210 41458; www.diktynna -travel.gr; Arhontaki 6) Organises a range of cultural and ecotourism activities, including cooking classes.
Tellus Travel (☎ 28210 91500; Halidon 108; www.tellus travel.gr; ☒ 8am-11pm) Rents cars, changes money, arranges air and boat tickets, accommodation and excursions.

SIGHTS

The massive fortifications built by the Venetians to protect their city remain impressive.

The best-preserved section is the western wall, running from the **Firkas Fortress** to the **Siavo Bastion**. It was part of a defensive system begun in 1538 by engineer Michele Sanmichele, who also designed Iraklio's defences. Entrance to the fortress is via the gates next to the Naval Museum. From the top of the bastion you can enjoy some fine views of the old town.

The Venetian **lighthouse** at the entrance to the harbour has been restored, though the new lighting along the sea wall could have been more subtle. It's a pleasant 1.5km walk around the sea wall to get there, especially in the early evening (you can cheat by taking the barge from the Fortezza café).

On the eastern side of the inner harbour you will see the prominent **Mosque of Kioutsouk Hasan** (also known as the Mosque of Janissaries), which has been restored and houses regular exhibitions.

Hania's **Archaeological Museum** (☎ 28210 90334; Halidon 30; admission €2; incl Byzantine Collection €3; ☒ 8.30am-3pm Tue-Sun; closes 7.30pm in summer but check) is housed in the superb 16th-century Venetian Church of San Francisco that became a mosque under the Turks, a movie theatre in 1913 and a munitions depot for the Germans during WWII. The museum houses a well-displayed collection of finds from western Crete dating from the Neolithic to the Roman eras. Artefacts from 3400 BC to 1200 BC, to the left as you enter the museum, include tablets with Linear A script (see p47). There is some exquisite pottery from the Geometric era (1200–800 BC) and a case of bull figurines. Among the Hellenistic and Roman exhibits, the statue of Diana is particularly impressive. There is a marble fountain in the pretty courtyard decorated with lions' heads from the Venetian period, while the Turkish fountain is a relic from the building's days as a mosque.

The **Naval Museum** (☎ 28210 91875; Akti Koundouri-oti; admission €3; ☒ 9am-4pm May-Sep) has an interesting collection of model ships dating from the Bronze Age, and naval instruments, paintings, photographs and memorabilia from the Battle of Crete. It is housed in the Firkas Fortress, once the old Turkish prison. An authentic replica of a Minoan ship, which sailed from Crete to Athens as part of the Athens 2004 Olympics ceremonies, will be the star attraction of the museum's new **Ancient and Traditional Maritime Museum** annexe in the Venetian ship sheds being created at the far end of the harbour.

The **Byzantine and Post Byzantine Collection of Hania** (☎ 28210 96046; Theotokopoulou; admission €2, I Archaeological Museum €3; ☒ 8.30am-3pm Tue-Sun) in the impressively restored Church of San lvatore. It has a small but fascinating collection of artefacts, icons, jewellery and coins, cluding a fine segment of a mosaic floor for a early Christian basilica and a prized icon St George slaying the dragon. The building as a mixed bag of interesting architectural atures from its various occupiers.

Hania's interesting **Cretan House Folklore useum** (☎ 28210 90816; Halidon 46; admission €2; ☒ 9.30am-3pm & 6-9pm) contains a selection of afts and implements including weavings ith traditional designs.

The **Historical Museum and Archives** (☎ 28210 606; Sfakianaki 20; admission free; ☒ 9am-1pm Mon-Fri), utheast of the old quarter, traces Crete's ar-torn history with a series of exhibits cusing on the struggle against the Turks. here are also exhibits relating to the German ccupation and a folklore collection.

The stunningly restored **Great Arsenal** ☎ 28210 40101; www.kam-arsenali.gr; Plateia Katehaki) now home to the Centre for Mediterranean rchitecture, which hosts regular events and xhibitions.

The restored **Etz Hayyim Synagogue** (Parodos ndylaki; ☎ 28210 86286; www.etz-hayyim-hania.org; ☒ 10am-8pm Tue-Fri, 5-8pm Sun, 10am-3pm & 5-8pm Mon) as a moving memorial to the Jews of Hania ho were annihilated by the Nazis.

Hania's three-level **Municipal Art Gallery** ☎ 28210 92294; www.pinakothiki-chania.gr; Halidon 98; mission €2, free Wed; ☒ 10am-2pm & 7-10pm Mon-, 10am-2pm Sat) hosts exhibitions of modern reek art.

You can escape the crowds of the Vene-an quarter by taking a stroll around the urkish **Splantzia quarter** – a delightful tangle f narrow streets and squares that is being ejuvenated and cut off to traffic. It is at-acting new boutique hotels, galleries and rtistic or alternative pursuits. Along Daliani, ou will see one of Hania's two remaining inarets and pass the restored 16th-century onastiri Tou Karolou (☎ 28210 50172; Daliani 22; ☒ 11am-late; closed Sun). Apart from the pleasant ourtyard café, which hosts occasional live usic and cultural events, the old monastery now the home, atelier and hairdressing alon of Hania's famous formerly Paris-based elebrity hairdresser-cum-sculptor Karolos ambelopoulos.

Hania's other remaining minaret is attached to the charmingly schizophrenic **Agios Nikolaos** formerly part of a Dominican priory, which has a belltower on the other side. Nearby you can see the restored Venetian church of **San Rocco**.

You can see excavation works at the site of **Ancient Kydonia**, to the east of the old harbour at the junction of Kanevaro and Kandaloneou.

Hania's magnificent covered **Agora** (Municipal Market; see p85) has some excellent eateries and is a worth a visit even if you don't want to shop. Sadly, the central bastion of the city wall was demolished to make way for this fine 1911 cruciform creation, modelled after the market in Marseilles.

ACTIVITIES
Hiking, Climbing & Biking

Trekking Plan (☎ 28210 60861; www.cycling.gr; Agia Marina) In Agia Marina, 8km southwest of the old town, Trekking Plan offers hikes to the Agia Irini and Imbros gorges, and climbs of Mt Gingilos, as well as canyoning, rappelling, rock-climbing and kayaking and mountain-bike tours.

Alpine Travel (☎ 28210 50939; 6932 252 890; www.alpine.gr; Boniali 11-19) Organises a range of eco-tourism, mountaineering and hiking programmes.

EOS (☎ 28210 44647; www.eoshanion.gr; Tzanakaki 90; ☒ 8.30am-10pm) The Hania branch of the Greek Mountaineering Association has information about serious climbing in the Lefka Ori, mountain refuges and the E4 trail, and runs regular weekend excursions.

Hellas Bike Tours (☎ 28210 60858; www.hellasbike.net; Agia Marina) In Agia Marina, this group rents out bikes and leads half and full-day bike tours around the region.

Nature Maniacs (☎ 28250 91017; www.naturmaniacs.com; Platanias) Specialises in nature, adventure and cultural travel programmes as well as a sea kayaking on the south coast around Loutro.

Diving

Blue Adventures Diving (☎ 28210 40608; www.blueadventuresdiving.gr; Arholeon 11) This outfit offers a PADI certification course (€370) and daily diving trips around Hania (two dives €75), including beginner dives. There are also snorkelling trips and cruise options if you just want to go along for the ride.

Swimming

The town beach at **Nea Hora** is crowded but generally clean if you need to cool off and get some rays. For better swimming, keep heading west and you'll come to the beaches (in order) of **Agioi Apostoli, Hrysi Akti** and **Kalamaki** (about 3.5km). There are regular local buses heading there and all the way to Platanias and beyond.

HANIA FOR CHILDREN

If your five-year-old has lost interest in Venetian architecture, head to the **public garden** between Tzanakaki and Dimokratias, where there's a playground, a small **zoo** with two resident kri-kri (Cretan goat) and a shady café. Eight kilometres south of town the giant water park **Limnoupolis** (☎ 28210 33246; Varypetro; day pass adult/ child 6-12 €17/12, afternoon pass €12/9; ⏰ 10am-7pm) has enough slides and rides to keep kids amused and cafés and pool bars for adults. Buses leave regularly from the KTEL bus station (€1.60).

TOURS

Boat excursions from the harbour take you to the nearby islands of Agii Theodoroi and Lazaretto and the Gulf of Hania. The **M/S Irini** (☎ 28210 52001; cruises €15; sunset cruises €8, children under 7 free) runs daily cruises on a lovely 1930s cruiser, including free snorkelling gear, and sunset cruises with complimentary fruit and raki.

The **F/B Alexandros** (☎ 28210 71514) runs daily cruises around Souda Gulf that stop at caves and beaches.

Several operators offer really short half-hour or one-hour cruises or rides on murky glass bottomed boats, but they are hardly worth it.

Sheffield-born photographer **Steve Outram** (☎ 28210 32201; www.steveoutram.com) runs photography tours twice a year for both amateur shutterbugs and more seasoned photographers.

FESTIVALS & EVENTS

In summer, the municipality hosts cultural events around the city, including the public gardens and the **open-air theatre** (www.chania.gr) on the outskirts of the city walls (on Kyprou), which has regular music and theatrical performances.

Hania commemorates the **Battle of Crete anniversary** with athletics competitions, folk dancing and ceremonial events during the last week of May.

SLEEPING

Hania's Venetian quarter is brimming with chic boutique hotels and family-run atmos-

pheric *pensions* in restored Venetian buildings. Most hotels are open year-round. Keep in mind many of the older and boutique hotels have no lift. The western end of the harbour and along Zambeliou is a good place to look, but it can be noisy at night, especially along the harbour – the price you pay for a view. There are cheaper rooms around the Splantzia quarter, where some reasonably priced boutique hotels have recently opened. Hotel complexes with pools can be found at Nea Hora and along the beach running west to Platanias and beyond.

Budget

Hania Camping (☎ 28210 31138; www.camping-chania .gr; Agii Apostoli; caravan/tent €7/4; 🏊) The nearest camp site is 3km west of town on the beach. The site is shaded and has a restaurant, bar and mini-market and pool. You can also rent a tent (€10). Buses heading west (every 15 minutes) from the southeast corner of Plateia 1866 can let you off at the camp site.

Pension Lena (☎ 28210 86860; lenachania@hotmail .com; Ritsou 5; s/d €35/55; 🖳) Lena's is a friendly, cosy *pension* in an old Turkish building where you can help yourself to a room if the owner is not there. It has an old-world feel and a scattering of antiques, though the front rooms are the most appealing. Originally from Hamburg, Lena makes guests feel welcome.

Ifigenia Rooms & Studios (☎ 28210 94357; www .ifigeniastudios.gr; Gamba 23 & Parodos Agelou; studio €35-140; 🖳) This network of refurbished houses around the Venetian port offers anything from simple rooms to fancy suites with kitchenettes, Jacuzzis and views. Some bathrooms are very basic, the faux old-world décor a little contrived and the renovations not always sympathetic.

our pick Pension Theresa (☎ /fax 28210 92798; Angelou 2; r €40-50; 🖳) This creaky old house with a steep spiral staircase and antique furniture is the most atmospheric *pension* in Hania. It attracts many artists and writers, and is often full. Some rooms have a view, but there's always the stunning vista from the rooftop terrace where you can use the communal kitchen. The rooms are spotless and all have TV, air-con and lofts with an extra bed for small families, though some are on the tight side and the ambience comes at a premium.

Monastiri Pension (☎ /fax 28210 41032; Agiou Markou 18 & Kanevarou; d & tr €40-55; 🗷) The stone arched entry and antique family furniture in the communal area give this older-style budget place a certain charm. Bathrooms are basic but rooms have a fridge and some have a TV. The front rooms have balconies with lovely views.

Midrange

Vranas Studios (☎ 28210 58618; www.vranas.gr; Agion Deka 10; studio €40-70; 🗷) This place is on a lively pedestrian street and has spacious, immaculately maintained studios with kitchenettes. All rooms have polished wooden floors, balconies, TVs and telephones. There's a handy internet café attached.

our pick Madonna Studios & Apartments (☎ 28210 94747; madonnastudios@yahoo.co.uk; Gamba 33; studio €70-110; 🗷) This charming small hotel has five attractive and well-appointed studios around a lovely flower-filled courtyard. They are furnished in traditional style and the front top room has a superb balcony, while the courtyard room has the original stone wash trough.

Nostos Hotel (☎ 28210 94743; www.nostos-hotel.com; Zambeliou 42-46; s/d/tr incl breakfast €60/80/120; 🗷) Mixing Venetian style and modern fixtures, this 600-year-old building has been remodelled into classy split-level accommodation, with kitchen, fridge, phone and TV. It also has a roof garden. Try to get a balcony room with harbour views.

Porto de Colombo (☎ 28210 70945; colompo@otenet .gr; Theofanous & Moshon; d/ste incl breakfast €84/103; 🗷) Once the French embassy and office of Eleftherios Venizelos, this Venetian townhouse is now a charming boutique hotel with 10 lovely, well-appointed rooms; the top suites have fine harbour views.

Bellmondo (☎ 28210 36216; www.belmondohotel .com; Zambeliou 10; d/ste incl breakfast €90/110; 🗷) This classy hotel has harbour views and a formal feel, with iron beds and traditional furnishings. It has Turkish and Venetian features, including part of an old *hammam* (Turkish bath) in one room. Children up to 12 stay free. The nicer rooms have balconies (€99).

Anemi Suites (☎ 28210 53001; www.anemisuites.gr; Sarpaki 41; s/d/tr €70/82/105; 🗷) A restored Venetian-Turkish building in the quiet Splantzia quarter has been turned into four comfortable suites.

Ionas Hotel (☎ 28210 55090; www.ionashotel.gr; Sarpaki & Sorvolou; d €50-80, ste €120; 🗷) This is one of the new breed of boutique hotels in the quiet Splantzia quarter. The historic building has a contemporary design and fit-out and the nine rooms with all the mod-cons and a small terrace on the roof. The price includes a buffet breakfast.

Splanzia Hotel (☎ 28210 45313; www.splantzia .com; Daskalogianni 20; d €100 incl buffet breakfast 🗷) This smart new designer hotel in an Ottoman building has eight stylish rooms, some decorated with four-poster timber beds and drapery. The back rooms overlook a lovely courtyard.

Top End

our pick Amphora Hotel (☎ 28210 93224; www.amphora.gr; Parodos Theotokopoulou 20; d with view €120, ste €145; 🗷) This historically evocative hotel is in an immaculately restored and kept Venetian mansion with rooms around a courtyard and in a second connected wing. The rooms are elegantly decorated and the top rooms have air-con and views of the harbour. The front rooms can be noisy in the summer and there are cheaper rooms without a view. Breakfast is €10.

our pick Casa Leone (☎ 28210 76762; www.casa -leone.com; Parodos Theotokopoulou 18; s & d incl breakfast €120-150; 🗷) This Venetian residence has been converted into a classy and romantic boutique hotel. The rooms are spacious and well appointed, with balconies overlooking the harbour. There are honeymoon suites, the usual mod cons and extras such as hairdryers.

Casa Delfino (☎ 28210 93098; www.casadelfino.com; Theofanous 7; ste & apt incl buffet breakfast €186-316; 🗷) This elegant 17th-century mansion is the most luxurious hotel in the Old Town. There are 22 individually decorated and well-appointed suites, including a palatial, split-level apartment with a Jacuzzi. The apartment sleeps up to four people. Breakfast is in the splendid pebble-mosaic courtyard.

EATING

Hania has some of the finest restaurants in Crete, some housed in roofless Venetian ruins. Unfortunately, most of the prime-position waterfront tavernas are generally mediocre, often overpriced and fronted by annoying touts, so head for the back streets.

Budget

Hania's famous covered **Agora** (Municipal Market; 🕙 Mon, Wed & Sat 8.30am-2pm, Tue, Thu & Fri 8.30am-1.30pm

& 6-9pm) is a good-value place for self-caterers to stock up on supplies, as well as stop for lunch.

Michelas (☎ 28210 90026; mains €5-7; ☺ 10am-4pm Mon-Sat) Near the meat section of the food market, this place has been serving great fresh, and cheap traditional cuisine for 75 years.

Iordanis Bougatsa (☎ 28210 90026l Kydonias 96; bougatsa €2.50) Continuing the business started by his great-grandfather in 1924, Iordanis churns out endless trays of delicious creamy *bougatsa* (filo pastry filled with *myzithra* cheese sprinkled with a little icing sugar). It's opposite the bus station.

Doloma (☎ 28210 51196; Kalergon 8; mayirefta €4.50-6; ☺ Mon-Sat) This unpretentious restaurant tucked behind the harbour is half-hidden amid the vines and foliage surrounding the outdoor terrace. The traditional cooking is faultless. Pick from the various trays of *mayirefta* (casseroles and bakes) cooked daily.

L'Artigiano Gelateria (☎ 28210 53612; Athinagora Plateia) There is almost always a queue for this delightful home-made Italian gelati.

There are plenty of snack food and souvlaki places on Halidon, but locals swear by the undeniably tasty souvlaki at the tiny old-style **Oasis** (Vouloudakidon 2; ☺ Mon-Sat; shopping hr only; souvlaki €2).

For breakfast, sandwiches and lighter meals you can try the popular **Aroma** (☎ 28210 41812; Akti Tombazi 4) next to the mosque or **Avgo Tou Kokkora** (☎ 28210 55776; Ag 10 & Sarpaki) behind the cathedral.

Midrange

our pick Portes (☎ 28210 76261; Portou 48; mains €6-8.50) Affable Susanna from Limerick cooks up Cretan treats with a difference at this superb restaurant in a quiet street in the Old Town. Try her divine marinated *gavros* (little fish), stuffed fish baked in paper, tasty meatballs with leek and tomato, or pretty much anything from the specials board.

To Karnagio (☎ 28210 53366; Plateia Katehaki 8; Cretan specials €5-10.50) This is a popular place with outdoor tables near the Great Arsenal. There is a good range of seafood (try the grilled cuttlefish) and classic Cretan dishes, plus a fine wine list.

Tamam (☎ 28210 96080; Zambeliou 49; mains €5.50-8.50) Housed in an old *hammam*, Tamam presents a superb selection of vegetarian specialities – try the spicy avocado dip on potato (€6) – and inspired dishes such as the Tas

kebab veal with spices and yogurt or the Beyendi chicken with creamy aubergine purée.

our pick Thalassino Ageri (☎ 28210 51136; Vivilaki 35; top fish €55 per kg; ☺ dinner) It can be tricky to find, but this solitary fish taverna in a tiny port among the ruins of Hania's old tanneries is one of the most delightful eateries in Crete. Apart from the superb setting they have fresh fish and excellent mezedes such as tender octopus in wine vinegar and melt-in-your-mouth calamari as well as a delicious fisherman's salad. Take a taxi or follow Venizelou around the coast turning left at Noel St as soon as you veer away from the coast.

Mesogeiako (☎ 28210 59772; Daliani 36; mezedes €3.20-5.60) This promising newcomer near the minaret in the revitalised Spantzia quarter is a trendy *mezedopoleio* serving an array of classic and more creative dishes. Try the pork meatballs and their excellent raki.

Monastiri (☎ 28210 55527; Akti Tombazi; mains €7.20-13.90) One of the few waterfront restaurants that gets the general thumbs up from discerning local and international diners, Monastiri, on the eastern side of the harbour, dishes up well-executed Cretan fare.

Faka (☎ 28210 42341; Plateia Katehaki; mains €6.20-12.90) This is another of those quiet, unassuming places that doesn't dish up bland fare. The cuisine is solid and genuine. Good local choices include or artichokes and broad beans. There's a children's menu and small playpen.

Pigadi tou Tourkou (☎ 28210 54547; Sarpaki 1-3; mains €10-14.50; ☺ dinner, closed Mon-Tue) Features from this former *hammam*, including the well it's named after (Well of the Turk), are incorporated into the cosy design of this popular restaurant, which has dishes inspired by Crete, Morocco and the Middle East. The service can, however, be indifferent and prices have crept up.

Ela (☎ 28210 74128; Kondylaki 47; mains €6.50-18; ☺ noon-1am) This 14th-century building was a soap factory, then a school, distillery and cheese-processing plant. Now Ela serves up a decent array of Cretan specialities, such as goat with artichokes, while musicians create a lively ambience. The tacky board outside tells you it's in every guidebook but the accolades are not undeserved.

Also recommended are the excellent Amphora Restaurant, on the port below the hotel and **Dinos** (☎ 28210 41865; Akti Enosis 3), in the cluster of fish tavernas at the far end of the harbour.

Top End

Akrogiali (☎ 28210 71110; Akti Papanikoli 20, Nea Hora; ✆ dinner only) One of the best seafood restaurants in Hania, Akrogiali is on the beach side of the new town. The fish is fresh and the accompaniments are superb. The airy restaurant opens onto the seafront giving you a great view of the sunset.

Apostolis I & II (☎ 28210 43470; Akti Enoseo; fish per kg up to €55) In the quieter eastern harbour, this is a well-respected place for fresh fish and Cretan dishes in two separate buildings. Apostolis II is the more popular as the owner reigns there, but the other store has the same menu at marginally cheaper prices. A seafood platter for two, including salad, is €30. Service is friendly and efficient, and there's a good wine list and harbour setting.

Nykterida (☎ 28210 64215; Korakies, on airport road) This highly regarded establishment just outside town has been around since 1933 and was converted to the German club during WWII. It has been graced over the years by the likes of Churchill, Melina Mercouri, Andreas Papandreou and Anthony Quinn (who the owner's father taught how to dance for his role in *Zorba the Greek*).

ENTERTAINMENT

The harbour's lively and prominent waterfront bars and clubs around the mosque are mostly patronised by tourists, while the row of clubs along Sourmeli are frequented by American soldiers from the nearby bases. There are some lively bars in the streets of the Old Town.

Synagogi (☎ 28210 96797; Skoufou 15) Housed in a roofless Venetian building that was once a synagogue, this popular lounge bar is the favourite haunt of young locals.

Fagotto (☎ 28210 71877; Angelou 16; ✆ 7pm-2am Jul-May) A Hania institution housed in a restored Venetian building, Fagotto offers the smooth sounds of jazz and light rock and blues. Jazz paraphernalia includes a saxophone beer tap.

Café Kriti (☎ 28210 58661; Kalergon 22; ✆ 8pm-late) Also known as Lyrakia, this rough-and-ready joint, with a decorative scheme that relies on saws, pots, ancient sewing machines and animal heads, is the place to hear live Cretan music.

Fortezza (☎ 28210 46546) This café, bar and restaurant, installed in the old Venetian ramparts across the harbour, is the best place in town for a sunset drink. A free barge takes you across the water, from the bottom of Sarpidona to the sea wall wrapping around the harbour.

Further along the harbour, the arty café-bar **Ta Duo Lux** (☎ 28210 52519; Sarpidona 8; ✆ 10am-late) remains a perennial favourite hangout for a younger alternative crowds and is popular day and night. Along this strip you will also find Bolero and Hippopotamos.

Serious party animals head to the flashy clubs in Platanias and Agia Marina, 11km west of Hania.

Koukouvagia (☎ 28210 27449; Venizelos Graves) If you have wheels then take a 10-minute drive up the hill to where the great statesman Eleftherios Venizelos is buried. The owl-themed café and bar (with an extraordinary owl décor collection) enjoys panoramic views of Hania. It's a cool place to hang on summer's nights. The pitta creations are excellent, as are the large selection of cakes and desserts.

SHOPPING

Hania offers the best combination of souvenir hunting and shopping for crafts on the island. The best shops are scattered through the back streets of the old town and around Theotokopoulou. Skrydlof is 'leather lane,' known as the 'Stivaniadika' because this was where you would pick up a pair of Cretan boots. You can still find them, but most of the goods on sale are handmade sandals, belts and bags. On Sifaka you will find the 'Machairadika', stores selling traditional Cretan knives.

There's an outdoor *laïki* (street market) Saturday mornings from 7am to 2pm on Minoos and another market on the waterfront west of the Firkas fortress on Thursdays.

Most stores in the old town tend to stay open until at least 11pm, while the new town shopping district keeps regular shop hours (see p210).

Exantas Art Space (☎ 28210 95920; Zambeliou & Moschon; ✆ 10am-2pm & 6pm-11pm) This classy store has great postcards with old photos, lithographs and engravings, handmade gifts, Cretan music as well as a good range of travel, coffee table and art books.

O Armenis (☎ 28210 54434; Sifaka 29) Owner Apostolos Pahtikos has been making traditional Cretan knives since he was 13 and has passed on the trade to his son. You can watch them work as they match the blades to carefully carved handles at the workshop (Sifaka 14). A kitchen knife costs €15.

Carmela (☎ 28210 90487; Angelou 7) This exquisite store has a tempting array of original jewellery designs with stones collected on their travels, as well as Carmela's unique ceramics using ancient techniques. They also have jewellery and ceramics by leading Greek artists.

Mat (☎ 28210 42217; Potie 51) A hobby that turned into an obsession for the late national chess champion Athanasios Diamantopoulos has put this tiny shop on the world map for chess enthusiasts. His wife continues to sell a large range of his original chess piece designs (from €60 to €1000), including the popular 'Athenians'.

Miden Agan (☎ 28210 27068; www.midenaganshop .gr; Daskalogianni 70; ⏰ 10am-3.30 Mon & Wed, 10am-2.15 & 6.15-10pm Tue & Thu-Sat) Foodies and wine lovers will be delighted with the range at this excellent shop, which stocks over 800 Greek wines, as well as its own wine and liquors. There's a variety of beautifully packaged local traditional gourmet deli foods, including oil and honey and their own line of spoon sweets (try the white pumpkin).

Paraoro (☎ 28210 88990; Theotokopoulou 16) Stamatis Fasoularis' distinctive series of metal boats are functional as well as decorative, such as his nifty steamship oil burner. The workshop also has unique ceramics by artist Yiorgos Vavatsis, including his trademark skewed drink ware. Their bigger gallery pieces are exhibited upstairs.

Roka Carpets (☎ 28210 74736; Zambeliou 61) This is one of the few places in Crete where you can buy genuine, hand-woven goods. You can watch the charming Mihalis Manousakis and his wife weave his wondrous rugs on a 400-year-old loom, using methods that have remained essentially unchanged since Minoan times.

Psimithio (☎ 28210 54606; Theotokopoulou 50) This small jewellery workshop just behind the cathedral has some interesting original designs in silver.

Karistianis (☎ 28210 93573; Skalidi 9-11) For outdoor clothing and hiking shoes to tackle gorges you could try this place or their hard core army supply store across the road for camping and climbing gear.

GETTING THERE & AWAY
Air

Hania's airport (CHQ; ☎ 28210 83800) is 14km east of town on the Akrotiri Peninsula.

Aegean Airlines (☎ 28210 63366; www.aegeanair .com)Four daily flights to Athens (€76-123) and one to Thessaloniki (€125-135).

Olympic Airlines (☎ 28210 58005; www.olympic airlines.com; Tzanakaki 88) Five daily flights to/from Athens (€76-106). Also four flights per week to/from Thessaloniki (€126-136).

Sky Express (☎ 2810 223 500; www.skyexpress.gr) Daily flights from Hania to Rhodes on 18-seater planes (from €104, one hour).

Boat

Hania's main port is at Souda, about 7km southeast of town. There are frequent buses to Hania (€1.15), as well as taxis (€7). The **Port Police** (☎ 28210 89240) can provide ferry information.

ANEK (☎ 28210 27500; www.anek.gr; Plateia Sofokli Venizelou) Has a daily boat at 9pm from Piraeus to Hania (€30, nine hours) and at 8pm from Hania to Piraeus. In July and August there is also a morning ferry from Piraeus (€30).

Hellenic Seaways (☎ 28210 75444; www.hellenic-seaways.gr; Plateia 1866 14) Has a high-speed catamaran service from Piraeus that take only 4½ hours (€53). It's a better option for getting to Hania as it arrives at 8.30pm, but the flight from Hania gets you to Athens rather inconveniently at 2am.

Bus

In summer, buses depart from Hania's **bus station** (☎ 28210 93052) during the week for the following destinations:

Destination	Duration	Fare (€)	Frequency
Elafonisi	2½hr	9.60	1 daily
Falasarna	1½hr	6.50	3 daily
Hora Sfakion	1hr 40min	6.50	3 daily
Iraklio	2¾hr	10.70	half-hourly
Kissamos-Kastelli	1hr	4	13 daily
Kolymbari	45min	2.80	half-hourly
Lakki	1¾hr	2.60	2 daily
Moni Agias Triadas	30min	2	2 daily
Omalos (for Samaria Gorge)	1hr	5.90	3 daily
Paleohora	1hr 50min	6.50	4 daily
Rethymno	1hr	6	half-hourly
Sougia	1hr 50min	6.10	2 daily
Stavros	30min	1.80	3 daily

Check with the bus station for off-peak services.

GETTING AROUND
To/From the Airport

There are three buses per day to the airport (€2, 20 mins) from the bus station. A taxi to the airport will cost about €18.

Bus

Local **blue buses** (☎ 28210 27044) meet the ferries at the port of Souda, just near the dock. In Hania, the bus to Souda (€1.15) leaves from outside the food market. Buses for the western beaches leave from the main bus station on Plateia 1866 and go as far as Panormo (€2).

Car, Motorcycle & Bicycle

Most motorcycle-hire outlets are on Halidon, but the companies at Agia Marina are competitive and can bring cars to Hania. Most of the old town is pedestrian only. The best place to park is in the free parking area near the Firkas fortress (turn right off Skalidi at the sign to the big supermarket car park on Pireos and follow the road down to the waterfront). Some of the new town streets have paid street parking so check for signs.
Europrent (☎ 28210 27810; Halidon 87)
Tellus Travel (☎ 28210 91500; www.tellustravel.gr; Halidon 108)

AKROTIRI PENINSULA & SOUDA BAY

AKROTIRI PENINSULA
ΧΕΡΣΟΝΗΣΟΣ ΑΚΡΩΤΗΡΙ

The Akrotiri (ak-roh-*tee*-ree) Peninsula, to the northeast of Hania, is a barren, hilly stretch of rock covered with scrub. It has a few coastal resorts, Hania's airport, a massive NATO naval base on Souda Bay and a two interesting monasteries. There are few buses and the poorly signposted roads can make it a difficult region to explore, but if you have a car it makes an interesting day trip where you can combine a swim and lunch with a visit to the monasteries. If you want to stay at the beach instead of Hania town, Kalathas and Stavros are a much quieter alternative to the resort strip west of town. The beach settlement of **Kalathas**, 10km north of Hania, has two sandy beaches lined by pine trees. It is the preferred weekend haunt of Haniots, many of whom own summer and weekend houses nearby.

Three kilometres north of Kalathas is the small beach settlement of **Tersanas**, signposted off the main Kalathas-Stavros road.

The village of **Stavros**, 6km north of Kalathas, is little more than a scattering of houses and a few restaurants and hotels. The main cove is a narrow strip of sandy beach dominated by a mammoth rock shelf that served as the dramatic backdrop for the final dancing scene in the classic movie *Zorba the Greek*. It can get crowded, but the sheltered cove is your best bet on a windy day. The area around Stavros is ripe with new villa development and is also home to the fancy **Perle Resort & Health Spa** (☎ 28210 39400; www .perlespa.com).

The impressive 17th-century **Moni Agias Triadas** (☎ 28210 63310; admission €2; ☼ 8am-7pm) is a visitor-friendly monastery. It was founded by the Venetian monks Jeremiah and Laurentio Giancarolo, who were converts to the Orthodox faith. There was a religious school here in the 19th century and it is still an active monastery with an excellent library. The church is worth visiting for its altarpiece as well as its Venetian-influenced domed façade. There is a small museum and a store selling the monastery's fine wine, oil and raki.

The 16th-century **Moni Gouvernetou** (Our Lady of the Angels; ☎ 28210 63319; ☼ 9am-noon & 5-7pm Mon, Tue & Thu, Sat & Sun 5am-11am & 5-8pm), 4km north of Moni Agias Triadas, may date as far back as the 11th century from a time when an inland sanctuary was an attractive refuge from coastal pirates. The building itself is disappointingly plain, but the church inside has an ornate sculptured Venetian façade. The monastery was attacked and burnt down during the war of independence but the monks were warned and managed to save the treasures (though not themselves) and had them shipped off to Mount Athos. The monastery is now run by four monks from the holy mountain who keep a strict regime and have banned tour buses. Visitors must park in the car park before the monastery and be dressed respectfully while on the grounds (they do not provide long pants or skirts) or will be asked to leave. Swimming is not permitted in the cove below.

From Moni Gouvernetou, it's a 20-minute walk (about 30 minutes on the uphill walk back) to the path leading down to the coast to the ruins of **Moni Ioannou Erimiti** (also known as Moni Katholikou). In disuse for many centuries, the monastery is dedicated to St John the Hermit who lived in the cave behind the ruins, at the bottom of a rock staircase. Near the entrance to the cave, there's a small pond of water believed to be holy. When

St John died in the cave, his 98 disciples are said to have died with him. His skull is kept in the monastery and brought out for a special service the first Sunday of every month.

On the eastern side of the peninsula is the pleasant beach of **Marathi**, a lovely spot past the military base with two sandy coves and turquoise waters on either side of a small pier. The ruins of **Ancient Minoa** are next to the car park. Marathi gets crowded with local families at weekends and has a couple of tavernas. Further south along this coastline is another pleasant swimming and snorkelling spot at **Loutraki**.

Sleeping & Eating

Esplanade Apartments (Kalathas; ☎ 28210 69810; www .esplandehotel.gr; studio & apt €40-85; 🔀 🖵 🕑) This two-storey hotel has roomy, light and breezy studios with phone, TV and well-stocked kitchenette.

Georgi's Blue Apartments (Kalathas; ☎ 28210 64080; www.blueapts.gr; studio & apt €85-130; 🔀 🕑) Georgi's is a tasteful, rather upmarket complex of well furnished studios and apartments with phone, satellite TV, fridge and kitchenette. There's a pleasant communal lounge area near the pool and a private little cove where you can swim off the rocks.

Paradisio Apartments (Stavros; ☎ 28210 39737; www .paradisiohotel.com; apt €85; 🔀 🕑) This is friendly family-run affair with apartments that can sleep up to five people. There's a swimming pool with a separate area for kids and the family provide guests with their own organic fruit, olive oil and honey.

Blue Beach (☎ 28210 39404; www.bluebeach-villas .com; d €50; 🔀 🕑) Right on the pretty spot on the beach, Blue Beach is a low-key resort hotel that welcomes independent travellers. The rooms are comfortable and self-contained with fridge, kitchenette, TV and there is a pool. Air-con is an extra €7.

Sun Set Beach Bar (☎ 28210 39780) Right on the western beach at Stavros, this attractive bar evokes a tropical paradise, tucked under a huge tree with a shady timber deck and thatched umbrellas. It's a great spot for a drink and they also serve a range of local an international-style snacks.

Patrelantonis (☎ 28210 63337; Marathi; fish per kg €34-50) This well-regarded fish taverna by the beach under the shady tamarisk trees puts on a decent seafood spread, best enjoyed with *horta* (wild greens) and their hand-cut potatoes.

Getting There & Away

There are six buses daily to Stavros beach (€1.80) that stop at Kalathas.

There are two buses Monday to Friday, at 6.30am and 2.15pm, to Moni Agias Triadas (€2, 40 minutes).

If you're coming by car from Hania follow signs to the airport and branch off at the turnoffs from there.

SOUDA ΣΟΥΔΑ

pop 5330

The harbour of Souda is one of Crete's largest, and is the port of entry if you come to Hania by ferry. The Venetians built a castle at the entrance of Souda Bay, which they held until 1715, even though the Turks had already seized the rest of the island. Souda is now the site of the Greek navy's main refitting station, which sees a sizeable military presence in the area.

The town of Souda, about 2km from the port, sprang up 130 years ago under Turkish rule, but little remains from that period. Today most of the activity and services – including travel agencies, banks and shops – are all clustered in the port close to the main plateia (square) near the ferry quay. Accommodation and dining opportunities are limited and you are much better off in Hania.

Gelasakis Travel (☎ 28210 89065; 🕑 8am-10.30pm), on the main plateia; changes money, handles air and boat tickets, and rents out cars.

Sleeping & Eating

Hotel Parthenon (☎ 28210 89245; El Venizelou 29; d €35; 🔀) Right across from the main plateia above a taverna, the rooms at this small hotel have a fridge and TV, if you need to spend a night in the port.

Vlachakis Brothers (☎ 28210 89219; 16 Ellis St) Over in Souda town, this simple fish taverna is widely known for its excellent seafood and its house specialty, the prawn omelette, washes down nicely with barrel wine.

Paloma (☎ 28210 89081; fish dishes €6-10) Further along from Souda on the coastal road leading to the airport, this fish taverna with classic blue chairs and chequered tablecloths is right by the sea overlooking the port. It's a pleasant walk past the cemetery.

Getting There & Away

Souda is about 9km east of Hania. There are frequent buses to Hania (€1.15) that meet the ferries. Taxis to Hania cost about €7.

GULF OF HANIA

The coastline west of Hania between the Akrotiri and Rodopou Peninsulas, which forms the Gulf of Hania, is an almost end-less 13km strip of hotels, domatia, souvenir shops, travel agencies, mini-markets and res-taurants. The former villages along this coast have become little more than entertainment strip malls. It's not the place to come if you're looking for a quiet, relaxing holiday, but the nightlife is good and it has all the services to cater to your needs.

The first tourist town is **Agia Marina**, 9km from Hania. While it caters primarily to package tourists, you will find a clutch of undistinguished domatia along the main road. The beach tends to be packed with lines of identical lounges and umbrellas, and the water is rather murky and uninspir-ing. Agia Marina is the first port of call for Hania nightclubbers.

Next along is **Platanias**, 12km from Hania and almost indistinguishable from Agia Ma-rina. This community of midrange accommo-dation, fast-food grills, bars, clubs and shops along busy main strip is teeming with Scan-dinavians. The streets of the old town, which sprawls over a steep hill on the south side of the road, are picturesque but touristy, though

there are great views from the top. The beach, as at Agia Marina, is crowded and mediocre.

Marginally better is **Gerani** at the far end of the strip, which is generally far less crowded. Further along, **Maleme** is a quiet, relatively undeveloped coastal resort. There are a few hotels and apartments near the fine pebble beach. Up on the hill, there is a moving, well-tended **German military cemetery** overlooking the airfield where more than 3000 German paratroopers killed in the Battle of Crete are buried.

SLEEPING

Many hotels lining the beach road have been given over to tour operators or function as private clubs.

Tassos Cottages (☎ 28210 61352; tassosgerani@hotmail .com; Gerani; apt €40-50) These well-equipped one and two-bedroom apartments surrounded by pleasant gardens are halfway between the beach and the main drag. They have a TV and fans. Call in at Tasso's taverna on the main street.

Ilianthos Village Apartments (☎ 28210 60667; www.ilianthosvillage.gr; Agia Marina; d incl breakfast from €172; ✷ ▨) This large resort on a wide stretch of beach is one of the more upmarket options in Agia Marina. It has children's facilities, and is accessible to people in wheelchairs and all the mod cons.

Indigo Mare (☎ 28210 68156; www.indigomare.gr; Platanias; studio/apt incl breakfast from €90/104; ✷ ▨) This upmarket apartment complex has well-fitted-out studios and apartments sleeping up to four people, and a lovely pool overlooking the beach.

EATING

Maria's (☎ 28210 68888; Kato Stalos; mains €5-9) For a good feed try the popular Maria's, on the eastern edge of Agia Marina, which serves Cretan and Mediterranean food on a plant-filled terrace. Try the local meat pie.

our pick **Drakiana** (☎ 28210 61677; mains €6-13) It is worth the lovely hike through 3km of olive and orange groves to get to this superbly located taverna under huge plane trees on a river bank. Look for a signposted turnoff from Platanias at the Mylos tou Kerata corner (see p92). Manolis Mavromatis serves excellent Cretan cuisine including a fennel pitta, meatballs in tomato sauce and special meat dishes such as suckling pig on the spit. There are also a picnic area, bar-becues and a children's playground nearby.

RESTING PLACE

About 1km west of Souda, is the im-maculately maintained **Souda Bay War Cemetery**, where about 1500 British, Aus-tralian and New Zealand soldiers who lost their lives in the Battle of Crete are buried. Beautifully situated at the water's edge, the rows of white headstones make a moving tribute to the Commonwealth's heroic defenders of Crete. More than half of the graves are unidentified as the bodies were relocated from German burial grounds in Hania, Rethymno, Iraklio and Galatas. Buses to Souda port that depart from outside the Hania food market on Giannari can drop you off at the cemetery.

Aidonisos (☎ 28210 83560; Gerani; mains €10.50-13.70; dinner only) This well-regarded newcomer offers contemporary Greek-style cuisine and some excellent desserts.

Mylos tou Kerata (☎ 28210 68578; Platanias; grills €8-15; ⏱ dinner from 6pm) One of the best restaurants in the area, it's located in an old water mill. The ambience is pleasant, the menu and wine list extensive and there's a huge range of grilled chicken, lamb and beef fillets.

ENTERTAINMENT

Platanias and Agia Marina are lined with summer clubs whose popularity, names and décor change year to year. In Platanias, the popular clubs were **Destil**, **Utopia** and **Milos**, with top-name DJs also leading big dance events at **Oceanos** in Agia Marina.

GETTING THERE & AWAY

Buses running between Hania and Kissamos-Kastelli stop in Platanias, Gerani and Agia Marina.

SFAKIA & LEFKA ORI

This region has some of the island's most spectacular sights, including the Samaria (sa-ma-*ria*) Gorge, the Lefka Ori Mountains and Mt Gingilos in the rugged interior. The province of Sfakia extends from the Omalos Plateau down to the southern coast and is Crete's most mountainous region.

Sfakia was the centre of resistance during the island's long centuries of domination by foreign powers, its steep ravines and hills making effective hideaways for Cretan revolutionaries. The Sfakian people are renowned for their proud fighting spirit, which even in the recent past has turned family against family in the form of murderous vendettas that have depopulated many of the region's villages (see the boxed text, p97).

Check out the website www.sfakia-crete .com for information on the region.

HANIA TO OMALOS

The road from Hania to the beginning of the Samaria Gorge is one of the most spectacular routes in Crete. After heading through orange groves to the village of **Fournes**, a left fork leads to **Meskla**, twisting and turning along a gorge offering beautiful views. Although the bottom part of the town is not particularly attractive

with boarded-up buildings, the road becomes more scenic as it winds uphill to the modern, multicoloured **Church of the Panagia**. Next to it is a 14th-century chapel built on the foundations of a 6th-century basilica that might have been built on an even earlier Temple of Aphrodite. At the entrance to the town a sign directs you to the **Chapel of Metamorfosis Sotiros** (Transfiguration of the Saviour) that contains 14th-century frescoes. The fresco of the Transfiguration on the south wall is particularly impressive.

The main road continues to the unspoilt village of **Lakki** (*la*-kee), 24km from Hania, which affords stunning views wherever you look. The village was a centre of resistance during both the uprising against the Turks and in WWII.

Rooms for Rent Nikolas (☎ 28210 67232; Lakki; d €35) has comfortable, simple rooms above a taverna, with magnificent views over the valley.

OMALOS ΟΜΑΛΟΣ
pop 30

Most tourists only hurry through Omalos, 36km south of Hania, on their way to the Samaria Gorge, but this plateau settlement deserves more of your time. During summer, the air is bracingly cool here compared with the steamy coast and there are some great mountain walks in the area. After the morning Samaria rush, there's hardly anyone on the plateau except goats and shepherds.

Omalos is little more than a few hotels on either side of the main road cutting through the plateau. The village is practically deserted in the winter. The town is about 4km before the entrance to the Samaria Gorge.

Sleeping & Eating

Generally, Omalos hotels are open when the Samaria Gorge is open, although winter tourism is evolving. Most hotels have restaurants that do a bustling trade serving breakfast to hikers and are open at meal times the rest of the day. Most will drive you to the start of the gorge.

Hotel Neos Omalos (☎ 28210 67269; www.neos-oma los.gr; s/d €20/30) has comfortable, modern, nicely decorated rooms which include phone, bath, with shower curtain and satellite TV. There's a pleasant lounge in the reception area.

Elliniko (☎ 28210 67169; s/d/tr €20/25/35) This is the nearest to the Samaria Gorge and has

---

DETOUR: THERISO

For a day trip or an alternative route to Omalos, you can take the scenic road to Theriso, 14km from Hania, via the village of Perivolia. This spectacular drive follows a running stream through a green oasis and the 6km Theriso Gorge. At the foot of the Lefka Ori Mountains, at 500m above sea level, the village was the site of historical battles against the Turks. These days it is popular for its fine tavernas that host marathon Sunday lunches.

Two tavernas vie for top billing. **O Leventis** (☎ 28210 77102) has a lovely courtyard under a giant canopy of plane trees and makes a delicious and sizeable *kreatotourta* (local meat pie), while **O Antartis** (☎ 28210 78943) also has excellent mezedes and Cretan food.

Just past the village on your right, there is a small **Museum of National Resistance** with an eerie monument outside paying tribute to a female resistance fighter. The old millstone was used by Turkish occupiers in 1821 to crush Chrysi Tripiti to death in the local olive press.

A steep and winding road takes you through rugged mountain terrain and around an ever-changing landscape of plane trees, olive, orange, eucalypt and pine through the villages of **Zourva** and **Meskla** to **Lakki,** where you can continue to Omalos or head back to Hania.

---

simple double rooms with TV, although they are a little cramped. There is also an attached restaurant that is often busy with tour buses during lunch.

Hotel Exari (☎ 28210 67180; www.exari.gr; s/d €20/30) This big stone-built hotel has pleasant, well-furnished rooms with TV, bathtub and balconies. The owner Yiorgos can deliver luggage to Sougia for groups. There is an attached taverna.

You could also try the friendly **Hotel Gingilos** (☎ 28210 67181; s/d/tr €20/25/35).

Located in the hills between Omalos and the Samaria Gorge, **Kallergi Hut** (☎ 28210 33199; dm without bathroom members/nonmembers €10/13) is maintained by the Hania EOS and makes a good base for exploring Mt Gingilos and surrounding peaks, though it is a hike to get there.

Getting There & Away

There are three daily buses to Omalos from Hania (one hour, €5.90). If want to hike the gorge and return to your room (and luggage) in Omalos, you can take the afternoon boat from Agia Roumeli to Sougia and get a taxi back to Omalos for about €35.

SAMARIA GORGE
ΦΑΡΑΓΓΙ ΤΗΣ ΣΑΜΑΡΙΑΣ

Hiking through the **Samaria Gorge** (☎ 28210 67179; admission €5; ☉ 6am-3pm 1 May–mid-Oct) is one of the 'must-dos' of Crete and attracts both serious hikers and people for whom it is clearly a one-off experience. Despite the crowds – more than 170,000 people walk the gorge each year – a hike through this stupendous gorge is still an experience to remember.

At 16km, the Samaria (sah-mah-rih-*ah*) Gorge is supposedly the longest in Europe. It begins just below the Omalos Plateau, carved out by the river that flows between the peaks of Mts Avlimaniko (1858m) and Volakias (2115m). Its width varies from 150m to 3m and its vertical walls reach 500m at their highest points. The gorge has an incredible number of wild flowers, which are at their best in April and May.

It is also home to a large number of endangered species, including the Cretan wild goat, the kri-kri. The gorge was made a national park in 1962 to save the kri-kri from extinction. You are unlikely to see too many of these shy animals, which show a marked aversion to hikers.

An early start (before 8am) helps to avoid the worst of the crowds, but during July and August even the early bus from Hania to the top of the gorge can be packed. There's no spending the night in the gorge so you are going to have to complete the hike in the time allocated. If you are not sure if you are fit enough, you could try the shorter (it's about half the length) but nonetheless picturesque Imbros gorge (p95).

The hike from Xyloskalo (the name of the steep stone pathway with wooden rails that gives access to the gorge), to Agia Roumeli (p95) on the coast takes from about four hours for the sprinters to six hours for the strollers. Early in the season it's sometimes necessary to wade through the stream. Later, as the flow drops, it's possible to use rocks as stepping stones.

HANIA

The gorge is wide and open for the first 6km, until you reach the abandoned settlement of **Samaria**. The inhabitants were relocated when the gorge became a national park. Just south of the village is a small church dedicated to **Saint Maria of Egypt**, after whom the gorge is named.

The gorge then narrows and becomes more dramatic until, at the 11km mark, the walls are only 3.5m apart – the famous **Iron Gates** (Sidiroportes). Here, a rickety wooden pathway leads hikers the 20m or so over the water and through to the other side.

The gorge ends at the 12.5km mark just north of the almost abandoned village of Old Agia Roumeli. From here it's a further uninteresting 2km hike to the welcoming seaside resort of Agia Roumeli, with its much appreciated fine pebble beach and sparkling sea, where most hikers can be seen between after noon taking a refreshing dip or at least bathing sore and aching feet. Be warned, falling rocks can be a hazard and people have been injured, including two fatal incidents in 2006. On extremely hot days the gorge is closed for safety reasons.

There are excursions to the Samaria Gorge from every sizable town and resort on Crete, but you can get there easily enough from Hania by bus (see Omalos), then catch a ferry from Agia Roumeli (see p96) back to Hora Sfakion or other south coast towns. Most travel agents have two excursions: 'Samaria Gorge Long Way' and 'Samaria Gorge Easy Way'. The first comprises the regular hike from Omalos; the second starts at Agia Roumeli and takes you up as far as the Iron Gates.

ASKYFOU ΑΣΚΎΦΟΥ
pop 444

The road to Hora Sfakion takes you across the war-torn plain of Askyfou, which was the scene of one of the most furious battles of the Cretan revolt of 1821. The Sfakiot forces triumphed over the Turks in a bloody battle here, which is still recounted in local songs. More than a century later the plain was the scene of more strife as Allied troops retreated towards their evacuation point in Hora Sfakion. The central town of the region is Askyfou, which stretches out on either side of a hill. The post office is at the top of the hill with a mini-market and several tavernas with fairly cheap rooms to rent.

As you enter Askyfou from Hania, signs direct you to the **military museum** (☎ 28250 95289; admission free; ☎ 8am-7pm Mon-Sat), which displays the gun and military odds-and-ends collection of Georgios Hatzidakis, who is eager to show you around.

For a glimpse of traditional Sfakian village life, it is worth veering right off the main road to arrive at a small square flanked by four *kafeneia* and statues of local resistance heroes. Just above the small square you'll probably see local black-clad gents under the mulberry tree of the old-style **kafeneio** (☎ 28250 95228), where apart from the local *myzithropita* (cheese pie) with honey you can normally get a basic meal such as local sausage, or at weekends traditional wild goat or lamb *tsigariasto* (sautéed) or *vrasto* (boiled), charged by the kilo. And lots of raki.

On the way to Imbros, the upscale **Lefkoritis Resort** (☎ 28250 95455; www.lefkoritis.com; apt summer €45-95) is a sizeable stone-built retreat popular with hunters that operates year-round and has a taverna. It has tasteful furnished rooms and apartments sleeping up to six and enjoys sweeping views of the surrounding mountains.

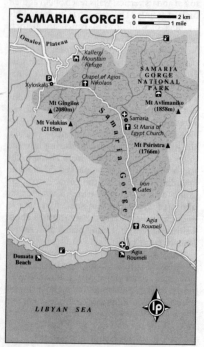

SAMARIA GORGE

0 — 2 km
0 — 1 mile

Omalos Plateau
Kallergi Mountain Refuge
Chapel of Agios Nikolaos
Xyloskalo
SAMARIA GORGE NATIONAL PARK
Mt Gingilos (2080m)
Mt Avlimaniko (1858m)
Mt Volakias (2115m)
Samaria
St Maria of Egypt Church
Mt Psiristra (1766m)
Iron Gates
Agia Roumeli
Domata Beach
Agia Roumeli
LIBYAN SEA

A SHORT SURVIVAL GUIDE TO THE GORGE

The Samaria Gorge hike is not a Sunday stroll; it is long and, at times, hard. Do not attempt it if you are not used to walking. If you find that the going is too tough within the first hour, there are park wardens with donkeys who will take you back to the beginning. They will be on the look out for stragglers.

Rugged footwear is essential for walking on the uneven ground, which is covered by sharp stones. Don't attempt the walk in unsuitable footwear – you will regret it. The track from Xyloskalo to Agia Roumeli is downhill all the way and the ground makes for generally uneven walking. Take a hat and sunscreen, plus a small bottle of water that can be refilled along the way in the many springs spurting cool water (it's inadvisable to drink water from the main stream). There is nowhere to buy food, so bring energy food to snack on.

IMBROS GORGE ΦΑΡΆΓΓΙ ΙΜΠΡΟΥ

The **Imbros Gorge** (admission €2; ☉ year-round), 57km southeast of Hania, is less hiked than its illustrious sister at Samaria but is just as beautiful. Cypresses, holm oaks, fig and almond trees gradually thin to just cypresses and Jerusalem sage deep within the gorge. The walls of rock reach 300m high, while the narrowest point of the ravine is only 2m wide. At only 8km the Imbros walk is also much easier on the feet. Most people begin the walk in the mountain village of **Imbros** but you can also do it from the southern village of **Komitades**. Both places are used by gorge hikers and have plenty of mini-markets and tavernas to fuel up at. There's nowhere to stay in Imbros village.

You'll find the well-marked entrance to the gorge next to Porofarango taverna on the road to Hora Sfakion. The track is easy to follow as it traces the stream bed past rockslides and caves. The gorge path ends at Komitades, from where you can walk 5km or take a taxi to Hora Sfakion (€17 to €20).

At the start of the gorge, the friendly family taverna **Porofarango** (☎ 28250 95450; mains €6-8) has a big balcony with great panoramic views of the gorge and serves good-value Cretan cuisine and generous raki. The meat is usually its own and it often has wild goat. Try the special *tsigariasto* pork.

There are three daily buses from Hania to Hora Sfakion (€6.50, 1¾ hours), which stop at Imbros. Buses from Hora Sfakion to Hania stop at Komitades.

The Happy Walker (p126), in Rethymno, organises hikes through Imbros.

SOUTHERN COAST

The rocky southern coast is dotted with laid-back beach communities such as Paleohora, Sougia, Frangokastello and Loutro. These are some of the best places in Crete to relax. Many of the beaches are inaccessible by road because of the mountains and gorges that slice though this part of the island, which spill out to the beaches. The Samaria Gorge ends at the village of Agia Roumeli. This region has some stunning walks and is the only place in Crete where you can boat-hop along the coast to isolated beaches.

AGIA ROUMELI ΑΓΙΑ ΡΟΥΜΕΛΗ
pop 123

These days most hikers emerging from the Samaria Gorge stop for a swim and lunch at the tiny beach settlement of Agia Roumeli before catching a boat, which is the only way out. Agia Roumeli is a pleasant enough stopover, although the surrounding mountains can make it very hot and stifling. The pebble beach gets exceptionally hot and thus impossible to sit on for long unless you hire a beach umbrella and sun lounge (€4).

DETOUR: DOURAKIS WINERY

Wine buffs will enjoy a stop at the **Dourakis winery** (☎ 28250 51761) near the Alikambos turn-off on the road to Hora Sfakion. Winemaker Andreas Dourakis is happy to show visitors around the stone-built winery and there is a pleasant tasting room upstairs where you can sample some of his 17 excellent wines, including an organic red and his well-known Logari label. Dourakis produces more than 180,000 bottles each year using local and foreign varietals.

If you're in no hurry to leave, there are quite a few places to stay and decent places to eat. There are no tourist facilities or banks, and not much to see, other than to walk up to the well-preserved ruins of a **Venetian castle** above the village (about 30 mins), or check out the **Panagia church** in the village, which has some surviving remnants of a Roman mosaic floor.

On Easter Saturday, the tavernas of Agia Roumeli put on a **post-resurrection feast**, which anyone in the village is free to join.

Sleeping & Eating

Gigilos Taverna & Rooms (☎ 28250 91383; gigilos@mycosmos.gr; mains €4-7; s/d/tr €25/35/40; ☒) Right on the beach at the western end of the village, the best rooms are at the front the beach road. They are clean and nicely furnished with decent new bathrooms and a communal fridge in the hall. The taverna has a pleasant huge shady deck on the beach.

Oasis (☎ 28250 91391; s/d/tr €25/30/35; ☒) The family who run these rooms live downstairs, giving this place a friendly and homy feel. The simply furnished rooms have dated but functional bathrooms, fridge and balconies.

Farangi Restaurant & Rooms (☎ 28250 91225; mains €4.50-8.50; d/tr €30/35; ☒) On the beach road, Farangi has a range of Cretan specials and taverna standards as well as friendly service and beer on tap. There are some tidy well-equipped rooms above the restaurant with a fridge, kettle and TV, some with sea views.

Getting There & Away

The boat **ticket office** (☎ 28250 91251) is a small concrete structure near the beach.

There are two afternoon boats daily (3.45pm & 6pm) from Agia Roumeli to Hora Sfakion (€7.50, one hour) via Loutro (€5, 45 minutes) that connect with the bus back to Hania, as well as the morning boat from Paleohora to Hora Sfakion. You can also head west catching a boat from Agia Roumeli to Paleohora (€11, 1.5 hours) at 4.45pm, calling in at Sougia (€6.30, 45 minutes).

HORA SFAKION ΧΟΡΑ ΣΦΑΚΙΩΝ
pop 302

Hora Sfakion (*ho*-ra sfa-ki-*on*) is the small coastal port where the hordes of walkers from the Samaria Gorge spill off the boat and onto the bus back to Hania. Most people pause only long enough to catch the next bus out, but the settlement can be a relaxing stay for a few days and there are several beaches accessible by boat or road, including the isolated **Sweetwater** and **Ilingas beach** to the west. It's also a convenient spot for heading westwards to other resorts or taking a ferry to Gavdos.

Under Venetian and Turkish rule Hora Sfakion was an important maritime centre and, as capital of the Sfakia region, the nucleus of the Cretan struggle for independence. The Turks inflicted severe reprisals on the town's inhabitants for their rebelliousness in the 19th century, after which the town fell into an economic slump that lasted until the arrival of tourism a couple of decades ago. Hora Sfakion played a prominent role during WWII when thousands of Allied troops were evacuated by sea from the town after the Battle of Crete.

Orientation & Information

The ferry quay is at the eastern side of the harbour. Buses leave from the square up the hill on the northeastern side. There is one ATM. The post office is on the square, opposite the police station.

Sfakia Tours (☎ 28250 91130), next to the post office, rent cars and can help with accommodation. There is parking near the bus stop and the ferry terminal. Check email at **Kenzo Club** (☼ 8am-late; €3 per hr).

Notos Mare Diving Centre (☎ 28250 91333; www .notosmare.com; from €42) offers a range of experiences for beginners and experienced divers, as well as snorkelling and boat excursions along the south coast.

You can also go **bungee jumping** off the Aradena (Aradhena) bridge (see p74).

Sleeping & Eating

Samaria & Lyvikon (☎ 28250 91261, 28250 91211; fax 28250 91161; s/d €20/30; ☒) These prominent neighbouring establishments have a range of decent, though dated, budget rooms. The Lyvikon has brighter rooms with bathtubs, fridge and TV and sea view balconies. They are virtually under the same management and the tavernas share a kitchen.

Rooms Stavris (☎ 28250 91220; stavris@sfakia-crete .com; s/d €21/24; ☒) Up the steps at the western end of the port, it has clean, basic rooms – some with kitchenettes and fridges. There were plans to refurbish them.

Lefka Ori (☎ 28250 9109; www.chorasfakion.com; s/d €23/27; ☒) This taverna at the western end of the port does some solid trade and has budget rooms behind the restaurant.

Xenia (☎ 28250 91490; fax 28250 91491; d €33-38; ❄) The best value rooms in town are the spacious seafront rooms in the modern wing of this refurbished hotel well-positioned at the western edge of town. The rooms in the main building are more cramped.

There are no standout dining options, though **Delfini** (☎ 28250 91002) is the pick of the bunch.

You can enjoy a lovely sunset and stunning views as far as Loutro from the Thalassa Café, about 1.5km along the road out of town.

Getting There & Away

BOAT

Boat tickets are sold in the **ticket booth** (☎ 28250 91221) in the car park. From June through August there is a daily boat from Hora Sfakion to Paleohora (€11, three hours) via Loutro, Agia Roumeli and Sougia. The boat leaves at Hora Sfakion at 1pm and stops for two hours at Agia Roumeli to catch the gorge walkers heading west. There are four additional boats between Hora Sfakion and Agia Roumeli (€7.50, one hour) via Loutro (€4, 15 minutes). From 1 June there are boats (€12, 1½ hours) to Gavdos island (see p106) on Friday, Saturday and Sunday.

BUS

There are four buses per day from Hora Sfakion to Hania (€6.50, two hours) – the afternoon buses at 5.30pm and 7pm wait for the boats from Agia Roumeli. In summer there are three daily buses to Rethymno via Vryses

(€6.50, 1 hour). There are two buses daily to Frangokastello (€1.50, 25 minutes).

AROUND HORA SFAKION

A scenic, hair-raisingly steep, 12km winding road west from Hora Sfakion takes you to **Anopoli** (Ανώπολη), a quiet village in a fertile plateau at the base of the Lefka Ori, with a memorial to resistance fighters in the main plateia (square). It was one of the few areas that did not fall to the Turks, which you can appreciate when you see its location.

The **Orfanoudakis bakery** (☎ 28250 91189) has some exceptional semi-sweet biscuits, rusks and sweet treats including mega-size Sfakianes pites. They also rent attractive and spacious new studios and apartments nearby (€35).

You can also reach Anopoli from an extremely steep path leading up from Loutro.

The virtually abandoned stone hamlet of **Aradena**, about 2km west of Anopoli, is famous for the **Vardinogiannis bridge** that crosses over the Aradena gorge. At the kantina next to the bridge you can get directions for a remote refuge at nearby Agios Ioannis.

At weekends you will see people launching themselves off the bridge 138m into the gorge – this is the highest **bungee jumping** (☎ 6937 615191; www.bungy.gr) bridge in Greece. For a less adrenalin-pumped experience, you can reach the gorge entrance by rambling through the ruins of the village. It takes two and a half hours to walk to **Marmara beach**, and the excellent **Dialeskari taverna** (☎ 6942 201456) perched above this idyllic (except at weekends and August) pebble cove. There are three basic rooms without power for rent.

CRETAN VENDETTAS

Cretans might be famously welcoming to strangers, but they are notorious throughout Greece for murderous family vendettas that have lasted for generations and caused hundreds of Cretans to flee the island.

Particularly prevalent among the harsh mountain people of Sfakia, where whole villages have been decimated due to vendettas, the disputes can start over the theft of sheep, an errant bullet at a wedding or anything deemed an insult to family honour. The insult is avenged with a murder, which must be avenged with another murder … and so the blood feud continues. Modernity has somewhat stemmed the carnage but there are still occasional mysterious cases where police can find no witnesses or people willing to come forward with information about a killing, including an incident in 2007 where an army conscript was shot in a barracks in Rethymno in front of his family and other witnesses but no one would identify the assailant. Avengers have also been known to pursue their targets across Greece and occasionally across the globe (as portrayed in the movie *Beware of Greeks Bearing Guns*).

HANIA

FRANGOKASTELLO
ΦΡΑΝΚΟΚΑΣΤΕΛΛΟ
pop 154

Frangokastello is a striking 14th-century fortress on a fine stretch of beach along the south coast, 15km east of Hora Sfakion. It is popular with day-trippers, but the scattered beach settlement around the castle is a peaceful retreat. The wide, white-sand beach beneath the fortress slopes gradually into shallow warm water, making it ideal for kids. Development has been kept to a minimum with most accommodation set back from the shore leaving the natural beauty largely untouched.

Frangokastello has an eventful history. The sand-coloured fortress was built by the Venetians as a defence against pirates and rebellious Sfakiots. The legendary Ioannis Daskalogiannis, who led a disastrous rebellion against the Turks in 1770, was persuaded to surrender at the Frangokastello Fortress but he was flayed alive. On May 17 1828, 385 Cretan rebels made a heroic last stand at the fortress in one of the bloodiest battles of the Cretan struggle for independence. About 800 Turks were killed along with the rebels.

Legend has it that at dawn each anniversary their ghosts, the *drosoulites,* can be seen marching along the beach. Others theorise that the 'ghosts' are an optical illusion created by peculiar atmospheric conditions and that the figures may be a reflection of camels or soldiers in the Libyan Desert. The name comes from the Greek word *drosia* meaning 'moisture', which in itself could refer to the dawn moisture that is around when the ghosts are said to appear.

There's no actual village centre in Frangokastello, just a series of scattered domatia, tavernas and residences that stretch either side of the main road from Hora Sfakion to the fortress, as well as a couple of mini-markets. The bus stops at several spots along the main road.

To the east of the castle is the stunning **Orthi Ammos** beach, with a long stretch of steep sand dunes (not pleasant on a windy day).

Sleeping & Eating

Accommodation is reasonably good value and mostly designed for longer stays. Those after value for money would be wise to avoid the over-the-top Kriti taverna, across from the castle.

Stavris Studios (☎ 28250 92250; stavris@sfakia-crete .com; studio €35-38; ※) This quiet, well-maintained place is on the right as you enter the town from Hora Sfakion. The rooms have kitchenettes and balconies and sea views and adjoining rooms for families.

Mylos (☎ 28250 92161; www.milos-sfakia.com; studio €35-50; ※) This old stone windmill in a pretty spot on the beach has been turned into an apartment and the four stone cottages under the tamarisk trees are now pleasant studios. There are also modern well-equipped studios nearby.

Fata Morgana & Paradisos (☎ 28250 92077; www .fatamorgana-kreta.com; studio €40-50; ※) Set among an olive grove above Orthi Ammos beach, this lovely complex has a range of attractive, spacious, fully-equipped studios and larger apartments for families, as well as two cosy mock castles (€55). There's a playground and a chook/bird pen to amuse the kids.

The best place to eat is the **Oasis Taverna** (☎ /fax 28250 92136; www.oasisrooms.com; mains €4.50-8), part of an excellent family-run studio and apartment complex at the western end of the beach. The taverna's well-executed Cretan specials include a delicious *kreatopita* (meat and cheese pie). The spacious rooms have full sized kitchens, are set among a lovely garden and you can walk to a quiet stretch of beach.

Taverna Babis & Popi (☎ 28250 92091; www.fran gokastello.de; specials €3-5.50) This taverna serves decent, good-value meals under a shady vine canopy tucked behind the family's rooms and minimarket.

Flisvos Taverna (☎ 28250 92069; mains €5.5-9) Enjoys a lovely setting right on the water under some tamarisk trees, and serves reasonable food. There are some rather cramped rooms above the taverna (€35) but they also have bigger apartments by the beach, as well as two restored houses in a nearby village.

Getting There & Away

In summer, two daily buses from Hora Sfakion to Plakias stop at Frangokastello (€1.50, 25 minutes). From Hania there's a daily afternoon bus (€7.20, 2½ hours). From Rethymno, you need to change at Vryses.

LOUTRO ΛΟΥΤΡΟ
pop 89

The small but densely built up fishing village of Loutro (loo-*tro*) lies between Agia Roumeli and Hora Sfakion. The town is little more than

WALKS AROUND LOUTRO *Graham Williams*

Loutro to Marble Beach via Livaniana

Distance: 6.5km
Duration: 3½ hours

Take the path beside the Hotel Daskalogiannis and follow the yellow/black E4 markers over the headland to Phoenix. As you descend there is a sign to Phoenix: take the right-hand path that goes around the houses. Cross the dirt road and head directly up the hill towards Livaniana in the distance. At the top of the hill take the path signposted to Livaniana and follow the blue-paint markers. Cross the road again and follow the obvious path that traverses up to the road on the outskirts of the village; 200m on is a taverna that sells cold drinks.

Walk on up the hill aiming for the church. Past the church, follow the blue markers to a sign pointing to Marble Beach. The markers take you around the field and along the edge of the old olive terrace. After 100m you come to a gap in a fence, where you look down into the Aradena Gorge. Look out for Bonelli's eagles riding the thermals. Turn left and follow the blue-paint markers, which lead you down towards the floor of the gorge. At the bottom turn left towards the sea and Marble Beach. The route is not always obvious with the faded red paint being the most reliable waymarking. Marble Beach has a taverna that serves simple meals.

To return to Loutro, follow the E4 path that starts behind the beach and the yellow/black paint spots. After half an hour you reach the hamlet of Likkos. Walk through the tavernas then follow the path (blue paint), which leads over the headland where you meet the path to Livaniana.

Loutro to Anopoli & the Aradena Gorge

Distance: 7km (9km if walking back to Loutro on the E4)
Duration: 5–6 hours

This is a strenuous, full-day's walk, which takes in an authentic country village, and spectacular gorge with a beach at the end of it.

Make an early start as all the hard effort is at the beginning – a 680m climb from the sea up to the plain of Anopoli. The path starts behind the Kri Kri taverna: go through the new metal gate, turn left and follow the path up the hillside. After an hour you reach a dirt road, cross it and keep going until you meet it again. Turn right and walk 100m until you reach a cistern on your left where you pick up the path again. After 200m the path forks: turn left and continue up the hill. You are aiming for the point below the walled compound you can see above you. At the top, enjoy the view, then follow the tarmac road to the town square where there are a couple of tavernas.

Follow the road sign to Aradena and follow it for 1.5km. Just as the ruins of Aradena come into view look for a small cairn and path on the right side of the road marked with faded blue spots. Walk along it pointing directly at Aradena, before descending into the gorge. At the bottom turn left. After 20 minutes you reach a staircase cut into the side of the gorge, follow it with care for 300m. In the past the Aradena Gorge was a tough proposition as getting around this section meant scrambling using fixed ropes and ladders.

Follow the cairns and faded red-paint spots until you reach the junction with the Livaniana path and continue as for the Loutro to Marble Beach via Livaniana walk above.

Hora Sfakion to Sweetwater Bay & Loutro

Distance: 5.5km
Duration: 2 hours

Follow the road west from Sfakion, signposted to Omalos. After 20 minutes you cross a culvert then ascend to the first switchback where there is an E4 sign to Sweetwater Bay. Follow the path marked with yellow/black paint marks and poles, which passes through a rock fall where the progress is slower, and arrives at Sweetwater after one hour. Across the bay the trail continues up beside the taverna to the top of the headland. Loutro is one hour further on, an easy if shadeless path.

A booklet called *Walks Around Loutro* is also available from shops in Loutro priced €5.

Graham Williams has been walking in Crete annually since 1988.

a crescent of white-and-blue domatia around a narrow beach. It's a pleasant, lazy resort that is never overwhelmed with visitors, although it can get busy and rather claustrophobic in July and August. It is a popular base for walkers (see p99).

Loutro is the only natural harbour on the south coast of Crete and is only accessible by boat or on foot. The absence of cars and bikes make it quiet and peaceful.

Its advantageous geographical position was appreciated in ancient times when it was the port for Phoenix and Anopoli. St Paul is said to have been heading to Phoenix from here when he encountered a storm that blew him off course past Gavdos Island and to eventually be shipwrecked in Malta.

Loutro is a good base for boat excursions along the southern coast. You can rent **canoes** (per hr/day €2/7) and a small ferry goes to nearby Sweetwater beach (€3.50, 15 mins).

Orientation & Information

There's no bank or post office, but there are places to change money at the western end of the beach. Boats dock in front of the Sifis Hotel. The ticket stall opens an hour before departures. There is **internet access** (per hr €4) at the Daskalogiannis Hotel.

Sleeping & Eating

Loutro has good budget accommodation options, with most places overlooking the harbour.

The Blue House (☎ 28250 91127; bluehouseloutro@ chania-cci.gr; d €40-45 ☒) has a mix of spacious, well-appointed rooms with big verandas overlooking the port. The nicer rooms are in the refurbished top floor section. The taverna downstairs serves excellent *mayirefta* (€5 to €7), including delicious garlicky spinach and a great *boureki* (small pastry pie) baked with zucchini, potato and goat's cheese.

Hotel Porto Loutro I & II (☎ 28250 91433; www .hotelportoloutro.com; s/d/tr €45/55/65 with breakfast; ☒) is the classiest hotel in Loutro, spread across two buildings. Rooms are simply decorated in understated island style, with quality linen and extra pillows, fridge and phone and small balconies overlooking the beach. They don't accept children under seven.

Apartments Niki (☎ /fax 28250 91259; www.loutro -accommodation.com; studio & apt €40-55; ☒) These beautifully furnished two- to four-person studios with beamed ceilings and stone floors

are just above the village. They have great views, ceiling fans and air-con, kitchenettes and balconies.

Faros (☎ /fax 28250 91334; d/tr €35/40; ☒) These spacious and airy rooms with beamed ceilings are a stone's throw from the beach, and have fridges and balconies. Air-con is €5 extra.

Rooms Sofia (☎ 28250 91354; d/tr €20/25) Above the Sofia mini-market, one street back from the beach, these are probably the cheapest rooms in town. They're plain and clean and a little cramped but most have a fridge and air-con.

You could also try **Keramos** (☎ 28250 91356; €35), which has simple budget rooms all brightly painted with Minoan murals. The top floor has air-con for €5 extra.

Given the captive market, the tavernas that line the waterfront in Loutro are surprisingly good. Most prominently display a wide range of *mayirefta* and you can't miss the dazzling range of cakes and sweets. Recommended are **Notos** (☎ 28250 91501) for excellent mezedes (€2.50-7), **Pavlos** (☎ 28250 91366; grills €6-8) for grills and **Ilios** (☎ 28250 91460) for fish.

Getting There & Away

Loutro is on the main Paleohora–Hora Sfakion boat route. From April to October there are four boats per day from Hora Sfakion (€4, 15 minutes), four from Agia Roumeli (€5, 45 minutes), and one boat per day from Paleohora (€13, 2½ hours). Taxi boats go to Sweetwater Beach and Hora Sfakion.

SOUGIA ΣΟΥΓΙΑ
pop 97

Sougia is one of the most laid back and refreshingly undeveloped beach resorts along the south coast, with a lovely wide curve of sand-and-pebble beach and a few tavernas and rooms along a shady tree-lined coastal road. It was once a popular remote hippy hangout and many nostalgic ex-hippies return religiously each year. It retains its chillout atmosphere and there is little to do other than relax and recharge depleted batteries for a few days.

Sougia's tranquillity has been preserved largely because of archaeological remains at eastern end of the beach that prohibit development. It lies at the foot of a narrow, twisting road that also deters most tour buses and passing traffic. There are a few small complexes of rooms, a few tavernas, a couple of lazy beach bars, two open-air clubs and a small settlement of campers and nudists at the eastern end of the beach. It is also great hiking territory, close to the Samaria and Agia Irini Gorges.

The ancient town was on the western side of the existing village. It flourished under the Romans and Byzantines when it was the port for Elyros, an important inland city (now disappeared). A 6th-century basilica that stood at the western end of the village contained a fine mosaic floor that is now in the Hania Archaeological Museum (p82).

There is one road into Sougia and the bus drops you on the coastal road in front of the Santa Irene hotel, where there is a ticket booth. There is an ATM next to Taverna Galini. Check out www.sougia.info for information about the town.

Roxana's snack store (☎ 28230 51668; ☉ 5am-late) sells boat tickets to Elafonisos. **Internet Lotos** (☎ 28230 51191; per hr €3; ☉ 7am-late) can get you online.

Sleeping

Aretousa (☎ 28230 51178; fax 28230 51178; s/d/studio €35/40/42; ☒) This lovely *pension* on the road to Hania has bright and comfortable refurbished rooms with new beds and linen, flat screen TVs, as well as studios with kitchenettes.

Captain George (☎ 28230 51133; g-gentek@otenet .gr; s/d/studio €35/40/48; ☒) Attractive, good value rooms and studios among a lovely garden with a resident kri-kri. The captain also runs taxi boat trips to nearby Lissos, Domata and other beaches.

Rooms Ririka (☎ 28230 51167; s/d €35/40; ☒) Small but homy rooms right on the eastern side of the beach over a lovely garden courtyard.

Santa Irene Hotel (☎ 28230 51342; www.sougia .info/hotels/santairene; s/d/apt €35/45/55; ☒ ☐) The rooms at this smart hotel on the beach have marble floors, TV and kitchenettes, while there are also two family rooms with baby cots available. Prices drop dramatically off season.

Arhontiko (☎ 28230 51200; r €40-50; ☒) Tucked behind the supermarket, Arhontiko has spacious, attractive new studios and apartments comfortable for longer stays.

Also recommended is **Pension Galini** (☎ /fax 28230 51488; s/d/tr €35/40/45; ☒) which has well-appointed rooms and barbecue facilities.

Eating

Polyfimos (☎ 28230 51343; mains €5.20-7.80; ☉ dinner) Tucked away off the Hania road behind the police station, ex-hippy Yianni makes his own oil, wine and raki and even makes *dolmades* (vine leaves stuffed with rice) from the vines that cover the shady courtyard. The food is excellent and service from the affable Savvas delightful.

Kyma (☎ 28230 51670; meat dishes €5.50-7) On the waterfront as you enter town, with the fish tank in the front, Kyma has a good selection of *mayirefta*, its own meat and fresh local fish supplied by the owner's brother. Try the *tsigariasto* (goat in wine) or the rabbit. If you are up for a splurge, try the langoustine spaghetti (€70 per kg).

Taverna Rembetiko (☎ 28230 51510; mezedes €2.30-3.80) On the road to Hania, this popular taverna has an extensive menu of Cretan dishes such as *boureki* and stuffed zucchini flowers. It has a great atmosphere and is known for its good Greek music.

Also recommended is the international-style cuisine of French-run Omikron, and Livykon taverna at the western end of the beach.

Entertainment

Sougia has two open-air clubs that can get surprisingly lively for such a small resort. Alabama on the eastern side of the beach is the perennial favourite, while Fortuna, on your left before the entrance to the town, has had an impressive makeover and is a great place for a late night drink. Both kick off after midnight.

Getting There & Away

There's a daily bus travelling from Hania to Sougia (€6.10, 1hr 50 mins). Sougia is also on the Paleohora-Hora Sfakion boat route. Boats leave in the morning for Agia Roumeli (€6.30, 13/4 hours), Loutro (€10, 1½ hours) and Hora Sfakion (€11, 13/4 hours). For Paleohora (€7, one hour) to the west there is a departure at 5.15pm.

AROUND SOUGIA

Twelve kilometres north of Sougia is the mouth of the pretty **Agia Irini Gorge**, which may not be as fashionable as Samaria Gorge (p93) but is less crowded and gruelling. The 7km gorge is carpeted with oleander and chestnut trees and is fragrant with rosemary, sage and thyme. You'll see the entrance to the gorge on the right if you're travelling from Sougia.

You'll cross a stream bed before coming to olive groves (where many trees were destroyed in a fire in 1994). From there, the path follows a dried-out river bed bordered by caves carved into the rock. There are a number of rest stops along the way and many tranquil places to stop and admire the scenery.

Paleohora travel agents (opposite) offer **guided walks** through the gorge but it's easy enough to organise independently – just catch the Omalos bus from Paleohora or the Hania bus from Sougia, and get off at Agia Irini.

Lissos Λίσσος

The ruins of ancient Lissos are 1½ hours walk from Sougia on the coastal path to Paleohora (see the boxed text, p106), which starts at the far end of Sougia's small port.

Lissos arose under the Dorians, flourished under the Byzantines and was destroyed by the Saracens in the 9th century. It was part of a league of city-states, led by ancient Gortyna, which minted its own gold coins inscribed with the word 'Lission'. At one time there was a reservoir, a theatre and hot springs, but these have not yet been excavated. Most of what you see dates from the 1st through 3rd centuries BC when Lissos was known for its curative springs. The 3rd-century-BC **Temple of Asklepion** was built next to one of the springs and named after the Greek god of healing, Asklipios.

Excavations here uncovered a headless statue of **Asclepius** along with 20 other statue fragments now in the Hania Archaeological Museum (p82). You can still see the marble altar base that supported the statue next to the pit in which sacrifices were placed. The other notable feature is the mosaic floor of multicoloured stones intricately arranged in beautiful geometric shapes and images of birds. On the way down to the sea there are traces of Roman ruins, and on the western slopes of the valley are unusual barrel-vaulted tombs.

Nearby are the ruins of two early Christian basilicas – **Agios Kirkos** and the **Panagia** – dating from the 13th century.

Lissos has a lovely beach to cool off after the walk, and if you come on July 15 you will stumble on the annual **festival**, held in honour of Agios Kirkos.

PALEOHORA ΠΑΛΑΙΟΧΩΡΑ

pop 2205

Paleohora (pal-ee-o-*hor*-a) was discovered by hippies back in the '60s and from then on its days as a tranquil fishing village were numbered. Despite the mid-sized hotels and package tourists, the place is still appealing and retains a laid-back feel. The number of backpackers is dwindling but it attracts many walkers in spring and autumn and people who come back year after year. The tourist profile has gone up an age bracket and it has become more of a family destination, though it gets much livelier in the peak of summer. It is also the only beach resort on Crete that does not go into total hibernation in winter.

The town lies on a narrow peninsula with a long, curving tamarisk-shaded sandy beach exposed to the wind on one side and a sheltered pebbly beach on the other. The most picturesque part of Paleohora is the maze of narrow streets around the castle.

On summer evenings the main street and beach road is closed to traffic and the tavernas move onto the road, giving the place a lively summer ambience.

Orientation & Information

Paleohora has an attractive seafront promenade, along with the main road (Venizelou) which is cut off to traffic – they are the centres of activity in the early evening. Boats leave from the old harbour at the southern end of the pebble beach. There are ATMs on the main drag.

Erato Internet (☎ 28230 8301; Eleftheriou Venizelou; per hr €3)

Municipal tourist office (☎ 28230 41507; ☯ 10am-1pm & 6-9pm Wed-Mon May-Oct) On the beach road near the harbour.

Notos Internet (☎ 28230 42110; Eleftheriou Venizelou 53; per hr €2; ☯ 8am-10pm)

Post office At the northern end of Pahia Ammos beach.

Wash & Go Laundry (wash €4; dry €4) Next to Notos, keeps the same hours.

Sights & Activities

It's worth clambering up the ruins of the 13th-century **Venetian castle** for the splendid view of the sea and mountains. The castle was built so the Venetians could keep an eye on the southwestern coast from this commanding position on the hill-top. There's not much left of the fortress, however, as it was destroyed by the Venetians, the Turks, the pirate Barbarossa in the 16th century, and the Germans during WWII.

There are several great beaches and walking trails nearby. From Paleohora, a six-hour walk along a scenic **coastal path** leads to Sougia, passing ancient Lissos (see opposite). You can also do an easier walk around Anydri (p105).

Aqua Creta Diving & Adventures (☎ 28230 41393; www.aquacreta.gr; Kondekaki 4) runs a range of diving courses from beginner dives (€50) to seven- to 10-day master courses (€580). They also run one-day beach-hopping and snorkelling excursions to remote beaches along the southern coast and as far as Gavdos (€50-60).

Museum of the Acritans of Europe (☎ 28230 42265; Next to the Panagia Church; admission free; ⏰ 10am-1pm & 6.30-9pm Wed-Sun) This obscure museum is dedicated to the border fighters and heroes of Europe's medieval and Byzantine times. It has a well-displayed historical exhibition along with musical instruments, weapons and other items from the period. The Paleohora connection remains a mystery.

Tours

You can hike the Samaria and Agia Irini Gorge from Paleohora, either through organised tours or the local KTEL bus service, returning by ferry.

In summer, you can take a day trip to **Elafonisos** by ferry (see p105). **Dolphin-watching trips** (€18; three hrs) leave at 5pm. They reckon you have a 50-50 chance of spotting one when it's not windy.

Tsiskakis Travel (☎ 28230 42110; www.notoscar.com; Eleftheriou Venizelou 53)
Selino Travel (☎ 28230 42272; selino2@otenet.gr)

Sleeping

Camping Grammeno (☎ /fax 28230 42125; per person/tent €4.27/3) This new camp site is at Grammeno Beach, about 5km west along the road to Koundoura.

Camping Paleohora (☎ 28230 41120; sites per person/tent €5/3) This large camp site is 1.5km

northeast of the town, about 50m from Pebble Beach. There is a taverna but no minimarket and facilities are a bit primitive, though the new management say they will improve things. You can rent tents (small/large €6/10).

Homestay Anonymous (☎ 28230 41509; www .anonymoushomestay.com; s/d/tr €17/24/28) This excellent small *pension* has great value rooms with private bathrooms and shared cooking facilities in the courtyard garden. The rooms are clean and tastefully furnished and the old stone walls have been exposed, adding to its character. The amiable owner, Manolis, is full of useful information for travellers and his mother next door looks after the place. Rooms can connect to accommodate families.

Oriental Bay Rooms (☎ 28230 41076; s/d/tr €30/35/38; 🅿) These immaculate rooms are in the large modern building at the northern end of Pebble Beach. Rooms have balconies with sea or mountain views and come with kettle and fridge.

Villa Anna (☎ 2810 346 428; anna@her.forthnet. gr; apt €42-80; 🅿) Set among a lovely shady garden bordered by tall poplars, these well-appointed, family-friendly apartments can sleep up to five people. There are cots, and swings and a sandpit in the garden and the grounds are secured.

Haris Studios (☎ 28230 42438; www.paleochoraholi days.com; d/apt €45/50; 🅿) Right on the dramatic rocky seafront around from the port, these friendly well-fitted studios are open all winter. The top rooms are nicer and have great views. The bathrooms are basic but functional. Scottish Flora cooks up a feast for guests once a week, often the day's catch from keen fisherman partner Haris.

Aris Hotel (☎ 28230 41502; www.aris-hotel.gr; s/d €40/50 with breakfast) This friendly good-value

---

LETTING IT ALL HANG OUT

In most places in Crete topless sunbathing is allowed, though it is wise in family areas to take heed of others around you or any signs asking you to keep your gear on.

Although naturism is not officially allowed, the remote south coast beaches have a more relaxed attitude and you'll find a sprinkling of naturists on the far ends of most remote beaches or in secluded coves. Many Greek naturists, free campers (though rarely locals) and old hippies frequent these beaches too, which despite the flesh factor can have a laid-back, even family ambience. Beaches that are currently popular with naturists include Kommos near Matala, Sweetwater Beach, the south end of the sandy beach in Paleohora and the east end of Sougia. Sweetwater, close to Loutro is an old standby as is Orthi Ammos, east of Frangokastello and Ditikos, west of Lendas.

hotel at the far end of the road skirting around the headland from the port welcomes independent travellers. There are bright garden and sea view rooms with some adjoining rooms and balconies for families, and you can get great rates off season.

Also recommended is the larger **Villa Marise** (☎ 28230 41162; www.villamarise.com; 🖳) complex, it's on the beach and has a great beach bar.

Eating

Paleohora has decent and generally good-value eateries.

Dionysos Taverna (☎ 28230 41243; mains €4.40-6.80) One of the oldest tavernas in town, the popular Dionysos is known for top-grade food, particularly its excellent *mayirefta*. There is a

good range of vegetarian dishes and grills. It has a roomy interior and tables spread across the main street.

ourpick Third Eye (☎ 28230 41234; mains €5) It's not just vegetarians who flock to the Third Eye, just inland from Pahia Ammos. Crete's only vegetarian restaurant has an eclectic menu of curries, salads, pastas and Greek and Asian dishes, much of it made from the family farm's organic produce. There is often live music on Saturdays. They also have good budget rooms and apartments (€20-40) upstairs with air-con, fridge and balconies.

Kyma (☎ 28230 41110; top fish €42 per kg) One of the better places for fresh, local fish, Kyma is run by a fisherman: the offerings are normally from his own catch. It has a pleasant setting

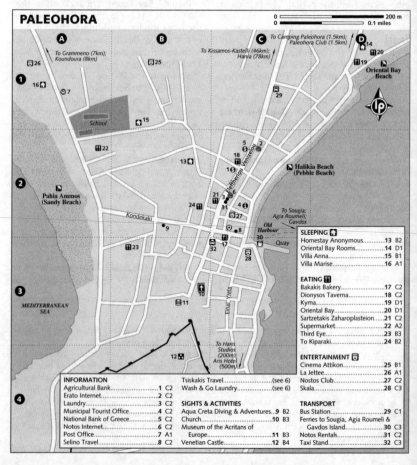

PALEOHORA

0 — 200 m
0 — 0.1 miles

To Grammeno (7km);
Koundoura (8km)

To Kissamos-Kastelli (46km);
Hania (78km)

To Camping Paleohora (1.5km);
Paleohora Club (1.5km)

Oriental Bay
Beach

School

Eleftheriou Venizelou

Halikia Beach
(Pebble Beach)

Pahia Ammos
(Sandy Beach)

Kondekaki

To Sougia;
Agia Roumeli;
Gavdos

Old
Harbour

Quay

MEDITERRANEAN
SEA

Einai Yria

To Hans
Studios
(200m);
Aris Hotel
(500m)

SLEEPING 🛏	
Homestay Anonymous	13 B2
Oriental Bay Rooms	14 D1
Villa Anna	15 B1
Villa Marise	16 A1

EATING 🍴	
Bakakis Bakery	17 C2
Dionysos Taverna	18 C2
Kyma	19 D1
Oriental Bay	20 D1
Sartzetakis Zaharoplasteion	21 C2
Supermarket	22 C2
Third Eye	23 B3
To Kiparaki	24 B2

ENTERTAINMENT 🎭	
Cinema Attikon	25 B1
La Jettee	26 A1
Nostos Club	27 C2
Skala	28 C3

INFORMATION	
Agricultural Bank	1 C2
Erato Internet	2 C2
Laundry	3 C2
Municipal Tourist Office	4 C2
National Bank of Greece	5 C2
Notos Internet	6 C2
Post Office	7 A1
Selino Travel	8 C2

Tsiskakis Travel	(see 6)
Wash & Go Laundry	(see 6)

SIGHTS & ACTIVITIES	
Aqua Creta Diving & Adventures	9 B2
Church	10 B3
Museum of the Acritans of Europe	11 B3
Venetian Castle	12 B4

TRANSPORT	
Bus Station	29 C1
Ferries to Sougia, Agia Roumeli & Gavdos Island	30 C3
Notos Rentals	31 C3
Taxi Stand	32 C3

right on the quiet end of the beach, with a few tables outside under the trees.

To Kiparaki (☎ 28230 42281; mains €8-9) This Dutch-run little place serves Asian-style food using only fresh produce for its daily changing menu. There are only eight tables in the little garden out the back.

Oriental Bay (☎ 28230 41322; mains €5-8) This beachside taverna is one of the best options on this side of the village. In addition to a range of cheap vegetarian choices, such as green beans and potatoes, there are dishes such as 'rooster's kiss' (chicken fillet with bacon) and 'drunk cutlet' (pork chop in red wine).

Also recommended are the excellent sweets and homemade ice cream at **Sartzetakis Zaharo-plasteion** (☎ 28230 41231) and the **Bakakis Bakery** (☎ 28230 41069) for snacks.

For excellent traditional Cretan food it is worth the trip to **Grammeno** (☎ 28230 41505; Cretan specials €4.50-9) just past the beach, about 5km west of Paleohora. The menu includes special-ties such as braised rooster, various wild greens, lamb in vine leaves and tender roast goat.

Right on Krios Beach – at the eastern end of Koundoura about 9km from Paleohora – there is a kantina that serves excellent and cheap Cretan food; try the *kalitsounia* (pastries filled with cheese or wild greens) or *Sfakianes pittes* (pancakes) with honey.

Entertainment

La Jettee, behind the Villa Marise hotel, is right on the beach and has a lovely garden, while Skala by the port is an old-time classic bar.

Most visitors to Paleohora spend at least one evening at the outdoor **Cinema Attikon** (tickets €7; ☽ screenings start 10pm).

Nostos Club (☎ 28230 42145; ☽ 6pm-2am) has an outdoor terrace bar and a small indoor club playing Greek and Western music. **Paleohora Club** (☎ 28230 42230; ☽ 11pm-late), next to the camp site, used to be popular for all-night, full-moon parties but is now a less-appeal-ing swanky indoor club. There's a shuttle bus from the port.

Getting There & Away

BOAT

Boat schedules change year to year so check with travel agents. In summer there is a daily morning ferry from Paleohora to Hora Sfakion (€14, three hours), via Sougia (€7, 50 minutes), Agia Roumeli (€11, 1½ hours) and Loutro (€13, 2½ hours). The same boat also continues three times per week in summer to Gavdos (€15, 2½ hours).

From mid-April M/B *Elafonisos* ferries people to the west-coast beach of Elafonisi (€7, one hour). The service increases from three times per week to daily in mid-May through September. It departs at 10am and returns at 4pm.

Tickets can be bought at **Selino Travel** (☎ 28230 42272; selino2@otenet.gr).

BUS

In summer there are four to six buses per day from the **bus station** (☎ 28230 41914) to Hania (€6.50, two hours). There is also one daily service, departing 6.15am, to Omalos (€5.50, 2 hours), for the Samaria Gorge, which also stops at the entrance to the Agia Irini Gorge (€4.50).

Getting Around

Notos Rentals (☎ 28230 42110; notosgr@yahoo.gr; Eleftheriou Venizelou) rents cars, motorcycles and mountain bikes.

The **taxi stand** (☎ 28230 41128; 6972 726 149) is near the port. Sample fares are Kissamos (€40), Hania (€60; airport €70) and Elafonisi (€60).

AROUND PALEOHORA

The village of **Anydri**, 5km northeast of Paleo-hora is a popular destination for walkers and is reached via a picturesque drive through a gorge. The founding fathers of the village were two brothers from Hora Sfakion fleeing a murderous vendetta, which is why most villagers have the same surname.

Many people walk a circuit route from Pale-ohora to Andyri via the gorge to return along the coast. Take the road that goes past the camp sites ground and follow the paved road that forks off to the left, which is bordered by steep rocks. As you enter the village you'll see a sign directing you to the **Anydri Gorge**. After a few hundred metres on a footpath you'll see an overgrown path on the left. Red markers direct you to the gorge. Alternatively, you can have a break in the village at the excellent **Kafeneio To Scholio** (☎ 28230 83001), a converted school, and take another path from there past the **Church of Agios Georgios** which has 14th-century frescoes.

After walking along the dried-out riverbed, signs direct you to wide **Gialiskari Beach** at the end of the gorge. The nicest stretch is the sandy beach with coarse sand at the eastern

---

PALEOHORA–SOUGIA COASTAL WALK

From the town centre of Paleohora, follow signs to the camp sites to the northeast. Turn right at the intersection with the road to Anydri and soon you'll be following the coastal path marked as the E4 European Footpath. After a couple of kilometres, the path climbs steeply for a beautiful view back to Paleohora. You'll pass **Anydri Beach** and several inviting **coves** where people may be getting an all-over tan. Take a dip because the path soon turns inland to pass over **Cape Flomes**. You'll walk along a plateau carpeted with brush that leads towards the coast and some breathtaking views over the Libyan Sea. Soon you'll reach the Minoan site of **Lissos** (see p102). After Lissos the path takes you through a pine forest. The road ends at Sougia Harbour. The 14.5km walk (allow about six hours) is nearly shadeless so take several litres of water and sunscreen. From June through August, it's best to start at sunrise in order to get to Sougia before the heat of the day.

---

end, left of the *kantina*. You can take a different path back to Paleohora following the E4 markers, which will take you along the coastal cliffs. The beach is accessible by a driveable dirt road, where it is signposted to the right well before the gorge.

GAVDOS ΓΑΥΔΟΣ
pop 81

Gavdos (*gav*-dos) is as much a state of mind as it is an island. If you want to get away from it all, there is no better place for peace and isolation. Gavdos attracts a loyal following of campers, nudists and free spirits seeking natural beaches, long walks and laid-back holidays. This is the place for chilling out, letting your beard grow, rolling cigarettes and spending the nights looking at the starry skies.

Located under Crete in the Libyan sea, 65km from Paleohora, it is the most southerly place in Europe. Geographically it's more akin to Africa than Europe and enjoys a very mild climate. You can swim as early as February. Gavdos is surprisingly green, with almost 65% of the island covered in low-lying pine and cedar trees and vegetation, although it has a rugged natural landscape. There are several stunning beaches, some of which are accessible only by foot or boat. Most of the beaches are on the northeastern coast, as the southern coastline is all cliffs.

Gavdos has three main 'villages', which are virtually abandoned and full of ruins, and one beach settlement that gets relatively lively in July and August. At its tourist peak, the island's permanent population of about 55 residents may swell to 1000.

Archaeological excavations indicate the island was inhabited as far back as the Neolithic period. In the Greco-Roman era Gavdos,

then known as Clauda, belonged to the city of Gortyna. There was a Roman settlement on the northwestern corner. Under the Byzantines, Gavdos was the seat of a bishopric, but when the Arabs conquered Crete in the 9th century the island became a pirates' nest.

Until the late 1960s Gavdos had little water and no electricity or phones, and most residents emigrated to Paleohora or other parts of Crete or Athens. While water is now plentiful, there can still be electricity shortages and blackouts (particularly in summer) as only part of the island has grid power – the rest use generators which are often turned off at night and in the middle of the day. It is wise to take a torch. Strong winds can leave visitors stranded for days on end, but you won't find too many people complaining.

Orientation & Information

The island's port is Karabe on the east side of the island, while the capital Kastri is in the centre. There is no bank but you can send mail in Sarakiniko. There are a couple of minimarkets for basic supplies and a medical clinic at Kastri. Mobile coverage is patchy but card phones are available. Gavdos has a short season, as most tavernas and rooms shut by early September when schools start.

Gavdos has a new port and a **police station** (☎ 228230 41109) at Karabe.

Sights & Activities

The biggest beach community is at **Sarakinikos**, in the northeast, which has a wide swathe of sand and several tavernas, as well as an **amphitheatre** for occasional performances. The stunning **Agios Ioannis** beach, on the northern tip, has a scraggly summer settlement of nudists and campers, though numbers swell in mmer. There are some wonderful beaches the northern coast such as **Potamos** and **rgos**, which you can reach by foot (about an ur) from Kastri if you follow the footpath ding north to Ambelos and beyond. Three nt arches carved into the rocky headland at **piti** – the southernmost tip of Europe – are e island's best-known natural feature. The ach is reached by boat or on foot (a 1¼-ur walk from Vatsiana).

The restored 1880 **lighthouse** on the road to e village of Ambelos has a museum and café. fore it was bombed by the Germans in 1941 was the world's second-brightest lighthouse ter Tierra del Fuego.

In **Vatsiana**, the island's priest has created a aall private **museum** (☎ 28230 42167; ⏰ 10am-6pm -Aug, knock next door at other times) in an old stone use with items collected from the island, in-ding agricultural and domestic tools, a loom d weavings. There is a small working trad-onal wood oven next door and the priest's fe, Maria, runs the quaint attached *kafeneio*, here you can try her ouzo and cake.

Despite the meagre population, there are 16 aall churches dotted around the island. Most at owners offer full- and half-day **cruises**, cluding trips to the remote, uninhabited and of Gavdopoula, although there are no od beaches there. Ask at the tavernas.

eeping & Eating

used to be considered upmarket if you had wer in Gavdos but a swathe of new ac-mmodation options has since sprung up, cluding some flashier places. Free camping popular. The tavernas all offer fairly good lue.

Nychterida Taverna & Rooms (☎ 28230 42120; d 0-50) has basic but comfortable rooms on rakinikos beach.

Akrogiali Taverna & Rooms (☎ 28230 42384; d/tr 5/40), on Korfos beach, offers fresh local fish d its own goat meat for hearty Cretan cook-g. The simple rooms have a fridge and a fan d overlook the beach.

Sarakiniko Studios (☎ 28230 42182; www.gavdo dios.gr; d/tr studio incl breakfast €50/60), above Sa-kiniko beach, has comfortable studios and w villas sleeping up to five (€80 to €100). ou can be picked up at the port or it is a 0-minute walk north. A camp site was set to gin operating nearby in 2008.

Taverna Sarakiniko (☎ /fax 28230 41103; gavdos@cha rthnet.gr; r/studio €60/85; ❄), run by Manolis the fisherman and his wife Gerti, serves Manolis' fresh catch daily. It has rooms with sea views, fridge and air-con (24-hour power) and stone studios nearby with pine furniture and basic kitchen facilities that sleep four. It also rents cars and bikes.

Theophilos taverna (☎ 28230 41311), above Agios Ioannis beach, has excellent trays of *mayirefta* catering to the campers coming up from the beach.

Getting There & Around

Services to Gavdos vary throughout the year and can take between 2½ to five hours depending on the boat and other stops, so it can be confusing. The most direct route to Gavdos is from Hora Sfakion, which has services to Gavdos on Friday, Saturday and Sunday (€15, 1½ hours). There are also two boats per week from Paleohora, increasing to three from mid-July to August, though they go via the southern ports and Hora Sfakion, making it a long five-hour trip. There is also a Tuesday morning post boat from Paleohora (via Sougia).

Only some ferries takes cars so check if you plan on taking one across.

You can rent a bike or car at the port or in Sarakiniko, though be wary that they may not have insurance.

WESTERN HANIA

Western Crete is less affected by tourism than the rest of Hania. The northern coast is de-fined by the virtually uninhabited Gramvousa and Rodopou Peninsulas. Kolymbari, at the foot of the Rodopou Peninsula, is the most developed tourist town.

The Kissamos province is a rugged region of scattered villages and towns that attracts few tourists. Its capital, Kissamos-Kastelli, is the port for boats from the Peloponnese. The west coast has two of Crete's finest beaches, both of which are surprisingly underdevel-oped: Falasarna in the northern corner and Elafonisi in the southern corner. The Selino Province includes the Innahorion region of small mountain villages.

RODOPOU PENINSULA

The barren, rocky Rodopou Peninsula has a few small villages clustered at its base but the rest is uninhabited. A paved road goes as far as Afrata, but then becomes a dirt track that meanders through the peninsula. If you are travelling by foot, jeep or motorcycle you can reach the Diktynna sanctuary at the end of the peninsula, but make sure you have planned your journey and are well supplied since there is not a drop of petrol or water, nor a morsel of food, beyond Afrata. From Afrata a road winds down to the small, gravelly pebbly **Afrata Beach**, which also supports a small seasonal snack bar.

Kolymbari Κολυμπάρι
pop 919

Kolymbari, 23km west of Hania, is at the base of the Rodopou Peninsula, and appeals to those seeking a quiet, relaxing holiday. Development of the fishing hamlet is in its embryonic stage, but that is changing fast as hotels and domatia arise to take advantage of the long pebbly beach. Kolymbari is a good base for a walk to Moni Gonias (right) and an excellent place to sample local fish at one of the well-regarded fish tavernas.

The bus from Hania drops you off on the main road, from which it is a 500m walk down to the settlement. There is an ATM on the main street and a post office in the centre of the village.

SLEEPING & EATING
Rooms Lefka (☎ 28240 22211; fax 28240 22211; s/d/tr €25/35/45;) On the way into town from the bus stop you will see this decent budget place on the right. Rooms are older-style but comfortable, with a fridge and rather wacky showers nozzles in the basin. They are well set up for families, and the taverna downstairs serves up good, honest Cretan food and a hearty breakfast (€6).

Aeolos Apartments (☎ 28240 22203; studio/apt €45/60;) Signposted to the left off the main road, this dated but well-maintained complex on the hill has big balconies with sea views and flower beds. Breezy studios and two-room apartments are spacious and comfortable, with carved timber beds, TV and kitchenettes with bar stools.

Argentina (☎ 28240 22243; fish per kg €30-48) Considered one of the best fish tavernas in the area, the classic Argentina has tables on the main road and across the street overlooking the sea. It serves seafood dishes such as octopus with olives, quality fish and there is a select wine list.

Diktina (☎ 28240 22611; top fish per kg €47) Th place has had an upmarket facelift and lool more like a city restaurant than a fish taverr but it has sea views and a range of reliab fish dishes.

Milos tou Tzerani (☎ 28240 22210) This café/b in a restored mill on the sea is a great plac for a coffee or an evening drink and also h light snacks and mezedes.

Also recommended is **Palio Arhondik** (☎ 28240 22124) on the beach.

GETTING THERE & AWAY
Buses from Hania to Kissamos-Kastelli stop Kolymbari (€2.80, 40 minutes, half-hourly)

Moni Gonias Μονη Γονιασ
Founded in 1618, **Moni Gonias** (☎ 28240 2231 Kolymbari; admission free, museum €2; 8am-12.30pr & 4-8pm Mon-Fri, 4-8pm Sat, 7am-noon & 4-8pm Sun) wa damaged by the Turks in 1645, but rebuil in 1662 and extended in the 19th century The monastery houses a unique collection o icons dating from the 17th and 18th centuries Some are in the church while others are in the monastery's two-room museum. The mos valuable icon is that of *Agios Nikolaos*, painte in 1637 by Palaiokapas (in the museum or your left). It perfectly exemplifies the Cretar school of icon painting that flourished in the 17th century. The monastery, which also incorporates Crete's Theological College, is easy to reach from Kolymbari. Take the beach road north from the town centre for about 500m.

Diktynna Δικτυνα
On the tip of the Rodopou Peninsula are the remains of a temple to the Cretan goddess Diktynna, which was the most important religious sanctuary in the region under the Romans. Diktynna was the goddess of hunting and she was worshipped fervently in western Crete.

Legend has it that her name derives from the word *diktyon*, which means 'net'. It was a fisherman's net that saved her when she leapt into the sea to avoid the amorous desires of King Minos. The temple dates from the 2nd century AD but it was probably built on the site of an earlier temple.

After the collapse of the Roman Empire the temple was desecrated but you can see the temple's foundations and a sacrificial altar as well as Roman cisterns. If you are 'templed out' you can relax on a lovely sandy beach.

Diktynna is only accessible by dirt road from Kolymbari, but travel agencies in Hania (p84) offer boat excursions.

KISSAMOS-KASTELLI
ΚΊΣΣΑΜΟΣ-ΚΑΣΤΕΛΛΙ
pop 3969

The largest town and capital of the Kissamos province is Kissamos-Kastelli, usually referred to simply as Kissamos. The north coast port town is where the ferries arrive from the Peloponnese or Kythira. It's a quiet town of mostly elderly residents that neither expects nor attracts much tourism, but is worth more than a passing glance. Many small family hotels have sprouted in recent years and tourism seems to be on the rise. The huge Bay of Kissamos has some fine pebble and sand beaches and the almost bucolic feel to the region is a welcome antidote to the bustling Crete further east. There's a string of waterfront tavernas and bars lining the seafront promenade but the place only ever gets busy in August. Kissamos is good base for walking and touring the area, with the Gramvousa Peninsula to the west and the Rodopou Peninsula to the east. Cruises to the Gramvousa Peninsula leave from Kissamos port.

History

In antiquity, Kissamos was the main town of the province of the same name. When the Venetians came along and built a castle here it became known as Kastelli. The name persisted until 1966 when authorities decided that too many people were confusing it with Crete's other Kastelli, near Iraklio. The official name reverted to Kissamos, though it is still often called Kastelli or Kissamos-Kastelli.

Ancient Kissamos was a harbour for the important city-state of Polyrrinia, 7km inland. Vestiges of Roman buildings have been unearthed, but most of the ancient city lies beneath the modern town of Kissamos and cannot be excavated. Kissamos gained independence in the third century AD and then became a bishopric under the Byzantines. It was occupied by the Saracens in the 9th century and flourished under the Venetians. Parts of the castle wall survive to the west of Tzanakaki square.

Orientation & Information

The port is 3km west of town. In summer a bus meets the boats, otherwise a taxi costs around €5. The bus station is on the main square, Plateia Tzanakaki, and the main commercial street, Skalidi, runs east from Plateia Tzanakaki. The post office is on the main through road, near Plateia Venizelou. There are a number of banks with ATMs along the highway and Skalidi. It's a 200m walk to reach the foreshore promenade.

Kissamos has a reasonably informative website, www.kissamos.net. **Horeftakis Tours** (☎ 28220 23250; www.horeftakistours.com; Skalidi) is a good source of information. You can buy foreign press and books at **Fountoulakis Bookshop** (☎ 28220 22361) on Skalidi. **Gamers Internet Cafe** (☎ 28220 22112; Skalidi 17; ☻ 10am-late; €1.70 per hr) has the full service.

Sights & Activities

The new **Archaeological Museum of Kissamos** (☎ 28220 83308; Plateia Tzanakaki; ☻ 8.30am-3pm; free admission), in an imposing two-level Venetian-Turkish building on the main square, has a well displayed collection of artefacts unearthed during archaeological digs in the area, including statues, jewellery, coins and a large mosaic floor from a Kissamos villa. There are exhibits from Falasarna and Polyrrinia and

---

DETOUR: RAVDOUHA

The unassuming fishing hamlet of **Ravdouha Beach,** on the western side of the rugged Rodopou Peninsula, is one of the area's hidden gastronomic treats. Follow the signs to Ravdoucha until you reach a fork in the road. To the left, a rough dirt road leads 700m to the **Waves on the Rock** (☎ 28240 23133) run by fisherman Theodoris Falelakis, who serves excellent fresh fish. If you really feel like getting away from it all there are also five **rooms** (€25-30) upstairs with kitchenette and air-con.

Turning right at the fork will lead you to a small pebbly beach with a pier and couple of tavernas, including an incongruous Italian restaurant **Don Rosario** (☎ 28240 23781; mains €9.50-22.50) run by a retired Italian chef, who dishes up scrumptious pans of seafood spaghetti and sophisticated Mediterranean cuisine on his shady terrace.

most of the collections spans the Hellenistic-Roman eras, though there are displays from Minoan excavations and Nopigia.

Run by Stelios Milonakis and his British wife Angela, **Strata Walking Tours** (☎ 28220 24336; www.stratatours.com) offers a range of walking tours for small groups, from leisurely day trips including taverna lunch in the surrounding countryside (€40) to full-on 15-day round trips (€895) reaching as far as the south coast. They also run jeep safaris to interesting off-road destinations (€40).

Sleeping

Camping Mithymna (☎ 2822031444; www.campingmithy mna.gr; Paralia Drapania; per person/tent €6/4) About 6km east of town, Camping Mithymna is an excellent shady site near the best stretch of beach with a restaurant, bar and shop. Take a bus to the village of Drapanias, from where it's a pleasant 15-minute walk through olive groves to the camp sites (or walk 4km along the beach).

Bikakis Family (☎ 28220 22105; www.familybikakis.gr; Iroön Polemiston 1941; s/d €20/25, studio €30; ✖ 🖵) This would have to be the best budget option in Kissamos town. The rooms and studios sparkle and most have garden and sea views, kitchenettes and extras such as TV, hairdryers and free internet. It maintains a family environment and owner Giannis makes guests feel very welcome. He is also an expert on herbal teas and the local environs. There are bigger studios and adjoining rooms for families and breakfast is available.

Thalassa (☎ 28220 31231; www.thalassa-apts.gr; Paralia Drapanias; studios €35-55; ✖ 🖵) The isolated Thalassa complex is an ideal spot to retreat to with a stack of books. The immaculate studios are airy and well-fitted out with irons, hairdryers and ADSL/wi-fi connections. There's a barbecue on the lawn and a small playground and it's just across from the beach, 100m east of Camping Mithymna.

Galini Beach (☎ 28220 23288; r €38-48) At the eastern end of the beach next to the soccer ground, this well-maintained, friendly, family-run hotel has spacious rooms decorated in cool tones, some with kitchenette, as well as adjoining family rooms.

Christina Beach Hotel (☎ 28220 83333; studio €60-80; 🅿 ✖ 🖵) This smart studio complex on the west side of Kissamos represents the upper end of accommodation in town. Right on the foreshore, the modern studios are large and airy and all have ISDN internet connection.

Eating

Kellari (☎ 28220 23883; Cretan specials €3-7.50) This well-regarded taverna on the eastern end of the beach strip has an extensive range of Cretan dishes, grills and fresh fish as well as a Greek-tasting menu for two (€16). Owned by the same family that runs Strata Walking Tours (p109), they use their own meat, wine, oil and other produce.

Papadakis (☎ 28220 22340; mains €5-8) One of the oldest tavernas in town, this place is well patronised by local diners. The taverna has a very relaxing setting overlooking the beach and serves well-prepared fish dishes such as oven-baked fish (€6) or fish soup.

O Stimadoris (☎ 28220 22057; fish per kg €30-45) This well-respected fish taverna is about 2km west of town, just before the small fishing harbour. The owners are fishermen and therefore the fish is always fresh. Try an unusual salad made of seaweed in vinegar, *salata tou yialou*. The small taverna is like a mini-museum while the room with sea views regularly hosts weddings.

Also recommended for fine home cooking and excellent value is **Violaki** (☎ 28220 23068) on the main through road and **Akroyiali**, well signposted before Kissamos, for excellent fresh fish on the beach.

Getting There & Away

BOAT

ANEN Ferries operates the F/B *Myrtidiotissa* at weekends on a route that takes in Antikythira (€9.40, two hours), Kythira (€16.40, four hours), and Gythio (€22.10, five hours). Sunday's service does serve Piraeus eventually but it's far quicker to go from Hania. You can buy tickets from **Horeftakis Tours** (☎ 28220 23250) and the **ANEN Office** (☎ 28220 22009; Skalidi).

BUS

From Kissamos' **bus station** (☎ 28220 22035), there are 14 buses per day to Hania (€4, 40 minutes), where you can change for Rethymno and Iraklio; two buses per day for Falasarna (€3, 20 minutes), one bus per day to Paleohora (€6.50, 1¼ hours) and one to Elafonisi (€5.90, 1¼ hours).

Getting Around

Moto Fun (☎ 28220 23440; www.motofun.info; Plateia Tzanakaki) Rents cars, bikes & mountain bikes.

AROUND KISSAMOS-KASTELLI

Polyrrinia Πολυρρηνια

The ancient city ruins of Polyrrinia (pol-ee-ren-*ee*-a) lie about 7km south of Kissamos-Kastelli, above the village of Ano Paleokastro (also called Polyrrinia). It's a steep climb to the ruins, but the sea and mountain views are stunning and the region is blanketed with wild flowers in spring. The city was founded by the Dorians in the 6th century BC and was constantly at war with the Kydonians from Hania. Coins from the period depict the warrior-goddess Athena, who was evidently revered by the warlike Polyrrinians.

Unlike their rivals the Kydonians, the Polyrrinians did not resist the Roman invasion and thus the city was spared destruction. It was the best-fortified town in Crete and the administrative centre of western Crete from the Roman through to the Byzantine period. The Venetians used it as a fortress. Many of the structures, including an **aqueduct** built by Hadrian, date from the Roman period.

The most impressive feature of the site is the **acropolis** built by the Byzantines and Venetians. There's also a church built on the foundations of a **Hellenistic temple** from the 4th century BC. Near the aqueduct is a **cave** dedicated to the nymphs; it still contains the niches for nymph statuettes.

It's a scenic two-hour walk from Kissamos-Kastelli to Polyrrinia. To reach the Polyrrinia road, walk east along the Kissamos-Kastelli main road and turn right after the OTE (public phone company) office. You can reach the site through the village on foot, passing by the interesting olive wood **workshop** (☎ 28220 24168) of Giorgos Tsichlakis.

If you are driving, take the perimeter road at the turn off for the **Acropolis Taverna** (☎ 28220 23678) which has lovely views. Behind the taverna there is a path to the left about 100m before the Agios Pateras church which leads to the acropolis. You can do a full circuit around the hill to take in the views but the path can be overgrown.

There are no buses to the site.

Sirikari Σηρικαρι

From Polyrrinia, many intrepid walkers continue the hike to the **Sirikari Gorge**, one of the area's most scenic and popular walks. The walk takes about two hours (and as much

again to reach Kissamos if you are doing it the other way around). From the tiny hamlet of Sirikari, the entrance to the gorge is near the Agios Apostoli church.

An appealing new accommodation option if you are after somewhere remote, is the **Kastania Traditional Guest House** (☎ 28220 51449; Sirikari; d €40-60 with breakfast). The owner, a retired air traffic controller, has restored the family home into four cosy traditional-style studios and makes a hearty breakfast (and can also provide good value home cooked meals). From here there are great walks through a verdant chestnut forest leading to Kambos.

GRAMVOUSA PENINSULA
ΧΕΡΣΟΝΗΣΟΣ ΓΡΑΜΒΟΥΣΑ

Northwest of Kissamos is the beautifully wild and remote Gramvousa Peninsula, whose main attraction is the stunning lagoon-like sandy beach of **Balos**, on Cape Tigani on the west side of the peninsula's narrow tip. The idyllic beach with turquoise waters is overlooked by the two islets of **Agria** (wild) and **Imeri** (tame), but day trippers can detract from its appeal.

The very rough but drivable dirt road (best in a four-wheel drive) to Balos begins at the end of the main street of **Kalyviani village** and follows the eastern slope of Mt Geroskinos. From here, the views over the shoreline and the Rodopou Peninsula are spectacular.

The road ends at a car park (with a kantina) from where the path to the beach is a 30-minute walk down the sandy cliffs (45 minutes on the way back up).

West-bound buses from Kissamos will let you off at the turn-off for Kalyviani, from where it is a 2km walk to the beginning of the path at the far end of the main street. The shadeless walk to Balos is around 3km – wear a hat and take plenty of water.

An easier way to get there are the three daily **cruises** (☎ 28220 24344; www.gramvousa.com; adult/concession cost €22/12; 55 mins). The morning boats stop at Imeri Gramvousa, which is crowned with a **Venetian castle** from which there are stunning views of the peninsula. It's a steep 20-minute walk to the top and there is a small beach below with a shipwreck. The beach gets crowded if the boats are full, as does Balos. Tickets can be bought on the day at Kissamos port. Departures are at 10am, 10.15am and 1pm and returns at 5.45pm and 8pm. The trip can be rough if it's windy.

HANIA

History

The offshore island of Imeri Gramvousa was an important vantage point for the Venetians, who built a fortress here to protect ships on their way to and from Venice. It was considered an impregnable fort and had a large cache of armaments. The Turks did not conquer Imeri Gramvousa along with the rest of Crete in 1645; the fort remained in Venetian hands. Eventually the Venetians left and the fort fell into disuse until it was taken over in 1821 by Cretan revolutionaries. It later became a notorious base for piracy before the Turks took it and used it to blockade the coast during the War of Independence. Local legend has it that the pirates amassed a fabulous fortune that they hid in caves around the island.

The **Kalyviani shipwreck**, rusting on the west side of Kalyviani beach, is a Lebanese-registered ship that struck trouble on its way from Libya to Crete in 1981.

Sleeping & Eating

A good base for touring this region is the village of Kalyviani, 7km west of Kissamos.

Kaliviani (☎ /fax 28220 23204; www.kaliviani.com; d & tr €40-55; ☒) An attractive stone-built guesthouse with comfortable, tastefully furnished rooms with fridge and balcony. The excellent restaurant (mains €4.80-8.50) serves up the genuine article, whenever possible using organic produce. Recommended is the *gramvousiano yiahni* – a tasty local goat stew (€7).

Olive Tree Apartments (☎ 28220 24336; www.olivetree.gr; apt €40-70; ☒ ☒) This attractive complex in an olive grove at the entrance to the village has spacious, comfortable and well-presented apartments suitable for families and longer stays, as well as an inviting pool.

Gramvousa (☎ 28220 22707; wood oven specials €.5.50-8.70) In the centre of the village, Gramvousa serves fine traditional Cretan cuisine in an attractively decorated stone building set in a superb garden. Try the wood oven specials such as the suckling pig or lamb with honey.

FALASARNA ΦΑΛΑΣΑΡΝΑ

pop 21

Falasarna, 16km west of Kissamos, was a Cretan city-state in the 4th century BC but there's not much of the ancient city left to see. It attracts a mixed bunch of travellers due to its long, wide stretch of sandy beach, which is considered one of the best in Crete. It is split up into several coves by rocky spits and is known for its stunning sunsets and the pink hues reflecting from the fine coral in the sand.

If you like solitude, Falasarna is your kind of place – apart from the rush of activity from mid-July to mid-August. There is no village nor facilities, just a scattering of widely spaced rooms and tavernas among the greenhouses that somewhat mar the approach to the beach. There is no organised 'beach scene', although there is a beach bar in the centre and the omnipresent beach umbrellas and lounges at different locations. The big beach to the south is the livelier spot, with the middle rocky cove frequented by nudists, and there's a quieter smaller beach to the north.

History

Falasarna has been occupied at least since the 6th century BC, but reached the height of its power in the 4th century BC. Although it was built next to the sea, the town's ruins are about 400m away from the water because the western coast of Crete has risen over the centuries. The town owed its wealth to the agricultural produce from the fertile valley to the south. It was the west-coast harbour for Polyrrinia but later became Polyrrinia's chief rival for dominance over western Crete. By the time of the Roman invasion of Crete in 67 BC, Falasarna had become a haven for pirates. Stone blocks excavated around the entrance to the old harbour indicate that the Romans may have tried to block off the harbour to prevent it from being used by pirates.

Sights

The **ruins** of the ancient city of Falasarna are the area's main attraction, although not much is visible. Signs direct you to the ancient city from the main road, following a dirt road at the end of the asphalt.

First you'll come to a large stone throne, the purpose of which is unknown. Further on there are the remains of the wall that once fortified the town and a small harbour. Notice the holes carved into the wall, which were used to tie up boats. At the top of the hill there are the remains of the acropolis wall and a temple as well as four clay baths.

Sleeping & Eating

Most accommodation is aimed at the independent traveller. The places on the beach are unfortunately the least attractive. There are numerous places for free camping, although like elsewhere it is officially frowned upon.

Rooms Anastasia-Stathis (☎ 28220 41480; fax 28220 41069; d/apt €40/50; 🔀) The airy, attractively furnished rooms with fridges and large balconies are perfect for stress relief, as the friendly owner Anastasia puts it. Her enormous breakfasts (€6) are open to all comers and guests can pick vegies from the garden.

Doma (☎ 28220 41726; www.domaapts.gr; studio €44, apt €50-70) This attractive complex in a garden setting has tastefully furnished studios and one- or two-room apartments that are well equipped for longer stays. There are big balconies and extras such as hairdryers and TV, while some have full-size kitchens.

Kavousi Resorts (☎ 28220 41251; www.kavoussi resorts.com; studio & apt €45-70 🔀) High above on the approach to Falasarna with sweeping views and spacious, comfortable new studios and apartments, though it's only feasible if you have a car.

Rooms for Rent Panorama (☎ 28220 41336; www .falasarna.gr; d/tr €48/55 🔀) One of the first places you will come across, signposted to the left along a gravel track, these refurbished studios are spotless and comfortable, and have a fridge or kitchenette. The well-run and friendly restaurant with a great view of the beach serves up good Cretan cooking.

Galasia Thea (☎ 28220 41421; mayirefta €4.50-6) On the cliff overlooking the great expanse of beach, this café has spectacular views from its huge terrace. There's a big range of baked dishes and *mayirefta* such as the Sfakiano lemon lamb.

Also recommended is **Sun Set** (☎ 28220 41204), a taverna for fish and classic Cretan food.

Getting There & Away

From June through August there are three buses daily from Kissamos to Falasarna (€2.60) as well as three buses from Hania (€6).

INNAHORION INNAXOPION

Innahorion is the highly scenic mountainous region south of Kissamos-Kastelli, which is renowned for its chestnut trees. It is often referred to as 'Ennia Horia', meaning nine villages, but there are actually more than nine villages dotting the region.

If you have your own transport you can drive through the region en route to Moni Hrysoskalitissas and Elafonisi or, with a little backtracking, to Paleohora. Alternatively, you

can take a circular route, returning via the coast road. Heading south from Kissamos you'll pass through some of the lushest and most fertile parts of the island.

You'll first come to the village of **Voulgaro**, which has two Byzantine churches. Three kilometres further south is the lovely village of **Topolia** with a cluster of whitewashed houses overhung with plants and vines.

After Topolia the road skirts the edge of the **Koutsomatados Ravine**, bending and twisting and affording dramatic views. Just before a narrow road tunnel there is a **snack bar** on the left, which is a good place to stop and take a photo of the ravine. Shortly, you will come to the **Agia Sofia cave**, which contains evidence of settlement from as far back as the Neolithic era. The cave is often used for baptisms and celebrates the patron saint's day on 13 April. A third of the way up the 250 rock-cut steps to the cave, the taverna **Romantza** has great views over the ravine and is run by the colourful Manolis, who wears traditional Cretan dress. It's a lovely drive to tiny **Koutsomatados**, followed by the village of **Vlatos**. Just south of Milia (see the boxed text, p115) and back on the main highway there is a turn-off for Paleohora via **Strovles** and **Drys**. While most maps suggest it is not a good road, it is actually paved and affords much quicker access to Paleohora than the more obvious route via Tavronitis.

Elos, the largest town and centre of the chestnut trade, stages a **chestnut festival** on the third Sunday of October. The plane, eucalyptus and chestnut trees around the main square make Elos a cool and relaxing place to stop. Behind the taverna on the main square you'll see the remains of the aqueduct that once brought water down from the mountains to power the mill.

Continuing south, you'll pass the atmospheric village of **Perivolia** and then come to **Kefali**, with its 14th-century frescoed church. Kefali has a handful of tavernas taking advantage of the lovely setting and view. From Kefali you can take either the road to Elafonisi or make a right turn and start the loop back along the picturesque west coast to your starting point. The coastal road from Kefali winds around cliffs with magnificent coastal views unfolding after every bend in the road. This is one of the most scenic drives in Crete.

Driving along the gorge you will first pass the little hamlet of **Pappadiana** then you'll start climbing through the mountains before coming to **Amygdalokefali**, which has beautiful sweeping sea views from a bluff outside town. About 50 minutes from Kefali you'll come to **Kambos** a tiny village on the edge of a gorge. It makes a good overnight stop since you can hike down the gorge to the beach, or alternatively take a hike back to Kissamos via a rough dirt track from Kambos. The trail, touted as an alternative to the better-known **E4 trail**, is known as the **F1 trail**.

Continuing northwards from Kambos, the road now circles around the other side of the gorge, eventually winding down to **Sfinari** after a further 9km. The languid, laid-back agricultural village stretches down to a sizeable beach, which is backed by a phalanx of greenhouses at the northern end but has a small gravelly cove, a basic camp site and a few fine fish tavernas on the beach.

After Sfinari you'll get more coastal views before the road drops down to **Platanos**, a quiet, tree-lined and rather scattered village of whitewashed houses. From here you can detour left to **Falasarna** or keep to the right for the downhill run back to Kissamos.

Sleeping & Eating

Accommodation throughout the region consists of rather scattered and largely underutilised domatia. There are no large tourist hotel complexes.

Panorama Taverna and Rooms (☎ 28220 51163; Katsomadatos; d €25) With a balcony overlooking the gorge, these simple, clean rooms make a great base for walks. There's no air-con but they are cool at night. Run by Manolis and his Dutch wife Antonia, the taverna has a range of *mayirefta* and can make meals to order for guest on longer stays.

Arhontas Taverna and Rooms (☎ 28220 51531; Katsomadatos; d €30) These are just below the main road is a shady spot virtually in the gorge, surrounded by the owner's fruit trees. The rooms are basic but functional and two have bathrooms added on to the balconies.

Kokolakis Rooms (☎ 28220 61258; Elos; d €30) The only accommodation in Elos is above the Kastanofolia taverna, right on the main road by the stream that runs through the village. The rooms are very basic and overpriced, given that the bathrooms are shared.

For a meal in Elos, try the friendly **Kamares Taverna** (☎ 28220 61332; main €5.50-7) for excellent *mayirefta*.

In Vlatos you can visit the organic olive oil farm **To Metohi Tou Monahogiou** (☎ 28220 51655) which has tastings and attractive though pricey accommodation (doubles, including breakfast €90) in a restored stone farm house in a lovely forest setting.

Polakis Rooms (☎ 28220 61260; Kefali; r €30) Simple accommodation with great views and ceiling fans.

For dining in Kefali, try **Elafos** (☎ 28220 96614) or the shady terrace of **Panorama** (☎ 28220 61208).

In Kambos, **Sunset Rooms** (☎ 28220 41128; s/d €15/25) has great views over the valley in otherwise basic but pleasant-enough rooms. The attached **Sunset Taverna** (dishes €2 to €5) serves up grills and large salads.

Hartzoulakis Rent Rooms (☎ 28220 41445; mano lis_hartzoulakis@yahoo.gr; Kambos; s/d €20/25) Small and basic but very clean, with large verandas. They make a good base for walkers. The taverna on the terrace serves up good Cretan fare and excellent raki.

our pick **Clara's** (☎ 28220 61537; Amigdalokefali; www.cafeclara.com; d €25-50) Danish accountant Lena Troelso has created a delightful home and hideaway just below the coastal road with breathtaking views. There's a lovely stone cottage with ensuite bathroom and two rustic rooms that share an outside bathroom, including a shower in a former grape press. She bakes bread every day and can provide meals. Ask at the kantina on the main road or call her for directions.

Captain Fidias (☎ 23220 41107; Sfinari Beach) One of three fish tavernas on Sfinari beach, this place is run by the amiable Fidias and his four strapping fishermen sons. When they run out they have been known to go home and get the fish destined for their dinner out of the fridge.

Andonis Theodorakis (☎ 28220 41125; Sfinari; mayirefta €4-7) Up on the main road to Platanos is Andonis' taverna and adjacent rooms. Food is all home-cooked, village style, and they serve local fresh fish. The chicken with okra is recommended. The simple homy rooms (s/d €15/24) have lovely sea views.

O Zaharias (☎ 28220 41285; Platanos; mayirefta €4-6) This pleasant and well-respected eatery just off the main highway on the road to Falasarna has traditional dishes such as *avgokolokytho* – an egg dish made with zucchini, tomato and olive oil. The large Obelix and Asterix-inspired mural was painted by the owner.

MONI HRYSOSKALITISSAS
ΜΟΝΗ ΧΡΥΣΟΣΚΑΛΙΤΙΣΣΑΣ

Five kilometres north of Elafonisi, is this beautiful **monastery** (☎ 28220 61261; admission €2; ☺ 7am-7pm) perched on a rock high above the sea. Hrysoskalitissa (hris-os-ka-*lee*-tiss-as) means 'golden staircase'. Some accounts suggest the top step of the 98 steps leading to the monastery was made of gold, but could only be seen by the faithful. Another version says one of the steps was hollow and used to hide the church's treasury. In any case, during the Turkish occupation the gold, along with much of the monastery's estate, was used to pay hefty taxes imposed by the Ottoman rulers.

The church is recent but the monastery is allegedly a thousand years old and may have been built on the site of a Minoan temple.

The monastery has created two small rudimentary **museums** on site, a folk museum with a selection of weavings and objects from rural life and an ecclesiastical museum with mostly icons and manuscripts. Buses to Elafonisi drop passengers here.

There are a handful of tavernas and accommodation options nearby, which is an alternative base for Elafonisi. **Glykeria** (☎ 28220 61292; www.glykeria.com; d €50 with breakfast; ☒ ☒) is a small and friendly family-run hotel with neat and simple rooms with fridges and balconies overlooking the sea, as well as an inviting pool and a taverna across the road. It's on the main road before the monastery.

ELAFONISI ΕΛΑΦΟΝΗΣΙ

pop 12

As one of the loveliest sand beaches in Crete, it's easy to understand why people enthuse so much about '. At the southern extremity of Crete's west coast, the beach is long, wide and is separated from the Elafonisi Islet by about 50m of knee-deep water. The clear, shallow turquoise water and fine white sand create a tropical paradise. There are a few snack bars on the beach and stalls to rent umbrellas and lounge chairs. The islet is marked by low dunes and a string of semi-secluded coves that attract a sprinkling of naturists. Unfortunately this idyllic scene can be spoilt by the busloads of day-trippers who descend in summer. There is some accommodation nearby for those who want to luxuriate in the quiet that descends in late afternoon, and several more options around Hrysoskalitissa.

Sleeping & Eating

Rooms Panorama (☎ 28220 61548; s/d studio €20/25) This place has a taverna overlooking the sea from its commanding position on a bluff. Rooms have a kitchenette and fridge, but many are rented by the month to itinerant workers.

Rooms Elafonisi (☎ 28250 61274, fax 28250 97907; s/d €30/35; ☒) The 21 spacious rooms here have fridges, and there are nicely furnished bigger rooms out the back among the olive groves, as well as apartments with kitchens. The outdoor patio has views and there's an attached restaurant.

Innahorion (☎ 28250 61111; d/tr €30/35; ☒) About 2.5km before the coast at Elafonisi, this restaurant is the best in the area, serving good Cretan food on the terrace. The accommodation is perhaps the least attractive of the three options, however. The 15 rooms each

---

MILIA VILLAGE

One of Crete's ecotourism trailblazers is the isolated mountain settlement of **Milia** (☎ 28220 51569; www.milia.gr; cottages incl breakfast €50-65-70). Inspired by a back to nature philosophy, sixteen abandoned stone farmhouses were restored into eco-cottages with only solar energy for basic needs (leave the laptop and hairdryer at home). The cottages have antique beds and rustic furnishing.

Milia is one of the most atmospheric and peaceful places to stay on the island, but it is also worth a visit just to dine at the superb taverna, which uses organic produce from its farm, including their own oil, wine, milk, cheese and free-range chickens, goats and sheep. Try the *boureki*, the stuffed rabbit with *myzithra* or yogurt, or pork with lemon leaves baked slowly overnight. We loved the winter favourite – potatoes, chestnuts and baby onions in red wine sauce. There is no Coke or anything processed.

There is a signposted turn-off on the right after the village of Vlatos. The rather narrow access road becomes a drivable 3km dirt road.

have a fridge and kitchenette, but are set back a fair way from the beach.

Getting There & Away
There is one boat daily from Paleohora to Elafonisi (€4.50, one hour) from mid-June through September, which leaves at 10am and returns at 4pm. There are also two buses daily from Hania (€8, 2¼ hours) and Kissamos (€3.40, 1½ hours), which return in the afternoon.

EASTERN HANIA

The northeastern corner of Hania prefecture contains some interesting sights, including the island's only natural freshwater lake, Lake Kournas, and beach resorts such as Kalyves, Almyrida and Georgioupolis, which retain more of a village feel than the resorts spread along the coast west of Hania. There are also the restored village of Vamos and the ancient site of Aptera, as well as traditional villages such as Gavalohori. Increased package tourism is changing the nature of the Apokoronas peninsula, as is the real estate construction frenzy for holiday homes for foreigners.

GEORGIOUPOLIS ΓΕΩΓΙΟΥΠΟΛΗ
pop 489
No longer the quiet getaway that it once was, Georgioupolis has been swamped by coastal hotel development. Popular with families and nature lovers, it still retains some of the ambience of a languid seaside tourist town. The town's most distinctive features are the eucalyptus trees lining the streets that fan out from the main square and the picturesque small chapel of Agios Nikolaos, jutting from a narrow rocky jetty in the sea.

Located at the junction of the Almyros River and the sea, Georgioupolis is a nesting area for the endangered loggerhead sea turtle. The **marshes** surrounding the riverbed are known for their bird life, especially the egrets and kingfishers that migrate into the area in April, as well as the hordes of mosquitoes in summer. The river spills its icy water near the smaller beach to the north of the port, where another small church, Agios Kyriakos, stands at the far end of the cove.

The long narrow stretch of hard-packed sand east of town, spliced by another river leading into the sea, becomes a long sandy beach that continues for about 10km towards Rethymno.

Georgioupolis was named after Prince George, High Commissioner of Crete from 1898 to 1906, who had a hunting lodge there. During classical times it was known as Amphimalla and was the port of ancient Lappa.

It is a handy base from which to explore Hania and Rethymno.

Orientation & Information
The main street from the highway leads to the town centre, where there are a number of travel agencies, tavernas and ATMs. **Ballos Travel** (☎ 28250 83088; www.ballos@gr) can organise boat tickets, excursions and accommodation, and also changes money, rents out cars and arranges money transfers. It also sell stamps – the town post box is outside. **Planet Internet Cafe** (☎ 28250 61732; www.alchemist.gr; per hr €3; ☻ 9am-late) is near the square. There is accommodation and other information on www.georgioupoli .net.

Sights & Activities
Yellowboat (per person per hr €6) rents pedalboats and canoes to go up the river.

If you don't have wheels, a **tourist train** (€6) runs trips to nearby Kournas Lake and Argiroupoli. **Zoraida's Horseriding** (☎ 28250 61745; www.zoraidas-horseriding.com) runs various trail rides around the area, including beach rides (€30) and special rides for children. **Adventure Bikes** (☎ 28250 61830; www.adventurebikes.org) rents bikes and runs bike tours around the region (€35-56).

Sleeping
Most of the big hotels on the beach are aimed at package tourists.

Andy's Rooms (☎ 28250 61394; d €29.50; studio €25-63; ☒) To the right of the main road opposite the church are these good-value large rooms with marble floor, mosquito screens, kitchenette, TV, ceiling fan and a big balcony. There are also larger apartments for families.

Porto Kalyvaki (☎ /fax 28250 61316; d €30-35; ☒ ☒) Located behind a taverna on the more isolated northern beach, Kalyvaki has a mix of rather plain studios spread across two buildings, and some quirky reconstructions of the Acropolis and other monuments scattered around the grounds.

Egeon (☎ 28250 61161; fax 28250 61171; studio €40; ☒) Near the bridge, these pleasant rooms are run by friendly Greek-American Polly and her fisherman husband, whose nets you may see laid out in the foyer. They've upgraded the furniture and installed screens on the windows, while some have kitchenettes, shower curtains and TV.

Nicolas Hotel (☎ 28250 61375; nicolashotel@yahoo .gr; d incl breakfast €55; 🔀) On the main road entering the village, this place has doubles attractively furnished in pine with a safe and home-cooked breakfast.

Apartments Sofia (☎ 28250 61325; www.river-side .gr; studios d/q €50/60; 🔀) This salmon-coloured building has balconies overlooking the sea and well-equipped rooms with kitchenette, CD player and hairdryer.

Eating

Poseidon Taverna (☎ 28250 61026; fish per kg €30-50) Signposted down a narrow alley to the left as you come into the village, this well-regarded place is run by a fishing family. You can choose from the fish and seafood laid out on the counter and enjoy an excellent meal under the mulberry trees in the lovely courtyard.

Arolithos (☎ 28250 61406; Greek specials €5.50-7.70) Near Andy's Rooms, Arolithos has an extensive selection of appetisers, traditional Greek dishes such as *spetsofai* (sausage and pepper stew), and some creative offerings such as the grilled chicken with orange sauce.

A good choice for fish is **Fanis** (☎ 28250 61374; € 35-58; seafood dishes €5.50-8.50), on the riverbank, which also serves reasonable Cretan cuisine and meat dishes.

For traditional home-style cooking you could also try Zorba's and Konaki, while the unassuming Plateia does some decent grills.

Entertainment

There's not much of a bar scene in Georgioupolis, though the new Tropicana Club, a massive two-level beach hut, was hoping to liven things up. Titos is the liveliest bar on the main square.

The sprawling Edem park complex on the beach has a large pool open to the public. It presents live Cretan music occasionally in the summer, as do some of the hotels and tavernas in town.

Getting There & Away

Buses between Hania and Rethymno stop on the highway outside Georgioupolis.

LAKE KOURNAS ΛΙΜΝΗ ΚΟΥΡΝΆΣ

Lake Kournas, 4km inland from Georgioupolis, is a lovely, restful place to have lunch or to pass an afternoon. The island's only natural lake, it is about 1.5km in diameter, 45m deep and is fed by underground springs. There's a narrow sandy strip around the lake and you can walk two-thirds of the way around. The crystal-clear water is great for swimming and changes colour according to the season and time of day. You can rent **pedalboats** and **canoes** (per hr €4) and view the turtles, crabs, fish and snakes that make the lake their home, although tourist buses can crowd the lake in the peak of summer.

There are a number of tavernas around the lake, but few of the older rent rooms above the tavernas were operating. The shady **To Mati tis Limnis** (☎ 28250 61695; mains €5.50-7) on the quieter end of the lake makes good traditional dishes such as rabbit *stifado* (braised with onions) or filling *mizythropites* (cheese pies).

You could also try **Omorfi Limni** (☎ 28250 61665) which dominates the other end of the restaurant strip, or stop for a drink and enjoy the stunning views of the lake and sea from up high at the oddly American Indian-themed **Empire Cafe** (☎ 28250 83008).

The lake is below **Kournas Village**, a steep 5km up a hill. Kournas is a traditional village of white-washed houses, a few stone homes and a couple of *kafeneia*. You can get a delicious meal at the **Kali Kardia Taverna** (☎ 28250 96278; grills €5) on the main street. Owner Kostas Agapinakis is known for his award-winning sausages, excellent *apaki* (smoked pork) and meats cooked on the grill outside the taverna. If you are lucky you might get to try his delicious *galaktoboureko* (custard pastry) while it is still warm.

As you enter the village there is an excellent **ceramics shop** (☎ 28250 96434; 🕒 9am-8.30pm) run by friendly Kostas Tsakalakis, who uses local clay and special lead-free glazes. There is a huge range and the prices are very reasonable.

A tourist mini-train runs from Georgioupolis to Lake Kournas in the summer, but no public transport.

KALYVES ΚΑΛΥΒΕΣ

pop 1408

Located 18km east of Hania on Souda Bay, Kalyves was once predominantly a farming village, but has now become a built up resort –

the biggest on the Apokoronas peninsula. It has morphed into a largely British and foreign enclave, thanks to the holiday home real estate boom in the area. The town is boasts a long sandy beach and retains a fairly low-key village ambience.

Kalyves has a post office and an ATM on the main road. You can rent cars and bikes from **Flisvos** (☎ 28250 31337; www.flisvos.com; ☼ 8.30am-1.30pm & 5.30-10pm). **Floppy Cafe** (☼ 8am-10pm; per hr €3) has high speed access, webcam and ice-cream.

Sleeping & Eating

Most of the private domatia are clustered at the western end of the village.

Thamiris (☎ 28250 31637; www.thamiris.georgioupoli .net; studio/apt €25-60; ☒) This friendly place just before the bridge has a range of well-maintained comfortable rooms and fully equipped studios in two complexes, as well as two attractive and more secluded studios right on the beach next to Piperia taverna. There's a daily cleaning service.

Maria (☎ 28250 31748; r €35; ☒) Maria has small rooms with kitchenette and sea views. Look out for the giant swan opposite the supermarket as you head into town.

Piperia (☎ 28250 31245; mains €6.50-7) Right on the beach just before town, this is one of the best restaurants in Kalyves, with a great selection of Cretan specials and seafood. The menu includes dishes made from organic produce and oil, including an exceptional organic Greek salad.

You could also try the well-regarded Provlita on the waterfront and Gialos at the other end of the beach. In the centre of Kalyves visit the Old Bakery for scrumptious cakes and homemade breads and biscuits.

Getting There & Away

There are seven buses daily (€2.10, 20 mins) to Kalyves from Hania.

ALMYRIDA ΑΛΜΥΡΙΔΑ
pop 119

The former fishing village of Almyrida, 14km east of Kalyves, is considerably less developed than its neighbour, although it's getting more so. Still, it's a reasonable spot to hang out for a few days and is probably a better option for independent travellers than Kalyves. Almyrida is popular for windsurfing because of its long, exposed beach. History buffs can check out the remains of an early **Christian basilica** at the western end of the village.

One road through the village runs along the beach. There's an ATM and you can check mail at **Internet Services** (☼ 11am-9pm) **Flisvos Tours** (☎ /fax 28250 31100; ☼ 8am-1.30pm & 5-9.30pm), just off the main road, rents out cars scooters and mountain bikes. The French-run **UCPA Sports** (☎ 28250 31443; www.ucpa.com), runs windsurfing (€8 per hour) and rents catamarans & kayaks. **Dream Adventure Trips** (☎ 6944 357 383) offers speedboat swimming and snorkelling trips to nearby caves, coves and Marathi beach (€15).

Sleeping & Eating

Almyrida Beach Hotel (☎ 28250 32284; www.almyrida beach.com; s & d incl breakfast €90-130; ☒ ☒) This hotel has two main hotel complexes across from the beach with a pool, including an incongruous white and grey modern wing with a range of rooms and suites (from €120).

Rooms Marilena (☎ 28250 32202; d €25) This place seems to be more popular with itinerant workers than the windsurfing fraternity these days, but has some smallish but decent budget rooms with ceiling fan, fridge and cooking ring upon request. It's behind the windsurf station.

Psaros (☎ 28250 31401; mains €6-10) Well located right on the far end of the beach, with classic blue and white chequered island décor, Psaros has fresh fish and friendly staff. Also recommended are **Lagos** (☎ 28250 31654) at the entrance to the town for good value traditional cooking in a lovely shaded terrace, and **Dimitri's** (☎ 28250 31303) family tavern for friendly service and produce from their farm.

PLAKA ΠΛΑΚΑ
pop 279

The village of Plaka, a pretty drive up from Almyrida, is unfortunately being swamped by a frenzy of development and look-alike holiday houses. Still, off the coast and around the main square (shaded by eucalyptus trees), the winding lanes and low-rise white buildings seem a world away from the tourist bustle. The town also has a few tavernas with lovely views down to the sea.

Eva Papadomanolakos, the owner of **Studios Koukourou** (☎ 28250 31145; fax 28250 31879; studio €35; ☒), has gone to a lot of trouble to create a homy Cretan atmosphere for her guests and has decorated her place with tropical plants and flowers. There's also a roof garden with panoramic views over the coast. The rooms are very clean and have kitchenettes. It's well signposted as you enter town.

APTERA ΑΠΤΕΡΑ

The ruins of the ancient city of **Aptera** (✹ 8am-3pm Tue-Sun), about 3km west of Kalyves, are spread out over two hills that loom over Souda Bay. Founded in the 7th century BC, Aptera was one of the most important city-states of western Crete and was continuously inhabited until an earthquake destroyed it in the 7th century AD.

It came back to life with the Byzantine reconquest of Crete in the 10th century, and became a bishopric. In the 12th century, the monastery of St John the Theologian was established; the reconstructed monastery is the centre of the site.

The site is still being excavated. Diggers recently exposed the remains of a fortified tower, a city gate and a massive wall that surrounded the city. You can also see Roman cisterns and a 2nd century BC Greek temple. At the western end there's a Turkish fortress, which was built in 1872 and enjoys a panoramic view of Souda Bay. The fortress was built as part of a large Turkish fortress-building programme during a period when the Cretans were in an almost constant state of insurrection. Notice the 'Wall of the Inscriptions' – this was probably part of an important public building and was excavated in 1862 by French archaeologists. The Greek Ministry of Culture is continuing to restore the site, installing signs and paths.

There's no public transport to Aptera.

VAMOS ΒΆΜΟΣ

pop 643

The 12th-century village of Vamos, 26km southeast of Hania, was the capital of the Sfakia province from 1867 to 1913 and was the scene of a revolt against Turkish rule in 1896. It is now the capital of the Apokoronas province. In 1995 a group of villagers banded together to preserve the traditional way of life of Vamos. They persuaded the EU to fund a project to showcase the crafts and products of the region and develop a new kind of tourism for Crete. They restored the old stone buildings of the village using traditional materials and crafts and turned them into guesthouses, and they opened shops and cafés where visi-

---

DETOUR: KOUMOS

One of the more quirky attractions of the Apokoronas area is **Koumos** (☎ 28250 32256; ✹ 10am-late) the huge stone fantasy of local builder Yiorgos Havaledakis. He has spent years collecting a hotchpotch of stones, pebbles and rocks of every shape colour and size from the surrounding mountains to create this bizarre sprawling open-air taverna and *kafeneio*. The grounds include a stone church, bridges, arches, sculptures, light poles – even the toilet block shows off his unique rock art.

---

tors could taste regional products. This operation has expanded and now dominates the village, which is nonetheless a pleasant stop or base for exploring the region. While the authentic village theme is a overrated, it is one of the better examples of this style of alternative tourism.

In late March or early April, Vamos celebrates **Hohliovradia** (Snail Night) with a festival of cooked snails, washed down with wine and raki.

The **Vamos Tourist office** (☎ /fax 28250 23251; www.vamossa.gr; ✹ 9am-9pm in summer) rents cars, books excursions and runs regular Cretan cooking lessons in a restored olive press. It arranges accommodation in a range of **Traditional Guesthouses** (cottage €75-120). The lovely restored stone cottages have kitchens, fireplaces and TVs and are decorated in traditional style. Most accommodate up to four people, but there are larger cottages including some with a pool.

The old stone taverna **I Sterna tou Bloumosifi** (☎ 28250 22932; mains €5-9.80) has a pleasant courtyard garden and is widely known for its excellent Cretan cuisine. For starters try the *gavro* (mild anchovy) wrapped in vine leaves, or the garlic and herb mushrooms, and then move on to the *hilopita* (tagliatelle) with rooster.

The other place to hang out is the understated **Liakoto** (☎ 28250 23251) café-bar-cum-art-gallery which has a lovely terrace overlooking the mountains and sea. Next door, you can buy local raki, herbs, organic oil and other Cretan products at the **Myrovolo Wine Store & General Store** (☎ 28250 22996).

There are six daily buses to Vamos from Hania (€2.80, 45 minutes).

AROUND VAMOS

The village of **Gavalohori**, 25km southeast of Hania, makes a pleasant stop. The main attraction is the **Folklore Museum** (☎ 28250 23222; admission €2; ☼ 9am-8pm Mon-Sat, 11am-6pm Sun), which is located in a renovated building that was constructed during Venetian rule and then extended by the Turks. The exhibits are well labelled in English and include examples of pottery, weaving, woodcarving, stonecutting and other Cretan crafts, including the fine *kapaneli* – intricately worked silk lace. A historical section documents Cretan struggles for independence.

Signs direct you to the **Byzantine wells**, **Venetian arches** and **Roman tombs** about 1.5km above the village.

The **Women's Cooperative** (☎ /fax 28250 22038; ☼ 10am-10pm Apr-Oct), on the main square, sells a few rare pieces of *kapaneli* (lacework) made by local women. You can normally see women hard at work on this painstakingly long process. Prices for quality lacework range from €15 to €1500, depending on the size.

VRYSES ΒΡΥΣΕΣ

pop 848

Most travellers just pass through Vryses, 30km southeast of Hania, on their way to or from the south coast, but this pleasant and sizeable village makes a good lunch-time interlude. The rivers Voutakas and Vrysanos run through the centre of the village watering the giant plane trees along the banks, where you can cool off in one of the shady tavernas. Vryses is a market centre for the region's agricultural products. Many locals stop here for yogurt and honey, a speciality of the town. The village centre is marked by a monument commemorating Cretan independence.

You will be tempted by the lamb or other tasty meat grilling on the spit outside **Taverna Progoulis** (☎ 28250 51086; grills €4.50-6), which has tables under the trees.

Near the crossroads in the town centre the modest **Vryses Way** (☎ 28250 51705) serves excellent gyros, *Sfakianes pittes* (traditional pancakes) and yogurt with honey.

Buses from Hania to Hora Sfakion stop at Vryses (€3.50, 30 minutes).

Rethymno Ρεθυμνο

Rethymno is Crete's most compact and mountainous prefecture, boasting the island's highest peak, Mt Psiloritis, in the east. Its central position makes it a good base for seeing the island's key sights and gives you a broad taste of what Crete has to offer. While it lacks the big draw cards of neighbouring Hania and Iraklio, Rethymno in not short of attractions.

Rethymno prides itself on being the cultural capital of the island, with a rich musical tradition and its historic importance during the Renaissance. The charming old town of Rethymno's capital is one of the island's architectural treasures, with its stunning fortress, picturesque Venetian harbour and mixture of Venetian and Turkish houses in the labyrinth of the old quarter. East of Rethymno town is Crete's longest stretch of sandy beach, home to a string of big hotel complexes, while further toward Iraklio are the smaller-scale resorts of Panormo and Bali.

Inland, you can explore diverse traditional villages, including the tiny agricultural villages of the Amari Valley, the town of Anogia, known for fine musicians and infamous huge weddings, and the pottery village of Margarites. Travellers on their way south stop at Spili to drink from its lion-head Venetian fountain, while the tavernas among the springs of Argyroupolis are a delightful respite from the summer heat.

Rethymno has three famous caves – Melidoni, Zoniana and the Ideon cave near Mt Psiloritis, where Zeus was allegedly reared. The south-coast resorts of Agia Galini and Plakias have their loyal following, while further west the rugged cliffs are interspersed with some of the island's finest unspoilt beaches. Rethymno also has two of Crete's most historically significant monasteries – Moni Arkadiou in the north and the Moni Preveli overlooking the Libyan sea.

HIGHLIGHTS

- Strolling the maze of narrow streets in Rethymno's **Venetian and Turkish old town** (p123)
- Cooling off by the springs of **Argyroupolis** (p130)
- Exploring the unspoilt southern beaches, from **Preveli** (p141) to **Agios Pavlos** (p141)
- Hitting the northern coastal resorts of **Bali** (p144) and **Panormo** (p143)
- Visiting the **Preveli monastery** (p140)
- Listening to *mandinades* (rhyming couplets) by moonlight in **Anogia** (p136)

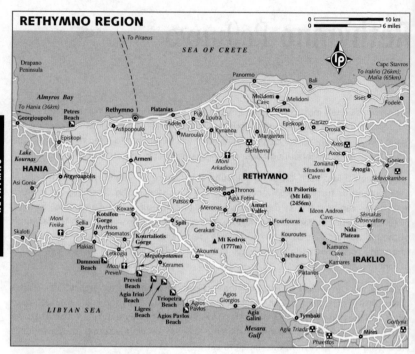

RETHYMNO REGION

RETHYMNO ΡΕΘΥΜΝΟ

pop 28,959

Rethymno (*reth*-im-no) is the island's third-largest town and one of the most picturesque, with a charming Venetian harbour and delightful old Venetian-Ottoman quarter.

The old quarter is a maze of narrow streets draped in floral canopies, graceful wood-balconied houses and ornate Venetian monuments, with minarets adding a touch of the Orient. While architectural similarities invite comparison with Hania, Rethymno has a character all its own.

HISTORY

The name Rethymno means 'stream of water' and evidence (to be found in the city's archaeological museum) indicates that the site of modern Rethymno has been occupied since Late Minoan times. In the 3rd and 4th centuries BC, 'Rithymna' emerged as an autonomous seat of sufficient stature to issue its own coinage. Ancient Rithymna probably lay at the base of Palekastro Hill but its remains have never been excavated, although later Roman mosaics have been found beneath the modern town.

The town prospered once more under the Venetians, who ruled from 1210 until 1645, and turned Rethymno (which they renamed Castel Vecchio) into an important commercial centre exporting wine and oil. The town flourished artistically under the Venetians and became the seat of a Venetian prefect. They built the harbour and began fortifying the town in the 16th century against the growing threat from the Turks. Michele Sanmicheli, the best military architect of the era, designed the thick outer walls, of which only the Porto Guora survives. The walls did not stop the city from being sacked by the pirate Barbarossa in 1538.

The Venetians then built the massive fortress on the hill, which nevertheless was unable to withstand the Turkish assault of 1646 and collapsed after a 22-day siege. Rethymno was an important seat of government under the Turks but it was also a centre of resistance to Turkish rule. The Turks inflicted severe reprisals upon the town for its role in the uprising of 1821, but the resistance continued.

Turkish forces held the town until 1897, when it was taken by Russia as part of the occupation of Crete by the Great Powers. Rethymno became an artistic and intellectual centre after the arrival of a large number of refugees from Smyrna in 1923.

These days, the city has a campus of the University of Crete, attracting a large student population that keeps the town lively outside the tourist season.

ORIENTATION

Rethymno is a fairly compact town with most of the major sights, accommodation and places to stay and eat within a small area off the old Venetian harbour. Most of the old town is pedestrian-only and parking can be a nightmare so you are better off leaving the car in one of the car parks (see Map pp124–5).

The old quarter occupies the headland north of Dimakopoulou, which runs from Plateia Vardinogianni on the western side to Plateia Iroön on the east. This is where you'll find the most atmospheric hotels and eateries. Banks and services are to the south on the edge of the new town.

The beach is on the eastern side of town, around from the Venetian harbour. One block back from the beach is Arkadiou, the main commercial and shopping street.

If you arrive by bus, you will be dropped at the rather inconveniently located terminal about 600m west of the Porto Guora, the historic gate to the old town. If you arrive by ferry, the old quarter is at the end of the quay.

INFORMATION
Bookshops
Book Store Mediterraneo (☎ 28310 23417; Mavrokordatou 2) English books, travel guides and foreign press.
Ilias Spondidakis bookshop (☎ 28310 54307; Souliou 43) Novels in English, books about Greece, tapes of Greek music; small secondhand section.
Xenos Typos (☎ 28310 29405; Ethnikis Antistaseos 21) Foreign press, guidebooks and maps.

Emergency
Tourist police (☎ 28310 28156; Delfini Bldg, Eleftheriou Venizelou; ☽ 7am-2.30pm) In the same building as the municipal tourist office.

Internet Access
Cybernet (Kallergi 44-46; per hr €3; ☽ 10am-5am)
Galero (☎ 28310 54345; Plateia Rimondi; per hr €3; ☽ 6am-late)

Laundry
Laundry Mat (☎ 28310 29722; Tombazi 45; wash & dry €9; ☽ 8.30am-2pm & 5.30-9pm Mon-Fri, 8.30am-2.15pm Sat) Next door to the youth hostel.

Left Luggage
KTEL (☎ 28310 22659; cnr Kefalogiannidon & Igoumenou Gavriil) The bus station stores luggage for €1.50 per day.

Medical Services
Rethymno Hospital (☎ 28210 27491; Triandalydou 17; ☽ 24hr)

Money
Alpha Bank (Pavlou Koundouriotou 29) Has a 24-hour automatic exchange machine and ATM.
National Bank of Greece (Dimokratias) On the far side of the square opposite the town hall.
National Mortgage Bank Next to the town hall, has a 24-hour automatic exchange machine and ATM.

Post
Post office (☎ 28310 22303; Moatsou 21; ☽ 7am-7pm Mon-Fri)

Toilets
There is a reasonable public toilet near the Venetian harbour just off Arkadiou.

Tourist Information
Municipal tourist office (☎ 28310 29148; www .rethymno.gr; Delfini Bldg, Eleftheriou Venizelou; ☽ 8.30am-8.30pm Mon-Fri, 9am-8.30pm Sat & Sun Mar-Nov).
Prefecture tourist office (☎ 28310 25571 www .rethymnon.gr; Dimokratias 1; ☽ 7.30am-3pm Mon-Fri).

Travel Agencies
Ellotia Tours (☎ 28310 24533; www.rethymnoatcrete .com; Arkadiou 155; ☽ 9am-9pm Mar-Nov) Helpful office that handles boat and plane tickets, changes money, rents cars and motorcycles, and books excursions.

SIGHTS
Rethymno's 16th-century **fortezza** (fortress; ☎ 28310 28101; Paleokastro Hill; admission €3.10; ☽ 8am-8pm Jun-Oct) is on the site of the city's ancient acropolis. Within its massive walls a great number of buildings once stood, of which only a church and a mosque survive intact. The ramparts offer good views, while the site has lots of ruins to explore. The main gate is opposite the Archaeological Museum on the eastern side of the fortress, but there were once

RETHYMNO

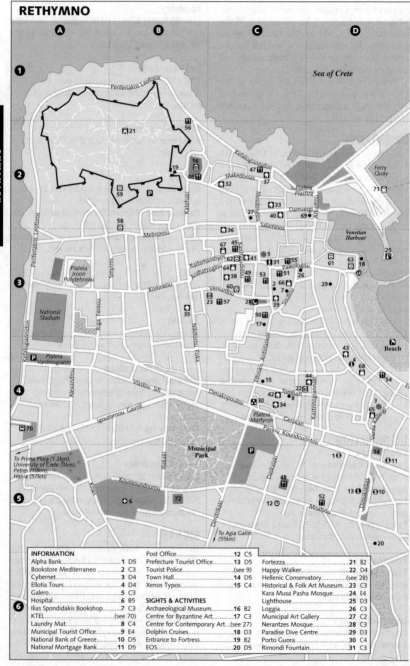

To Prima Plora (1.2km);
University of Crete (3km);
Petres (10km);
Hania (57km)

To Agia Galini
(55km)

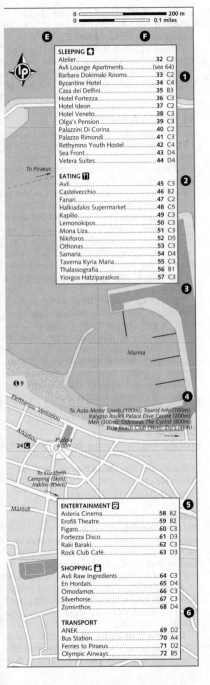

two other gates on the western and northern sides for the delivery of supplies and ammunition. In summer it is a stunning concert venue for the Renaissance Festival (p126).

Rethymno's tiny **Venetian harbour** is crammed with fish tavernas and cafés fronted by touts, but you can get a better sense of it by walking along the old harbour walls past the fishing boats to the landmark **lighthouse**, built later by the Turks.

The small **Archaeological Museum** (☎ 28310 54668; admission €3; ☻ 8.30am-3pm Tue-Sun), near the entrance to the fortress, was once a prison. The exhibits are well labelled in English and contain Neolithic tools, Minoan pottery excavated from nearby tombs, Mycenaean figurines and a 1st-century-AD relief of Aphrodite, as well as an important coin collection. There are also some excellent examples of blown glass from the classical period. Various displays outline the history of archaeological excavations in the region. Rethymno's **Historical & Folk Art Museum** (☎ 28310 23398; Vernardou 28-30; admission €3; ☻ 9.30am-2.30pm Mon-Sat) gives an excellent overview of the area's rural lifestyle, with its collection of clothing, baskets, weavings and farm tools, and useful explanatory labels. It is in a lovely historic Venetian building.

Pride of place among the many vestiges of Venetian rule goes to the **Rimondi Fountain** with its spouting lion heads and Corinthian capitals, built first in 1588 and rebuilt in 1626 by a rector of the city, A Rimondi. Another major landmark is the 16th-century **Loggia** (a Venetian version of a gentleman's club), once a meeting house for Venetian nobility, now a museum shop selling good-quality reproductions.

At the southern end of Ethnikis Antistaseos is the well-preserved **Porto Guora** (Great Gate), a remnant of the defensive wall that was once topped with the symbol of Venice: the Lion of St Mark, now in the Archaeological Museum. Around the Porto Guora lies a network of old streets built by the Venetians and rebuilt by the Turks. The **Centre for Byzantine Art** (☎ 28210 50120; Ethnikis Antistaseos; ☻ 10am-2pm & 7pm-late) is a great example of a restored Venetian-Turkish mansion and has exhibitions, workshops and a terrace café with great views of the old town. Other Turkish legacies in the old quarter include the **Kara Musa Pasha Mosque**, which has a vaulted fountain, and the **Nerantzes Mosque**, which was converted from a Franciscan church in 1657. It now houses the **Hellenic**

RETHYMNO

Conservatory (☎ 28310 22724; Vernadou 1; ☒ closed August) and makes a lovely venue for concerts and recitals. The management is happy for you to have a look around. The building's minaret, built in 1890, was being restored at the time of writing.

The **Municipal Art Gallery** (☎ /fax 28310 52530; Himaras 5 & Melissinou; ☒ 9am-2pm Tue-Sun, 5-9pm Wed) near the fortezza houses a permanent exhibition of works by Rethymno painter Lefteris Kanakakis, as well as contemporary Greek artists since 1950. It is part of the **Centre for Contemporary Art** (www.rac.gr; ☒ 9am-1pm & 7-10pm Tue-Fri, 11am-3pm Sat & Sun) , which holds periodic exhibitions. The pleasant **municipal park** offers a respite from the heat and crowds.

ACTIVITIES
Hiking
The **Happy Walker** (☎ /fax 28310 52920; www.happy walker.com; Tombazi 56; ☒ 5pm-8.30pm) runs various walks in the region, including complete walking holidays.

Rethymno's chapter of the Greek Mountaineering Club **EOS** (EOS; ☎ 28310 57766; www.eos .rethymnon.com; Dimokratias 12; ☒ 8.30-10.30pm) can give advice on the region.

Bike Riding
Cycling enthusiast and Greek Paralympic champion **Odyseas the Cyclist** ☎ /fax 28310 58178; odyseasthecyclist@hotmail.com; Velouhioti 31) runs small guided rides in the area including half-day tours to Arkadi, Margarites and Argyroupoli (€40) and full-day rides to Preveli (€60). He has top brand bikes for hire and also runs tailored tours for people with disabilities.

Diving
The **Paradise Dive Centre** (☎ 28310 26317; www.diving -center.gr) runs diving activities and PADI courses for all grades of divers from their base at Petres, about 15 minutes west of Rethymno. **Kalypso Rock's Palace Dive Centre** (☎ 28310 20990; www.kalypsodivingcenter.com; Eleftheriou Venizelou 42) runs a slick diving operation, mostly from its diving base in Plakias (Map p122) on the southern coast.

TOURS
Rethymno is well placed for boat excursions. Along the harbour front there are several companies that offer boat trips, including **Dolphin Cruises** (☎ 28310 57666), which offers three-hour trips on the 'pirate ship' to nearby caves, Pan-

ormo and Bali (adult/child under 12 €25/12), all-day trips to Marathi beach (€34/17), and fishing trips on a speedboat (€25).

Travel agents sell a range of coach excursions to key sites, including the Samaria Gorge (€28), Elafonisi (€26) and Gramvousa (€24). Prices exclude admission charges and boat fares.

FESTIVALS & EVENTS
Rethymno's main cultural event is the annual **Renaissance Festival** (☎ 28310 51199; www.rfr .gr;), which runs from July to September. Held primarily in the open-air **Erofili Theatre** at the fortezza, it features performances by Greece's leading theatre companies, as well as dance, music and acts from around Europe. It promotes both the Cretan and European Renaissance, so you will get anything from Shakespeare and Molière to Cretan playwrights. Get programmes and tickets at the **town hall** (☎ 28310 88279; ☒ 9am-1.30pm Mon-Fri) or from the Erofili Theatre one hour before performances.

Most years there's a **Wine Festival** in mid-July, which is held in the municipal park and offers a good opportunity to sample local wine and cuisine. Ask the tourist office for details. Rethymno is also renowned for its annual **carnival celebration** (http://carnival-in-rethymnon -greece.com), a three week pre-Lent celebration of dancing and masquerading, games and treasure hunts and a grand street parade. It usually falls around January or February.

SLEEPING
The old town has an ample supply of lovely restored mansions, boutique hotels and friendly pensions to cater for all budgets, and many hotels are open all year. To the east is an endless stretch of hotels and resorts.

Budget
Elizabeth Camping (☎ 28310 28694; www.camping elizabeth.com; sites per person €6.54, tent small/large €4.85/5.65) Located near Mysiria beach, 3km east of Rethymno, this is the nearest camping ground. There's a taverna, snack bar and mini-market, plus a communal fridge, free beach umbrellas and sun lounges, and a weekly beach BBQ. An Iraklio-bound bus can drop you here.

Rethymno Youth Hostel (☎ 28310 22848; www.yh rethymno.com; Tombazi 41; dm with shared bathroom €9; ☐) The hostel is friendly and well run with free hot showers. Breakfast is available from €2 and there's a bar in the evening. There is no curfew and the place is open all year.

Barbara Dokimaki Rooms (☎ 28310 24581; alicedok@ yahoo.com; Damvergi 14; s €30, d €45-60, tr €70; ✱) This well-located complex of rooms in a Venetian building with a newer 2nd-floor addition is set around a pleasant courtyard. The rooms are simple with timber floors and some period features. They have TV and dated but functional bathrooms.

Sea Front (☎ 28310 51981; www.forthnet.gr/elotia; Arkadiou 159; d €35-45; ✱) This conveniently located pension on the beach has pleasant budget rooms with timber floors and fridge. They also have cheerful studio apartments with sea views and ceiling fans further towards the town beach, and rooms in another building nearby.

ourpick Atelier (☎ 28310 24440; atelier@ret.forth net.gr; Himaras 27; d €35-45) One of the best value options are these clean and attractively refurbished rooms attached to a pottery workshop. Both are run by Froso Bora. They have exposed stone walls and many Venetian architectural features, as well as small flat-screen TVs, new bathrooms and kitchenettes.

Olga's Pension (☎ 28310 28665; Souliou 57; s/d/tr €35/45/65) Friendly Olga's is tucked away on touristy but colourful Souliou. It has a faded charm, with a quirky décor and a network of terraces bursting with flowers and greenery that connect a range of dated but colourful rooms. Most have a fridge, TV, fan and basic bathrooms. Rates include breakfast at Stella's kitchen downstairs.

Byzantine Hotel (☎ 28310 55609; Vosporou 26; d incl breakfast €45) The excellent-value small hotel in a historic building near the Porta Guora maintains a traditional feel. The rooms are simply decorated with carved timber furniture and some have bathtubs. The back rooms overlook the old mosque and minaret. At the time of writing there were plans to install air-con.

Midrange

Hotel Fortezza (☎ 28310 55551; www.fortezza.gr; Melissinou 16; s/d incl breakfast €62/75; **P** ✱ ✱) Housed in a refurbished old building in the heart of the old town, the tasteful rooms have TVs and telephones. After a day of roaming through Rethymno, it's pleasant to relax by the swimming pool.

Casa dei Delfini (☎ 28310 55120; kzaxa@reth.gr; Nikiforou Foka 66-68; studios €45-70, ste €80-140; ✱) Turk-

ish and Venetian architectural features have been cleverly maintained in this elegant pension, including an old stone trough and the *hammam* (Turkish bath) ceiling in one of the studio bathrooms. There is a range of traditionally decorated rooms, all with kitchenettes, through the most impressive is the massive maisonette with a large private terrace.

Hotel Ideon (☎ 28310 28667; www.hotelideon.gr; Plastira 10; s/d €54/75, studio/apt incl breakfast €90/105; ✱) This polished central establishment is one of the oldest hotels in town, spread over two restored old buildings and a modern wing. The rooms are nicely decorated and well appointed and there are balconies with sea views. The courtyard pool spares you the long walk to Rethymno's beach.

Hotel Veneto (☎ 28310 56634; www.veneto.gr; Epimenidou 4; studio/ste incl breakfast €124/143; ✱) The oldest part of the hotel dates from the 14th century and many traditional features have been preserved without sacrificing modern comforts. There's a stunning pebble mosaic in the foyer and the eye-catching rooms of polished wood floors and ceilings have iron beds, satellite TV and kitchenettes. Rates drop significantly out of high season.

Top End

ourpick Vetera Suites (☎ 28310 23844; www.vetera .gr; Kastrinogiannaki 39; d €85-150; ✱) These six elegant suites stand out for their attention to detail, from the lace curtains to the mastic bath products and china tea sets for breakfast. Each room is stylishly decorated with iron beds and antiques, and comes with a neatly concealed kitchenette. The bathroom tiles feature paintings by the owner's favourite artist, Degas, and there are DVD players and other mod cons, including access for laptops.

Palazzo Rimondi (☎ 28310 51289; www.palazzo rimondi.com; Xanthoudidou 21 & Trikoupi 16; d studio/ste incl breakfast €160-190; ✱) This charming Venetian mansion in the heart of the old city has exquisite individually decorated studios with kitchenettes. There's a small splash pool in the courtyard where breakfast is served.

Palazzini di Corina (☎ 28310 21205; www.corina .gr; Damvergi 9; d €120, ste €160-220; ✱ ✱) This regal Venetian mansion right near the harbour is one of the classiest boutique hotels in town. Decorated with antique furniture, it has been beautifully restored, with exposed stone walls, timber vaulted ceilings and a lovely internal mosaic courtyard. Prices include breakfast.

Avli Lounge Apartments (☎ 28310 58250; www .avli.gr; cnr Xanthoudidou 22 & Radamanthyos; r incl à la carte breakfast €199-239; ❄) These decadent eclectic suites are spread over two beautifully restored Venetian buildings in Rethymno's historic old town. There are ornate iron or wooden beds, antiques, exquisite furnishings and *objets d'art*. A fitting place to retire after spoiling yourself with dinner in Avli's ambient courtyard garden.

EATING
The waterfront along Eleftheriou Venizelou is lined with similar tourist restaurants staffed by fast-talking touts, as is the Venetian harbour except that the setting is better and the prices higher. The best places are in the web of side streets inland from the harbour, while a couple warrant a trip outside the tourist zone.

Budget
Taverna Kyria Maria (☎ 28310 29078; Moshovitou 20; Cretan dishes €2.50-6.50) This good value traditional taverna behind the Rimondi Fountain has outdoor seating and birdcages hanging from the leafy trellis. Meals normally end with a complimentary dessert and shot of raki.

Zisi's (☎ 28310 28814; Old Rethymno-Irakion Rd Mysiria; grills €3.20-6; ❤ closed Tue) Locals swear by Zisi's for cheap, quality Cretan food, particularly the charcoal-grilled meats and the 25 or so daily trays of home-style dishes. It's a little out of town along the stretch of beachfront hotels and resorts (on right just before the Creta Palace), but is worth the trip. Kids will love the new playground.

Samaria (☎ 28310 24681; Eleftheriou Venizelou; mayirefta €4-6.50) Of the waterfront tavernas, this is one of the few where you'll see local families eating. There's a large range of *mayirefta* (casseroles), and the soups and grills are excellent.

Nikiforos (☎ 28310 55403; Moatsou 40; mains €4-7; ❤ noon-10pm) It may lack the atmosphere of the old town, but this traditional *mayireio* in the new town churns out trays of home-style cooking for hungry locals and does a decent takeaway trade.

Kapilio (☎ 28310 52001; Xanthoudidou 7; set menu for 1 €12.50-13.80) Popular with students, this Serb-run *mezedopoleio* has a mixed menu with a range of special set menus that include raki, wine, salad and a main dish.

Midrange
our pick Thalassografia (☎ 28310 52569; Kefalogiannidon 33; mezedes €3.80-7.30) This excellent *mezedopoleio* is the place to watch the sunset and try some fine mezedes, as well as a few pastas and more hearty meals. It's a casual place with a breathtaking setting under the fortezza, taking in views over the sea. The grilled sardines are excellent, as are the creamy mushrooms.

Fanari (☎ 28310 54849; Kefalogiannidon 15; mezedes €2.50-10) West of the Venetian harbour, this welcoming waterfront taverna serves good mezedes, fresh fish and Cretan cuisine. The *bekri mezes* (pork with wine and peppers) is excellent, or try the local speciality, *apaki* (smoked pork). The homemade wine is decent, too.

Castelvecchio (☎ 28310 55163; Himaras 29; mains €7-16; ❤ dinner only Jul & Aug, lunch & dinner Sep-Jun) The affable Valantis will make you really feel at home in the garden terrace of this family taverna located on the edge of the fortezza. Try the *kleftiko* (slow oven-baked lamb).

Lemonokipos (☎ 28310 57087; Ethnikis Antistaseos 100; mains €5.80-9) Dine among the lemon trees in the lovely courtyard of this well-respected taverna in the old quarter. It's good typical Cretan fare, with a decent range of vegetarian dishes and lots of tasty appetisers.

Also recommended is **Othonas** (☎ 28310 55500; Petihaki 27) for traditional Cretan food. It looks touristy on the outside but is decent. It's a member of Concred (p57) and uses quality produce.

Top End
our pick Avli (☎ 28310 26213; www.avli.com; cnr Xanthoudidou 22 & Radamanthyos; mains €13.50-30). This former Venetian villa is the place for a romantic evening out, or at least one with maximum ambience. The nouveau-Cretan style food is superb and there's an idyllic garden courtyard bursting with pots of herbs, bougainvillea canopies, fruit trees and works of art. The sleek wine bar in the adjacent old stables boasts more than 400 Greek wines. They've also opened the more casual Raki Baraki (Radamanthyos 16) mezedes bar, with live music Thursday to Sunday.

Prima Plora (☎ 28310 24925; Akrotiriou 2, Koumbes; seafood mezedes €5.50-16) This stylish modern restaurant on the developing beachfront strip on the western side of town is worth the hike. It has an exceptional setting with tables right on the water near an old Venetian water pump with views of the fortezza. It has a sophisticated menu of top-quality seafood dishes such as prawn risotto, and uses organic vegetables.

ENTERTAINMENT
Bars & Clubs

The bars and cafés along El Venizelou fill up on summer evenings with pink-skinned tourists nursing tropical drinks. Rethymno's livelier nightlife is concentrated around Nearhou and Salaminos near the Venetian harbour, as well as the waterfront bars off Plastira Square. Students frequent the lively *rakadika* (cafés serving carafes of raki or wine with mezedes) on Vernadou.

Fortezza Disco (Nearhou 20; ☼ 11pm-dawn) The town's veteran disco is big and flashy with three bars, a laser show and an international crowd that starts drifting in around midnight.

Rock Club Café (☎ 28310 31047; Petihaki 8; ☼ 9pm-dawn) is one of Rethymno's classic hang-outs; tourists fills the club nightly.

Figaro (☎ 28310 29431; Vernardou 21; ☎ 11am-late) Housed in a cleverly restored old building, Figaro is an atmospheric 'art and music' all-day bar that attracts a subdued crowd.

Baja Beach Club (☎ 28310 20333; Platanias) On the old highway east of the town, this massive beach bar is like a tropical paradise with palm trees and bars around a big pool. At night it morphs into a happening club. The turn-off is just before the bridge.

Cinemas

Asteria Cinema (☎ 28310 22830; Melissinou 21; tickets €7; ☼ 9pm) A small open-air cinema showing new-release movies.

SHOPPING

Rethymno's shopping strip is relatively compact, with an assortment of shops selling everything from souvenirs to high-end jewellery. You'll find better quality mainstream merchandise on Arkadiou. Colourful Souliou is crammed with little shops. The Thursday market on Dimitrakaki along the public gardens has fresh produce, clothing and odds and ends.

Omodamos (☎ 28310 58763; www.omodamos.com; Souliou 3) The original ceramic designs in this shop are made by leading ceramicists from around Greece.

Zominthos (☎ 28310 52673; Arkadiou 129) This shop has an eclectic selection of jewellery from contemporary Greek designers as well as some ceramics and sculptures.

En Hordais (☎ 28310 29043; Varda Kalergi 38) This tiny store packed with handmade musical instruments is the place to get that Cretan *lyra* (a three-stringed instrument similar to a violin), bouzouki or other Greek musical instruments.

Silverhorse (☎ 28310 51401; www.silverhorse.gr; Radamanthios 10) This place specialises in handmade belts, leather goods, saddles and other interesting leather paraphernalia, which it can make to order.

Avli Raw Materials (☎ 28310 58228; Arabatzoglou 38-40) Foodies will love this store packed with a huge range of gourmet delights from around Greece, including an excellent selection of wine.

GETTING THERE & AWAY
Boat

Note that some ferries leave from the port and others from the marina further east.

ANEK (☎ 28310 29221; www.anek.gr; Arkadiou 250) Ferry three times a week between Rethymno and Piraeus (€29, 10 hours), leaving both Rethymno and Piraeus at 8pm.

NEL LINES (☎ 28310 24295; www.nel.gr) Runs a high-speed service between Rethymno and Piraeus (€57, five

---

SWEET TREATS

One of the last traditional filo masters in all of Greece, **Yiorgos Hatziparaskos** (☎ 28310 29488; Vernardou 30) still makes super-fine pastry by hand in his traditional workshop. The highlight is when he throws the dough into a giant bubble before stretching it over a huge table. His wife Katerina encourages passers-by to watch the spectacle and try some of best *baklava* and *kataifi* they will ever eat.

At **Mona Liza** (☎ 28310 23082; Paleologou 36), around the corner from the Loggia, Nikos Skartsilakis is legendary for his 'crema' ice cream made from sheep's milk, as well as his excellent sweets. Try the *galaktoboureko* (custard pastries), the walnut pie, or *vrahaki*, chocolate with almonds.

Loukoumades, the donut-like concoctions with honey and cinnamon, have been perfected by **Kanakakis** (☎ 28310 22426; Plateia Martyron), just outside the Porto Guora, while locals swear by the ice cream at **Meli** (☎ 28310 50847; S Venizelou 7) on the waterfront.

hours) daily from July to September (four times a week May to June).

SeaJets (www.seajets.gr) Runs the Superjet catamaran high-speed service on Thursday and Saturday between Rethymno and Santorini (€37.90, two hours 40 minutes), Ios, Naxos and Mykonos (€58).

Bus

From the **bus station** (☎ 28310 22212; Igoumenou Gavriil) there are hourly summer services to both Hania (€6, one hour) and Iraklio (€6.50, 1½ hours). There are also six buses a day to Plakias (€3.50, one hour); six to Agia Galini (€5.30, 1½ hours); three to Moni Arkadiou (€2.40, 40 minutes); two to Omalos (€11.90, two hours); two daily from Monday to Friday to Margarites (€3, 30 minutes); two daily Monday to Friday to Anogia (€4.50, 1¼ hours); and four to Preveli (€4, 1¼ hours). There are daily buses to Hora Sfakion via Vryses. Services are greatly reduced in the low season.

GETTING AROUND

Auto Motor Sports (☎ 28310 24858; www.auto motosport.com.gr; Sofoklis Venizelou 48) rents cars and motorbikes.

AROUND RETHYMNO

The hinterland villages of Rethymno make for pleasant excursion if you have your own wheels. The hills are not too taxing, the roads not too busy and the scenery is pleasantly verdant. There are at least a couple of villages to the southwest of Rethymno that make for an ideal afternoon jaunt.

Episkopi, 23km west of Rethymno, is a pretty, traditional town of winding lanes and tiny houses, overlooking the valley. The springs and waterfalls of Argyroupolis (right) are a delightfully cool surprise. **Maroulas** (p132), 10km southeast of Rethymno, is a delightful historic town with commanding sea views.

The lovely village of **Asi Gonia** will give you some insight into traditional life in Crete. Every year around St George's day (23 April), Asi Gonia hosts an amazing spectacle with its stock-breeder's festival, when thousands of goats and sheep are gathered in and around the church to be blessed and milked (the milk given out to the crowd). The festivities continue into the evening.

THE VILLAGE TAVERN

The mountain village tavern, one of the delights of travelling through Crete, is experiencing a revival. A spate of new tavernas serving traditional Cretan cuisine, albeit in more stylish surrounds, are breathing new life into rural villages. Around Rethymno, you are spoilt for choice. One of the best tavernas is **O Kipos Tis Arkoudenas** (☎ 28310 61607) near Episkopi, east of Rethymno, which has superb organic produce and many dishes cooked in the wood oven. Another excellent new arrival is **Goules** (☎ 28310 41001) in a lovely restored stone *kafeneio* in the tiny village of Goulediana, south of Rethymno.

ARGYROUPOLIS ΑΡΓΥΡΟΎΠΟΛΗ
pop 398

When the summer heat becomes too intense for the beach, you'll find a natural, outdoor air-conditioning system at Argyroupolis, 25km southwest of Rethymno. At the bottom of this village is a watery oasis formed by mountain springs that keeps the temperature markedly cooler than on the coast. Running through aqueducts, washing down walls, seeping from stones and pouring from spigots, the gushing spring water supplies the entire city of Rethymno.

Towering chestnut and plane trees and luxuriant vegetation create a shady, restful spot for lunch among the waterfalls and fountains that have been incorporated into all the tavernas. Argyroupolis is built on the ruins of the ancient city of Lappa. The villagers maintain a traditional lifestyle, largely undisturbed by tourism, but are proud of their heritage and eager to show you around. The innovative Stelios Manousakas at the **Lappa Avocado Shop** (☎ 28310 81070), just off the main square, is a good source of information and provides town maps (he is also the town mayor). You can also pick up a supply of his excellent avocado-based creams and skin products, which are made from the family's avocado plantation and exported to Athens and France.

The turn-off to the springs and tavernas is signposted to your right before the village.

Sights

The main square is recognisable by the 17th-century Venetian **Church of Agios Ioannis**. There is a quaint private **museum of village life** on the main street above a mini-market run by the Zografakis family (see below). The dynamic Eleftheria has amassed an eclectic collection of family heirlooms and historic items from nearby villages. If it is closed, call in at the taverna or shop and they will give you a private tour.

The old town is entered through the stone archway opposite the church. Roman remnants are scattered amid the Venetian and Turkish structures.

The main street will take you past a **Roman gate** on the left with the inscription *Omnia Mundi Fumus et Umbra* (all things in this world are smoke and shadow). In a few metres a narrow street to the right leads down to a 3rd-century-BC **marble water reservoir** with seven interior arches.

Returning to the main road and continuing in the same direction you will see on the left a **Roman mosaic floor**, dating from the 1st century BC. With 7000 pieces in six colours, the well-preserved floor is a good example from the Geometric Period (1200–800 BC).

A couple of signposted roads lead to the tavernas clustered around the springs below the town, but it's best to get a map from the Lappa Avocado Shop (opposite). A path from the bottom of the Paleos Mylos tavern (below) leads to a well-preserved 17th-century water-driven **fulling machine**, which was used to thicken cloth by moistening and beating it. Nearby you can find a **Roman bath** and **St Mary's Church**, built on a temple devoted to Neptune.

North of the town, a footpath on the right takes you about 50m to a **Roman necropolis** with hundreds of tombs cut into the cliffs. The path leads on to a **plane tree** that is supposed to be 2000 years old.

Sleeping & Eating

Lappa Apartments (☎ 28310 81204; d €30-35;) Right in the village, these homely apartments set around a courtyard with a lovely garden enjoy great views of the mountains. They are fully equipped with good-sized fridges, decent bathrooms and there are BBQ facilities. It is perfect for longer stays or families.

Zografakis (☎ 28310 81269; d €25-30) On the main road, the Zografakis family rent decent clean and cheap rooms above the taverna.

The tavernas at the springs are a little touristy and overpriced, but you can't go too wrong and the setting is spectacular.

You will struggle to hear yourself over the sound of the running water and cicadas at the old water mill **Paleos Mylos** (☎ 28310 81209; mains €6-9.90), the last taverna on you right down the hill. The verdant location is superb and the grills and salad are a safe bet. Across the road, **Athivoles** (☎ 28310 81101) has excellent fresh trout, local meat and Cretan cuisine.

Getting There & Away

There are two daily buses from Rethymno (€2.80, 40 minutes) to Argyroupolis, Monday to Friday.

MONI AGIA IRINIS
ΜΟΝΗ ΑΓΙΑ ΕΙΡΗΝΣ

About 5km south of Rethymno, before the village of the same name, you will come across the fortress-like **Moni Agia Irinis** (☎ 28310 27791; 9am-1pm & 4pm-sunset). The Byzantine building was badly damaged by the Turks and was abandoned for more than 150 years until its restoration began in 1989 by the dynamic nuns who run the monastery today. It has become a centre for the preservation of handicrafts and needlework and has a permanent exhibition of weaving and embroidery. It also sells handicrafts and icons produced by the nuns. Parts of the historic building have been restored, including the stables, wine press and refectory.

ARMENI ΑΡΜΕΝΟΙ

Heading south from Rethymno, there is a turn-off to the right to the Late Minoan **Cemetery of Armeni**, 2km before the modern village of Armeni. Some 200 tombs were carved into the rock here between 1300 and 1150 BC, in the midst of an oak forest. The curious feature of this cemetery is that there does not seem to have been any sizable town nearby that would have accounted for so many tombs. Pottery, weapons and jewellery excavated from the tombs are now on display at the Archaeological Museum (p125) in Rethymno.

At Armeni an excellent place to stop for lunch is **Alekos Kafeneio** (☎ 28320 41185) next to a small square off the main road. This unexpected gem that's been run by the same family for three generations has a small but superb daily selection of traditional dishes such as lamb *tsigariasto* with a hint of yogurt, served with an impressive house salad. The rabbit is also recommended.

RETHYMNO

THE HINTERLAND

Rethymno's mountainous hinterland offers a diverse range of routes and interesting detours. In the lush Amari Valley you'll come across unspoilt bucolic villages. On the way to the historic Arkadi monastery you can stop at the pottery village of Margarites and see the ruins of Ancient Eleftherna. Heading east you can explore some historic caves and have coffee in the squares of one of Crete's most famous and traditional towns, Anogia.

AMARI VALLEY ΚΟΙΛΆΔΑ ΑΜΑΡΙΟΥ

You'll need your own transport to explore the Amari Valley, southeast of Rethymno, between Mts Psiloritis and Kedros. This region harbours around 40 well-watered, unspoilt villages set amid olive groves, almond and cherry trees and many lovely Byzantine churches. The valley begins in the picturesque village of **Apostoli**, 25km southeast of Rethymno, reached via a scenic drive through a wild and deserted gorge bordered by high cliffs. The turn-off for Apostoli is on the coast 3km east of Rethymno. The road forks at Apostoli and

then joins up again 38km to the south, making it possible to do a circular drive around the valley; alternatively, you can continue south to Agia Galini.

Taking the left fork from Apostoli you'll come to the village of **Thronos** with its Church of the Panagia constructed on the remains of

---

CRETAN BEER

When Düsseldorf-born mathematician Bernd Brink moved to Crete after marrying a Cretan girl, he did what any self-respecting German would do – open a brewery. Since opening in 2001, the boutique **Rethymniaki Brewery** (☎ 28310 41243; 🕑 2pm-late Thu-Mon Jul-Oct) – Crete's only brewery – has progressed from cleaning bottles and labelling by hand to a sophisticated operation producing about 150,000 bottles per year. Its well-regarded organic Rethymnian blonde and dark lagers are sold all over Greece. You can drop by and sample them, along with some meze, at the mini-taverna and beer garden on site. It's about 12km south of Rethymno near Armeni.

DETOUR: MAROULAS

Enjoying a stunning position perched on a rise with panoramic sea views, the protected historic settlement of Maroulas, 10km southeast of Rethymno, is spotted by a well-preserved 44m tower jutting above the village. The fortified town has a mix of late Venetian and Turkish architecture, including 10 olive presses. Much of it was being restored and is a delight to wander through.

Maroulas is home to **Marianna's Herb Workshop** (☎ 28310 72432; 🕑 10am-2pm & 4.30-8pm summer) a treasure trove of alternative herbal remedies and concoctions. Marianna collects aromatic medicinal herbs from the mountains to make her unique range of teas and oils from natural extracts using traditional methods. She has products for all manner of ailments, as well as skin products and herbs for cooking. Her teas in include Sarantovotano, a mix of 40 herbs that midwives used to boil up so that they might pass the baby through the steam for its first breath.

Marianna's interest in alternative therapies took her back to her roots to ancient remedies and her hobby became a full-time obsession when she moved to Maroulas in the mid-1990s. She hit the mountains and consulted older locals about identifying Crete's various herbs. 'This knowledge shouldn't be lost,' she says. 'People should recognise every plant and know what it's for. "Our medicine is our food," they used to say in ancient times.' Marianna says animals were another guide to herbs and flowers, as they don't touch toxic plants. Indeed, Kri Kri goats were observed using Crete's endemic *diktamo* to heal their wounds, while other historic accounts refer to wounded goats eating *diktamo* to expel the hunter's arrow. The plant is one of the hardest to find as it can only be collected in gorges and from the rocky tops of mountains where goats can't tread.

While in Maroulas you can enjoy sensational views out to sea from the quirky café **Farmhouse Katerina** (☎ 28310 71627), which has an animal pen attached. If you call in advance they can make you a meal from their own meat (thankfully pre-slaughtered). The taverna **Ofou to Lo** (☎ 28310 71670) also enjoys a lovely setting and has good food.

an early Christian basilica. The 14th-century frescoes are faded but extraordinarily well executed; the oldest are in the choir stalls. Ask at the *kafeneio* (coffeehouse) next door for the key.

Returning to Apostoli continue south along the main road. The next town is **Agia Fotini**, which is a larger town with a supermarket. The road twists and turns along the scenic valley before it comes to **Meronas**, a little village with big plane trees, and a fine Church of the Panagia. The oldest part of the church is the nave, which was built in the 14th century. The southern side of the church with its elegant portal was added under the Venetians. The highlight of the church is the beautifully restored 14th-century frescoes.

The road continues south to **Gerakari**, an area known for its delicious cherries. From Gerakari a new road continues on to Spili.

Near the alluring little village of Patsos is the **Church of Agios Antonios**, in a cave above a picturesque verdant gorge. The cave was an important sanctuary for the Minoans and the Romans, and is still a pilgrimage destination on 17 January. You can take the scenic route along the Spili–Gerakari road, following driveable dirt road to Patsos, where you turn left. The entrance to the gorge is clearly signposted and it is a short walk to the cave. There are lovely spots with picnic tables along the way.

SPILI ΣΠΗΛΙ
pop 698

Spili (*spee*-lee) is a pretty mountain village with cobbled streets, rustic houses and plane trees. Its centrepiece is the unique Venetian fountain in the square that spurts water from 19 lion heads, though its recent refurbishment was ill-advised. Bring along your own water containers and fill up with the best water on the island.

Spili is no longer an undiscovered hideaway. Tourist buses on their way to the southern coast regularly stop in the town during the day, but in the evening Spili belongs to the locals. It is a great base for exploring the region, as well as being a good spot for lunch. There are two ATMs and a post office on the main street and you can check your email at Fabrica Cafe near the fountain.

Sleeping & Eating

Heracles Rooms (☎ /fax 28320 22411; heraclespapadakis@hotmail.com; s/d €29/40; ❄) Spotless, nicely furnished rooms with insect screens, fridge and great mountain views. Friendly Heracles is keen to impart his knowledge of the area.

Costas Inn (☎ 28320 22040; fax 28320 22043; d incl breakfast €40) These well-kept rooms have satellite TV, radio, ceiling fans and use of a washing machine. Some have a fridge. Breakfast (their own fresh eggs) is downstairs at the taverna.

Yianni's (☎ 28320 22707; mains €4-7) Past the fountain this friendly place has a big courtyard and excellent traditional cooking such as the delicious rabbit in wine, and mountain snails. It also has a decent house red.

Stratidakis (☎ 28320 22006; specials €4.50-6) This place has meat grilling on the spits outside and the specials of the day in pots you can check out in the taverna. There's a lovely balcony out the back.

Panorama (☎ 28320 22555) Pantelis Vasilakis and his wife Calliope run a fine traditional taverna in a picturesque spot on the outskirts of town on the road to Agia Galini, with great views from the terrace. Traditional family recipes and old-style hospitality are the go.

DETOUR: ADELE

For a glimpse of rural life past and present it's worth a visit to **Agreco** (☎ 28310 72129; www.grecotel.gr; admission free but call in advance), which has recreated a 17th-century farm and mini village on a huge estate near the village of Adele, about 13km south east from Rethymno. The working farm prides itself on being a showcase of organic, environment-friendly traditional farming methods and has modern equipment as well as old machinery, including an old donkey-driven olive press, watermill and wine press. You can observe the various activities of the farm – including the making of cheese, bread, raki and wine – as well as wander around the stockyard and garden. The estate is owned by the Daskalantonakis family, who own the Grecotel hotel chain. There is also a *kafeneio* (coffee house) and shop selling traditional products from the farm and the region. You can end your visit with a meal at the excellent taverna overlooking the vineyard, which serves authentic Cretan cuisine using the farm's produce.

The bread is usually homemade, the mezedes excellent and mains include specialities such as kid goat with wild greens. It's an accredited Concred taverna (p57).

Kambos (☎ 6974 924 833) A lone taverna on the road to Gerakari, about 6km from Spili, an area renowned for its wild tulips and orchids, this no-frills family run place is generally known only by locals. They cook simple, traditional Cretan food from their own meat and vegetables.

Getting There & Away

Spili is on the Rethymno–Agia Galini bus route (see p130), which has six daily services.

MONI ARKADIOU ΜΟΝΗ ΑΡΚΑΔΊΟΥ

This historic 16th-century **monastery** (Arkadi Monastery; ☎ 28310 83136; admission €2; ⏰ 9am-7pm Apr-Oct) stands in attractive hill country 23km southeast of Rethymno. The exterior is coldly impressive but the Venetian church inside dates from 1587 and has a richly decorated Renaissance façade with eight slender Corinthian columns topped by an ornate triple-belled tower (it used to feature on the old 100 drachma note).

In November 1866 the Turks sent massive forces to quell insurrections gathering momentum throughout the island. Hundreds of men, women and children who had fled their villages used the monastery as a safe haven. When 2000 Turkish soldiers staged an attack on the building, the Cretans, rather than surrender, set light to a store of gun powder. The explosion killed everyone, Turks included, except for one small girl who lived to a ripe old age in a village nearby. A bust of this woman, and the abbot who lit the gun powder, stand outside the monastery.

To the left of the church there is a small **museum** commemorating the history of the monastery. The striking bare cypress trunk in the courtyard, scorched by the Turkish fire, still has a bullet embedded in its bark. It is worth checking out ossuary in the former windmill outside the museum grounds, which has a macabre collection of skulls and bones of the 1866 fighters.

There are three daily buses from Rethymno to the monastery (€2.40, 30 minutes).

ELEFTHERNA ΕΛΕΥΘΕΡΝΑ

The site of ancient Eleftherna, 25km southeast of Rethymno, is perched on a spectacular location between two gorges. Eleftherna was built by the Dorians in the 8th century BC and became an important settlement. Much of the area is still being excavated by Greek archaeologists, who recommended excavations in 1985 (the British abandoned theirs in 1929).

You can approach Eleftherna from Arkadi Monastery or from Margarites. At the fountain, signs point you to the **Acropolis**, which is past the car park at the newer Akropolis taverna (leave the car there) and the remains of a **tower**. A path leads you down to the vast **Roman cisterns** carved into the hills, which are eerie to explore. You can see the new excavations in the valley below. A **necropolis** which yielded evidence of human sacrifice has also been uncovered nearby in the area known as Orthi Petra, along with a **Hellenistic bridge** to the north.

The new excavations of the **ancient town** are best reached by driving back to the main road towards Margarites and following the dirt road to the site. The Hellenistic and Roman ruins are currently fenced off, but you can get a glimpse. The site is expected to be made more visitor-friendly.

MARGARITES ΜΑΡΓΑΡΊΤΕΣ

pop 330

Known for its fine pottery, this tiny town is invaded by tour buses in the morning but by the afternoon all is calm. Then you can enjoy wonderful views over the valley from the taverna terraces on the main square, dominated by giant eucalyptus trees.

The town has only one road, which runs through town to the town square, where the bus stops. There is no bank, post office or travel agency, but you'll find more than 20 ceramic studios on and around the main street. The pottery is of mixed quality and taste, but if you skip the garish pieces that line the main street, there are some authentic local designs and quality pieces at a few places. Septuagenarian potter **Manolis Syragopoulos** (☎ 28340 92363) comes from a long line of potters and is the only one left to use manual wheels and a wood-fired kiln – to make pottery the way his great grandfather did. His traditional workshop is about 1km outside the town on your left.

The finer pieces in town can be found at Konstantinos Gallios' excellent studio **Ceramic Art** (☎ 28340 92304) in a lane at the far end of town, and the slick **Kermeion** (☎ 28340 92135) on the main street, where George Dalamvelas is happy to explain the techniques and history of the town. Dalamvelas uses largely local clay and has many pieces based on Minoan designs. The traditional potters use local clay, collected from about 4km away at the foot of Mt Psiloritis. The clay is of such fine quality it needs only one firing and no glazing – the outside being smoothed with a pebble. You will see many pieces bearing the special flower motif of the area.

Sleeping & Eating

Kouriton House (☎ 28340 55828; www.kouritonhouse .gr; r incl breakfast €45-100) Just outside Margarites in Tzanakiana, this beautifully restored 1750 mansion is a protected historic monument. Philologist Anastasia Friganaki is keen to show guests around the area's natural and historic attractions, and demonstrate traditional methods of making honey, picking herbs and greens, and cooking Cretan and Minoan cuisine.

Mandalos (☎ 28340 92294) On the shady main square with lovely views, this well-regarded taverna and *kafeneio* is a good place to stop for lunch.

Getting There & Away

There are two buses daily from Rethymno Monday to Friday (€3, 30 minutes).

PERAMA TO ANOGIA

The province of Mylopotamos has some of the more dramatic scenery in northern Crete. The hilly interior contains a scattering of villages and farming towns that are just beginning to attract some tourism. The roads leading southeast from the small commercial centre of **Perama** to Anogia pass through a series of cosy villages and bustling market towns along the foothills of Mt Psiloritis.

From Perama, take the northeast turn-off to the **Melidoni cave** (☎ 28340 22650; admission €3; 9am-6pm Mar-Oct) also known as Gerontospilios. More than 300 villagers took refuge from the Turkish army in the cave in 1824. When the villagers refused to emerge, the Turks threw burning materials through a hole in the top of the cave and asphyxiated everyone. After paying your respects to the martyrs at a monument in the Heroes Room, you can wander through chambers filled with several stalactites and stalagmites.

Continuing east turn left towards the pretty village of **Garazo**, which has a couple of tavernas and a post office. On the way, there is a turn-off at the village of Moutzana for **Episkopi**, a charming tiny village that was once the bishopric under Venetian rule. The town has many stone houses, including several well-preserved Venetian mansions that are being restored and turned into private museums. There are some frescoes still evident in the ruins of the 15th-century **Church of Episkopi** and a Venetian **water fountain** at the end of the town next to the bridge.

From Episkopi you can continue southeast on a scenic route that takes you past the area's largest town, **Zoniana**. In this region everyone seems to be dressed in black and drives a pick-up truck.

Look for signs to the **Sfendoni Cave** (☎ 28340 61734; www.zoniana.gr; 10am-5pm Apr-Nov, 10am-3pm weekends Dec-Mar), arguably the most spectacular cave on the island. Stalactites, stalagmites and strange rock formations make for an eerie experience. The front of the cave was a hideout for Greek fighters against the Turks, but most of the large cave (3000 sq metres) was undisturbed and is still not accessible to visitors. You can walk a fair way into a cave, however, through a series of walkways, but it's still important to watch your step as it can be slippery. The lighting changes colour, illuminating various parts of the cave. You normally have to enter the cave in groups with a guide.

At Zoniana you can visit the quirky **Potamianos Wax Museum** (☎ 28340 61087; admission €3.50; 10am-sunset), Crete's answer to Madame Tussaud's. It has 103 wax dummies of Crete's historic figures in some impressive recreations of historic moments, including a secret school and macabre execution scenes. The private collection was created over 25 years by septuagenarian Dionysis Potamianos and his wife. The road continues to the village of **Axos**, which has the kind of lazy Cretan ambience that has made it a popular stop for tour buses. During the day the village is quiet, but at night the tavernas with open-air terraces host 'Cretan folklore evenings' for tourists.

ANOGIA ΑΝΩΓΕΙΑ

pop 2125

If ever there was a village in Crete that embodies the quintessential elements that make up the 'real' Crete, it is Anogia, a bucolic village perched on the flanks of Mt Psiloritis.

RETHYMNO

RETHYMNO

Anogia is well known for its rebellious spirit and its determination to hang on to its undiluted Cretan character. It's a macho town where the *kafeneia* on the main square are frequented by moustachioed men, the older ones often wearing traditional dress (baggy pants and headdress), the younger ones driving mean-looking 4WD utilities (pick-ups). The women stay behind the scenes or flog the traditional crafts that hang all over the shops in town.

Anogia is also known for its stirring music, and the town has spawned a disproportionate number of Crete's best-known musicians (see p49), including the legendary Nikos Xylouris (the house in the main square where he was born is a mini-shrine; its quasi *kafeneio* is run by his sister).

During WWII Anogia was a centre of resistance to the Germans, who massacred all the men in the village in retaliation for their role in sheltering Allied troops and aiding in the kidnap of General Kreipe. The black shirts men still wear today are to demonstrate their mourning.

Today, Anogia is the centre of a prosperous sheep husbandry industry and a burgeoning tourist trade, bolstered as much by curious Greeks as by foreign travellers seeking a Crete away from the hype of the coastal resorts. You may still come across a spontaneous, lively *mandinades* (traditional Cretan rhyming songs) session in one of the tavernas or cafés, particularly during the sheep-shearing season in July, accompanied by copious amounts of raki. Pistol shots often ring into the night air.

Behind the main square of the lower village is the small **Grilios museum** (☎ 28340 31593) with quirky sculptures in stone and wood by local Alkiviadis Skoulas. It is run by his son Yiorgos, who is known to hold impromptu *lyra* performances. Knock next door or ask at the square if it's not open.

Orientation & Information

The town is spread out on a hillside with the textile shops in the lower half and most accommodation and businesses in the upper half, so getting around involves some steep climbing. There's an ATM and post office in the upper village.

Infocost (☎ 28340 31808; per hr €3; ♥ 5pm-late) in the upper village has internet access.

Festivals & Events

Most weekends there is usually some event (official or not) taking place in Anogia.

A **wedding** in Anogia often involves the entire village (see boxed text, opposite). In late July, the town hosts cultural events and concerts as well as the **Yakinthia Festival** (www .yakinthia.com), organised by the musician Loudovikos ton Anogion, which includes open-air concerts at a site on the slopes of Mt Psiloritis. Look around for posters in Anogia from mid-July onwards, or check online for details.

Sleeping & Eating

Kitros (☎ 28340 31429; d €25) This is the only accommodation in the lower village. Rooms are reasonably priced but share a bathroom between two rooms. It is above the taverna (grills €4-7), which does a presentable job of dishes like *gigandes* (lima beans), or baked lamb and potatoes. The homemade wine and raki is good too.

Rooms Aris (☎ 28340 314817; d €30) Aris enjoys perhaps the best views in Anogia. Rooms are clean and cosy and all have new bathrooms. It is next door to the Aristea.

BACK TO THE FARM

Agrotourism is picking up in Crete, and Axos' **Enagron** (☎ 28340 61611; www.enagron.gr; studios & apt €78-130) is a fine example of the new school of classy rural developments. Enagron is part of the trend towards year-round ecotourism. This farm and accommodation complex hosts occasional cooking seminars on Cretan cuisine and local produce, and allows guests to participate in cooking and any aspect of its agricultural and productive life, from raki and cheese-making classes with the local shepherd to picking wild greens. It's hardly roughing it – there is a pool in the middle overlooking the mountains, comfortable traditionally furnished stone-built studios with fireplaces, a lovely taverna serving its own organic produce, and a communal area with antiques and a country-estate feel. It also runs guided walks and horse or donkey rides in the surrounding countryside. Accommodation is 20% cheaper in summer.

You can visit the farm and eat at the restaurant by booking ahead.

A CRETAN AFFAIR

Anogia is famous for its wild and extravagant wedding celebrations, which traditionally take place in the village squares – 2000 guests are not uncommon and most of the village joins in. Family and friends gather to accompany the groom with a musical procession through the village to the bride's house.

The staccato rattle of a machine gun, or the crack of pistols fired into the air signal the start of the groom's walk (moves to ban this practice have met with mixed success). At the bride's house, the groom's party is met with more machine gun fusillades. The combined parties then make their way to the church for the ceremony, after which the party starts in one of the village squares (or taverna). There is copious food – mostly chunks of lamb and watermelon – and an obscene amount of drink, and then the music and dancing begins and continues until dawn. If the event is being held in the square, they don't mind visitors discretely joining the festivities. Don't join the dancing unless you are invited as each song is normally paid for by the group dancing so others don't cut in. Ask around if you are in Anogia on a weekend; you might just score an invite to a most memorable event. Otherwise just follow the pick-up trucks carting piles of meat, and the sound of gunfire.

Hotel Aristea (☎ 28340 31459; d incl breakfast €40) In the upper village, the friendly Aristea enjoys good views and cool breezes in simple but well-outfitted rooms with TV, private bathrooms and balconies. The owner also runs the excellent modern studios next door.

Ta Skalomata (☎ 28340 31316; grills €4-8) This, the oldest restaurant in town, provides a wide variety of grills and Cretan dishes at very reasonable prices. Zucchini with cheese and aubergine is very tasty, as is the home-baked bread. The restaurant is on the eastern side of the upper village and enjoys great views.

Aetos (☎ 28340 31262; grills €5-8.50) This popular taverna in the upper village has a giant charcoal grill cooking meat out the front and fantastic mountain views out the back. It is traditionally furnished and has good Cretan cooking. A regional special is *ofto*, a flame-cooked lamb or goat. Aetos also serves the local mainstay – spaghetti cooked in stock with cheese.

The capacious **Delina** (☎ 28340 31701) is owned and occasionally patronised by renowned Cretan lyra player Vasilis Skoulas but is better suited to big functions than intimate dining. It is next to the new **Delina Mountain resort** (www.delina.biz), a swanky year-round retreat with indoor pool, sauna and *hammam*, about 2km along the road to the Nida Plateau.

If the square in the lower village is a bit intimidating for a coffee stop, head further up to the lovely shady square next to Agios Yiorgos church, where you must try the divine sheep's milk ice cream and *galaktoboureko* (custard pastries) at **Skandali Zaharoplasteio** (☎ 28340 31236).

Getting There & Away

There are four buses daily from Iraklio (see p158; €3.40, one hour), and two buses daily Monday to Friday from Rethymno (€4.50, 1¼ hours).

MT PSILORITIS ΟΡΟΣ ΨΕΙΛΟΡΙΤΗΣ

Imposing Mt Psiloritis, also known as Mt Idi, at 2456m is the highest mountain in Crete. At the eastern base of Mt Psiloritis is the **Nida Plateau**, a wide expanse used for sheep grazing that lies between a circle of imposing mountains. The winding, 22km paved road leading up to the plateau from Anogia is carpeted with wild flowers in the early spring and you'll notice many *mitata* (round stone shepherd's huts) along the way (beware, some are guarded by dogs).

The surreal space-age domed structures on a lunar-like landscape you will spot to the east is the **Skinakas Observatory**, the country's most significant star-gazing vantage point, at height of 1750m. It is possible to drive up to the site for spectacular views, but the nocturnal astronomers don't appreciate daytime visitors. The observatory does, however, open to the public once a month during the full moon from May to September, between 5pm and 11pm (English-speaking guides in July and August only). Check the website (www.skinakas.org.gr).

Psiloritis' important feature is the **Ideon Andron Cave** – the place where, according to legend, the god Zeus was reared. The cave may have been inhabited in the early Neolithic period. It is accessible to visitors but its attraction is

RETHYMNO

more historical, as it is one huge and relatively featureless cavern, strewn with old timber and disused rail tracks.

THE SOUTH COAST

As you near the coast from Spili the scenery becomes more dramatic and takes in marvellous views of the Libyan sea. Heading west then south towards the coast at Plakias you will pass through the dramatic **Kourtaliotis Gorge** through which the river Megalopotamos rumbles on its way to the sea at **Preveli Beach**. North of Plakias is the spectacular **Kotsifou Gorge**.

PLAKIAS ΠΛΑΚΙΑΣ
pop 186

Plakias is one of the liveliest resort towns on the southern coast. The well run youth hostel helps attract a younger crowd than many of the resorts nearby. The mid-size hotels and *domatia* in town attract a mix of package and independent travellers. Off-season it attracts many families and an older crowd.

Plakias has some decent eating options, good regional walks, a large sandy beach and enough activities and nightlife to keep you entertained. It is also a good base from which to explore the region, with a number of excellent beaches nearby.

Orientation & Information
It's easy to find your way around. The main street skirts the beach and another runs parallel one block back. The bus stop is at the middle of the waterfront.

Plakias has two ATMs, while **Monza Travel Agency** (☎ 28320 31882), near the bus stop, arranges car and bike hire and excursions. The post office is on the street off Monza Travel. You can check mail at **Frame** (☎ 28320 31522; per hr €4; 9am-late) above the supermarket or at the **Youth Hostel Plakias** (☎ 28320 32118; per hr €3.60).

Activities
There are well-worn **walking paths** to the scenic village of Sellia, the Moni Finika, Lefkogia, and a lovely walk along the spectacular Kourtaliotis Gorge to Moni Preveli. An easy 30-minute uphill path to Myrthios begins just before the youth hostel.

For guided walking tours, including a walk to Preveli beach that gets you back by boat (€30), contact **Anso Travel** (☎ 28320 31712; www.anso travel.com). You can arrange to go horse riding through the **Alianthos Beach Hotel** (☎ 28320 31196), which also offers pony rides for children.

There are a several diving operators in town. One of the first was **Kalypso Rocks' Palace Diving Centre** (☎ 28320 31895; www.kalypsodivingcenter .com), which has an impressive dive base nearby offering a range of scuba diving and snorkelling activities. Another well-respected operation is **Phoenix Diving Club** (☎ 28320 31206; www .scubacrete.com).

For **boat trips** (return €12) to Preveli try the fisherman owner of Tasomanolis taverna (right).

Avid readers will appreciate the **Plakias Lending Library** (9.30am-12.30pm Sun, Mon & Wed, 5-7.30pm

---

HIKING ON MT PSILORITIS

From the Nida Plateau you can join the east–west E4 trail for the ascent to the summit of Psiloritis known as **Timios Stavros** (Holy Cross). The return hike to the summit can be done in about seven hours from Nida. While you don't need to be an alpine mountaineer, it is a long slog and the views from the summit may be marred by heat haze or cloud cover. Shortly after leaving Nida a spur track leads to **Ideon Andron Cave**, with an altitude of 1495m. Along the way to the summit a number of *mitata* provide occasional sheltering opportunities should the weather turn inclement, while at the summit of Psiloritis itself is a twin-domed, small dry-stone chapel.

An alternative access or exit route begins (or ends) at **Fourfouras** on the edge of the Amari Valley and a further 3½-hour hike to the west from the summit. There is a mountain refuge about halfway along this trail. From Fourfouras you can find onward transport, or continue to follow the E4 to **Spili**. A third access/exit route from the mountain runs to the south and meets the village of **Kamares** (five hours). Halfway along this track you will pass the **Kamares cave**, in which a large collection of painted Minoan urns was found, and which is a popular day hike in its own right for visitors to the southern side of Psiloritis.

The best map for walking in this region is the Anavasi 1:25,000 map of Psiloritis (Mt Ida) (see p215).

, Thu & Sat), just past the Youth Hostel, which s amassed an excellent collection of books, deos and DVDs in several languages.

eeping

ost accommodation is signposted on comunal wooden sign boards on the main road. heck www.plakias-filoxenia.gr for additional tel information.

Camping Apollonia (☎ 28320 31318; per adult/tent 50/3.50; 🚇) On the right of the main apoach road to Plakias, the site is shaded, but ther scruffy and run down.

Youth Hostel Plakias (☎ 28320 32118; www.yhplakias m; dm €9; 💻) For independent travellers this *the* place to stay in Plakias. British manager ris has created a friendly place with spotless orms, refurbished toilets and showers, green wns, a shady porch, volleyball court and Inrnet access. The atmosphere is helped along Chris' eclectic music collection. It's a 10-inute signposted walk from the bus stop.

Castello (☎ /fax 28320 31112; r/studio €30/33; P 🐕) is the relaxed owner Christos and his leafy d shady garden that makes this place a ppy haven. All rooms are cool, clean and dge-equipped and most have cooking facilis and big shady balconies. There are also big ro-bedroom apartments ideal for families 45 to €55). Air-con is an extra €5.

Paligremnos Studios (☎ 28320 31835; www.paligrem s.com; r €35-40; 🐕) At far eastern end of the each, these family-run studios are dated t are a decent budget option. They have tchenettes and some have great sea views m the balconies. There is an attached shady verna.

Pension Thetis (☎ 28320 31430; thetisstudios@gmail m; studios €45-70; 🐕) This is a very pleasant d clean family-oriented set of studios. The furbished rooms have fridge, basic cooking cilities, coffee maker and satellite TV. Relax the cool and shady garden where there is a hall playground for kids.

Alianthos Garden Hotel (☎ 28320 31280; www.al thos.gr; d incl breakfast €70; 🐕 🚇) This modern tel is at the entrance to town next to the ad overlooking the sea. It's comfortably rnished in traditional Cretan style.

ting

he waterfront restaurants that tout picture enus are generally mediocre.

Taverna Christos (☎ 28320 31472; specials €5-11) is established waterfront taverna has a romantic tamarisk-shaded terrace overlooking the sea. It has a good choice of Cretan dishes and fresh fish and a daily specials board.

Lisseos (☎ 28320 31479; dishes €5.30-8.50; 🕓 from 7pm) The location below the road near the bridge is uninspiring, but this place is well known for specialising in *mayirefta* – the best home-style cooking in town.

Tasomanolis (☎ 28320 31129; mixed fish for 2 €16.50) This traditional fish taverna on the western end of the beach is run by a keen fisherman. You can sample his catch on a pleasant terrace overlooking the beach, grilled and accompanied with wild greens and wine.

our pick **Iliomanolis** (☎ 28320 51053; mains €4-6) It's worth the drive through the spectacular Kotsifou Gorge to eat hearty home-style Cretan food at in the village of Kanevos, in a lovely setting with the gorge on one side and a forest on the other. This place is renowned for its excellent food, and owner Maria is happy to show you the tempting array of food in the kitchen (between 20 and 25 dishes each day). The meat is mostly their own produce and they sell their own wine, olive oil and raki.

A popular and cheap *souvlaki* place frequented by the hostel crowd is **Nikos Souvlaki** (☎ 28320 31921), but locals reliably swear by the souvlaki and grills at **To Xehoristo** (☎ 28320 31214). Also recommended are **Sifis** (☎ 28320 31001) for grills and **Siroko** (☎ 28320 32055) just past Tasomanolis.

Entertainment

Plakias has a good nightlife scene in the summer. Travellers tend to gravitate to a couple of key hang-outs, including the excellent beach bar in the middle of the beach. The younger hostel crowd congregate at Ostraco, while Finikas is also popular.

Getting There & Away

In summer there are six buses a day to Rethymno (€3.50, one hour). It's possible to get to Agia Galini from Plakias by catching a Rethymno bus to the Koxare junction (referred to as Bale on timetables) and waiting for a bus to Agia Galini. Plakias has good bus connections in summer, but virtually none in winter. The bus stop has a timetable.

Getting Around

Cars Alianthos (☎ 28320 31851; www.alianthos.com) Reliable car-hire outlet.

Easy Ride (☎ 28320 20052; www.easyride.gr) Close to the post office. Rents out mountain bikes, scooters and motorcycles.

AROUND PLAKIAS
Myrthios Μύρθιος
pop 208

This pleasant village perched on a hillside above Plakias is an alternative to staying in Plakias. It is within easy reach of the beach and action if you have a car (it's about 20 minutes from Plakias on foot) and enjoys some spectacular views over Plakias Bay.

Niki's Studios & Rooms (☎ 28320 31593; r/studio/tr €25/30/40; ⌘) has basic comfortable rooms, plus studios with kitchenette, fridge and air-con.

our pick **Anna Apartments** (☎ 6973 324 775; www .annaview.com; d studios €39-55; ⌘) boasts attractive and spacious studios and apartments that are perfect for longer stays. They have big balconies, full-size kitchens, and are more comfortable and homey than the norm.

Stefanos Village (☎ 28320 32252; www.plakias.com; studio/apt from €68/88; ⌘), on the outskirts of the village, is an excellent midrange option, with an enticing horizon pool with panoramic views. The family-run three-level complex has self-catering studios and apartments with spacious balconies and sea views. Most have fully equipped kitchens.

our pick **Plateia** (☎ 28320 31560; mains €5.50-9), better known as Friderikos' (after the friendly owner), has good views from the stone-built courtyard and excellent food that appeals to a more discerning local palate. Pork fricassee served with potatoes is a good bet, along with a drop of the house wine.

Moni Preveli Μονή Πρέβελη

The well-maintained **Moni Preveli** (☎ 28320 31246; www.preveli.org; admission €2.50; ⌘ 8am-7pm mid Mar-May, 9am-1.30pm & 3.30-7.30pm Jun-Oct) stands in splendid isolation high above the Libyan sea. On the way up there is a prominent war memorial on the cliffs with statues of a gun-toting priest and a Commonwealth soldier. From the car park outside the monastery, there's a lookout with a stunning panoramic view over the southern coast.

The origins of the monastery are unclear because most historical documents were lost in the many attacks inflicted upon it over the centuries. The year '1701' is carved on the monastery fountain but it may have been founded much earlier. Like most of Crete's

---

DETOUR: ASOMATOS

On the road to Plakias and Preveli, in the village of **Asomatos**, is the fascinating private **Museum of Papa Mihalis Georgoulakis** (☎ 28320 31674; www.plakias.net; admission €2.50; ⌘ 10am-3pm). The octogenarian priest has amassed an extraordinary collection of ecclesiastical and historical artefacts, memorabilia, weapons, letters and posters from the Cretan resistance, icons and household items. It is displayed in a quirky, cluttered house in the middle of the village, which has a charming internal courtyard and a small café where you can buy the family's raki and oil.

---

monasteries, it played a significant role i the islanders' rebellion against Turkish rul It became a centre of resistance during 186 causing the Turks to set fire to it and destro surrounding crops. After the Battle of Cret in WWII, many Allied soldiers were shel tered here before their evacuation to Egyp In retaliation, the Germans plundere the monastery.

The monastery's **museum** contains a can delabra presented by grateful British soldier after the war. Built in 1836, the church is wort a visit for its excellent collection of more tha 100 icons, some dating back to the early 17t century. There are several fine works by th monk Mihail Prevelis, including a wonderfu icon screen containing a gaily painted *Adan and Eve in Paradise* in the middle of the alta

About 1km before the monastery, a roa leads downhill to a large car park (€2) from where a steep foot track leads you 425 step down to Preveli Beach.

From June through August there are fou buses daily from Rethymno to Moni Prevel (€3.90, 1¼hr).

Preveli Beach Παραλία Πρέβελη

Known officially as Paralia Finikodasou (Palm Beach), Preveli Beach, at the mouth o the Kourtaliotis Gorge, is one of Crete's mos photographed and popular beaches. The rive Megalopotamos meets the back end of th beach before it conveniently loops aroun its assorted bathers and empties into th Libyan sea. It's fringed with oleander bushe and palm trees and used to be popular wit freelance campers before that simple pleasure was officially outlawed. The beach is mainly sand, has some natural shade at either end – although umbrellas and loungers can be hired – and enjoys cool and clean protected water that is ideal for swimming and diving. There are a couple of seasonal snack bars.

Walk up the palm-lined banks of the river and you'll come to cold, freshwater pools ideal for a swim. There are also pedal boats for hire.

A steep path leads down to the beach from a car park about 1km before Moni Preveli. Alternatively, you can drive to within several hundred metres of the beach by following a signposted, 5km-long, drivable dirt road from a stone bridge just off the Moni Preveli main road, where it's worthwhile stop for lunch or refreshments at **Gefyra** (☎ 6936704126). The road ends at Amoudi beach, from where you can walk 500m west over the headland and you're home. You can also get to Preveli Beach from Plakias by boat from June through August or by taxi boat from Agia Galini.

Beaches Around Plakias

Between Plakias and Preveli Beach there are several secluded coves popular with freelance campers and nudists. **Damnoni Beach** is pleasant out of high season, despite being dominated by the giant Hapimag tourist complex.

To the west is **Souda**, a quiet beach with some rooms and a couple of tavernas. Continuing west via the village of Sellia and **Rodakino** are the low-key beach settlements of **Polyrizos-Koraka** (also known as Rodakino) with only a handful of tavernas and a few small hotels scattered along a pleasant stretch of beach. It's ideal if you want a quiet beach to chill out at for a few days.

Panorama (☎ 28320 32179; d €30-40; ⊗), at the far western end of Rodakino beach, has decent, budget rooms with a view built on a rise above the beach, behind the thatched-roof taverna. The best rooms are the newer self-catering studios, with tasteful tiles floors, well-stocked kitchenettes, double beds, reading lights and new furniture.

AGIOS PAVLOS & TRIOPETRA
ΑΓΙΟΣ ΠΑΥΛΟΣ & ΤΡΙΟΠΕΤΡΑ

It's not surprising that the fabulous remote sandy beaches of Agios Pavlos and Triopetra have been chosen for yoga retreats (see p211). These unspoilt and peaceful beaches surrounded by sand dunes and rugged cliffs are arguably one of the most beautiful and serene stretches of unspoilt coastline in Crete.

Agios Pavlos claims to be the location from where Icarus and Daedalus took their historic flight in ancient mythology, although nearby Agia Galini makes the same claim.

Agios Pavlos is little more than a few rooms and tavernas around a small picturesque cove with a sandy beach. There are some stunning rock formations in the cliffs leading to the first of three spectacular sandy coves (about a 10-minute walk, then it gets tougher). The sand dunes reach all the way to the top, which is stunning but can get a bit nasty on very windy days. The furthest coves are the least busy, although there are a few thatched umbrellas and lounges scattered around for your comfort.

Triopetra, named after the three giant rocks jutting out of the sea just off the coast, can be reached from Agios Pavlos (about 300m is drivable dirt road) or via a 12km windy asphalt road from the village of Akoumia, on the Rethymno-Agia Galini road. Just past Akoumia there is the Byzantine church of **Metamorphosis tou Sotira**, which has fine frescoes dating from 1389.

There is also an asphalt road leading to **Agia Irini beach**, via the village of Kerames.

While the roads to these beaches were sealed a few years ago – and were being extended to Ligres, with plans to go as far as Preveli in future – they have so far not been spoilt by overdevelopment. There is no public transport to any of these beaches.

Sleeping & Eating

Agios Pavlos Hotel & Taverna (☎ 28320 71104; www.agiospavloshotel.gr; Agia Irini; d €30-40) A family-run place on Agia Irini beach with simple rooms in the main building. It has small balconies overlooking the sea, as well as rooms under the shady terrace below the taverna (*mayirefta* €4.50 to €7), which has good Cretan food. The café-bar next door is the place for breakfast and drinks, and has internet facilities. The same family also has large self-contained studios at the Kavos Melissa complex (r €45) further up on the cliff.

Yirogiali Taverna & Rooms (☎ 6974 559 119; Triopetra; d/tr €35/40; ⊗) Right on the Triopetra's long beach is this place run by two brothers, with their mother cooking in the kitchen. The rooms are a recent addition, with marble floors and bathrooms, attractive timber furniture, fridge, TV and balconies.

Pavlos Taverna Pension (☎ /fax 28310 25189; www
.triopetra.com.gr; d/tr/q €30/35/45) For real isolation,
this *pension* on the smaller eastern beach at
Triopetra has decent rooms with small kitchens and great sea views behind the taverna,
which serves local meat and fresh fish and lobster (that Pavlos, the owner, normally catches)
and home-grown organic produce.

Another isolated option is the **Ligres Beach
Taverna** (☎ 6972 524 425), a small family-run place
with simple rooms next to a stunning beach.
It's signposted from Kerames village.

AGIA GALINI ΑΓΙΑ ΓΑΛΗΝΗ
pop 855
Agia Galini (a-ya ga-*lee*-nee) is another erst-
while picturesque fishing village where tourism and overdevelopment has spoilt much of
the original charm. Agia Galini was once a
port of the ancient settlement of Sybritos.

Hemmed in against the sea by large
sandstone cliffs and phalanxes of hotels and
domatia, Agia Galini can be rather claustrophobic. It is probably the most touristy
southern beach resort, though inoffensive
compared to the north coast. While it still
gets lively during peak season, and has a
great atmosphere at night, it has become a
more sedate resort attracting a middle-aged
crowd and families. It's a convenient base to
visit Phaestos and Agia Triada, and although
the town beach is crowded there are boats to
better beaches.

Orientation & Information
You can get information at www.agia-galini
.com. The bus station is at the top of the approach road. The post office is just past the
bus stop. There are ATMs and travel agencies with currency exchange. Many cafés have
internet access, including **Hoi Polloi** (☎ 28320
91102; per hr €4; ☼ 9am-late), and there is a **laundry**
(☼ 10am-2pm & 5-9pm) in the street opposite the
post office.

Tours
Near the port, **Cretan Holidays** (☎ 28320 91241)
can assist with accommodation and offers a
range of bus tours including Knossos (€42);
a western Crete tour that includes Hania,
Rethymno and Arkadi (€45); Samaria Gorge
(€44); and a tour of villages and farms where
you sample local cuisine (€45). It also has
day-long boat trips to Agiofarango, including
lunch (€44).

Sleeping
There is no shortage of places to stay in Agia
Galini, but a large percentage of the accommodation is pre-booked by tour operators in
peak season.

Adonis (☎ 28320 91333; www.agia-galini.com; r €50-
120; ☒ ☒) This pleasant hotel is spread over
several buildings but the rooms, studios and
apartments all have use of the large pool.
Rooms are light and clean and most have
been refurbished. Some have balconies with
sea views.

Stohos Rooms & Taverna (☎ 28320 91433; d incl
breakfast €40-45; ☒) On the main beach, with
apartments upstairs with kitchenettes and big
balconies, and huge studios downstairs which
are ideal for families or groups. Friendly Fan-
ourios presides over the excellent taverna
downstairs. Try the *kleftiko* or other clay-oven
dishes (€8.50).

Erofili Hotel (☎ 28320 91319; hotelerofili@hotmail
.com; d incl breakfast €30-40; ☒) Run by the laid-
back Miro and his turtle mascot, this pleasant
10-room hotel has more character than most.
There are plain rooms and some with air-con,
fridge and TV. All have great sea views and
the lower rooms have a garden terrace. It's
signposted to the right off the main road. Miro
runs the music bar Yamas.

Hotel Rea (☎ /fax 28320 91390; www.hoter-rea.messara
.de; s/d €30/35; ☒) On the main road near the
port, this budget hotel is dated but has clean,
reasonably sized twin and double rooms
with pine furniture. The bathrooms are basic
but the front rooms have balconies with
sea views.

Agapitos Rooms (☎ 28320 91164; d/tr/q €30/35/40;
☒) They don't have a view but these homely
studios halfway down the hill are reasonable
value, with balconies and back porches, and
some have new bathrooms.

Agia Galini Camping (☎ 28320 91386; sites per person
€6, tents €4) Next to the beach, 2.5km east of
the town, this well-run camping ground is
signposted off the Iraklio-Agia Galini road.
It's well shaded and has a pool, restaurant
and mini-market.

Eating
Madame Hortense (☎ 28320 91351; Greek dishes
€4.50-13) The most atmospheric and elegant
restaurant in town is on the top floor of the
three-level Zorbas complex enjoying great
views of the harbour. Cuisine is Greek Mediterranean, and they do steaks (€12).

La Strada (☎ 28320 91053; pizzas €5.50-7.50, pastas €5-6) On the first street left of the bus station, this place has excellent pizzas, pastas and risottos.

Faros (☎ 28320 91346; fish dishes €7-11) Inland from the harbour, this no-frills place is one of the oldest fish tavernas in town, dishing up reasonably priced fresh fish (€45 per kg) as well as a range of grills and *mayirefta*.

Kostas (☎ 28320 91323; fish dishes €6-27) Right on the beach at the eastern end, this established fish taverna decked out in classic blue and white is known for its excellent fresh fish and seafood and is always packed with locals. There's a big range of mezedes and pricey but excellent seafood.

Also recommended are Romantika, at the eastern end of the beach and Stohos Taverna (see opposite). The Petrino *ouzeri* in town has an authentic atmosphere and fine mezedes.

Getting There & Away
BUS
In peak season there are six buses each day to Iraklio (€7.10, two hours), six to Rethymno (€5.30, 1½ hours) and five to Phaestos and Matala (€2.80, 40 to 45 minutes).

TAXI BOAT
In summer there are daily boats from the harbour to the beaches of Agios Giorgios, Agiofarango and Preveli Beach, with fares ranging from €10 to €20.

Getting Around
Opposite the post office, **Mano's Bike** (☎ 28320 91551) rents out scooters and motorcycles, while **Monza Travel** (☎ 28320 91278) rents out cars and organises bus excursions.

THE NORTHEAST COAST

Once you clear the resort strip, the coastline east of Rethymno is indented and pockmarked with watery caves and isolated coves that are only accessible by boat. The chief resorts along the north coast are Bali and Panormo.

PANORMO ΠΑΝΟΡΜΟ
pop 873
Panormo is one of the lesser-known and relatively unspoilt beach towns on the northern coast. It has a couple of good sandy beaches and is easy to get to from Rethymno. While the beaches are not always the most pristine, the village does have a relaxed folksy atmosphere and makes for a quieter alternative to the occasionally claustrophobic scene immediately east of Rethymno and at nearby Bali. There are a couple of big hotel complexes to the west of the town, but Panormo itself retains an authentic village feel. In summer, concerts and cultural events are held in the cultural centre in a restored carob factory behind the bus stop.

Panormo was once a busy commercial port for citrus and carob exports. The village was built on the site of an ancient settlement, of which little is known. Coins found here indicate that the village flourished from the 1st to the 9th centuries AD, when it was destroyed by the Saracens. There was once an early Christian basilica, probably built around the 6th century, and there are the ruins of a Genoese castle on the harbour.

Orientation & Information
The bus stop is on the main road outside of town. The post office is one block behind the remains of the castle. There is an ATM in one of the hotels just outside Panormo. A tourist mini-train leaves from the main street for the nearby Melidoni Cave (p135) and the pottery village of Margarites (p134). A well-regarded Cretan cooking course is run from Panormo; see p63 for details.

Further information can be found at www
.panormo.com.

Sleeping & Eating
Villa Kynthia (☎ 28340 51102; www.kynthia.gr; d €129-171; ✕ ⓡ) This historic old mansion in the village centre has been lovingly restored and converted into a charming B&B-style hotel decorated with iron beds, antique furnishings and murals. One of the rooms has an elaborate frieze of the *Odyssey*. There is one family-size apartment. The pool and breakfast area are in a beautiful private garden courtyard.

Lucy's Pension (☎ 28340 51212; www.lucy.gr; d/studio €40/45; ✕) Well signposted in the centre of town, the owner Lucy has dated but well-maintained simple rooms with kitchenette and balconies. The top rooms have sea views. She also manages the Castello apartments on the waterfront, which are light-filled, spacious and have TV and small kitchens.

Konaki Studio-Apartments (☎ 28340 51026; www .geocities.com/konakihotel; studios €50; ⓡ) The garden

RETHYMNO

and pool of this small complex are nicer than the rooms, but this friendly hotel is one of the more pleasant options. It's up above the beach on the northern side of town.

To Steki tou Sifaka (☎ 28340 51230; mains €5-7.50) This cosy taverna-cum-*ouzerie* is on a paved street a block back from the waterfront. It has good home-style Cretan food. Pick from the specials board out front.

Angira (☎ 28340 51022; grills €5.50-8) A giant anchor on the eastern end of the harbour points you to this respected seaside fish taverna, which serves fresh locally caught fish and seafood, as well as the usual grills and Cretan specialties.

You could also try **Captains' House** (☎ 28340 51352) on the western end of the port for fresh fish, or the faux castle **Taverna Kastro** (☎ 28340 51362), near the bus stop, which has a pleasant courtyard and good mezedes.

Getting There & Away
Buses from Rethymno go to Panormo every 20 minutes (€2, 25 minutes). Buses from Rethymno to Iraklio stop on the main road just outside of town.

BALI ΠΠΑΛΙ
pop 330
Bali, 38km east of Rethymno and 51km west of Iraklio, has one of the most stunning settings on the northern coast, with a series of little coves strung along the indented shore, marked by hills, promontories and narrow sandy beaches. But helter-skelter development around the coast has significantly marred the natural beauty of this former fishing hamlet and the narrow beaches are overcrowded and claustrophobic in the summer. Still, it's not a bad place to rent a boat and get the full effect of the dramatic landscape.

The name Bali has nothing to do with its tropical namesake in Indonesia; it means 'honey' in Turkish, as excellent honey was once collected and processed here. In antiquity the place was known as Astali, although no traces of ancient Astali now remain.

Orientation & Information
Bali is a rather spread-out settlement and it is a long and undulating walk from one end to the other – 25 minutes or more. The village is punctuated by a series of coves that are better known by the hotels or taverns that dominate them than by their proper names. So you have the big

Livadi Beach (Paradise), followed by Varkotopo (Kyma) and then the port beach Limani (Bali Beach), now connected to the smaller Limanakia beach. Over the bluff at the northern end is the tiny Karavostasi cove (Evita), reached on foot along a coastal path from the port or a circuitous drive over the cliff tops.

There is an ATM near the coast guard or you can change money in one of the travel agencies or at Racer Rent-a-Car (see opposite), on the left as you enter town.

Behind the port, **Bali Net Cafe** (☎ 28340 94110; per hr €3; ☺ 10am-midnight) has high-speed access, full services and a separate games room. If you don't have your own wheels, you can get around to the different beaches on the minitrain **Bali Express** (one way €2).

Activities
Bali and it is a popular base for divers and has a variety of water sports. Near the port, **Hippocampos Dive Centre** (☎ 28340 94193; www.hippo campos.com; dives incl equipment from €31) is a well-run operation offering a range of beginner's and advanced dives and snorkelling. On the port, **Water Sports Lefteris** (☎ 28340 94102; cat _cruises@yahoo.gr) will rent you a pedal boat or canoe (€8 to €10 an hour), a motorboat (€30 for two hours) or a jet ski (€40 for 15 minutes). Parasailing costs €40 for a 15-minute flight and there are day-long and sunset cruises (€25).

Sleeping
There is little budget accommodation in Bali, with most of it being designed for couples and families on longer holidays, or taken over by package-holiday groups. Bookings are wise in high season.

Sunrise Apartments (☎ 28340 94267; d/apt €40/50; 🏊) Right on Evita Beach, the rooms are very clean, pleasant and spacious, with fridge and basic cooking facilities. The owners will pick up guests from Iraklio airport.

Bali Blue Bay (☎ 28340 20111; mooky@otenet.gr; d incl breakfast €50; 🏊 🖳) This sleek modern hotel has great views over Bali from the rooms and rooftop pool. The rooms are spacious and boast a tasteful, contemporary design and are equipped with TV, fridge and hairdryers.

Apartments Ikonomakis (☎ 28340 94125; d/q €35/65; 🏊) This place is centrally located on a quiet street slightly inland from the port, and was recently refurbished. The rooms are comfortable and have kitchenettes.

Sea View Apartments (☎ 28340 94214; d €60; ✹) Around the bluff from the port (or accessed by car from the back road) this pastel-coloured apartment complex has a great waterfront setting. The two-room apartments are spacious and comfortable, thought the décor is uninspiring.

Eating
Taverna Karavostasi (☎ 28340 94267; Greek specials €4.50-6.50) Belonging to Sunrise Apartments, this cosy little eatery 30m back from Evita Beach offers simple home cooking and snacks. Okra with lamb is a popular dish.

Taverna Nest (☎ 28340 94289; grills €5-9) This family taverna just up from the port near the car park is not on the waterfront, but dishes out home-style cooking and excellent grills on a pleasant vine-covered terrace. They predominantly use their own fresh produce and meat.

Panorama (☎ 28340 94217; mains €5-8.50) With a prime position overlooking the port, this place is popular and specialises in fresh fish and home-style Cretan food. It's one of the oldest and most respected establishments in town.

Getting There & Around
Buses from Rethymno to Iraklio (€5.90) drop you at the main road, from where it is a 2km walk to the port of Bali. For rentals, **Racer Rent-a-Car** (☎ 28340 94149; fax 28340 94249) has an office at the entrance to town and one at the port.

RETHYMNO

Iraklio Ηρακλειο

Iraklio is Crete's most brash and dynamic region, home to almost half the island's population, the bulk of its commercial and agricultural activity and Crete's most important and fascinating archaeological sites. The island's rich and unique cultural heritage comes alive when traipsing through the Minoan palaces of Knossos, Phaestos, Agia Triada, Gortyna and Malia. The many treasures unearthed at these sites are in the exceptional collection of the archaeological museum in the city of Iraklio – the island's capital and usual port of entry.

However, Iraklio is a diverse region that embodies some of the best and worst of Crete. Sadly, much of the northern coast has surrendered to tourism, with endless hotels lining the beaches. The overdeveloped resorts of Malia and Hersonisos are the island's contribution to the party scene, though they are struggling to deal with the less savoury elements of this type of tourism. Amongst it all, the north is also home to some exclusive resorts, Crete's only international standard golf course and a new aquarium.

But venturing away from the north coast, you enter the region's rural heart and the centre of the island's wine industry, which is becoming more sophisticated and visitor-friendly. Exploring traditional inland villages you can get a glimpse of the old Crete, while in Arhanes, you will see a thriving modern village. The region's natural beauty can be enjoyed in villages such as Zaros, where you can walk the Rouvas Gorge and visit lovely monasteries in the mountains. The southern mountains are popular climbing country.

In the quieter and less accessible southern coast, the ex-hippy hangout of Matala is the only really developed resort. For a more tranquil experience, you can escape to quieter beaches at Kastri and Keratokambos or for total isolation, a dramatic mountain drive leads to the laid-back community of Lendas and the remote surrounding beaches.

IRAKLIO

HIGHLIGHTS

- Exploring the ruins of the Minoan civilisation at **Knossos** (p158), **Phaestos** (p169) and **Malia** (p178)
- Indulging in the lively nightlife and café scene of the island's capital, **Iraklio** (p156)
- Viewing the extraordinary collection of Iraklio's **archaeological museum** (p149)
- Unwinding on the lovely beaches of **Matala** (p172) and **Lendas** (p176) on the south coast
- Enjoying the cool mountain air and monasteries of **Zaros** (p166)

IRAKLIO ΗΡΑΚΛΕΙΟ

pop 137,390

Bustling Iraklio (also called Heraklion) can be a shock to the senses when you first arrive with a Greek island holiday in mind. Crete's hectic, noisy and traffic-ridden capital is a sprawling modern metropolis of concrete apartment blocks that lacks the architectural charms of Rethymno and Hania.

Yet Greece's fifth-largest city has undergone a significant makeover in recent years and is experiencing a period of urban renewal. The waterfront redevelopment has made a marked difference and the city's historic centre has been turned into pleasant pedestrian precinct where its historic monuments are brought to the fore.

The archaeological museum in Iraklio and the palace at Knossos are a window into Minoan culture, but Iraklio abounds in other reminders of its turbulent history. The 14th-century Venetian walls and fortress underscore the importance of Iraklio (then called Candia) to the Venetians, and many monuments date from Venetian occupation, notably the Morosini Fountain, the Venetian Loggia and Agios Markos Basilica.

Iraklio has a certain urban sophistication, with a thriving café and restaurant scene, the island's best shopping and lively nightlife. It can grow on you if you take the time to explore its nuances, but people wanting to a relaxing holiday tend to stay long enough for an obligatory visit to the museum and Knossos, before escaping to more immediately inviting parts of the island.

HISTORY

Iraklio is believed to have been settled since the Neolithic age. Little is known about the intervening years, but in AD 824 Iraklio was conquered by the Saracens and became known as Rabdh el Khandak (Castle of the Ditch), after the moat that surrounded their fortified town. It was reputedly the slave-trade capital of the eastern Mediterranean and the launching pad for the region's notorious pirates.

Byzantine troops finally ousted the Arabs after a siege, in AD 961, that lasted almost a year. The Byzantine leader Nikiforos Fokas made a lasting impression upon the Arabs by chopping off the heads of his prisoners and throwing them over the fortress walls.

The city became known as Handakas until Crete was sold to the Venetians in 1204 and they named it Candia. The Venetians built magnificent public buildings and churches, and barricaded themselves inside the fortress when necessary to protect themselves against a rebellious populace.

Under the Venetians, Candia became a centre for the arts and home to painters such as Damaskinos and El Greco. When the Turks captured Constantinople, the walls of Candia's fortress were extended in anticipation of the growing Turkish menace. Although the Turks quickly overran the island in 1648, it took them 21 years to penetrate the walls of Candia.

Other European countries sent defenders and supplies from time to time, but it was mainly the strength of the walls that kept the Turks at bay. The Turks finally resorted to bribing a Venetian colonel to reveal the wall's weak points and thus were able to capture Candia in 1669. Casualties were high on both sides; the Venetian defenders lost 30,000 men and the Turks lost 118,000.

Under the Turks the city became known as Megalo Kastro (Big Castle) and a cloud of darkness descended. Artistic life withered and many Cretans fled or were massacred.

In August 1898, a Turkish mob massacred hundreds of Cretans, 17 British soldiers and the British Consul. Within weeks, a squadron of British ships steamed into Iraklio's harbour and ended Turkish rule.

Hania became the capital of independent Crete at the end of Turkish rule, but Candia's central location soon saw it emerge as the commercial centre. It was renamed Iraklio and resumed its position as the island's capital in 1971.

The city suffered badly in WWII, when most of the old Venetian and Turkish town was destroyed by bombing.

ORIENTATION

Iraklio's has two main squares. Plateia Venizelou, better known as the Lion Square because of its landmark Morosini Fountain, is in the heart of the city, while the sprawling Plateia Eleftherias is towards the harbour. The pedestrian streets leading off the fountain are the hub of the city's lively café and dining scene.

Iraklio has two intercity bus stations (see p158). The ferry port is 500m to the east of the old port. The airport is about 5km east of the centre.

IRAKLIO

IRAKLIO

IRAKLIO REGION

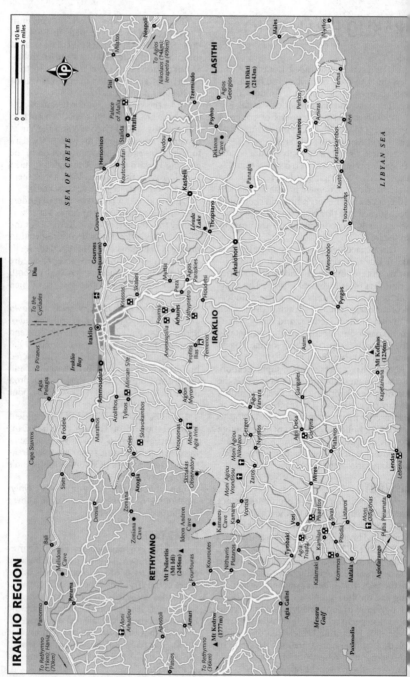

NFORMATION

Bookshops

Newsstand (☎ 2810 220 135; Plateia Venizelou) Foreign press and magazines, guidebooks, maps and books on Crete.

Planet International Bookshop (☎ 2810 289 605; Handakos 73) Excellent selection of literature, history and travel books.

Road Editions (☎ 2810 344 610; Handakos 29) A specialist travel bookshop with a great selection of maps and guidebooks.

Emergency

Tourist police (☎ 2810 210 171; Dikeosynis 10; ☺ 7am-10pm)

Internet Access

In Spot Internet Cafe (☎ 2810 300 225; Koraï 6; per hr €2.40, midnight-noon €1.20; ☺ 24hr) High-speed access, printers, burners and games.

Netc@fe (1878 4; per hr €1.50; ☺ 10am-2am) Has full services.

Sportc@fe (cnr 25 Avgoustou & Zotou; per hr €1; ☺ 24hr) Dimly lit, smoky and packed with gamers.

Internet Resources

www.heraklion-city.gr The municipality site

Laundry

Most laundries charge from €6 for a wash and dry.

Inter Laundry (☎ 2810 343 660; Mirabelou 25; ☺ 9am-9pm Mon-Sat)

Laundry Perfect (☎ 2810 220 969; Idomeneos & Malikouti 32; ☺ 9am-9pm Mon-Sat)

Wash Centre (☎ 2810 242 766; Epimenidou 38; ☺ 9am-9pm Mon-Fri, 9am-8pm Sat)

Left Luggage

Bus Station A (☎ 2810 246 538; per day €2; ☺ 6.30am-8pm)

Iraklio Airport Luggage Service (☎ 2810 397 349; from €2.50-5; ☺ 24hr) Near the local bus stop.

Laundry Washsalon (☎ 2810 280 858; Handakos 18; per day €3)

Medical Services

Apollonia Hospital (☎ 2810 229 713; Mousourou) Inside the old walls.

University Hospital (☎ 2810 392 111) At Voutes, 5km south of Iraklio, it's the city's best equipped medical facility.

Money

Most banks are on 25 Avgoustou.

National Bank of Greece (25 Avgoustou 35) Has a 24-hour exchange machine.

Post

Post office (☎ 2810 289 995; Plateia Daskalogianni; ☺ 7.30am-8pm Mon-Fri, 7.30am-2pm Sat)

Tourist Information

EOT (Greek National Tourism Organisation; ☎ 2810 246 299; Xanthoudidou 1; ☺ 8.30am-8.30pm Apr-Oct, 8.30am-3pm Nov-Mar) Has brochures and maps if you are lucky; opposite the archaeological museum. There is also a tourist information office inside Bus Station A.

Travel Agencies

Skoutelis Travel (☎ 2810 280 808; www.skoutelis-travel.gr; 25 Avgoustou 24) Helpful agent, makes airline and ferry bookings, arranges excursions, accommodation and car hire and has useful ferry information online.

SIGHTS

Archaeological Museum of Iraklio

This outstanding **museum** (☎ 2810 279 000; Xanthoudidou 2 (temp entry from Hatzidakis); admission €4, incl Knossos €10; ☺ 1-7.30pm Mon, 8am-7.30pm Tue-Sun Apr-Oct; 8am-3pm Tue-Sun, noon-3pm Mon late Oct-early Apr) is second in size and importance only to the National Archaeological Museum in Athens because of its unique and extensive Minoan collection. The museum was undergoing a major €21 million restoration, with the revamped museum expected to open in 2009. In the meantime, highlights of the collection are on display in a compact temporary exhibition being housed in another annexe on the site.

The collection covers Cretan civilization from Neolithic times until the Roman empire and includes pottery, jewellery, figurines and sarcophagi, as well as some famous frescoes, mostly from Knossos and Agia Triada. All testify to the remarkable imagination and

IRAKLIO

HERCULEAN CITY

After King Minos' wife, Pasiphae, gave birth to the Minotaur, her lover (the bull) went wild and laid waste to the Cretan countryside. Fortunately, help was at hand in the form of iron-man Hercules (Heracles), the man who killed a lion with his bare hands. His voyage to Crete to kill the bull was the seventh of his 12 mighty labours. As the monstrous animal belched flames and fumes, Hercules captured it single-handedly and took it away. The ancient Cretans were so grateful that they named Minos' port city after their superman.

IRAKLIO

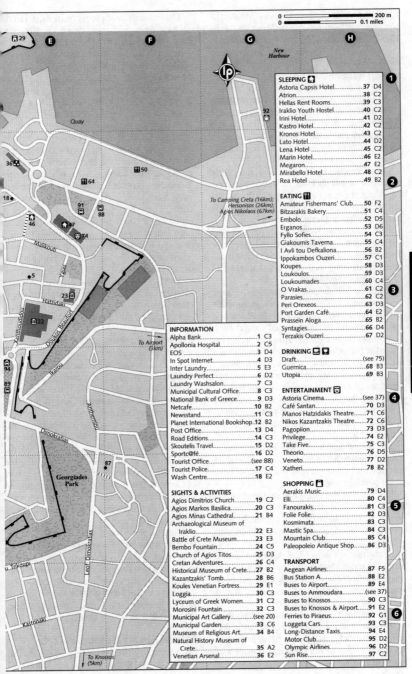

New Harbour

Quay

To Camping Creta (16km);
Hersonisos (26km);
Agios Nikolaos (67km)

Malikouti

Hatzidaki

To Airport
(3km)

Ikarou

Dimokratias

Georgiades
Park

u Trikoupi

Leof. Dimokratias

Kastrinaki

To Knossos
(5km)

IRAKLIO

SLEEPING 🏠
Astoria Capsis Hotel..............**37** D4
Atrion.................................**38** C2
Hellas Rent Rooms...............**39** C3
Iraklio Youth Hostel.............**40** C2
Irini Hotel...........................**41** D2
Kastro Hotel........................**42** C2
Kronos Hotel.......................**43** C2
Lato Hotel...........................**44** D2
Lena Hotel..........................**45** C2
Marin Hotel.........................**46** E2
Megaron............................**47** E2
Mirabello Hotel...................**48** C2
Rea Hotel **49** B2

EATING 🍴
Amateur Fishermans' Club......**50** F2
Bitzarakis Bakery..................**51** C4
Embolo..............................**52** D5
Erganos.............................**53** D6
Fyllo Sofies.........................**54** C3
Giakoumis Taverna...............**55** C4
I Avli tou Defkaliona.............**56** B2
Ippokambos Ouzeri..............**57** C1
Koupes..............................**58** D3
Loukoulos...........................**59** D3
Loukoumades.......................**60** C4
O Vrakas............................**61** C2
Parasies.............................**62** B2
Peri Orexeos.......................**63** D3
Port Garden Café.................**64** E2
Prassein Aloga....................**65** B2
Syntagies............................**66** D4
Terzakis Ouzeri...................**67** D2

DRINKING 🍷 🍸
Draft...............................(see 75)
Guernica............................**68** B3
Utopia...............................**69** B3

ENTERTAINMENT 🎭
Astoria Cinema...................(see 37)
Café Santan........................**70** D3
Manos Hatzidakis Theatre......**71** C6
Nikos Kazantzakis Theatre......**72** C6
Pagopiion..........................**73** D3
Privilege............................**74** E2
Take Five............................**75** B3
Theorio..............................**76** D5
Veneto..............................**77** D2
Xatheri..............................**78** B2

SHOPPING 🛍
Aerakis Music......................**79** D4
Elli....................................**80** C4
Fanourakis..........................**81** C3
Folie Folie..........................**82** D3
Kosmimata..........................**83** C3
Mastic Spa..........................**84** C3
Mountain Club.....................**85** C4
Paleopoleio Antique Shop......**86** D3

TRANSPORT
Aegean Airlines....................**87** F5
Bus Station A.......................**88** E2
Buses to Airport...................**89** E4
Buses to Ammoudara............(see 37)
Buses to Knossos..................**90** C3
Buses to Knossos & Airport......**91** E2
Ferries to Piraeus..................**92** G1
Loggeta Cars.......................**93** C3
Long-Distance Taxis..............**94** E4
Motor Club.........................**95** D2
Olympic Airlines...................**96** D2
Sun Rise.............................**97** C2

INFORMATION
Alpha Bank...........................**1** C3
Apollonia Hospital.................**2** C5
EOS....................................**3** D4
In Spot Internet.....................**4** D3
Inter Laundry.........................**5** E3
Laundry Perfect......................**6** D2
Laundry Washsalon..................**7** C3
Municipal Cultural Office...........**8** C3
National Bank of Greece............**9** D3
Netcafe..............................**10** B2
Newsstand...........................**11** C3
Planet International Bookshop....**12** B2
Post Office...........................**13** D4
Road Editions.......................**14** C3
Skoutelis Travel......................**15** D2
Sportc@fé............................**16** D2
Tourist Office......................(see 88)
Tourist Police........................**17** C4
Wash Centre.........................**18** E2

SIGHTS & ACTIVITIES
Agios Dimitrios Church............**19** C2
Agios Markos Basilica.............**20** C3
Agios Minas Cathedral............**21** B4
Archaeological Museum of
   Iraklio.............................**22** E3
Battle of Crete Museum............**23** E3
Bembo Fountain....................**24** C5
Church of Agios Titos.............**25** D3
Cretan Adventures.................**26** C4
Historical Museum of Crete......**27** B2
Kazantzakis' Tomb..................**28** B6
Koules Venetian Fortress.........**29** E1
Loggia................................**30** C3
Lyceum of Greek Women..........**31** C2
Morosini Fountain..................**32** C3
Municipal Art Gallery...........(see 20)
Municipal Garden..................**33** C6
Museum of Religious Art..........**34** B4
Natural History Museum of
   Crete...............................**35** A2
Venetian Arsenal....................**36** E2

advanced skills of the Minoans. While the temporary exhibition only includes 400 of the 15,000 artefacts that had been on display in the museum, it is presented to international museum standards and comprises the key masterpieces of the collection. Among the highlights are the famous Minoan frescoes from Knossos, including the **Procession fresco**, the **Griffin Fresco** (from the Throne Room), the **Dolphin Fresco** (from the Queen's Room) and the amazing **Bull-Leaping Fresco**, which depicts a seemingly double-jointed acrobat somersaulting on the back of a charging bull.

Other frescoes include the lovely, recently restored **Prince of the Lilies**, as well as two frescoes from the new Palace period – the priestess archaeologists have dubbed **La Parisienne** and the **Saffron Gatherer**.

Also on display from the palace at Knossos are **Linear A and B tablets** (the latter have been translated as household or business accounts), an ivory statue of a **bull leaper** and some exquisite **gold seals**.

From the Middle Minoan period, the most striking piece is the 20cm black stone **Bull's Head**, a libation vessel, with a fine head of curls, gold horns and lifelike painted crystal eyes. Other fascinating exhibits from this period include the tiny, glazed colour reliefs of Minoan houses from Knossos, called the **town mosaic**.

Finds from a shrine at Knossos include figurines of a bare-breasted **snake goddess**.

Among the treasures of Minoan jewellery is the beautiful, fine gold bee pendant found at Malia depicting two bees dropping honey into a comb.

The prized find from Phaestos is the fascinating **Phaestos Disk**, a 16cm circular clay tablet inscribed with pictographic symbols that have never been deciphered.

Examples of the famous elaborate **Kamares pottery**, named after the sacred cave of Kamares where the vases were first discovered, include a superbly decorated vase from Phaestos with white sculpted flowers.

Finds from the palace at Zakros include the gorgeous **crystal rhyton** vase that was found in over 300 pieces and painstakingly put back together again, as well as vessels decorated with floral and marine designs.

The spectacular Minoan **sarcophagus from Agia Triada**, a stone coffin painted with floral and abstract designs and ritual scenes, is regarded as one of the supreme examples of Minoan art.

Other significant pieces from Agia Triada include three celebrated vases. The **Harvester Vase** – of which only the top part remains – depicts a light-hearted scene of young farm workers returning from olive picking. The **Boxer Vase** shows Minoans indulging in two of their favourite pastimes – wrestling and bull-grappling. The **Chieftain Cup** depicts a more cryptic scene: a chief holding a staff and three men carrying animal skins.

Finds from Minoan cemeteries include two small clay models of groups of figures that were found in a *tholos* tomb. One depicts four male dancers in a circle, their arms around each other's shoulders. The dancers may have been participating in a funeral ritual. The other shows two groups of three figures in a room flanked by two columns, with two large seated figures being offered libations by a smaller figure. It is not known whether the large figures represent gods or departed mortals.

Another highlight providing an insight into Minoan life is the elaborate **gaming board** decorated with ivory, crystal, glass, gold and silver, from the New Palace period at Knossos.

Historical Museum of Crete

A fascinating collection from Crete's more recent past is presented at the excellent **Historical Museum** (☎ 2810 283 219; www.historical-museum .gr; Sofokli Venizelou; admission €5; ◷ 9am-5pm Mon-Fri, summer; 9am-3pm Mon-Sat winter). The ground floor covers the period from Byzantine to Turkish rule, displaying plans, charts, photographs, ceramics and maps. On the 1st floor are the only two El Greco paintings in Crete – *View of Mt Sinai and the Monastery of St Catherine* (1570) and the tiny recent addition, *Baptism of Christ*. Other rooms contain fragments of 13th- and 14th-century frescoes, coins, jewellery, liturgical ornaments and vestments, and medieval pottery.

The 2nd floor has a reconstruction of the **library of author Nikos Kazantzakis**. Another room is devoted to Rethymno-born former prime minister Emmanouil Tsouderos. Some dramatic photographs of a ruined Iraklio are displayed in the **Battle of Crete** section, which was being revamped. There is an outstanding **folklore collection** on the third floor.

Natural History Museum of Crete

Established by the University of Crete, this leading **Natural History Museum** (☎ 2810 282 740;

www.nhmc.uoc.gr; Leof Venizelou; adult €3, adults accompanying children free; 10am-2pm Mon-Sat, 10am-7pm Sun) has relocated to impressive new five-level premises in the restored former electricity building on the waterfront. Only two wings had opened at the time of research, including an impressive interactive discovery centre for kids, compete with labs and excavation projects. Apart from the broader evolution of humankind, the museum explores the flora and fauna of Crete, the island's ecosystem and habitats, and its caves, coastline and mountains. It also looks at the Minoan environment, including a reconstruction of a Minoan cottage and its inhabitants. It's a pleasant 10-minute walk along the coast.

Other Attractions

Iraklio burst out of its **city walls** long ago, but these massive Venetian fortifications, with seven bastions and four gates, are still very conspicuous, dwarfing the concrete structures of the 20th century.

The 16th-century **Koules Venetian fortress** (Iraklio Harbour; admission €2; 8.30am-3pm Tue-Sun) stands at the end of the Old Harbour jetty (though it was sinking and underwent significant restoration recently). Built by the Venetians who called it Rocca al Mare, it stopped the Turks for 22 years and then became a Turkish prison for Cretan rebels. The impressive exterior has reliefs of the Lion of St Mark. The interior has 26 overly restored rooms and good views from the top. The rooms on the ground level are used for art exhibitions, while music and theatrical events are held in the upper level. The vaulted arcades of the **Venetian Arsenal** are located on the harbour front, opposite the fortress.

Several other notable vestiges from Venetian times survive. Most famous is **Morosini Fountain** on Plateia Venizelou, which spurts water from four lions into eight ornate U-shaped marble troughs. The fountain, built in 1628, was commissioned by Francesco Morosini while he was governor of Crete. A marble statue of Poseidon with his trident used to stand at the centre, but was destroyed during the Turkish occupation. Opposite is the three-aisled 13th-century **Agios Markos Basilica**, reconstructed many times and is now the **Municipal Art Gallery** (2810 399 228; 25 Avgoustou; admission free; 9am-1.30pm & 6-9pm Mon-Fri; 9am-1pm Sat). A little north of here is the attractively reconstructed 17th-century **Loggia**, a Venetian

version of a gentleman's club, where the male aristocracy came to drink and gossip. It is now the town hall.

The delightful **Bembo Fountain**, at the southern end of 1866, is shown on local maps as the Turkish Fountain, but it was actually built by the Venetians in the 16th century. It was constructed from a hotchpotch of building materials including an ancient statue. The ornate hexagonal edifice next to the fountain was a pump house added by the Turks, and now functions as a pleasant *kafeneio* (coffee house).

The **Museum of Religious Art** (2810 288 825; Monis Odigitrias; admission €2; 9.30am-7.30pm Mon-Sat Apr-Oct; 9.30am-3.30pm winter) is housed in the former Church of Agia Ekaterini, next to **Agios Minas Cathedral**. It has an impressive collection of icons, frescoes and elaborate ecclesiastical vestments. The premier exhibits are the six icons painted by Mihail Damaskinos, El Greco's mentor.

The **Church of Agios Titos** (Agio Titou) was constructed after the liberation of the Crete in AD 961 and was converted to a Catholic church and then a mosque. Twice rebuilt after being destroyed by the big fire in 1554 and then the 1856 earthquake, it has been an Orthodox Church since 1925.

You can pay homage to Crete's most acclaimed contemporary writer, Nikos Kazantzakis (1883–1957; see p53), by visiting his **tomb** at the Martinengo Bastion (the largest and best preserved bastion) in the southern part of town. The epitaph on his grave, 'I hope for nothing, I fear nothing, I am free', is taken from one of his works. You can actually walk along the **city walls** all the way to the waterfront from here (about an hour), or you can climb up from the steps next to the arches at Plateia Kyprou.

The **Battle of Crete Museum** (2810 346 554; cnr Doukos Beaufort & Hatzidaki; admission free; 8am-3pm) chronicles this historic battle through photographs, letters, uniforms and weapons.

The quaint **Lyceum of Greek Women** (2810 286 594; www.leher.gr; Monis Agarathou 9; admission free; 10.30am-12.30pm Mon-Fri) has a fine collection of Cretan costumes, weavings and other handicrafts.

IRAKLIO FOR CHILDREN

The **Natural History Museum of Crete** (opposite) is a safe bet for kids, as is an excursion to the **Cretaquarium** (see p161). If the children are museumed out, the waterfront **Port Garden Cafe** (☎ 2810 242 411; Paraliaki Leoforo; ☎ 7am-late) has indoor and shaded outdoor play areas, including jumping castles and swings. You can also escape the heat and let the kids run around in **Georgiades Park**, where there is a pleasant shady café.

ACTIVITIES
Hiking
Cretan Adventures (☎ 2810 332 772; www.cretanadventures.gr; Evans 10, upstairs) is a well-regarded local company run by two intrepid brothers who can organise hiking tours, mountain biking, and other specialist and extreme activities. The **Mountaineering Club of Iraklio** (EOS; ☎ 2810 227 609; www.cretanland.gr/orivatikos; Dikeosynis 53, Iraklio; ☎ 8.30pm-10.30pm) arranges excursions across the island most weekends.

Swimming & Diving
For a dive in Crete's clear warm waters try **Diver's Club** (☎ 2810 811755; www.diversclub-crete.gr; Agia Pelagia), about 20km west of Iraklio, for boat and beach dives at various sites. Ammoudara, about 4km west of Iraklio, is the closest beach to the city but you are better off heading further afield to Agia Pelagia in the west, or Koundoura to the east.

TOURS
Iraklio's travel agents run coach tours the length and breadth of Crete. There are also daily cruises to Santorini. Try the helpful **Skoutelis Travel** (☎ 2810 280808; www.skoutelistravel.gr; 25 Avgoustou 24).

FESTIVALS & EVENTS
Iraklio's **Summer Arts Festival** presents international orchestras and dance troupes as well as local talent. The principal venue for performances is the huge open-air **Nikos Kazantzakis Theatre** (☎ 2810 242 977; Jesus Bastion; box office ☉ 9am-2.30pm & 6.30-9.30pm), near the moat of the Venetian walls, the nearby Manos Hatzidakis theatre and the Koules Venetian fortress (p153). Programmes are posted last-minute on www.heraklion-city.gr or ask at the **municipal cultural office** (☎ 2810 399 211; Androgeiou 2; ☉ 8am-4pm) behind the Youth Centre café.

SLEEPING
Iraklio's central accommodation is weighted towards business travellers, and the few budget hotels are often not enough to cope with the number of travellers in the high season. Most hotels were upgraded in the lead-up to the 2004 Olympics.

Budget
Camping Creta (☎ 28970 41400; fax 2897 041 792; per tent/person €5.50/4) The nearest camp sites are at Gouves, 16km east of Iraklio. The camping ground is a flat, shadeless area, but there is a sand- and- pebble beach.

Iraklio Youth Hostel (☎ 2810 286 281; heraklioyouthhostel@yahoo.gr; Vyronos 5; dm/d/tr without bathroom €10/25/35) This scruffy, run-down Greek Youth Hostel Organisation establishment is the source of many complaints from travellers. The dorms are as basic as you can get. It's a last-resort option.

Hellas Rent Rooms (☎ 2810 288 851; fax 2810 284 442; Handakos 24; dm/d/tr without bathroom €10.50/30/42) This friendly and relaxed de facto youth hostel has a reception area and rooftop garden bar three flights up. The rooms have fans and a washbasin and the shared bathrooms are basic but clean. All rooms have balconies. You can have breakfast on the terrace from €2.50.

Mirabello Hotel (☎ 2810 285 052; www.mirabello-hotel.gr; Theotokopoulou 20; s/d without bathroom €35/44, d with bathroom €65; ✳) One of Iraklio's most pleasant budget hotels, the relaxed Mirabello is on a quiet street in the centre. The rooms are immaculate, though some are a little cramped, with TV, phones, balconies and upgraded bathrooms. Some rooms share single-sex bathrooms.

Lena Hotel (☎ 2810 223 280; www.lena-hotel.gr; Lahana 10; s/d without bathroom €35/45, with bathroom €45/60; ✳) On a quiet street, this friendly hotel has 16 comfortable, airy rooms with phone, TV, fans and double-glazed windows. Most have private bathrooms but even the communal bathrooms are pleasant and upgraded.

Rea Hotel (☎ 2810 223 638; www.hotelrea.gr; Kalimeraki 1; d shared/private bathroom €34/44) Popular with backpackers, the family-run Rea has an easy, friendly atmosphere. Rooms all have fans and sinks, although some bathrooms are shared. There's a small, basic communal kitchen and they also have family rooms (€60).

Midrange
Kronos Hotel (☎ 2810 282 240; www.kronoshotel.gr; Sofokli Venizelou 2; s/d €48/60; ✳ 💻) This well-maintained older waterfront hotel has comfortable rooms with double-glazed windows

and balconies, phone and TV, and most have a fridge. It is one of the better value two-star hotels in town. Ask for one of the rooms with sea views.

our pick Kastro Hotel (☎ 2810 284 185; www.kastro-hotel.gr; Theotokopoulou 22; s/d/tr incl breakfast from €50/75/90; 🅿 🖵) A refurbished, modern, cheery hotel in the back streets, the Kastro is an excellent choice. The large rooms have fridges, TV, hairdryers, phones and ISDN internet connectivity.

Marin Hotel (☎ 2810 300 018; www.marinhotel.gr; Doukos Beaufort 12; s €75, d €95-125; 🅿 🖵) The front rooms of this modern hotel have great views of the harbour and fortress, and some have big balconies. Rooms are attractive and well-appointed and staff are attentive. The price includes breakfast.

Irini Hotel (☎ 2810 229 703; www.irini-hotel.com; Idomeneos 4; s/d incl breakfast €71/100; 🅿) Close to the old harbour, Irini is a mid-sized establishment with 59 large, airy rooms with TV, radio and telephone, and plants and flowers on the balconies. You can get a lower rate if you skip breakfast.

Atrion Hotel (☎ 2810 246 000; www.atrion.gr; Hronaki 9; s/d incl breakfast €95/110; 🅿 🖵) This refurbished hotel is one of the city's more pleasant options. Rooms are tastefully decked out in neutral tones, with TV, fridge, hairdryers and data ports. The top rooms have sea views and small balconies.

Top End

our pick Lato Hotel (☎ 2810 228 103; www.lato.gr; Epimenidou 15; s/d/ste €100/127/175; 🅿 🖵) This friendly boutique hotel overlooking the old and new harbours is one of Iraklio's prime hotels. It has a smart contemporary design and furnishings, and excellent service. Most rooms have spectacular views, especially the spacious suites. There are great views from the rooftop restaurant and bar, while downstairs is the funky new Brilliant (☎ 2810 334 959) gourmet restaurant.

Megaron (☎ 2810 305 300; www.gdmmegaron.gr; Doukos Beaufort 9; s/d €190/215, ste from €247; 🖵 🅿 🖵) This once-derelict historic building on the harbour has been stunningly transformed with top design and fittings throughout. There are comfortable beds, jacuzzis in the VIP suites, plasma-screen TVs and a fax in every room. The rooftop restaurant and bar have fine harbour views and there's a unique glass-sided pool.

EATING

Iraklio has restaurants to suit all tastes and pockets, from excellent fish tavernas to exotic international cuisine and formal dining options. You'll find the all-night souvlaki joints around the Lion Fountain and a few atmospheric tavernas around the market, as well as on the waterfront. Note that the majority of restaurants are closed on Sunday.

Budget

Giakoumis Taverna (☎ 2810 280 277; Theodosaki 5-8; mayirefta €4-6) This is one of our favourites among the tavernas clustered around the 1866 market side streets. There's a full menu of Cretan specialities and vegetarian options. Turnover is heavy, which means that the dishes are fresh, and you can see the meat being prepared for the grill.

0 Vrakas (☎ 6977 893973; Plateia 18 Anglon; seafood mezedes €4.20-12) This small street-side *ouzerie* (serving ouzo and light snacks) grills fresh fish alfresco in front of diners. It's unassuming and the menu is limited, but still very popular with locals. Grilled octopus with ouzo is a good choice.

Ippokambos Ouzeri (☎ 2810 280 240; Sofokli Venizelou 3; mezedes €4.50-9.50) Many locals come to this classic Iraklio haunt at the edge of the tourist-driven waterfront dining strip. Take a peek inside at the fresh trays and pots of *mayirefta* such as baked cuttlefish, and dine at one of the sidewalk tables or on the promenade across the road.

Fyllo...Sofies (☎ 2810 284 774; Plateia Venizelou 33; bougatsa €2.20; 🕙 5am-late) Next to the Lion Fountain, this place does a roaring morning trade when both the tourists off the early boats and the post-club crowd head straight for a delicious *bougatsa* pastry. Try the custard version or the less sweet *myzithra* cheese sprinkled with sugar.

Bitzarakis Bakery (☎ 2810 287 465; 1821 7) Sells excellent freshly baked *kalitsounia* (lightly fried pastries) along with many other delectable snacks, sweets and traditional Cretan products made by the Kroussonas women's cooperative (see boxed text, p163).

Loukoumades (☎ 2810 285 567; 1821 9; six pieces €2; 🕙 5am-10pm Mon-Sat) Delicious fluffy *loukoumades* (fritters) drizzled with honey, sesame seeds and cinnamon.

Midrange

Koupes (☎ 6977 259038; Agiou Titou 22; mezedes €2.50-6.50) One of a row of *rakadika* (café-style eateries serving raki or wine with mezedes) along this pedestrian strip popular with students, this place opposite the school has a good range of mezedes.

Terzakis Ouzeri (☎ 2810 221 444; Marineli 17; mezedes €3.60-10.20) On a small square opposite the Agios Dimitrios church, this excellent *ouzerie* has a good range of mezedes, *mayirefta* and grills. Try the sea urchin salad or, if you are really game to try a local speciality, ask if they have *ameletita* (unmentionables, fried sheep testicles).

Embolo (☎ 2810 284 244; Miliara 7; mains €4.50-8) Run by former musician Giannis Stavrakakis from Anogia, Embolo dishes up fine Cretan food – excellent grills, *pites* (pies) and large salads – and has occasional live music.

our pick **I Avli tou Defkaliona** (☎ 2810 244 215; Prevelaki 10; mains €6-8.90; ☽ dinner) This popular taverna with traditional wicker chairs, checked tablecloths and plastic grapevines is known for its broad range of mezedes, home-style dishes and quality meat and seafood, as well as its lively atmosphere.

Peri Orexeos (☎ 2810 222 679; Koraï 10; mains €7-8) Right on the busy Koraï pedestrian strip, this restaurant offers excellent modern Greek food with creative takes such as creamy chicken-filled *kataïfi* (angel-hair pastry) with creamy chicken, huge salads and solid Cretan cuisine. There's also a wicked chocolate dessert.

Syntagies (☎ 2810 241 378; Koziri 3; mains €9.50-19) Housed in one of Iraklio's few surviving 1920s neoclassical mansions, this elegant place has original painted ceilings (including damaged sections from WWII) and tables in the flower-filled courtyard garden. It serves well-executed classic Greek/Cretan dishes alongside international cuisine. The pastrami pastries are stand-out starters.

Also recommended is **Parasies** (☎ 2810 225 009; Plateia Istorikou Mouseiou) in the corner of the square next to the Historical Museum; for good-value fresh seafood, the **Amateur Fisherman's Club** (☎ 2810 223 812), in a concrete building on the waterfront opposite the bus station; and **Erganos** (☎ 2810 285 629; Georgiadi 5) opposite the Jesus Bastion for reliable Cretan food at decent prices.

Top End

our pick **Prassein Aloga** (☎ 2810 283 429; cnr Handakos & Kydonias 21; mains €12-18) This little rustic-style café/restaurant has excellent innovative Mediterranean food from an ever-changing menu.

It has some dishes based on ancient Greek cuisine, such as pork medallions with dried fruit on wild rice.

Loukoulos (☎ 2810 224 435; Korai 5; mains €15-32) Loukoulos offers luscious Mediterranean specialties served on fine china and accompanied by soft classical music. You can either opt for the elegant interior or take your meal on the outdoor terrace under a lemon tree.

Also recommended is the superb food at Pagopiion (below), before it gets too noisy.

ENTERTAINMENT

When not being used by live performers in the summer (see p154), the Nikos Kazantzakis theatre operates as an **open-air cinema** (☎ 2810 242 977; Jesus Bastion).

Astoria Cinema (☎ 2810 226 191; Plateia Eleftherias) screens the latest movies, mostly in English. A new cinema multiplex and entertainment complex was due to open along the waterfront towards the Natural History Museum.

The best way to find any live Cretan music in town is by asking at the Aerakis Music store (see opposite), spotting posters around town, or trying your luck at **Xatheri** (☎ 2810 332 757; Handakos 36) and **Theorio** (☎ 2810 288 390; Pediados 22) which have regular live music on Friday and Saturday nights (November to May).

Cafés & Bars

Iraklio has an astounding number of cafés and bars, the most concentrated and lively area being the pedestrian strips around Korai and Perdikari. Most morph into lively bars after 11pm. Along Handakos you'll find relaxed and cosy places more suitable for conversation than people-watching.

Pagopiion (☎ 2810 346 028; Plateia Agiou Titou; ☽ 10am-late) This former ice factory with an arty edge is a perennial favourite that becomes a lively bar after 11pm.

Guernica (☎ 2810 282 988; Apokoronou Kritis 2; ☽ 10am-late) A great combination of traditional décor and contemporary music make this one of Iraklio's hippest bar/cafés. The rambling old building has a delightful terrace garden for the summer.

Veneto (☎ 2810 223 686; Epimenidou 9) This café has the best view of the harbour and fortress from its lovely terrace. It's in an historic building near Hotel Lato.

Take Five (☎ 2810 226 564; Akroleondos 7; ☽ 10am-late) This old favourite on recently pedestrianised El Greco Park has been rather swamped

by louder new arrivals. Next door, Draft
(☎ 2810 301 341; Arkoleondos 9) grill and
beer house has more than 40 beers, though
they don't come cheap (from €5.50).

Utopia (☎ 2810 341 321; Handakos 51) This almost
formal old-style café specialises in teas, hot
chocolates, fondues and has an assortment
of equally wicked icecreams.

Café Santan (☎ 6976 285 869; Korai 13) The city's
first oriental café, with *shishas*, sofas and eth-
nic oriental dance music, including live belly
dancers from 11pm.

Nightclubs

Iraklio has the smartest and most sophisticated nightlife on Crete. The clubs are scattered around town, along Leoforos Ikarou,
just down from Plateia Eleftherias, and Epi-
mendou. In summer, the action moves to the
clubs by the waterfront, where a new club
and entertainment precinct is emerging with
open-air clubs. Some venues open around
midnight. The cover charge usually starts at
about €6 and should include a drink.

Privilege (Doukos Beaufort 7) Iraklio's smart set
packs this dance club that can easily hold 1000
people. Like many of Crete's dance clubs,
there's international music (rock, techno
etc) until about 2am, when Greek club music
takes over.

The most popular waterfront club is the
pretentious but nonetheless classy **Big Fish**
(☎ 2810 288 011; Makariou 17 & Venizelou; ☼ all day),
in a stunningly restored old stone building.
There is also the club next door, Desire.

SHOPPING

Iraklio has the most extensive and sophisticated shopping on Crete, so it's a good
place to pick up the latest fashion, replace
a suitcase or shop for luxury goods. Pedestrian Dedalou and Handakos are lined with
mostly mainstream shops. The busy narrow market street, 1866, has stalls spilling
over with sponges, herbs, fruits, vegetables,
T-shirts, nuts, honey, shoes and bags. For
leading designers and jewellers, head to Ka-
lokerinou and 1821 where you'll find Greek
jewellers like **Fanourakis** (☎ 2810 282 708; Plateia
N Foka).

Aerakis Music (☎ 2810 225 758; Daedalou 37; www
.seistronmusic.gr) Offers the best range of Cretan
music, from old and rare recordings to the
latest releases – many on their own record
label, Seistron Music.

Paleopoleio Antique Shop (☎ 2810 240 155; Agiou
Titou 52) One of the few surviving antique
stores in a city obsessed with the latest brand
names, this old store has a small assortment
antiques and collectables, icons and old books,
the showpiece being an old diver's costume
hanging in the window.

Kosmimata (☎ 2810 346 888; Handakos 31) Designer
Lily Haniotaki-Besi and her jeweller husband
make all the modern and unique jewellery in
this delightful small silver workshop.

Mountain Club (☎ 2810 280 610; Evans 15) If you
haven't come prepared for hikes and adventures, you'll find outdoor clothing and
footwear as well as camping, climbing and
biking gear here.

Folli Follie (☎ 2810 346 354; Daedalou 23) Greece's
internationally successful handbag and jewellery chain.

Mastic Spa (☎ 2810 390 567; Kantanoleon 2) Has
unique products made from Chios Island
mastic, including foodstuffs and skin care.

GETTING THERE & AWAY
Air
Nikos Kazantzakis International Airport (code HER;
☎ 2810 228 401)

DOMESTIC
Olympic (☎ city 2810 244 824, airport 2810 337 203; www
.olympicairlines.com; 25 Avgoustou 27) and **Aegean** (☎ city
2810 344 324, fax 2810 344 330, ☎ Airport 2810 330 475;
www.aegeanair.com; Leof Dimokratias 11) each have at
least five flights daily to Athens (from €85)
from Iraklio' as well as daily flights to Thessaloniki (from €106). Olympic also flies to
Rhodes (from €89). Both airlines have regular
special fare deals, although rarely in peak season. Aegean's early bird internet bookings are
excellent value but dates cannot be changed.
For flying last-minute, Olympic is normally
cheaper. **Sky Express** (☎ 2810 223 500; www.skyex
press.gr) has daily flights to Rhodes and several
weekly flights to Santorini, Lesvos, Kos, Samos
and Ikaria (from €79) on its 18-seater planes.

INTERNATIONAL
Iraklio has charter flights from all over Europe, with flights to London available from
€80 to €150. Skoutelis Travel (p154) is a
good place to ask. **GB Airways** (www.gbairways
.com) also has weekly scheduled flights from
Gatwick. Aegean Airlines had direct scheduled flights from Iraklio to Rome, Larnaca,
Stuttgart, Dusseldorf and Monaco.

Boat

The **Iraklio Port Authority** (☎ 2810 244 912) at the port has ferry schedule information.

Minoan Lines (☎ 2104 145 700, 2810 229 624; www .minoan.gr) operates ferries between Iraklio and Piraeus (seven hours), departing from both Piraeus and Iraklio at 10pm. Fares start at €29 for deck class and €54 for cabins. The Minoan Lines' high-speed boats, the F/B *Festos Palace* and F/B *Knossos Palace,* are more modern and comfortable than their ANEK rivals.

In summer, Minoan runs extra 6½ hour services (deck class €37) on weekends and some weekdays, departing Iraklio and Piraeus at 11am and arriving at 5.30pm.

GA Ferries (☎ 2810 222 408; www.gaferries.gr) runs four ferries weekly from Iraklio to Thessaloniki (€46.50, 31 hours) via Santorini (€16, 4½ hours) Ios (€18.80, 6½ hours) and Paros (€24.30, 10 hours), stopping at several other islands en route. GA also has a weekly ferry from Iraklio (leaving Friday 5pm) to Rhodes (€26.40, cabin €39.20, 14½ hours) via Kasos (€19.40, six hours) and Karpathos (€17.40, eight hours).

Hellenic Seaways (www.hellenicseaways.gr) has a daily high-speed service to Santorini (€31, 1¾ hours), Ios (€36.70, 2½ hours) Paros (€47.80, 3¼ hours), Naxos (€41.70, 4¼ hours) and Mykonos (€48.70, 4¾ hours).

ANEK Lines (☎ 28102 44912; www.anek.gr) has daily ferries between Iraklio and Piraeus (regular €32, cabin €58, eight hours) at 8.30pm.

LANE Lines (☎ 2810 346 440; www.lane.gr) leaves Iraklio for Sitia, Kasos (€19.50, six hours), Karpathos (€19.50, eight hours), Diafani (€17.90, nine hours), Halki (€18.20, 11hours) and Rhodes (€27, 14 hours).

BUSES FROM BUS STATION A

Destination	Duration	Fare (€)	Frequency
Hania	3hr	10.50	18 daily
Rethymno	1¾hr	6.50	18 daily
Agia Pelagia	45min	3.10	3 daily
Agios Nikolaos	1½hr	6.20	half-hourly
Arhanes	30min	1.60	hourly
Hersonisos/Malia	45min	3.50	half-hourly
Ierapetra	2½hr	9.50	8 daily
Knossos	20min	1.15	3 hourly
Lasithi Plateau	2hr	4.70	1 daily
Milatos	1½hr	4.70	2 daily
Sitia	3½hr	13.10	5 daily

BUSES FROM BUS STATION B

Destination	Duration	Fare (€)	Frequency
Agia Galini	2hr	7.10	6 daily
Anogia	1hr	3.40	4 daily
Matala	2½hr	6.80	5 daily
Phaestos	1½hr	5.70	8 daily

Bus

Iraklio has two intercity bus stations. **Bus Station A** (☎ 2810 246 534), which serves eastern and western Crete (including Knossos), is on the waterfront near the quay, though there were plans to relocate it. **Bus Station B**, (☎ 2810 255 965) just beyond Hania Gate, west of the centre, serves Phaestos, Agia Galini and Matala.

Services reduce on weekends. Check out www.ktel-herakl io-lassithi.gr.

Long-Distance Taxi

For destinations around Crete, **Long-Distance Taxis** (☎ 2810 210 102) have cabs at Plateia Eleftherias outside the Astoria Capsis Hotel, and at Bus Station B. Sample fares include Agios Nikolaos (€60), Rethymno (€70) and Hania (€120).

GETTING AROUND

Bus No 1 goes to and from the airport every 15 minutes between 6am and 1am. The bus terminal is near the Astoria Capsis Hotel on Plateia Eleftherias. A taxi to the airport costs around €7 to €10. Try **Ikarus Radio Taxi** (☎ 2810 211 212).

The airport has a full range of car-rental companies including the big multinationals, but you'll get the best deal from local outlets, which are largely located on 25 Avgoustou. **Loggetta Cars** (☎ 2810 289 462; www.loggetta.gr; 25 Avgoustou 20)

Motor Club (☎ 2810 222 408; www.motorclub.gr; Plateia 18 Anglon) Opposite the fortress, has the biggest selection of bikes.

Sun Rise (☎ 2810 221 609; 25 Avgoustou 46) Just off pedestrian street.

AROUND IRAKLIO

KNOSSOS ΚΝΩΣΟΣ

Once the capital of Minoan Crete, **Knossos** (☎ 2810 231 940; admission €6, incl Iraklio Archaeological Museum €10; ☻ 8am-7.30pm Apr-Oct, 8am-3pm Nov-Mar) is the island's major tourist attraction. The palace site is in an evocative location, about 5km south of Iraklio, surrounded by green hills and shaded by pine trees, though the road leading up to it is an uninspiring gauntlet of souvenir shops. The ruins of Knossos (k-nos-*os*) were uncovered in 1900 by the British archaeologist Sir Arthur Evans (p162). Heinrich Schliemann, the legendary discoverer of ancient Troy, had his eye on the spot, believing an ancient city was buried there, but he was unable to strike a deal with the local landowner in Turkish-controlled Crete. Intrigued by Schliemann's discovery of engraved seals in Crete, and later pottery finds in Kamares, Evans sailed to Crete in 1894 and set in train the purchase of a share of the Knossos site, which gave him exclusive rights to the excavation. He returned

five years later and began digging with a group of Cretan workmen.

The first treasure to be unearthed in the flat-topped mound called Kefala was a fresco of a Minoan man, followed by the discovery of the Throne Room. The archaeological world was stunned that a civilisation of this maturity and sophistication had existed in Europe at the same time as the great pharaohs of Egypt. Some even speculated that it was the site of the lost city of Atlantis to which Plato referred to many centuries later, though this is highly disputed.

Evans 'realistic' reconstruction methods continue to be controversial – with both visitors and archaeologists believe Evans got carried away by his own fantasy. Unlike other

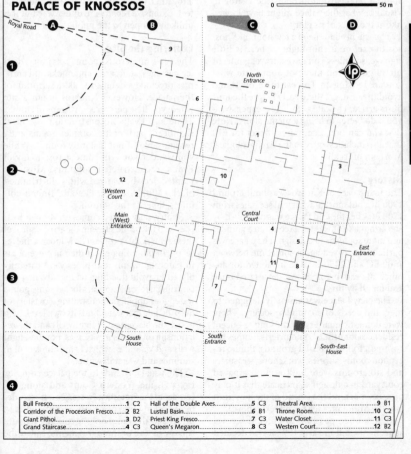

PALACE OF KNOSSOS

Bull Fresco...........................**1** C2	Hall of the Double Axes...........**5** C3	Theatral Area...........................**9** B1
Corridor of the Procession Fresco...**2** B2	Lustral Basin...........................**6** B1	Throne Room...........................**10** C2
Giant Pithoi...........................**3** D2	Priest King Fresco...................**7** C3	Water Closet...........................**11** C3
Grand Staircase...................**4** C3	Queen's Megaron...................**8** C3	Western Court...........................**12** B2

IRAKLIO

IRAKLIO

THE LABYRINTH

Legend has is that after King Minos failed to sacrifice a magnificent white bull in honour of Poseidon, the god took his revenge by making the king's wife, Pasiphae, fall in love with the beast. To help her lure the bull, Daedalus, chief architect at Knossos and all-round handyman, made her a hollow wooden cow structure in which she could conceal herself. The bull apparently found her irresistible and their bizarre union produced the Minotaur: a hideous half-man, half-bull monster.

King Minos had Daedalus build a labyrinth in which to confine the Minotaur. He enraged the Athenians by demanding that Athens pay an annual tribute of seven youths and seven maidens to feed the monster, to compensate for the Athenians killing Minos' son Androgeos. The Athenian hero Theseus vowed to kill the Minotaur and sailed to Crete posing as one of the sacrificial youths. He fell in love with Ariadne, King Minos' daughter, who promised to help him if he would take her away with him. Ariadne gave him the ball of twine that he unwound on his way into the labyrinth and used to retrace his steps after slaying the monster. They eventually fled Crete together.

---

archaeological sites in Crete, however, substantial reconstruction helps the visitor to visualise what the palace might have looked like at the peak of its glory.

You will need to spend a few hours at Knossos to explore it thoroughly. There is little signage, so unless you have a travel guide, or hire a guide, you may not appreciate what you are looking at. To beat the crowds and avoid the heat, get there early before the tour buses arrive. The café at the site is expensive – you'd do better to bring a picnic along. Note that you can buy a combined ticket for €10 that also includes entry to the Archaeological Museum of Iraklio.

History

The first palace at Knossos was built around 1900 BC, but most of what you see dates from 1700 BC after the Old Palace was destroyed by an earthquake. It was then rebuilt to a grander and more sophisticated design. The palace was partially destroyed again sometime between 1500 BC and 1450 BC and inhabited for another 50 years before it was devastated once and for all by fire.

The New Palace was carefully designed to meet the needs of a complex society. There were domestic quarters for the king or queen, residences for officials and priests, homes for common folk and burial grounds. Public reception rooms, shrines, workshops, treasuries and storerooms were built around a paved courtyard in a design so intricate that it may have been behind the legend of the labyrinth and the Minotaur (see boxed text, above).

It was once possible to enter the royal apartments, but in early 1997 it was decided to cordon this area off before it disappeared altogether under the continual pounding of feet. Extensive repairs are under way but it is unlikely to open to the public again.

Exploring the Site

The site's numerous rooms, corridors, dog-leg passages, staircases, and nooks and crannies preclude a detailed walk description of the palace. However Knossos is not a site where you'll be perplexed by heaps of rubble. Thanks to Evans' reconstruction, the most significant parts of the complex are instantly recognisable (if not instantly found). While you wander you will come across many of Evans' reconstructed columns. Most are painted deep brown-red with gold-trimmed black capitals. These, like all Minoan columns, taper at the bottom.

Strategically placed copies of Minoan frescoes help infuse the site with the artistic spirit of these remarkable people. The Minoan achievements in plumbing equal their achievements in painting: drains and pipes were carefully placed to avoid flooding, taking advantage of centrifugal force. It appears that at some points water goes uphill, demonstrating a mastery of the principle that water finds its own level. Also notice the placement of light wells and the relationship of rooms to passages, porches, light wells and verandas, which kept rooms cool in summer and warm in winter.

The usual entrance to the palace complex is across the Western Court and along the **Corridor of the Procession Fresco**. The fresco depicted a long line of people carrying gifts to present to the king; only fragments remain. A copy of one of these fragments, called the

Priest King Fresco, can be seen to the south of the Central Court.

An alternative way to enter is to have a look at the Corridor of the Procession Fresco, then walk straight ahead to enter the site from the northern end. If you do this you will come to the **theatral area**, a series of steps whose function remains unknown. It could have been a theatre where spectators watched acrobatic and dance performances, or the place where people gathered to welcome important visitors arriving by the Royal Road.

The **Royal Road** leads off to the west. The road, Europe's first (Knossos has lots of firsts), was flanked by workshops and the houses of ordinary people. The **Lustral Basin** is also in this area. Evans speculated that this was where the Minoans performed a ritual cleansing with water before religious ceremonies.

Entering the **Central Court** from the north, you will pass the relief **Bull Fresco**, which depicts a charging bull. Relief frescoes were made by moulding wet plaster and then painting it while it was still wet.

Also worth seeking out in the northern section of the palace are the **giant pithoi**, ceramic jars used for storing olive oil, wine and grain. Evans found over 100 of them at Knossos (some were 2m high). Once you have reached the Central Court, which in Minoan times was surrounded by the high walls of the palace, you can begin exploring the most important rooms of the complex.

From the northern end of the west side of the palace, steps lead down to the **Throne Room**. This room is fenced off but you can still get a good view of it. The centrepiece, the simple, beautifully proportioned throne, is flanked by the **Griffin Fresco**. Griffins were mythical beasts regarded as sacred by the Minoans.

The room is thought to have been a shrine, and the throne the seat of a high priestess, rather than a king. Certainly, the room seems to have an aura of mysticism and reverence rather than pomp and ceremony. The Minoans did not worship their deities in great temples but in small shrines, and each palace had several.

On the 1st floor of this side of the palace is the section Evans called the **Piano Nobile**, for he believed the reception and staterooms were here. A room at the northern end of this floor displays copies of some of the frescoes found at Knossos.

Returning to the Central Court, the impressive **grand staircase** leads from the middle of the eastern side of the palace to the royal apartments, which Evans called the **Domestic Quarter**. This section of the site is now cordoned off. Within the royal apartments is the **Hall of the Double Axes**. This was the king's megaron, a spacious double room in which the ruler both slept and carried out certain court duties. The room had a light well at one end and a balcony at the other to ensure air circulation.

The room takes its name from the double axe marks on its light well. These marks appear in many places at Knossos. The *labrys* (double axe) was a sacred symbol to the Minoans, and the origin of our word 'labyrinth'.

A passage leads from the Hall of the Double Axes to the **queen's megaron**. Above the door is a copy of the **Dolphin Fresco**, one of the most exquisite Minoan artworks. A blue floral design decorates the portal. Next to this room is the queen's bathroom, complete with terracotta bathtub and a **water closet**, touted as the first ever to work on the flush principle; water was poured down by hand.

Getting There & Away

Bus No 2 leaves Bus Station A in Iraklio every 10 minutes for Knossos. From the coastal road there are signs directing you to Knossos. Beware of touts trying to usher you into private paid parking areas. There are several free car parks further along closer to the site.

CRETAQUARIUM

The massive **Cretaquarium** (☎ 2810 337 788; www .cretaquarium.gr; adult/child 4 & over €8/6; ☻ 9am-9pm May-mid-Oct, 10am-5.30pm Oct-Apr) is part of the Thalassocosmos marine-science complex established by the Hellenic Centre for Maritime research at the former American base at Gournes, 15km east of Iraklio. It is the largest aquarium in the Eastern Mediterranean region. There are several large tanks with an amazing display of marine life, though it is light on really big fish. There are some interactive multimedia features and displays in several languages. It's right on the beach, so you incorporate a swim.

North coast buses (€1.60, 30 minutes) can drop you on the main road, from there it's a 10-minute walk. The turn-off to Kato Gouves is well signposted on the new national road.

FODELE ΦΟΔΕΛΕ

pop 521

The pretty village of Fodele, 25km west of Iraklio, is famous as the birthplace of El Greco (p49).

IRAKLIO

While this is disputed, there is a small **museum** (☎ 2810 521 500; admission €2; ☺ 8am-7pm Tue-Sun) dedicated to the great artist in a lovely stone building on the outskirts to the village where he is supposed to have lived as a child. There are a few reproductions of his work but little enlightenment about the man and his life. Opposite the museum, is the cruciform Byzantine domed **Church of the Panayia**, built on the site of an earlier basilica. Unfortunately it is normally closed.

Fodele is nonetheless an attractive village in a fertile and verdant valley with a river running through it and a few Byzantine chapels. Women sit crocheting outside stores selling crafts and souvenirs that line the main street, and there are café tables along the riverbank. Locals come here in winter and spring to eat meat at the tavernas by the river.

AROLITHOS ΑΡΟΛΙΘΟΣ

On the road to Tylisos, 11km southwest of Iraklio, the faux Cretan village of **Arolithos** (a-*ro*-li-thos) has an **agricultural and folklife museum** (☎ 2810 821 050; www.arolithosvillage.gr; adult/child €3/1.50; ☺ 9am-9pm Mon-Fri, 9am-5pm Sat & Sun summer; 9am-5pm Mon-Fri, 10am-6pm Sat winter). Built in the mid-1980s, this family-run stone-built village has pottery, weaving and blacksmiths' workshops, a taverna, *kafeneio*, village shop with local handicrafts and a huge square that regularly hosts real Cretan weddings and baptisms. The three-level

museum has a decent collection of household and agricultural items in themed displays about rural life. There is also comfortable traditional-style **accommodation** (d with breakfast €55).

On the road from Iraklio, you will spot **Koumbedes** taverna, in a restored Ottoman mosque. It has good food and pleasant views over the valley.

TYLISOS ΤΥΛΙΣΟΣ

The **Minoan site** (☎ 2810 831 498; admission free; ☺ 8.30am-3pm Mon-Sat) at the small village of Tylisos (*til*-is-os), 13km southwest of Iraklio, is for the insatiable archaeology enthusiast. Amid the village houses, three large villas dating from different periods have been excavated. Buses from Iraklio to Anogia go through Tylisos. They also go past another Minoan site at **Sklavokambos**, 8km closer to Anogia. The ruins date from 1500 BC and were probably the villa of a district governor.

MYRTIA ΜΥΡΤΙΑ

Myrtia, some 15km south of Iraklio, is the ancestral village Crete's most famous writer (see p53) and now home to the **Nikos Kazantzakis Museum** (☎ 2810 742 451; www.kazantzakis-museum.gr; adult/student & child €3/free; ☺ 9am-7pm Mar-Oct, 10am-3pm Sun Nov-Feb). The museum has an excellent collection of memorabilia about the author and his works, including movie and theatre posters from his works from around the world.

SIR ARTHUR EVANS & KNOSSOS

Sir Arthur John Evans (1851–1941) was the British scholar who discovered the ruins of the lost palace at Knossos and named the civilisation Minoan after the legendary King Minos. An avid amateur journalist and adventurer, he was curator of the Ashmolean Museum in Oxford from 1884 to 1908. His special interest in ancient coins and the writing on stone seals from Crete brought him to the island for the first time in 1894. He had a hunch that the mainland Mycenaean civilisation derived originally from Crete. With the help of the newly formed Cretan Archaeological society, he began negotiating the purchase of the land, eventually securing it in 1900 after Greek laws changed. Digging began and the palace quickly revealed itself.

Evans was so enthralled by his discovery that he spent the next 25 years and £250,000 of his own money excavating and reconstructing sections of the palace, unearthing the remains of a Neolithic civilisation beneath the remains of the Bronze Age Minoan palace. He also discovered some 3000 clay tablets containing Linear A and Linear B script and wrote his own definitive description of his work at Knossos in a four-volume opus called *The Palace of Minos*. Evans received many honours for his work and was knighted in 1911.

Many archaeologists have disparaged Evans' reconstruction, believing he sacrificed accuracy to his overly vivid imagination. Evans maintained that he was obliged to rebuild columns and supports in reinforced concrete or the palace would have collapsed, but many archaeologists feel that the site was irretrievably damaged. Certainly archaeologists today would not be allowed to use so much fanciful conjecture.

DETOUR: KROUSONAS

In the foothills of Mt Psiloritis, the women of the village of Krousonas have created a unique cottage industry making traditional Cretan pastry and local delicacies from their grandmother's recipes. The **Kroussaniotissa Cooperative** (☎ 2810 711 989; ☾ 8am-11pm) has 25 women producing a mouth-watering range of sweet and savoury *kalitsounia* (pastries), almond biscuits, rusks, pasta, *baklava*, *galaktoboureko* (custard pastries) and other sweets. Their specialty is the *kouloura* (ornate bread) for weddings and baptisms that can take two women eight hours to decorate. The cooperative is the biggest business in the village, catering for many weddings and social functions, and exporting all over Greece and as far as Germany.

After stocking up on Cretan treats you can visit the nearby **Moni Agia Irini**. This picturesque monastery dates from the last years of Venetian rule, but was destroyed by the Turks in 1822 and all the monks were killed. Rebuilt in 1940, today it's occupied by nuns.

If you want to stay in this area, a good alternative to Iraklio, an excellent option is the **Viglatoras Traditional Apartments** (☎ 2810 711 332; www.viglatoras.gr) on a farm in the nearby village of Sarhos.

There are two buses daily from Iraklio (€2.20, 30 minutes).

TEMENOS ΤΕΜΕΝΟΣ

Above the village of Profitis Ilias, 24km south-southeast of Iraklio, the Byzantine castle of Temenos dominates the twin peaks of Roka Hill, whose strategic position overlooking the north coast and the surrounding mountain peaks made it a perfect place for a fortress. Byzantine ruler Nikiforos Fokas built the castle in 961 to protect Iraklio. There are two pathways leading to its ramparts, which are an hour's walk from the top of the village.

Despite its proximity to Iraklio, the agricultural region maintains a traditional character and sees few tourists. The best information on the area is from local nature enthusiast Dimitris Kornaros who runs **Axas Outdoor Activities** (☎ 2810 871 239; axas@yahoo.gr).

In July and August, concerts are held in a unique venue near the nearby village of Kyparissi – a stone-built amphitheatre in the middle of fields known as **Theatro Agron**. Ask around or at Aerakis music store in Iraklio for a program.

This area is best explored by car.

CENTRAL IRAKLIO

Although most travellers zip through the region between Iraklio and the south coast, several sights make it well worth a stop, but you need your own wheels to explore the area.

The main roads leading south from Iraklio pass through a series of bustling commercial centres and agricultural villages that see very few tourists. Arhanes, with a couple of interesting Minoan sites nearby and excellent tavernas, makes a worthwhile stop and Zaros is a good base to explore the surrounding region.

Peza is the heart of the country's wine production, while the village of Thrapsano makes the giant Minoan-style pottery.

ARHANES ΑΡΧΆΝΕΣ
pop 3824

Arhanes, 14km south of Iraklio, is in the heart of Crete's main wine-producing district. The fertile basin of Arhanes has been settled since the Neolithic period. The ancient Minoans built a grand palace that was an administrative centre for the entire Arhanes basin, but it was destroyed along with the other great Minoan palaces. The town came back to life under the Mycenaeans, flourishing until the Dorian conquest in 1100 BC.

Today Arhanes is a vibrant town with meticulously restored old houses and pleasant squares. It's considered a model of rural town redevelopment and the new road from Iraklio, which makes it an easy commute, is bringing people back to the village.

Irakliots regularly visit to eat at Aharnes' fine tavernas, while locals hang out in the cafés around the main square. There is small but excellent archaeological museum and a few excellent accommodation options in restored old buildings.

Orientation & Information

The village is divided into two, but the interest is in Ano (upper) Arhanes. It's a bit of a maze getting around the one-ways streets and narrow alleys so it's best to park on the outskirts and follow the signs to the post office. The bus stops at the start of the village and close to the main square. There are several ATMs. You can find accommodation and information at www.archanes.gr.

Sights

Only scraps of the **palace** (signposted from the main road) remain and most of the small sites scattered around town are not open to the public. The small but well-arranged **Archaeological Museum of Arhanes** (☎ 2810 752 712; admission free; 8.30am-2.30pm Wed-Mon) has several interesting finds from regional excavations. Exhibits include clay *larnakes* (coffins) and musical instruments from Fourni, and an ornamental dagger from the Anemospilia temple (see boxed text, opposite) used for human sacrifice.

The **Folk Museum of Arhanes** (☎ 2810 752 891; admission €1; 9am-1pm Mon & Wed-Fri) in a restored stone building, is set up like a traditional home, with a worthy collection of furniture, embroideries and handicrafts and the tools of rural life, including bloomers and kids' toys. It's signposted from the Archaeological museum. On the outskirts of Kato Arhanes the **Cretan Historical and Folk Museum** (☎ 2810 751 853; admission €3; 9.30am-5pm) has an interesting private collection from various periods of Crete's history, including personal effects of the infamous German General Kreipe (see p35).

Sleeping & Eating

Neraidospilios (☎ 2810 752 965; www.neraidospilios.gr; studio & apt €40-70;) These superbly appointed and spacious studios and apartments, on the outskirts of the village overlooking the mountains, are run by the brothers at the Diahroniko café. Go there and they will direct you. The pool is an added attraction.

Villa Arhanes (☎ 2810 390 770; www.maris.gr; apt €129-194;) This intimate upmarket complex is in a tastefully restored 19th-century Cretan mansion high in the village. Guests can participate in rural work or other seasonal village activity.

Also recommended is the **Arhontiko guest house** (☎ 2810 751 007).

All the tavernas in town have a good reputation. On the square you could try **Likastos** (☎ 2810 752 433) or **To Spitiko** (☎ 2810 751 591),

while **Ambelos** (☎ 2810 751 039), opposite the Agricultural cooperative, is a good choice for local specialties.

It is worth exploring the back streets to find **Fabrica Eleni** (☎ 2810 751 331; www.oilvisit.com), a bar-cum-*rakadiko* housed in a restored olive-oil press, complete with original olive press and mini-museum featuring some of the owner's father's ingenious inventions.

Getting There & Away

There are buses hourly from Iraklio to Arhanes (€1.60, 30 minutes). Drivers should take the more scenic Knossos road which has some interesting detours. There are several roads into the village, the second turn-off leading you close to the main square.

AROUND ARHANES

The round stone 'beehive tombs' at **Fourni**, dating from around 2500 BC, form the most extensive Minoan cemetery on the island. One of the tombs contained the remains of a Minoan noble woman whose jewellery is on display in the Archaeological Museum of Iraklio. From the bus stop in Arhanes follow signs up a steep trail to the burial grounds.

About 5km south of Arhanes, **Vathypetro Villa** (admission free; 8.30am-3pm Tue-Sun), dating from about 1600 BC, was probably the home of a prosperous Minoan noble. Archaeologists discovered wine and oil presses, a weaving loom and a kiln in storerooms. There isn't any public transport to the site, although several travel agencies in Iraklio include a visit to the villa as part of their tours. It is well signposted from the town.

Some 1.5km northwest of Ano Arhanes is the Minoan site of **Anemospilia** (Wind Cave). Discovered in 1979, this middle-Minoan sanctuary is significant because it demonstrated that human sacrifice played at least some role in Minoan society (see boxed text, opposite). Unfortunately, the site is not open to the general public without special permission.

From Arhanes, it is a 4.2km drive or walk up to **Mt Yiouhta**, where there are great views and the remains of a Minoan peak sanctuary on the northern side.

HOUDETSI ΧΟΥΔΕΤΣΙ
pop 864

The otherwise unremarkable village of Houdetsi, is home to **Labyrinth Musical Workshop** and a **Museum of musical instruments**

(☎ 2810 741 027; www.labyrinthmusic.gr; admission €3; ⊙ 10am-4pm Mar-Oct), created by much-lauded musician and honorary Cretan Ross Daly. With the help of the local municipality, Daly has transformed a derelict stone manor into a museum exhibiting part of his extensive collection of mostly stringed instruments from around the world. More than 250 rare and priceless instruments are on display and an interactive audio system allows you to hear the sound of each one.

Each summer, leading international traditional musicians attend workshops and master classes and hold concerts in the lovely grounds outside the centre. Don't be surprised if you see Turks, Afghanis, Pakistanis, Bulgarians and Mongolians hanging out in Houdetsi. Daly, who is of Irish descent, is one of the leading exponents of the Cretan lyra and master of the modal non-harmonic music of Greece, the Balkans, Turkey, the Middle East, North Africa and North India. He has released more than 25 recordings (see p52).

A new accommodation option in Houdetsi is the restored stone **Petronikolis Traditional House** (☎ 2810 743 203; www.petronikolis.gr; apt €60-70; ❉ ▣). Four spacious apartments are decorated in traditional style (except for the Indonesian dining settings), including some original agricultural equipment from the family estate. The family also has an attractive farmhouse 1.5km away in the middle of a vineyard and olive grove that sleeps up to four.

In town, the best dining option is **Roussos Taverna** (☎ 2810 742 189; ⊙ Jun-Oct lunch & dinner, Nov-May dinner only Tue-Sun), known for excellent Cretan cooking.

The steep dirt road above the village takes you over the hill to breathtaking views of the new **Tamiolakis Winery** (see p166).

There are three buses daily to Houdetsi (€2.20, 45 minutes).

THRAPSANO ΘΡΑΨΑΝΟ

pop 1381

Thrapsano, 32km south of Iraklio, attracts few visitors other than those visiting the town's **pottery workshops**. Thrapsano is a thriving centre for the production of huge distinctive Minoan-style *pithoi* that grace countless hotels, restaurants and homes across the island and are exported throughout the world. An annual pottery festival takes place in mid-July.

MURDER IN THE TEMPLE

Human sacrifice is not commonly associated with the peace-loving Minoans, but the evidence found at the site of Anemospilia near the village of Arhanes, 18km south of Iraklio, irrefutably suggests otherwise. During excavations at a simple three-room temple in the 1980s, scientists found the remains of a young man placed on an altar and trussed, with a huge sacrificial bronze dagger incised with the shape of a boar-like beast amid the bones. The remains of two other skeletons nearby – probably those of a priestess and an assistant – seemed to indicate that the boy's death was part of a sacrificial rite. Perhaps the sacrifice was made just as the 1700 BC earthquake began, in a desperate attempt to appease the gods.

Workshops scattered around the town are normally happy to let visitors see them at work. You can watch the giant pots being made at the traditional **Nikos Doxastakis workshop** (☎ 2891 041 160) up towards the municipal offices, while **Vasilakis Pottery** (☎ 2891 041 666), just past the lake turn-off, has smaller pieces you can take home, as has **Koutrakis Art** (☎ 2891 041 000), on the road into town.

Beyond some well-preserved frescoes in the 15th century two-aisled **Timios Stavros church** in the middle of the village, there's little to see or do.

Just outside the town on the road north to Apostoli is the **Livada Lake**, a preserved wetland with a bird-watching lookout and a run-down covered picnic area. The lake has doubled in size over time as potters have extracted clay from the lakebed. At the time of writing, a massive pottery museum was being constructed near the lake.

On the way to the lake you will pass the **Panagia Pigadiotissa church**, past the cemetery, where a monument has been built around an old 'miracle' well. Local legend has it that when anything (including people) fell into the well, the water rose to the top and saved them from drowning.

From Iraklio, Thrapsano is best reached via the Knossos road, turning off at the village of Agies Paraskies, near Peza. There are four buses daily to Thrapsano from Iraklio (€3.10, one hour).

IRAKLIO

WINE COUNTRY

The region south of Iraklio is Crete's prime vineyard, with about 70 per cent of wine produced in Crete coming from the Peza area. Along with Arhanes and Dafnes, these areas cultivate many Cretan grape varieties and produce designated appellation of origin wines.

There are growing opportunities for wine tasting. The impressive **Boutari Winery** (☎ 2810 731 617; www.boutari.gr; 1hr tour & tasting €4.50, tasting only €4; ◷ 9am-6pm Mon-Fri, 10am-6pm Sat & Sun), near Skalani, about 8km from Iraklio, is set on a hill in the middle of the Fantaxometoho estate, with an elegant tasting room and showroom overlooking the vineyard. Tours of the vineyard and winery include a quirky futuristic video on Crete in the cellar cinema, where you watch the high-tech show wearing headphones (choice of four languages) and learn how to taste wine.

You can also taste local wines in the heart of the wine region at Peza. The massive **Minos winery** (☎ 2810 741 213; www.minoswines.gr; tasting free, video & tour €2; ◷ 9am-4pm Mon-Fri, 9am-3pm Sat) and the **Pezas Union of local producers** (☎ 2810 741 945; www.pezaunion.gr; admission free; ◷ 9am-4pm Mon-Sat) have tastings and videos, as well as mini-museums of the local wine industry. All sell wine at cheaper than retail prices.

A new boutique winery worth visiting is the superbly located **Tamiolakis Winery** (☎ 2810 742 083; ◷ 9am-5pm Mon-Sat) in Houdetsi. This organic winery is one of Crete's excellent new generation wineries, with Bordeaux-trained winemakers, state-of-the art equipment, visitor friendly facilities – and some fine wines using Cretan varietals. Their elegant tasting room overlooks the vineyards in a picturesque valley.

AVDOU ΑΒΔΟΥ
pop 320

The sleepy agricultural village of Avdou is only a 20-minute drive from the north coast town of Malia, but the two worlds could not be further apart. Half the houses in the village seem to be abandoned, while the rest are spruced up and flower-filled, including some restored by foreigners.

If you follow the signs to the town centre you will pass a mini-market and, turning left at the giant plane tree, come to a small square with a café, with a store and a couple of tavernas further along. There are four Byzantine churches around the village but the only one you can normally find open is the **Agios Antonios church**, which has some surviving frescoes. Ask a taverna for the key if it is locked.

Apart from the odd griffin vulture, a common sight in the skies above Avdou is the paragliders from the Avdou-based **International Centre of Natural Activities** (☎ 2897 051 200; www.icna.gr).

You can go horse riding up in the hills at **Odysseia Stables** (☎ 2897 051 080; www.horseriding.gr), in a stunning location about 2km along a dirt road from Avdou. Manolis Frangakis and his Dutch wife Sabine also run the adjacent classy **Velani Country Hotel** (www.countryhotel.gr; r €50-70), a relaxing place with simple, stylish rooms and a lovely pool overlooking the valley. It is worth the trip just to eat at the attached **taverna**.

Accommodation options in Avdou are at the extreme ends of the spectrum. The two totally basic rooms in the village above Michalis Markantonakis' **Pantopoleion** (☎ 2897 051 243; r incl breakfast €20) are clean but barely fit two beds and share a communal wash basin and toilet on the balcony. You have to go to the owner's home to shower. Michalis also runs the taverna opposite, so you can have your dinner grilled downstairs and pour your own wine from the barrels in the storeroom across the street.

Avdou Villas (☎ 2810 300 540; www.avdou.com; apt €129-240; ☒ ☒) is a significantly more upmarket rural complex on a farm just outside the village with fully self-contained apartments with all the modcons.

You can get a decent meal at **Strovili** (☎ 2897 051 039) on the main road next to the church, opposite the children's playground.

There are two buses daily to Avdou from Iraklio (€3.50, 30 minutes). From the main coastal highway, turn off at Malia for the village of Mohos.

ZAROS ΖΑΡΟΣ
pop 2081

If the name rings a bell, it's probably because 'Zaros' is the label on the litres of mineral water you've been guzzling. Around 46km southwest of Iraklio, Zaros is a refreshingly unspoilt traditional village that's known for its spring water and bottling plant. Various excavations in the region indicate that the Minoans and the Romans settled here, lured by the abundant supply of fresh water. The spring water from Zaros also supplied the great Roman capital of Gortyna: Byzantine monasteries are nearly as abundant as the spring water. You can visit several of them and also walk the stunning Rouvas gorge. Zaros makes an ideal base for walkers and is relatively close to the nearby beaches of Kommos and the area's archaeological sites.

Orientation & Information

The business end of Zaros is at the southern entrance of the town. The post office and a supermarket are across the street from the police station. There's an ATM on the main street.

Sights & Activities

If you have your own wheels, the Byzantine monasteries and traditional villages tucked away in the hills are worth exploring. Take the road that leads west from Zaros and you will see a sign directing you to **Moni Agiou Nikolaou**, which is at the mouth of the verdant **Rouvas Gorge**. The monastery still houses several monks and the church contains some 14th-century paintings. A few kilometres further is the **Moni Agiou Andoniou Vrondisiou**, which is noteworthy for its 15th-century Venetian fountain and early 14th-century frescoes from the Cretan School.

The drive to the monasteries and further on to the traditional mountain villages of **Vorizia** and **Kamares** is particularly scenic. From there, you can hike inland and up to Mt Psiloritis. You have a choice of heading westwards along the E4 trail down the mountain to Fourfouras or eastwards along the same trail down to the Nida Plateau. There is also a paved road to the village of Anogia.

The Zaros **bottling plant** in the northern end of town will usually allow you to take a look at operations. A short distance before the plant you will come to a lovely shady park, **Votomos**, with a small lake, a taverna and a children's playground, which makes a great picnic stop. From the lake, there is a walking path to Moni Agiou Nikolaou (900m) and the entry to Rouvas Gorge (2.5km), although it would be better to do it the other way around and end up at the lake for lunch.

On the main road in town is the **lyra workshop** (☎ 2894 031 249) of well-known instrument maker Antonis Stefanakis, whose hand-made lyras are sold around the world. The workshop was to relocate to his newly built studios in the top of the village, where he was planning to display his collection of costumes from his days as a leading folk dancer.

Sleeping & Eating

Studios Keramos (☎ /fax 2894 031 352; s/d incl breakfast €30/45; ⊠) Close to the village centre, this homely hotel run by the friendly Katerina is decorated with Cretan crafts, weaving and family heirlooms. Many of the rooms and studios have antique beds and furniture, some have TV and kitchenette. Katerina is up early cooking up a scrumptious and copious traditional Cretan breakfast – don't miss it.

Eleonas (☎ 2894 031 238; www.eleonas.gr; apts €56; ⊠ ⊠) This is an attractive upscale mountain retreat set among the olive groves and terraced along the hillside overlooking a verdant valley. The smartly appointed apartments have all the mod cons including satellite TV and DVD players and cooking facilities. Horse riding, archery, mountain bikes and guided walking tours are on offer or you can just hang by the pool. There's a decent taverna attached.

I Limni (☎ 2894 031 338; trout per kg €22; ☺ 9am-late) Right on the lake, this taverna is a peaceful oasis serving fresh grilled trout and Cretan specialties. The basket of starters that comes out with the bread adds a nice touch.

our pick Vengera (☎ 2894 031 730) On the main street, this excellent taverna is run by vivacious Vivi and her mother Irini, who cook five or six traditional dishes daily. They also do special €25 meal- and- accommodation deals in nearby studios.

Votomos (☎ 2894 031 0710; trout per kg €27) Trout is the speciality at this taverna and trout farm just outside town past the Idi hotel.

A short drive from Zaros, in the neighbouring village of Nyvritos, the traditional-style *kafeneio* **Nivritos** (☎ 2894 031 296) has superb home-style food and doubles as an outlet for herbalist owner Dimitris Tsakalakis' range of Cretan herbs.

Getting There & Away

There are two buses daily to Zaros from Iraklio (€4.10, one hour).

SOUTHERN IRAKLIO

The main highway that runs from Tymbaki to Pyrgos divides the northern part of the Iraklio prefecture from the southern coastal resorts. Along the highway are busy commercial centres, such as Tymbaki, Mires, Agii Deka and Pyrgos, that market the agricultural produce from the surrounding region. Although these towns hold little interest for tourists they do give a sense of the dynamism of the Cretan economy.

The south-central region of Crete is blessed with a trio of important archaeological sites – Phaestos, Agia Triada and Gortyna – and a cluster of minor sites spanning Cretan history from the Minoans to the Romans. Getting from one to the other ideally requires private transport or joining a comprehensive sites tour from Iraklio. Either way, allow some time to see the sites and consider basing yourself here for a day or two.

When you get tired of poking around ancient ruins, the south-coast beaches of Matala, Kommos, Kalamaki and Lendas beckon with long stretches of sandy beach. The road to the Agiofarango gorge takes you past the historic Moni Odigitrias. Further to the east are the quiet beach communities of Kastri and Keratokambos.

GORTYNA ΓΟΡΤΥΝΑ

The archaeological site of **Gortyna** (☎ 2892 031 144; admission €4; ☒ 8am-7.30pm, to 5pm winter), 46km southwest of Iraklio, is the largest in Crete and one of the most fascinating. Also called Gortyn or Gortys, Gortyna (gor-tih- nah) doesn't have much from the Minoan period because it was little more than a subject town of powerful Phaestos until it began accumulating riches (mostly from piracy) under the Dorians. By the 5th century BC, however, it was so influential as Knossos. When the island was under threat from the Romans, the Gortynians cleverly made a pact with them and, when the Romans conquered the island in 67 BC, they made Gortyna the island's capital. The city blossomed under the Roman administrators who endowed it with lavish public buildings, including a Praetorium, amphitheatre, public baths, a music school and temples. Except for the 7th century BC Temple of the Pythian Apollo and the 7th century AD Church of Agios Titos, most of what you see in Gortyna

dates from the Roman period. Gortyna's centuries of splendour came to an end in AD 824 when the Saracens raided the island and destroyed the city.

The vastness of the site indicates how important Gortyna city was to the Romans. The city sprawls over a square kilometre of plains, foothills and the summit of Mt Agios Ioannis. At one time there must have been ducts and an aqueduct that brought water from the springs of Votomos lake, 15km away, to service their elaborate systems of fountains and public baths. There also must have been streets and a town square, but these have not been excavated.

Although Italian archaeologist Federico Halbherr first explored the site during the 1880s, excavations are continuing.

Beginning south of the main road you'll first come to the **Temple of the Pythian Apollo**, which was the main sanctuary of pre-Roman Gortyna. Built in the 7th century BC, the temple was expanded in the 3rd century BC and converted into a Christian basilica in the 2nd century AD. Nearby is the **Praetorium** that was the palace of the Roman governor of Crete, an administrative building with a basilica and a private residence. Most of the ruins date from the 2nd century AD and were repaired in the 4th century. To the north is the 2nd-century **Nymphaeum**, a public bath supplied by an **aqueduct** bringing water from Zaros. It was originally adorned with statues of nymphs. South of the Nymphaeum is the **amphitheatre**, which dates from the late 2nd century AD.

The most impressive monument within the fenced area is the **Church of Agios Titos**, which is the finest early-Christian church in Crete. It was probably built on the site of an earlier church, but this construction dates from the 6th century. The stone cruciform church has two small apses and contains three levels, with the surviving apse providing a hint of its former magnificence. Nearby is the **Odeion**, a theatre built around the 1st century BC. Behind the Odeion is a plane tree that, according to legend, served as a love nest for Zeus and Europa.

Beyond the Odeion is the star attraction – the stone tablets engraved with the 6th-century-BC **Laws of Gortyna**. The 600 lines written in a Dorian dialect were the earliest law code in the Greek world. Ancient Cretans were preoccupied with the same issues that drive people into court today – marriage, divorce, property transfers, inheritance and adoption, as well as criminal offences. They provide an insight into the social organisation of pre-Roman Crete. It was an extremely hierarchical society, divided into slaves and several categories of free citizens, each of whom had strictly delineated rights and obligations.

It's a bit of a hike but it's worth visiting the **Acropolis** at the top of the hill in the northwest corner of the site. Following the road along the stream near the Odeion you will come to a gate beyond the theatre that marks the start of the path to the top. In addition to a bird's-eye view of the entire site, the acropolis contains impressive sections of the pre-Roman ramparts.

Buses to Phaestos from Iraklio also stop at Gortyna; see p171 for details.

PHAESTOS ΦΑΙΣΤΟΣ

The Minoan site of **Phaestos** (☎ 2892 042 315; admission €4/2, incl Agia Triada €6; ☉ 8am-7.30pm Jun-Oct, 8am-5pm Nov-Apr), 63km from Iraklio, was the second-most important palatial city in all of Minoan Crete. With amazing, all-embracing views of the Mesara Plain and Mt Psiloritis,

Phaestos (fes-*tos*), has the most awe-inspiring location of all the Minoan sites. The layout of the palace is similar to Knossos, with rooms arranged around a central court.

Pottery deposits indicate that the site was inhabited in the Neolithic era around 4000 BC, when the first settlers established themselves on the slopes of Kastri Hill. The first palace was built around 2000 BC and then destroyed by the earthquake that levelled many Minoan palaces. The ruins were covered with a layer of lime and debris, which formed the base of a new palace that was begun around 1700 BC. It, too, was destroyed in the catastrophe that befell the island in 1450 BC. In the intervening centuries Phaestos was the political and administrative centre of the Mesara Plain. Ancient texts refer to the palace's importance and note that it minted its own coins. Although Phaestos continued to be inhabited in later centuries, it fell into decline as Gortyna rose in importance. Under the Dorians, Phaestos headed a battling league of cities that included Matala and Polyrrinia in western Crete. Phaestos was defeated by Gortyna in the 2nd century BC.

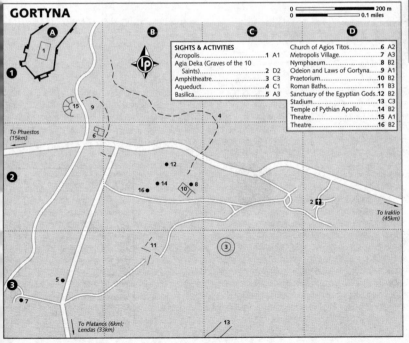

GORTYNA

0 ——— 200 m
0 ——— 0.1 miles

SIGHTS & ACTIVITIES

Acropolis..................................1 A1	Church of Agios Titos...............6 A2
Agia Deka (Graves of the 10	Metropolis Village.....................7 A3
Saints)..................................2 D2	Nymphaeum.............................8 B2
Amphitheatre..........................3 C3	Odeion and Laws of Gortyna......9 A1
Aqueduct.................................4 C1	Praetorium..............................10 B2
Basilica...................................5 A3	Roman Baths............................11 B3
	Sanctuary of the Egyptian Gods.12 B2
	Stadium..................................13 C3
	Temple of Pythian Apollo..........14 B2
	Theatre..................................15 A1
	Theatre..................................16 B2

To Phaestos (15km)

To Iraklio (45km)

To Platanos (6km); Lendas (33km)

IRAKLIO

IRAKLIO

Excavation of the site began in 1900 by Professor Federico Halbherr of the Italian School of Archaeology, which continues the excavation work. In contrast to Knossos, Phaestos has yielded few frescoes; it seems the palace walls were mostly covered with a layer of white gypsum. There has been no reconstruction of these ruins. The difficulty of visualising the structure of the palace is further compounded by the fact that the site includes remains of the Old Palace and the New Palace.

Exploring the Site

Past the ticket booth, the **Upper Court** that was used in both the Old and New Palaces contains the remains of buildings from the Hellenistic era. A stairway leads down to the **Theatral Area** that was once the staging ground for performances. The seats are at the northern end, and the southern end contains the **west façade of the Old Palace**. The 15m-wide **grand stairway** leads to the **Propylon**, which was a porch. Below the Propylon are the **storerooms** that still contain *pithoi* (storage urns). The square hall next to the storerooms is thought to have been an **office**, where tablets containing Linear A script were found beneath the floor in 1955. South of the storeroom a **corridor** led to the west side of the **Central Court**. South of the corridor is a **lustral basin**, rooms with benches and a **pillar crypt** similar to that at Knossos. The Central Court is the centrepiece of the palace, affording spectacular views of the surrounding area. It is extremely

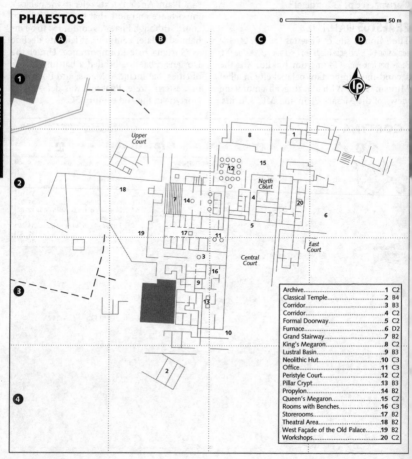

PHAESTOS

0 — 50 m

Archive	1 C2
Classical Temple	2 B4
Corridor	3 B3
Corridor	4 C2
Formal Doorway	5 C2
Furnace	6 D2
Grand Stairway	7 B2
King's Megaron	8 C2
Lustral Basin	9 B3
Neolithic Hut	10 C3
Office	11 C3
Peristyle Court	12 C2
Pillar Crypt	13 B3
Propylon	14 B2
Queen's Megaron	15 C2
Rooms with Benches	16 C3
Storerooms	17 B2
Theatral Area	18 B2
West Façade of the Old Palace	19 B2
Workshops	20 C2

well preserved and gives a good sense of the magnificence of the palace. Porticoes with columns and pillars once lined the long sides of the Central Court. Notice the **Neolithic hut** at the southwestern corner of the Central Court. The best-preserved parts of the palace complex are the reception rooms and private apartments to the north of the Central Court, where excavations continue. Enter through the **Formal Doorway** with half columns at either side, the lower parts of which are still in situ. The corridor leads to the north court; the **Peristyle Court**, which once had a paved veranda, is to the left of here. The royal apartments (**Queen's Megaron** and **King's Megaron**) are northeast of the Peristyle Court but they are currently fenced off. The celebrated Phaes-

tos Disk (above) was found in a building to the north of the palace. It now resides in the Archaeological Museum of Iraklio (p149).

Getting There & Away

Eight buses a day head to Phaestos from Iraklio (€5.70, 1½ hours), stopping at Gortyna. There are also buses from Agia Galini (€2.80, 45 minutes, five daily) and Matala (€1.60, 30 minutes, five daily).

AGIA TRIADA ΑΓΙΑ ΤΡΙΑΔΑ

The small Minoan site of **Agia Triada** (☎ 2892 091 564; admission €3, incl Phaestos €6; ☼ 10am-4.30pm summer, 8.30am-3pm winter) is 3km west of Phaestos in an enchanting landscape surrounded by hills and orange groves. Like the site of Phaestos,

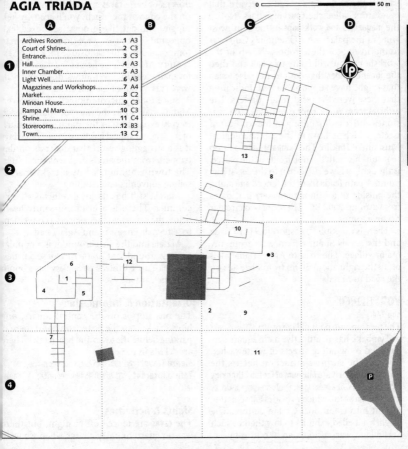

AGIA TRIADA

0 — 50 m

Archives Room	**1** A3
Court of Shrines	**2** C3
Entrance	**3** C3
Hall	**4** A3
Inner Chamber	**5** A3
Light Well	**6** A3
Magazines and Workshops	**7** A4
Market	**8** C2
Minoan House	**9** C3
Rampa Al Mare	**10** C3
Shrine	**11** C4
Storerooms	**12** B3
Town	**13** C2

IRAKLIO

it appears that Agia Triada has been occupied since the Neolithic era.

Masterpieces of Minoan art, such as the vases now in the Archaeological Museum of Iraklio (p149), were found here, but the palace was clearly not as important as the palace at Phaestos. Its principal building was smaller than the other royal palaces, but the fact that is was built to a similar design and the opulence of the objects found indicate that it was a royal residence, possibly a summer palace of Phaestos' rulers.

After the entrance, you will first pass the ruins of a **Minoan House** before reaching the **shrine** that dates from the early 14th century BC. It once contained a frescoed floor painted with octopuses and dolphins, which is now in the Archaeological Museum of Iraklio. Northwest of the shrine is a paved courtyard that excavators called the **Court of Shrines**. Notice the **magazines and workshops** in the southwest wing of the palace; the 'Chieftain's Cup' was found in one of these rooms. North of the workshops you will come to a **hall** and then the **inner chamber** that contains a raised slab that might have supported a bed, indicating that these were the residential quarters. The **archives room** once contained over 200 seal stones and a wall painting of the wild cat of Crete, which is now in the Archaeological Museum of Iraklio. The **Rampa al Mare**, a ramp that runs beneath the north side of the palace, is thought to have run down to the sea at one point. A path leads from the fenced site along the hillside to a Minoan **cemetery** that dates from around 2000 BC. There are two circular beehive tombs.

There is no public transport to Agia Triada and the site is about a 5km walk from any major village. The road to Agia Triada takes off to the right about 500m from Phaestos on the road to Matala.

VORI ΒΩΡΟΙ
pop 744
The pleasant unspoilt village of Vori, 4km east of Tymbaki, has an attractive main square surrounded by winding streets of whitewashed houses. The surprise attraction here is the outstanding private **Museum of Cretan Ethnology** (☎ 2892 091 112/0; admission €3; ☼ 10am-6pm Apr-Oct, by appointment in winter), which provides a fascinating insight into traditional Cretan culture. The English-labelled exhibits follow themes such as rural life, war, customs, architecture, music,

and the herbs, flora and fauna that form the basis of the Cretan diet. There some are some beautiful weavings, furniture, woodcarvings and musical instruments. The museum is well signposted from the main road.

There are a few tavernas around the lovely main square. Signposted about 400m up from the museum are the **Portokali Apartments** (☎ 2892 091 188; www.portokali.messara.de; studio €30 ⊠), four excellent good-value studios set in a garden with BBQ facilities and lots of homely touches. They have bikes for guests.

MATALA ΜΑΤΑΛΑ
pop 101
Matala (*ma*-ta-la), on the coast 11km southwest of Phaestos, was once one of Crete's best known hippie hang-outs. When you see the dozens of eerie **caves** speckling the rock slab on the edge of the beach, you'll see why '60s hippies found it, like, groovy (see boxed text opposite). The caves were originally Roman tombs cut out of the sandstone rock in the 1st century AD and have been used as dwellings for many centuries. Windows, doors and beds were carved out of the soft rock.

Since those halcyon hippy days, however, Matala has gone the way of many beach towns, expanding to the point where much of its original appeal has been lost. These days it is a struggling resort that depends on day trippers from the area's archaeological sites. The town is dominated by a tacky market selling souvenirs and clothing.

Matala still has its loyal returnees every summer. There is a beautiful sandy **beach** below the caves and the resort is a convenient base to visit Phaestos and Agia Triada.

Matala and the area around it is a popular nesting ground for *Caretta caretta* sea turtles. The Sea Turtle Protection Society has a booth near the car park.

Orientation & Information
The bus stop is on the central square, one block back from the waterfront, and there is parking before the town and beach (€2). There are ATMs in the village.
Monza Travel (☎ 28920 45757) Changes money.
Zafiria Internet (☎ 28920 45496; per hr €4; ☼ 8am-late)

Sights & Activities
The **caves** are fenced off at night, but there was no guard or entry charge when we were

there. For a less crowded beach, head to **Kokkini Ammos** (Red Beach). It's about a 30-minute scramble south over the rocks and attracts a smattering of nudists.

You can also take a beach or mountain ride in the area through **Melanouri Horse Farm** (☎ 2892 045 040; www.melanouri.com) in nearby Pitsidia.

Sleeping & Eating

The street running inland to the left of the main drag is lined with budget accommodation, which makes it easy to haggle for the best deal. Hotels are reasonably priced off-season.

Matala Community Camping (☎ /fax 2892 045 720; sites per person/tent €4.30/3) A reasonable, shaded, although rather uneven, site just back from the beach.

Fantastic Rooms to Rent (☎ 2892 045 362; fax 2892 045 292; s/d/tr €20/25/25, d & tr with kitchen €30; 🍴) Has been here since the hippie heydays, and has added a newer block at the back. The rooms are plain but comfortable, many with kitchenette, phone, kettle and fridge.

Pension Andonios (☎ 2892 045 123; fax 2892 045 690; d/tr €25/30) Run by the genial Antonis, this comfortable pension has attractively furnished rooms set around a lovely courtyard, many with kitchenette, and the top rooms have balconies.

Hotel Zafiria (☎ 2892 045 366; fax 2892 045 725; d incl breakfast €40; P 🍴 🛰) The sprawling Zafiria takes up a whole block on Matala's main street. There is a spacious lobby bar and the comfortable rooms have balconies, sea views and telephones, and there's a pool a beneath the cliffs.

Eating in Matala is hardly an experience in haute cuisine, and little to distinguish any of the tourist joints on the waterfront. Overlooking the beach, **Lions** (☎ 2892 045 108; specials €6-9) has been popular for many years and the food is better than average. It is also a good place for a drink as it gets lively in the evening.

Gianni's (☎ 2892 045 719; mains €5-7), towards the end of the main street, is a no-frills place that has good-value grills, including a mixed grill with salad and potatoes (€7).

Head out of town 1.2km to the **Mystical View** (☎ 6944 139 164) tavern with spectacular sunset views over Kommos beach.

Getting There & Away

There are five buses daily between Iraklio and Matala (€6.80, 2½ hours), and Matala and Phaestos (€1.60, 30 minutes).

AROUND MATALA

There are several other bases from which to explore this southern pocket of Iraklio, especially if you stay in an inland village.

Pitsidia, 5km northeast of Matala off the main road, is quiet during the day when most people are at the beach, but has a pleasant village ambience in the evenings. **Pension Aretoussa** (☎ 2892 045 555; www.pensionaretoussa.com; s/d/tr €27/33/45) on the main road has garden terrace out the front for breakfast. The rooms are clean, nicely decorated with paintings by the owner, Michalis, and nice touches like mosquito nets. The back rooms have access to a private garden making them ideal for families.

Apart from the great wood-oven pizzas, **Bodikos Rooms & Pizzeria** (☎ 2892 045 438; www.bodikos-matala.com; d €35) place has large comfortable studios and rooms upstairs, as well as some family accommodation nearby.

In town, the places to hang out in the evening are the friendly **Mike's** (☎ 28920 45007) and **Eva and Nikos** (☎ 2892 045 497), a popular taverna on the main square.

Buses to Matala stop on the main road. The village square is inland.

IRAKLIO

THE HIPPIE CONNECTION

Long before Mykonos was hip and Ios was hot, Matala was host to a colony of flower children and alternative lifestylers who, in the late 1960s and early 1970s, turned Matala into a modern troglodyte city.

Drawn by the lure of free cave accommodation, a gorgeous beach, a smattering of low-key, cheap tavernas, free love and copious pot, Matala's hippies came in droves and hung around – wearing little more than headbands and guitars. They moved ever higher up the cliff to avoid sporadic attempts by the local police to evict them. Singer Joni Mitchell was among the hippies who lived in the caves. In 'Carey' from her 1970's album *Blue* she sang: *but let's not talk about fare-thee-wells now, the night is a starry dome and they're playin' that scratchy rock and roll beneath the Matala moon.*

DETOUR: Towards the Agiofarango Gorge

There is something truly divine about this isolated southwest pocket of Iraklio, which combines a visit to a monastery, a picturesque and easy gorge walk and rewards you with a swim in an isolated cove.

About 7km from the turn-off for Sivas is **Moni Odigitrias** (☎ 2892 042 364; ⊙ 9am-8pm), a historic monastery with a preserved tower from which the monks fought off the Turks, Germans and the odd pirate. These days they'll let you climb up for superb views. The monastery was a base for many monks who lived as hermits in the surrounding caves and remote chapels. There is small museum with the original olive and wine presses, giant pots, a raki still and other agricultural tools. The Panagia church has some 15th-century frescos and icons.

A signposted track opposite the monastery marks the trail to the less-traversed **Agiofarango** (Holy gorge). From this point it is an hour walk to the start of the gorge. You can drive further along down a dirt road and leave the car at a point where it is only about 20 minutes to the gorge entrance, but it can be pretty rough. The picturesque gorge is bedecked with oleander and its steep rock face makes it a popular spot for climbers. There are caves and makeshift chapels and hermitages in the cliffs, and right in the gorge at the half way point is the Byzantine chapel of **Agios Antonios**. The gorge emerges at a lovely pebble cove and crystal-clear beach, which most of the time is only occupied by other walkers (and the occasional excursion boat).

On the way back, reward yourself with a stop at the **Kafeneio Xasou** (☎ 2892 042 804; mezedes €2.50-4; ⊙ Tue-Sat 4pm-11pm, Sun 10am-11pm) on the main road as you pass the village of Listaros. The owners moved here from Athens for a quiet life and are active environmentalists. Sylla is also a mean cook, experimenting with traditional recipes with superb results.

Further north from Pitsidia, about 2km inland from the main road is the pretty village of **Sivas**, which has a lively main square and many heritage-protected stone buildings.

our pick **Sigelakis** (☎ 28920 42748; mains €5-6; ⊙ dinner only) is a popular dinner option just off the square. Friendly owner Yiorgos is renowned for his traditional cooking and dishes such as the delicious goat in tomato sauce, the grilled mushrooms and a tasty eggplant slice with garlic and tomato. He has also built comfortable and attractive new **studios** (www .sigelakis-studios.gr; r €45-50) nearby.

KOMMOS ΚΟΜΜΟΣ

The archaeological site of Kommos, 12km southwest of Mires along a beautiful beach, is still being excavated by American and Canadian archaeologists. Although the site is fenced off it's easy to get an idea of it from the outside. Kommos is believed to have been the port for Phaestos and contains a wealth of Minoan structures. It's even possible to spot the layout of the ancient town, with its streets and courtyards, and the remains of workshops, dwellings and temples. Notice the Minoan road paved in limestone that leads from the southern section inland towards Phaestos; the ruts in the road from Minoan carts and a sewer on its northern side are still visible.

Kommos is about 3km north of Matala and makes for a pleasant walk.

KAMILARI ΚΑΜΗΛΑΡΙ

pop 263

Built on three hills, Kamilari is a traditional village with impossible narrow streets winding through the centre of town. It's no secret, but it has not yet been adversely affected by tourism. Most of the accommodation is on the outskirts of town and locals generally outnumber visitors. Its proximity to Kalamaki Beach and central location make it a good base to explore the south-coast beaches and archaeological sites.

In the middle of fields about 3km from the village is an important and extraordinarily well-preserved circular **Minoan tomb** with stone walls still standing two metres high. Clay models depicting the funerary rituals unearthed by excavators are in the Archaeological Museum of Iraklio (p149). The road to the tomb is signposted at the entrance to Kamilari. It is a good half-hour walk.

Sleeping & Eating

Apartments Ambeliotissa (☎ /fax 2892 042 690; www .ambeliotissa.com; studio €25-50; ⊠ ⊜) This family-friendly place has pleasant furnished studios and apartments with balconies overlooking the garden and kitchen facilities. There's an outdoor BBQ and playground and they have bikes for guests. They also run Studios Pelekanos nearby.

Plaka Apartments (☎ 2892 042 697; www.plakakreta .com; d €30-35; ✖) These lovely well-appointed apartments on a hill just outside the village have balconies with sea views and are decorated in cool blue and white shades. There is a garden with sun lounges in the back. Ask at Taverna Mylonas.

Asterousia Apartments (☎ 28920 42832; www .asterousia.com; studio €35-50) The hammock out the front, a scattering of antiques and brightly painted open-plan rooms give this place a great ambience. There's a big old table on the veranda and a nice garden, making it a good base for longer stays and families.

Taverna Mylonas (☎ 2892 042 156; mains €5.50-6.50) This place has good home-cooked Cretan food in the centre of the village, and they have also added some Italian and Chinese-style dishes. There are great views of the surrounding mountains from the tables on the terrace.

Kentriko (☎ 2892 042 191; mains €5.50-6.50) In a restored stone *kafeneio* on the narrow main drag, this place is run by the friendly Greek-Australian Irini, who has black- and- white photos of village families on the walls. It also has internet access.

Getting There & Away
There is one bus daily from Iraklio's Bus Station B via Mires (€6, 1½ hours).

KALAMAKI ΚΑΛΑΜΆΚΙ
pop 71
The wide, sandy beach that stretches for many kilometres in either direction is Kalamaki's best feature and makes for a pleasant walk. Located 2.5km southwest of Kamilari, tourism here is in its embryonic stage. It's a quiet place to stay and the swimming is good.

There is one main road leading into the village square, which is right behind the beach. **Monza Travel** (☎ /fax 28920 45692; ✖ 9am-2pm & 5-10pm) handles car and bike rentals, hotel reservations, air and boat tickets, and excursions around Crete.

Sleeping & Eating
Kostas (☎ /fax 28920 45692; www.kreta-kalamaki.com; d €25-70; ✖) These rooms above Monza Travel have fridges, TV and coffee-making equipment, and enjoy a communal roof garden that

is great at night. Rooms of different sizes and configurations sleep up to six.

Pension Galini (☎ 2892 045 042; www.kreta-kalamaki .com; r & apt €30-60; ✖) About 30m away from the beach, this attractive complex has spacious rooms and apartments sleeping up to six, with balconies, fully equipped kitchens satellite TV and internet connectivity. There's also a rooftop terrace with sea views.

Yiannis (☎ 2892 045 685; mixed mezedes spread €7-9) It's easy to miss this tiny place, behind the hotels that blocked the sea views. But Yiannis retains a loyal following for his excellent no-nonsense mezedes at reasonable prices – he usually makes about 18 types of mezedes (€1.80 to €2.50), including lots of vegetarian dishes, and there's always a complimentary glass of raki.

Delfinia (☎ 2829 045 697; fish per kg €30-45) This fish taverna at the northern end of the beach is one of the most highly regarded in the area. They also do a great range of mezedes.

Getting There & Away
There is one bus daily from Iraklio's Bus Station B via Mires (€6.80, two hours).

KAPETANIANA ΚΑΠΕΤΑΝΙΑΝΑ
pop 98
There are two main reasons to take the journey through the Mesara plain and make the winding steep ascent to the remote mountain hamlet of Kapetaniana – climbing and walking. Perched on the lower slows of Mt Kofinas (1231m), about 60km from Iraklio, Kapetaniana (from the word 'captain') was where the Cretan rebel leaders lived and where, much later, some hippies from Matala came hiding from the police. Today this wild and picturesque spot is popular territory for serious walkers and nature lovers. Mt Kofinas is also the most popular climbing destination in Crete (see p74). The village is divided into an upper and lower village.

In Ano (upper) Kapetaniana, the delightful guesthouse **Pension Kofinas** (☎ 28930 41440; www .korifi.de; s/d €20/25) is operated by Austrian ex-hippies Gunnar and Louisa, who moved there in the '80s when there was no sealed road (it was finished in 2005). They run guided walks and organise hiking tours. They have only four rooms, one with dorm bunks, which all share an external toilet. Bookings are essential. Gourmet chef Gunnar rustles up a scrumptious dinner for guests (€12-15 including

IRAKLIO

wine) on the terrace, which has superb views of Kofinas and out to sea.

In Kato Kapetaniana, about 15 houses were being restored and turned into rural retreats.

LENDAS ΛΕΝΤΑΣ
pop 78

The major appeal of the small beach settlement at Lendas is its remoteness and laid-back feel. Reached via a long and winding road with a dramatic last few kilometres descending to the village, Lendas clings to the cliff over the beach and has a pleasant view over the Libyan Sea. The narrow pebbly beaches are pleasant enough, but there are some better beaches to explore nearby and some stunning rock formations. Lendas attracts mostly independent travellers, including regulars who have been coming for 20 years. It retains an appealing intimacy, plus a peacefulness that comes from not having any passing traffic. There is a lively beach scene, with a couple of beach bars.

Within walking distance there is an archaeological site and the **Diskos** (or Dytikos) naturist beach where old hippies from Matala camp on the beach.

Orientation & Information

As you enter the village, a left fork takes you to the eastern car park, while the right fork goes to the main 'square'. The bus stops outside the eastern car park. Lendas has only a couple of mini-markets for essential supplies and an **Internet café** (☎ 2829 095 206; per hr €3) on the main square. Make sure you have plenty of petrol as you are a long way from the nearest supply.

To get to Dytikos beach follow the main road west for 1km or the path alongside the coastal cliffs.

Sights

The archaeological site of **Lebena** is right outside the village. Lebena was a health spa that the Romans visited for its therapeutic springs. Only two granite columns remain of a temple that dates from the 4th century BC. Next to the temple was a treasury with a mosaic floor that is still visible. Very little else is decipherable and the springs have been closed since the 1960s.

Sleeping & Eating

Bungalows Lendas (☎ 28920 95221; s/d €22/25-40; ☒) This quiet complex west of the main square has great sea views from the balconies. The rooms are simple but clean, with basic bathrooms and a fridge. There's a central communal kitchen. The gruff family matriarch runs the Elpida taverna on the beach and is well knows for her traditional cooking.

Studios Gaitani (☎ 2892 0953 41; www.studios-gaitani.gr; studio €30-50; ☒) It doesn't get more beachfront than this. These modern studios are a few steps down to the sand. They have kitchenettes, TV and fridge, and the larger ones can fit up to four.

our pick El Greco (☎ 2892 095 322; www.lentas-el greco.com; specials €4.50-9) This friendly taverna run by three brothers has an excellent selection of *mayirefta* and traditional Greek and international dishes in a garden setting overlooking the sea. There are decent sea-view rooms with air-con behind the taverna and spacious studios across the road (€30 to €40).

Also recommended is the **Akti** (☎ 2892 095 206; mains €6-10) taverna next door, for good quality food and a decent selection of wines.

Across the way in Dytikos (see left), **Villa Tsapakis** (☎ 2892 095 378; www.villa-tsapakis.com; d/studio €25/30-35; ☒) is a friendly hotel with well-appointed, good-value rooms around central courtyard.

Getting There & Away

There's a daily bus from Iraklio (€7.10, 2½ hours).

KASTRI & KERATOKAMBOS
ΚΑΣΤΡΙ & ΚΕΡΑΤΟΚΑΜΠΟΣ
pop 316

At the twin mini-resorts and now contiguous villages of Kastri and Keratokambos, 13km downhill, there's a pleasant tree-lined beach and a number of eating and sleeping choices. The tranquillity of this tiny resort is its chief asset. Many Germans have moved in and bought property here. If you like peace and quiet and have a few books to read, this is your kind of place. There are no facilities other than a mini-market.

Sleeping & Eating

Filoxenia Apartments (☎ /fax 2895 051 371; studio €25-30; ☒) These lovely two- to- three-person studios, wrapped in a flower-filled garden, are equipped with kitchenette, fridge and TV, and make for a very pleasant base. They are right across from the beach.

Komis Studios (☎ 2895 051 390; www.komisstudios.gr; Keratokambos; apt incl breakfast €60-75; ☒) These classy upmarket apartments are attractively decorated in rustic style, with iron beds and old TVs and movie posters on the walls. They are well out-fitted with telephone, TV, hairdryers and can accommodate two to four people.

The tavernas along the beach generally offer very good value. **Taverna Nikitas** (☎ 2895 051 477; mains €4-6) offers consistently high-quality and delicious grills. The goat in red sauce is highly recommended, as is the local swordfish. **Taverna Livyko** (☎ 2895 051 290; grills €5.50-7) makes tasty grills from its own meat, along with fresh fish and Cretan specials such as boiled goat and lamb with artichokes. The setting is delightful. Also recommended is the cheery Morning Star Taverna decked out in classic blue and white.

Getting There & Away
There is no public transport available to Kastri and Keratokambos.

NORTHEASTERN COAST

Ever since the national road along the northern coast opened in 1972, the coast between Iraklio and Malia has seen a frenzy of unbridled development, particularly in the seaside towns of Hersonisos and Malia. There's not much here for individual travellers since the hotels deal almost exclusively with package-tour operators who block-book hotel rooms months in advance.

The village of Koutouloufari, above Herso-nissos, is the most appealing place to stay in this area. The Minoan palace at Malia is the only significant site of cultural interest, and there is an important aquarium in Gournes. Amid the low-brow establishments, there are several high-end resorts and Crete's only world-class 18-hole golf course.

HERSONISOS & MALIA
ΧΕΡΣΟΝΗΣΟΣ/ΜΑΛΙΑ
The northern resorts of Hersonisos and Malia have seen better days. Hersonissos, 27km east of Iraklio, began its days as a small fishing village on a hill, but these days the resort that grew along the long sandy beach is a brash, expansive mecca of cheap package tourism, with a long coastal strip of neon-lit restaurants and look-alike hotels. While there are a few big and high-end resort hotels in the area, the towns themselves holds little appeal. Admit-tedly, Hersonissos has the liveliest nightlife on the island, which is fine if you want to party all night and crash on a crowded beach (or stay cocooned in a resort). Or is this author just a snobbish killjoy?

Malia, about 7km east, is Crete's 'wildest' party resort and has become even more notorious (and irredeemable) since they cracked down on the hooligan element in Faliraki (Rhodes), bringing the worst elements of young British holidaymakers to Crete. Crowded and noisy, Malia is full of pubs, bars, tacky eateries, and sunburnt topless Brits hooning around on quad bikes, making it seem like one big fun park (or nightmare). The scale of overdevelopment is confronting to the senses. Many hotels only deal with tour operators, but the travel agents in town can usually recommend places they have deals with.

The only noteworthy attraction in the area is the excellent **Lychnostatis Museum** (☎ 2897 023 660; www.lychnostatis.gr; admission €4.50; ⏰ 9.30am-2pm Sun-Fri). Instead of selling out or building a hotel on the family land right next to the beach, the Markakis family have commendably created this unique open-air museum dedicated to Cretan rural life. There are displays about all aspects of traditional rural life from weaving to raki-making, a Cretan herb garden, as well as a small *kafeneio*. Instead of inscriptions there are clever *mandinades* (traditional rhyming songs), including the verses painted on the walls of the mill dedicated to the owner's wife.

On the other side of the highway about 7km south of Hersonisos is the 18-hole **Crete Golf Club** (☎ 2897 026 000; www.crete-golf.gr; 18 holes €67). It's a tough desert-style course on the hills that's definitely not for hackers. It's cheaper to play at twilight (€42).

There are buses to Hersonisos and Malia from Iraklio every 30 minutes (€3.50, 45 minutes).

KOUTOULOUFARI ΚΟΥΤΟΥΛΟΥΦΑΡΗ
pop 538
Uphill from the madness, past the old villages of Hersonisos and Piskopiniana, is the more appealing village of Koutouloufari, which although touristy retains some semblance of charm. The main road is closed off at night, creating a festive atmosphere. It's a safe distance from the sprawling resort town below but close enough to check it out.

IRAKLIO

Sleeping & Eating

Villa Iokasti (☎ 2897 022 607; www.iokasti.gr; apt €70–80; ❌ 🏊) One- and two-bedroom apartments in an attractive garden setting off the main drag towards the end of the village. It has a well-regarded taverna and café with pleasant sea views.

Elen Mari Apartments (☎ 2897 025 525; Koutouloufari; apt €40; ❌) The fully equipped studios are neat and well maintained and some have excellent views over Hersonisos.

Emmanuel Taverna (☎ 2897 021 022; Plateia Eleftheriou Venizelou, specials €10) Managed by a Greek-Australian family, this homely taverna specialises in spit-roasted meats and dishes cooked in the wood oven out the front. The owner

recommends their specialty lamb in rose wine with bay leaves, or anything from the spit or oven, which are fired up every night.

Fabrica (☎ 2897 023 981; crepes €2.50–7.50) In the evening, head to this café-bar with a great rooftop terrace with views below to Hersonisos. It's in an old stone building to the right past Sergiani. Take the turn off to the right as soon as you get off the Hersonisos turn-off.

PALACE OF MALIA ΑΝΑΚΤΟΡΑ ΜΑΛΙΩΝ

The **Palace of Malia** (☎ 2897 031 597; admission €4; ☿ 8.30am-3pm Tue-Sun), 3km east of Malia, was built at about the same time as the two other great Minoan palaces at Phaestos and Knos-

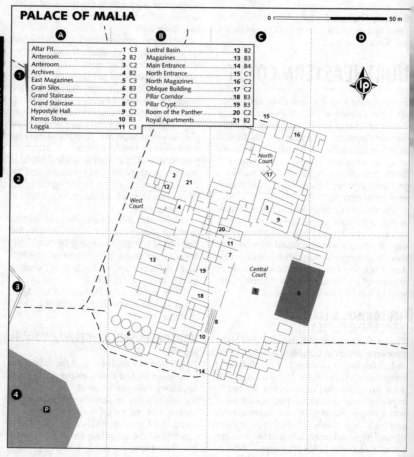

PALACE OF MALIA

0 -------- 50 m

Altar Pit...................................1 C3	Lustral Basin.............................12 B2	
Anteroom.................................2 B2	Magazines................................13 B3	
Anteroom.................................3 C2	Main Entrance..........................14 B4	
Archives...................................4 B2	North Entrance.........................15 C1	
East Magazines.........................5 C3	North Magazines.......................16 C2	
Grain Silos...............................6 B3	Oblique Building.......................17 C2	
Grand Staircase.........................7 C3	Pillar Corridor...........................18 B3	
Grand Staircase.........................8 C3	Pillar Crypt...............................19 B3	
Hypostyle Hall...........................9 C2	Room of the Panther..................20 C2	
Kernos Stone...........................10 B3	Royal Apartments......................21 B2	
Loggia....................................11 C3		

MASS TOURISM

While some people clearly enjoy the scene at Hersonisos and Malia, most travellers wanting to see Crete will have the same first instinct as they approach the resorts – get out fast. The local population itself has retreated to the villages up the hill behind the main road and left the lower beachfront area to wallow in sleazy commercialism. Everything is designed for tourist consumption and mostly aimed at young party animals.

Both resorts chase bargain-hunting package tourists but Hersonisos has a few luxury hotels on the outskirts. The crowds are generally young in both towns, but in Malia you'll feel decrepit if you're over 22. Consuming copious quantities of alcohol is the main game. In Hersonisos you drink to get drunk, dance and wake up with a stranger, while at Malia you drink to get drunk, fall down and wake up on the pavement. If that sounds good to you, you know where to go. But try to visit Crete one day.

---

sos. The first palace was built here around 1900 BC and rebuilt after the earthquake of 1700 BC. What you see is the remains of the newer palace where many exquisite artefacts from Minoan society were found. Excavation began in 1915 by Greek archaeologists and is being continued by French archaeologists. Because the ground plan has been well preserved, it is an easy site to comprehend. The exhibition hall has reconstructions of the site and interesting photos, including aerial shots. There is a shady spot to rest and take in the site and a café. The beach nearby (about 300m on the right) is one of the best swimming spots in the area.

Exploring the Site

Access to the ruins is from the **West Court**. Head south through the **Magazines** and at the extreme southern end you'll come to the eight circular pits which archaeologists think were **grain silos**. To the east of the pits is the main entrance to the palace, which leads to the southern end of the **Central Court**. Moving northeast you'll come to the **Kernos Stone**, a disk with 24 holes around its edge. Archaeologists have yet to ascertain its function, but it probably had a religious purpose. Adjacent

to this is the **Grand Staircase**, which might have led to a shrine. To the north is the **Pillar Corridor** with interconnecting rooms and next to it is the **Pillar Crypt** with the Minoan double-axe symbol engraved up on the pillars. The impressive **Central Court** is 48m long and 22m wide and contains remains of the Minoan columns. Notice the covered altar pit in the centre of the courtyard.

At the northern end of the western side of the court is the **Loggia**, which was probably used for ceremonial purposes. Next to the Loggia is the **Room of the Panther** in which a 17th-century-BC stone axe shaped like a panther was found. Northwest are the **Royal Apartments** with a **Lustral Basin**. At the north end of the central court is the **Hypostyle Hall**, with benches on the side indicating that it may have served as a kind of council chamber. Other rooms include the **archives room** in which tablets containing Linear A script were found. The covered area off the central court are the **East Magazines**. On your way out through the north entrance take note of the giant *pithoi* in the **North Court**.

Any bus going to or from Iraklio along the north coast can drop you at the site.

IRAKLIO

Lasithi Λασιθι

Crete's easternmost prefecture may receive far fewer visitors than the rest of the island, but the exclusive resorts around Elounda and Agios Nikolaos are the stronghold of Crete's high-end tourism. Elounda has become synonymous with luxury hotels – among them one of the world's top resorts – while the capital, Agios Nikolaos, is the region's contribution to the party scene.

The rest of the prefecture, however, is largely refreshingly undeveloped compared with the rest of Crete, mostly due to the isolated locations, winding access roads and lack of international charter flights.

At the far eastern end of the north coast is the pleasant town of Sitia, the centre of the region's olive oil industry. The famous palm-lined beach of Vai is in the far east, near one of the island's historic monasteries.

The fertile region of the Lasithi Plateau provides excellent cycling opportunities through quiet rural villages to the Dikteon Cave, where legend has it that Zeus was born and hidden from his murderous father. The hinterland has many traditional villages, and lonely plateaus and mountain ranges to explore.

The southern coast extends from the seaside village of Myrtos in the west to the commercial centre of Ierapetra, and beyond to the rugged coast and largely untouched beaches of Xerokambos.

In the far east, Zakros combines some of the best experiences of Crete – a walk through a beautiful gorge to the evocative ruins of a Minoan Palace, just 200m from an underpopulated beach with a few good tavernas.

Lasithi has its share of sleepy fishing villages, such as Mohlos in the north and Plaka to the east, and Spinalonga Island continues to intrigue visitors.

HIGHLIGHTS

- Cycling around the **Lasithi Plateau** (p191)
- Wandering among the fascinating ruins on **Spinalonga Island** (p190)
- Exploring the Minoan palace near the beach at **Kato Zakros** (p199)
- Relaxing on **Vai** (p197), Crete's only palm-lined beach
- Visiting the **Moni Toplou** (monastery) (p196)

NORTH COAST

AGIOS NIKOLAOS ΑΓΙΟΣ ΝΙΚΟΛΑΟΣ

pop 11,286

Lasithi's capital, Agios Nikolaos (*ah-yee-os nih-ko*-laos) may lack the historic character of Crete's other major towns but its natural advantage is a striking position on a hill overlooking Mirabello Bay, with a small picturesque lake connected to the sea and a pleasant harbour.

In the early 1960s the former fishing village became a chic hideaway for the jet set and the likes of Jules Dassin and Walt Disney, but by the end of the decade package tourists were arriving in force and it became an overdeveloped tourist town.

After a slump in recent years, 'Agios' appears to have bounced back and found a different rhythm. It's become a town for locals as much as tourists. It still draws people from the resorts that stretch all the way to Elounda, especially at night, when the cafés and restaurants around the lake and port light up and the ambience turns more vibrant and cosmopolitan. While it's not the party town it once was, it has a lively nightlife. Agios Nikolaos remains the epicentre of Crete's luxury resort industry, but also attracts a mixed and relatively subdued older crowd and families.

While there is superficially little to attract the independent traveller, there is reasonable accommodation, prices are not too horrendous and there are enough activities to cater for all tastes.

It was the first town in Crete to install free wi-fi in the harbour area and the centre of town.

History

Agios Nikolaos emerged as a port for the city-state of Lato (p187) in the early Hellenic years, when it was known as Lato-by-Kamara. The harbour assumed importance in the Greco-Roman period after the Romans put an end to the piracy that had plagued the northern coast.

The town continued to flourish in the early Christian years and, in the 8th or 9th century, the small Byzantine Church of Agio Nikolaos was built.

When the Venetians bought Crete in the 13th century, the Castel Mirabello was built on a hill overlooking the sea and a settlement arose below. The castle was damaged in the earthquake of 1303 and was burned by pirates in 1537, before being rebuilt according to plans by the military architect Sammicheli. When the Venetians were forced to abandon the castle to the Turks in 1645 they blew it up, leaving it in ruins. There's no trace of the Venetian occupation now except the name they gave to the surrounding gulf – Mirabello ('beautiful view').

The town was resettled in the mid-19th century by fleeing rebels from Sfakia and was later named capital of the Lasithi region.

Orientation

The **bus station** (☎ 28410 22234) has been rather inconveniently relocated to the northwestern side of town, about 800m from central Plateia Venizelou. The de-facto town centre is around Voulismeni Lake. Most banks, travel agencies and shops are on Koundourou and parallel pedestrian street 28 Oktovriou. The main roads have a one-way traffic system, so if you are driving follow the signs to the port area or one of the car parks near the harbour.

Information

Anna Karteri Bookshop (☎ 28410 22272; Koundourou 5) Well stocked with maps, guide books and literature in English and other languages.

General Hospital (☎ 28410 66000; Knossou 3) On the west side of town.

Municipal Tourist Office (☎ 28410 22357; www .agiosnikolaos.gr; ☽ 8am-9.30pm Apr-Nov) Right by the bridge; has helpful information and maps, changes money and assists with accommodation.

National Bank of Greece (Nikolaou Plastira) Has a 24-hour exchange machine.

Peripou Café (☎ 28410 24876; 28 Oktovriou 13; per hr €4; ☽ 9am-2am) Has computers and wi-fi.

PK's Internet (☎ 28410 28004; Akti Koundourou 1; per hr €2; ☽ 9am-2am) Has a full printing, burning, Skype (phone calls via internet) and video-cams set-up.

Post Office (☎ 28410 22062; 28 Oktovriou 9; ☽ 7.30am-2pm Mon-Fri)

Tourist Police (☎ 28410 91408; Erythrou Stavrou 47; ☽ 7.30am-2.30pm Mon-Fri)

Sights

It is worth the hike up to the **Archaeological Museum** (☎ 28410 24943; Paleologou Konstantinou 74; admission €4; ☽ 8.30am-3pm Tue-Sun; ☖), which has

LASITHI REGION

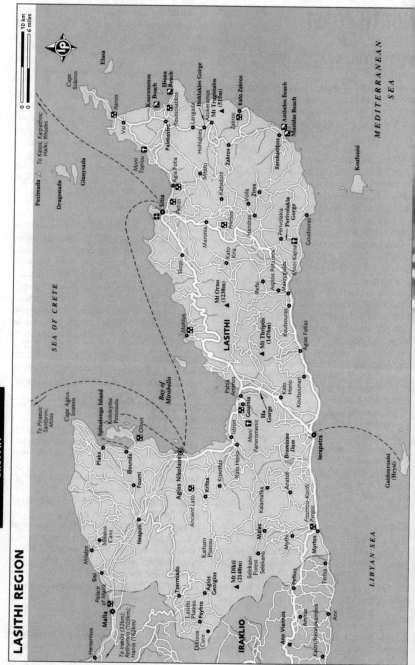

an extensive and well-displayed collection from eastern Crete. While it has no major showpiece, it is probably the second most significant Minoan collection and includes clay coffins, ceramic musical instruments and gold from the island of Mohlos. The chronological exhibits begin with Neolithic finds from Mt Tragistalos, north of Kato Zakros, and early Minoan finds from Agia Fotia, then finds from Malia and Mohlos. The highlight is the odd-looking *Goddess of Myrtos*, a clay jug from 2500 BC found near Myrtos. Another stand-out Minoan item is a stone ritual vessel in the shape of a shell, found in a late Minoan shrine at Malia, which features two Minoan demons and a goddess. Noteworthy exhibits from the Hellenistic and Roman periods include an athlete's skull, with gold wreath and a coin in his mouth for safe passage to the underworld, and a winged Eros figurine.

The **folk museum** (☎ 28410 25093; Paleologou Konstantinou 4; admission €3; ☽ 10am-2pm Tue-Sun), next to the tourist office, has a small, well-displayed collection of traditional handicrafts and costumes.

The compact **Iris Museum** (☎ 28410 25899; 28 Oktovriou 21-23; admission €2; ☽ 9am-9pm Mon-Fri) has displays of dried herbs and the flora of Crete, and also sells local essential oils.

Activities

The town beaches of **Ammos** and **Kytroplatia Beach** are smallish and can get rather crowded. The sandy beach at **Almyros**, about 1km south of town, is the best of the lot and tends to be quieter. It can be reached on foot via a coastal path starting at the end of the road just past the stadium. There's not much shade but you can hire umbrellas. **Ammoudara Beach**, 3km from town, is a little better and supports a fairly busy restaurant and accommodation scene.

You can venture further towards Sitia to the pleasant coves with long stretches of sandy beach and turquoise waters at the signposted **Golden Beach** (Voulisma Beach) and around **Istron Bay**.

The wooden sailboat **M/S Manolis** (☎ 6974 143 150) runs fishing trips that include a barbecue and swim at Kolokytha island, as well as private charters.

Sailing trips and private charters around the Mirabello gulf are run by **Zaharias** (☎ 69373 74954; www.sailcrete.com).

There is a **children's playground**, **swimming pool** and **mini golf** at the municipal beach on the south side of Agios Nikolaos.

Three diving centres offer boat dives and PADI-certification courses.

Creta Underwater Centre (☎ 28410 22406; www .cretaunderwatercenter.com) In the Mirabello Hotel.

Happy Divers (☎ 28410 82546; www.cretashappydiv ers.gr) In front of the Coral Hotel.

Pelagos (☎ 28410 24376; www.divecrete.com) In the Minos Beach Art Hotel.

Tours

Travel agencies offer bus tours to Crete's top attractions and the boats along the harbour advertise their various excursions. Boat trips to Spinalonga (€17) include a swim at Kolokytha.

Minotours Hellas (☎ 28410 23222; www.minotours .gr; 28 Oktovriou 6) organises guided coach tours of Phaestos, Gortys and Matala (€33), the Samaria Gorge (€45), the Lasithi Plateau (€34), Knossos (€30) and other destinations.

Festivals & Events

In July and August Agios Nikolaos hosts the **Lato Cultural Festival**, with concerts by local and international musicians, folk dancing, *mandinades* (rhyming couplets) contests, theatre and art exhibitions. Ask at the tourist office for details. **Marine Week**, during the last week of June in even-numbered years, has swimming, windsurfing and boat races.

Sleeping
BUDGET & MIDRANGE

Pension Mary (☎ 28410 23760; Evans 13; s/d/tr €15/25/30; ⊠) This is one of those friendly places where the owner lives downstairs and bonus homemade sweets are almost guaranteed. The rooms are basic but clean and most have private bathrooms, fridges, balconies with some sea views and access to a communal kitchen. The top room is cramped but has a private terrace with barbecue. Breakfast is €5.

Pergola Hotel (☎ /fax 28410 28152; Sarolidi 20; d with view €20-40; ⊠) This family-run hotel has a homy feel. Rooms are comfortable and all have fridges, TV and air-con. There is a pleasant veranda under a pergola to relax or have breakfast. Front rooms have balconies and sea views. The owners can pick you up from the bus station.

Mylos Pension (☎ 28410 23783; Sarolidi 24; d €40; ⊠) From the fake flowers on the bed to the family photos and icons on the walls, this quaint *pension* is an extension of the friendly elderly owner's home. The front rooms have sensational views (try for room 2) and all have a fridge and TV. The sprightly Georgia swears by the hard mattresses.

Hotel Doxa (☎ 28410 24214; www.doxahotel.gr; Idomeneos 7; s/d incl breakfast €55/65; ✕) The plant-filled lobby sets a homy tone for this hotel, which has an attractive terrace for breakfast or drinks. Pleasant and clean rooms are equipped with fridges, hairdryers and satellite TVs and some have views. It's close to the marina and Ammos beach.

Lato Hotel (☎ 28410 24581; www.lato-hotel.gr; Amoudi s/d €46/59; ✕ 🖳 🖵) If you have your own wheels, this friendly hotel at Ammoudi beach is a good option. There's a small pool and it's a 15-minute walk into town along the waterfront. The same management runs the charming Karavostasi studios in a stone carob warehouse on an isolated cove about 8km east.

our pick Du Lac Hotel (☎ 28410 22711; www.dula chotel.gr; 28 Oktovriou 17; s/d/studio €40/60/80; ✕) This refurbished hotel on the lake has standard rooms and spacious fully fitted-out studios. Both have stylish contemporary furnishings and nice bathrooms. It's in a great central location, with lovely views over the lake.

TOP END

Palazzo (☎ 28410 25080; www.palazzo-apartments.gr; apt €90-110; ✕ 🖵) Opposite Kytroplatia Beach, these classy apartments sleeping up to four are the closest thing to a boutique hotel in town. The 10 charming, individually decorated apartments have mosaic-tiled floors, marble bathrooms and lovely balconies with views (in the front rooms). There's free email downstairs.

Minos Beach Art Hotel (☎ 28410 22345; www.bluegr .com; r from €180; ✕ 🖵) This classy resort in a superb location just out of town is a veritable art gallery, with sculptures from leading Greek and foreign artists adorning the grounds right down to the beach. Crete's first luxury resort continues to reinvent itself, but its low-rise design and understated style maintains its position as one of the island's best hotels. The sign on the hotel says Minos Beach Hotel.

Eating

The well-positioned lakeside restaurants tend to push inevitably bland and often overpriced tourist 'Greek' food. Hit the back streets or head further afield for the genuine article.

BUDGET & MIDRANGE

our pick Taverna Itanos (☎ 28410 25340; Kyprou 1; mains €4-9) This friendly taverna with beamed ceilings and stucco walls is popular with locals wanting traditional home-style Cretan cooking. You can pick from the trays of excellent *mayirefta* (casseroles and oven-baked dishes) out the back, such as goat with artichokes or lamb fricassee.

Sarri's (☎ 28410 28059; Kyprou 15; mains €6-8) Tucked away in the back streets, Sarri's is a good spot for breakfast, lunch or dinner on the shady garden terrace. Check the daily specials board.

Aouas Taverna (☎ 28410 23231; Paleologou Konstantinou 44; mezedes €5.20-9.60) This family-run place on the road to the museum has a range of Cretan specialities such as herb pies and pickled bulbs, as well as tasty grills. The interior is plain but the garden courtyard is refreshing and the mezedes are good.

Pamtomaca (☎ 28410 82394; Paleologou 52; 7pm-midnight) This colourful Catalano-Mediterranean combo is another good budget option.

our pick Gargadoros (☎ 28410 22599; Gargodoros Beach; mains €6-14) This stylish restaurant opposite a relatively quiet beach on the way to Almyros is a recent and promising addition to Agios Nikolaos' dining scene. It's light and cheery with colourful chairs and tables and a relaxed feel. The food is well executed, with modern takes on traditional dishes and emphasis on Greek and Mediterranean flavours. It's a longish walk from town along the beach front (there's a path).

Barko (☎ 28410 24610; Kytroplatia Beach; mains €8.50-13.80) This place has gone upmarket since moving to flashier premises opposite the beach. There are still excellent Cretan-style dishes but the menu includes more creative Mediterranean-style cuisine such as a light risotto with pumpkin and *anthotyro* (a soft whey cheese). There's a decent wine list, too.

TOP END

Migomis (☎ 28410 24353; Nikolaou Plastira 20; mains €14-20) Overlooking Voulismeni Lake from up high, Migomis is one of the classic and pricier lakeside eating places. The cuisine is Greek/international and the views and ambience are impressive, complete with the baby grand

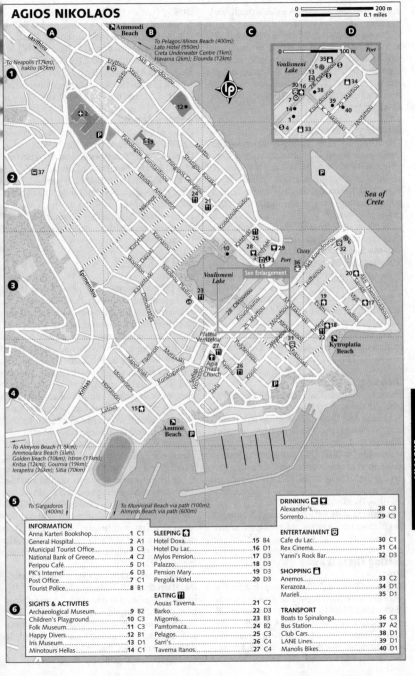

AGIOS NIKOLAOS

LASITHI

piano. The fancy menu includes ostrich, and has Asian influences..

Pelagos (☎ 28410 25737; Katehaki 10; appetisers €4-8.50) For an excellent selection of fresh fish and seafood, this place is generally considered the best (and priciest) restaurant in Agios Nikolaos. The mezedes are excellent. It's in a beautifully restored house with an ambient garden.

Drinking & Entertainment

The waterfront cafés lining Akti Koundourou come alive from late afternoon and later morph into lively bars. The dance clubs are in 'little Soho' on 25 Martiou. Yanni's Rock Bar (Akti Koundourou 3) is a classic and popular haunt where not even the décor has changed in years.

Tourists tend to congregate on the opposite side of the port, particularly the popular **Sorrento** bar and around the corner at the flashing lights of **Alexanders**, which has added more recent tunes to their '60s to '80s selection.

For eclectic listening and soothing views over Voulismeni Lake try **Café du Lac** (☎ 28410 26837; 28 Oktovriou 17).

Rex Cinema (☎ 28410 83681; M Sfakianaki 35) screens the latest releases, as well as art-house movies on Thursdays.

Shopping

There are shops selling all the basics and souvenirs in town.

Anemos (☎ 28410 23528; Koundourou 12) Has unique pieces by jewellers from around Greece.

Kerazoza (☎ 28410 22562; Koundourou 42) Handmade masks, marionettes and figurines derived from ancient Greek theatre, along with some good-quality sculptures, ceramics and jewellery by local artisans.

Marieli (☎ 28410 28813; 28 Octovriou 33) A cute little gift store with a range of Greek handicrafts and jewellery.

Getting There & Away

BOAT

LANE Lines (☎ 28410 89150; www.lane.gr) has ferries twice per week from Agios Nikolaos to Piraeus (deck/cabin €34/€46, 14 hours), via Santorini (€20.20, five hours) and Milos (€20.60, nine hours). There is also a service from Piraeus via Milos to Agios Nikolaos, Sitia, Kasos, Karpathos, Halki and Rhodes.

BUS

Buses leave from Agios Nikolaos' **bus station** (☎ 28410 22234; www.crete-buses.gr) for Elounda (€1.30, 16 daily, 20 minutes), Ierapetra (€3.30, eight daily, 1 hour), Iraklio (€6.20, half-hourly, 1½ hours), Kritsa (€1.30, 10 daily, 15 minutes) Lasithi Plateau (€3.50, two daily, 3 hours) and Sitia (€5.90, seven daily, 1½ hours).

Getting Around

Car- and motorcycle-hire outlets can be found on 28 Oktovriou and the northern waterfront. **Club Cars** (☎ 28410 25868; www.clubcars.net; 28 Oktovriou 30) has cars for hire from €32 per day.

Manolis Bikes (☎ 28410 24940; 25 Martiou 12) has a huge range of scooters, motorcycles and quad bikes. Prices begin at €20 a day for a scooter and go up to €50 a day for a Yamaha XT 660. It also has top-of-the-range mountain bikes (from €10).

KRITSA ΚΡΙΤΣΑ

pop 1626

The pretty mountain village of Kritsa (krit-sah), perched 600m up the mountainside 11km from Agios Nikolaos, is renowned for its strong tradition of needlework and weaving. It appears to have morphed into a tourist attraction, with weaving and embroidery draped on every available surface. Busloads of tourists swarm through the streets all summer and the villagers are eager to cater to these customers. It creates a colourful atmosphere, but not much of the stuff on sale these days is handmade or necessarily authentic. It's still possible to find the traditional geometric designs of Crete and the odd finely crocheted blanket or tablecloth, but they are becoming a rarity (and are – justifiably – not cheap, due to the labour-intensive work involved and the few women still willing and able to do it).

Apart from the needlework, **Olive Wood** (☎ 28410 51585) is one of the few shops in town that has handmade local crafts. You can order a pair of Cretan boots at **Detorakis** (☎ 28410 51349), who has been making them for 50 years.

Most years, Kritsa stages a massive **traditional wedding** (€20 including food and drink) in August, as long as one lucky couple agrees to make their nuptials a totally public affair. The event includes a feast, traditional customs and dancing, and attracts quite a crowd. It usually takes place the first Sunday after the 15 August Assumption Day holiday.

LASITHI

One narrow street runs through Kritsa, but there are car parks at the top and bottom of the village. The post office is near the lower car park. There is an ATM halfway up the hill.

Sleeping & Eating

Rooms Argyro (☎ 28410 51174; www.argyrorentrooms .gr; s €20, d €30-35; 🛜) A friendly place with 12 immaculate and basic rooms with balconies and a little shaded restaurant downstairs for breakfast and light meals. It's on your left as you enter the village.

Olive Press (☎ 28410 51296; www.olivepresscenterall .com; d/apt €55/70) This Belgian-run B&B is in a lovingly restored stone olive press in the upper part of the village, near Agios Yiorgos church. One apartment incorporates the original olive press.

Platanos (☎ 28410 51230; mains €4.80-6.50) This taverna/*kafeneio* retains a traditional feel and has a lovely setting under a giant plane tree and vine canopy. There's a standard menu of grills and *mayirefta* and it's well regarded by locals.

To Plai (☎ 28410 51196; mains €4.40-10) On the road to Katharo just past the car park, this simple taverna has authentic Cretan cooking such as boiled goat or mutton, goat in wine, and wild greens including *stamnagathi* when in season. There are tables on the balcony with views over the valley.

Saridakis Kafeneio (☎ 28410 51577) This original old-style *kafeneio*, serving only Greek coffee (€1.50) and a few homemade sweets, is a rarity these days.

Getting There & Away

There are hourly buses from Agios Nikolaos to Kritsa (€1.30, 15 minutes).

AROUND KRITSA

The tiny triple-aisled **Church of Panagia Kera** (☎ 28410 51806; admission €3; 🕑 8.30am-3pm Mon-Fri, 8.30am-2pm Sat), 1km before Kritsa, contains the most outstanding Byzantine frescoes on Crete. The oldest part of the church is the 13th-century central nave, but most of the frescoes date from the early to mid-14th century. The dome and nave are decorated with four gospel scenes: the Presentation, the Baptism, the Raising of Lazarus and the Entry into Jerusalem. On the west wall are a portrayal of the Crucifixion and grimly realistic depictions of the Punishment of the Damned. The vault

of the south aisle recounts the life of the Virgin; the north aisle is an elaborately worked-out fresco of the Second Coming. Nearby is an enticing depiction of Paradise next to the Virgin and the Patriarchs – Abraham, Isaac and Jacob. Judgement Day is portrayed on the west end, with the Archangel Michael trumpeting the Second Coming.

From Kritsa it is a 16km scenic climb up to the spectacular **Katharo Plateau,** which is cultivated by people from Kritsa and virtually inhabited only by sheep and goats – and even then only in summer. On the road to Katharo you pass by the village of **Kroustas**, where locals go for very traditional local cuisine. The popular **O Kroustas** (☎ 28410 51362) has excellent Cretan food, including a superb (albeit high-calorie) *lazania* (twisted handmade pasta also called *stroufikta*) cooked in stock with *anthotyro* and excellent rusks made in the wood oven.

ANCIENT LATO ΛΑΤΩ

The ancient city of **Lato** (admission €2; 🕑 8.30am-3pm Tue-Sun), 4km north of Kritsa, is one of Crete's few non-Minoan ancient sites. Lato (la-*to*) was founded in the 7th century BC by the Dorians and at its height was one of the most powerful cities on Crete, until it was destroyed in 200 BC. It sprawls over the slopes of two acropolises in a lonely mountain setting, commanding stunning views down to the Bay of Mirabello.

The city's name is derived from the goddess Leto whose union with Zeus produced Artemis and Apollo, both of whom were worshipped here.

The site is barely signposted so can be a bit of a guessing game.

The **city gate** is the entrance to the site and leads to a long, stepped street. The wall on the left contains two towers, which were also residences. Follow the street to reach the **agora**, built around the 4th century BC, which contained a cistern and a small rectangular sanctuary. Excavations of the temple have revealed a number of 6th- century BC figurines. The circle of stones behind the cistern was a threshing floor. The western side of the agora contains a **stoa** with stone benches. There are remains of a pebble mosaic nearby. A terrace above the southeast corner of the agora contains the remains of a **rectangular temple**, probably built in the late 4th or early 3rd century BC. Between the two towers on the northern end of the agora there are steps leading to the **prytaneion**, the administrative centre of the city-state. The centre of the prytaneion contained a hearth with a fire that burned day and night. On the east side of the prytaneion is a colonnaded court. Below the prytaneion is a semicircular **theatre** that could seat about 350 people next to an **exedra** (stage), which has a bench around the walls.

There are no buses to Lato. The road to the site is signposted to the right on the approach to Kritsa. It's a pleasant 30-minute walk through olive groves.

ELOUNDA ΕΛΟΥΝΤΑ
pop 1561

There are magnificent mountain and sea views along the 11km road north from Agios Nikolaos to Elounda (el-*oon*-da). A cluster of luxury resorts occupy the lovely coves along the coast. The first elite hotel was built here in the mid-1960s, quickly establishing Elounda as the playground for Greece's glitterati and high flyers – soon after, the world's rich and famous followed suit. Elounda boasts some of the most exclusive resorts in Greece, which monopolise most of the nice beaches in the area.

Past the resorts, the once-quiet fishing village of Elounda bristles with tourists in summer, although it is calmer than its larger neighbour Agios Nikolaos. Busloads of day-trippers rock up on their way to Spinalonga Island. Elounda's attractive harbour is somewhat spoilt by the huge ugly neon signs on many restaurants and central car park. The pleasant but unremarkable sandy town beach, to the north of the port, can get very crowded. There's another beach on the other side past Alykes, the now largely submerged salt mines established by the Venetians. This sheltered lagoon-like stretch of water is formed by the Kolokytha 'island', which you can reach via a narrow stone peninsula.

Orientation & Information

The main square with a prominent clock tower and car park is next to the harbour. The bus stops nearby, where there are a couple of ATMs and the post office.

Babel Internet Café (☎ 28410 42336; Akti Vritomartidos) On the waterfront, north of the clock tower.

Eklektos (☎ 28410 42086) Sells maps and new and used English-language books.

Municipal Tourist Office (☎ 28410 42464; 8am-11pm Jun-Oct) Helps with accommodation and information, and changes money.

Olous Travel (☎ 28410 41324) Handles air and boat tickets and finds accommodation.

Tours & Activities

Boats from Elounda offer trips to Spinalonga Island, swimming and fishing trips, and four-hour cruises that include Spinalonga, swimming and a visit to the sunken city of Olous (opposite).

The area around Elounda offers excellent diving. Try the PADI **Blue Dolphin Diving Centre** (☎ 28410 41802; www.dive-bluedolphin.com; dive €39) at the Grecotel Elounda Village hotel.

Sleeping

If you're not lucky enough to be staying at one of the swanky resorts, it almost defeats the purpose of hanging out in Elounda. Many hotels are fully booked by tour operators.

BUDGET & MIDRANGE

Delfinia Studios & Apartments (☎ 28410 41641; www .pediaditis.gr; studio/apt €30-40;) The pleasant rooms here have balconies overlooking the sea and there is a range of options for larger groups and families. Run by the same family as the bookshop on the main road, who also run the Milos apartments nearby.

Hotel Aristea (☎ 28410 41300; www.aristeahotel .com; s/d/tr incl breakfast €30/45/55;) In the town centre is this uninspiring but decent and clean budget option. Most rooms at least have a sea view, double-glazed windows, TV, fridge and a hairdryer.

Corali Studios (☎ /fax 28410 41712; www.coralistu dios.com; studio €60-70;) On the northern side, these handy self-catering studios are set in lush lawns with a shaded patio.

Portobello Apartments (2-/4-bed apt €65-75;) Next door to Corali Studios and under the same management, these spacious apartments are a good option for two or more people.

Elounda Island Villas (☎ 28410 41274; www.eloun daisland.gr; d from €70; 4-person apt €105;) A secluded option on Kolokytha island, reached along the narrow peninsula. The split-level apartments are set amid a pleasant garden and decorated with traditional furnishings. Kitchens are well equipped, bathrooms functional and there is an attached tavern. It's a 20-minute walk into town.

TOP END

Elounda's resorts are the stuff most people only dream about. **Elounda Beach** (☎ 28410 41412; www.eloundabeach.gr; r from €250; ⊠ ⓢ), one of the world's great luxury resorts, is the epitome of luxury, attracting some elite clientele. You can upgrade all the way to the royal suites with a private indoor swimming pool, personal fitness trainer, butler and cook (for a mere €15,000 per night).

Eating

Nikos (☎ 28410 41439; fish per kg €35-40) While it lacks the ambience of the seafront eateries, no-frills Nikos on the main street is a good choice for fish and lobster because it generally catches its own. There are outdoor tables under a canopy across in the square. Service can be erratic but the food is very reasonably priced.

Megaro (☎ 28419 42220; fish per kg up to €45; mains €4-8) This recently refurbished place on the corner of the square is popular with locals around the district. The owner fishes from his own boat and the menu also includes Cretan specialities.

Paradosiako (☎ 28410 42444; mains €5.50-8.50) Recommended for grilled and oven-baked meat dishes. It's opposite the playground.

Ferryman (☎ 28410 41230; local fish platter for 2 €44) With a lovely setting on the waterfront, the Ferryman claims its moment of fame from being featured in the TV series *Who Pays the Ferryman*. The food and service is excellent (they even clean the fish for you), though it is on the pricey side. Its speciality is fish and lobster, but there's a broader menu of Cretan specialties

Entertainment

There are several bars and clubs at Elounda, but it's no Agios Nikolaos.

Katafygio (☎ 28410 42003) has tables along the water and is housed in a former carob-processing plant. It has Cretan and Greek nights and belly dancing.

Alyggos Bar (☎ 28410 41569), on the main street, is popular with tourists and has an impressive display of soccer jumpers and matches on TV. **Babel** (☎ 28410 42336; Akti Vritomartidos) is another good place for a drink or you can get into the Greek groove at **Venue** (☎ 28410 41355) next to Olous Travel.

Getting There & Around

Boats go across to Spinalonga every half-hour (adult/child return €10/5)

There are 13 buses daily from Agios Nikolaos to Elounda (€1.30, 20 minutes).

Cars, motorcycles and scooters can be hired at **Elounda Travel** (☎ 28410 41800; www.eloundatravel .gr) in the town centre.

KOLOKYTHA PENINSULA
ΧΕΡΣΟΝΗΣΟΣ ΚΟΛΟΚΥΘΑ

Just before Elounda (coming from Agios Nikolaos), a sign points right to **ancient Olous**, which was the port of Lato. The city stood on and around the narrow isthmus (now a causeway) that joined the southern end of the Kolokytha Peninsula to the mainland. Olous was a Minoan settlement that flourished from 3000 to 900 BC. Around 200 BC it entered into a treaty with Rhodes as part of the island's desire to control eastern Crete and put an end to the piracy that was ravaging the Aegean. Excavations indicate that

---

GOOD FOR THE SOUL

Elounda is home to some of Europe's most luxurious spas and thalassotherapy centres, which – as the name suggests – promote the therapeutic benefits of the sea with seawater pools and hydrospas, marine algae body wraps and every imaginable sea-themed pampering and rejuvenation treatment.

The state-of-the-art **Elounda Spa & Thalassotherapy Centre** (☎ 28410 65660; www.bluepalace.gr; full-day treatments from €140), in the Blue Palace Resort just before Plaka, also incorporates Cretan nutrients into unique treatments, including exfoliation with sugar and olive oil, a traditional olive oil massage and hydromassage baths using Cretan herbs. There is even a treatment using raki – not your traditional rakotherapy!

There are packages and discounts for non-guests if you can't manage a stay at the resort for the full treatment.

Another world class spa in Elounda is the new **Six Senses Spa** (☎ 28410 68000; www.portoelounda .com; signature treatment package €220) at the Porto Elounda Hotel.

lonelyplanet.com

Olous was an important trade centre with the eastern islands and minted its own currency. Little is known about the settlement during the Greek, Roman and Byzantine eras, but it appears that it was destroyed by the Saracens in the 9th century.

The isthmus sank as a result of the earthquakes that have repeatedly devastated Crete. In 1897 the occupying French army dug a canal across the isthmus connecting Spinalonga Bay to the open sea. Most of the ruins lie beneath the water, which makes it a popular place for snorkelling. The shallow water appears to be paradise for sea urchins and the area is known for the many birds that nest there. An early Christian mosaic near the causeway was part of an early Christian basilica.

There is an excellent sandy **beach** 1km along a narrow but graded dirt road on the eastern side of the peninsula. The beach is sheltered, the water pristine and few people use it, other than visitors with small *caiques* (little boats).

PLAKA ΠΛΆΚΑ
pop 38

The small fishing village of Plaka, 5km north of Elounda, used to supply the leper colony on Spinalonga. Today, Plaka has been somewhat dwarfed by the giant Blue Palace Resort at the entrance to the village, but it's still an attractive and quiet place, with a reasonable stretch of pebble **beach** overlooking Spinalonga. In a pretty waterfront setting, a handful of fish tavernas are housed in row of stone buildings.

Ask around at the boats at the port or one of the tavernas and local fishermen can take you over to Spinalonga Island (€7). You can also go across by sea kayak with Driros Beach-based **Spinalonga Windsurf** (☎ 69935 24738; www.spinalonga-windsurf.com; €15).

The popular waterfront **Taverna Giorgos** (☎ 28410 41355; Cretan specials €6.50-8) is run by a local fisherman and his family, who will dish up a decent fresh seafood meal as well as Cretan specialities.

Stella Mare Studios (☎ 28410 41814; studio €50-60; ❄) has simple studios and apartments with homy touches such as lace curtains and tapestries on the walls. They are set around a courtyard garden; some have balconies with sea views and there are goats grazing across the road.

The **Pefko** (☎ 28410 42510) *kafeneio* is a charming place for a drink.

SPINALONGA ISLAND
ΝΗΣΟΣ ΣΠΙΝΑΛΟΓΚΑ

Spinalonga Island lies just north of the Kolokytha Peninsula and was strategically important from antiquity to the Venetian era. The island's massive **fortress** (☎ 28410 41773; admission €2; ⏰ 10am-6pm) was built by the Venetians in 1579 to protect the bays of Elounda and Mirabello. It was considered impregnable and withstood Turkish sieges for longer than any other Cretan stronghold, but finally surrendered in 1715 some 40 years after the rest of Crete. The Turks used the island as a base for smuggling. Following the reunion of Crete with Greece, Spinalonga became a leper colony, which closed in 1953, and the island has been uninhabited ever since.

Regular excursion boats visit Spinalonga from Agios Nikolaos (€15) (see p183). Ferries can take you across from Elounda (€10) or you could also take a cheaper boat from Plaka. Boats from Agios Nikolaos pass the uninhabited Bird Island and Kri-Kri Island, one of the last habitats of the kri-kri, Crete's wild goat. Both are designated wildlife sanctuaries.

MILATOS ΜΥΛΑΤΟΣ

Milatos, the north coast's easternmost beach settlement, is refreshingly mellow after the overdeveloped coastal strip east of Iraklio. Milatos beach is little more than a main square, with the Church of Analipsis in the middle, and a string of tavernas, dwellings and accommodation lining the beach. The actual village of Milatos is 2km up the hill.

There is little to see of Ancient Milatos, to the east of the beach, but you can explore the series of caverns in the **Milatos Cave**, about 3km east of the village (best to have a torch). More than 2000 Cretans were holed up in the cave for 15 days in 1823 but were massacred when they surrendered. There is memorial chapel inside the cave.

Panorama (☎ 28410 81213; top fish per kg €45) on the western end is run by a fishing family and uses mostly local organic vegetables. It also has spacious studios in a complex behind the taverna (€40).

At the other end of the beach **To Meltemi** (☎ 28410 81286; mains €5.50-8.50) is a friendly, family-run place with excellent local cuisine – try the *hortopitakia* (pies with greens).

Another worthwhile taverna in this area is **Volosyros** (☎ 28410 71601; mains €6.50-8.50) which has a wood oven and a lovely garden terrace out the back. It's on the road to Milatos, in the upper village of Sisi.

LASITHI PLATEAU
ΟΡΟΠΕΔΙΟ ΛΑΣΙΘΙΟΥ

The Lasithi Plateau, 900m above sea level, is a vast expanse of pear and apple orchards, almond trees and fields of crops. It would have been a stunning sight when it was dotted by some 20,000 metal windmills with white canvas sails built by the Venetians in the 17th century. There are less than 5000 still standing today and few are in service, most having been replaced by less-attractive mechanical pumps.

The plateau's rich soil has been cultivated since Minoan times. The inaccessibility of the region made it a hotbed of insurrection during Venetian and Turkish rule. Following an uprising in the 13th century, the Venetians drove out the inhabitants of Lasithi and destroyed their orchards. The plateau lay abandoned for 200 years, preserving a rich forest and biotope, as a lack of drainage meant the plain flooded each spring with melted snow. Food shortages led the Venetians to cultivate the area and build the irrigation trenches and wells that still service the region.

There are 20 villages dotted around the periphery of the plateau. Tour buses regularly pass through the region, which relies heavily on tourism but is essentially an agricultural area with traditional rural villages that return to pastoral serenity when the tourists leave. It is worth an overnight stay to get a sense of rural Crete.

You can approach the plateau from several points, the main routes being from Iraklio via the Kastelli road or Malia, or the commercial town of Neapoli, with other turn-offs near Agios Nikolaos.

The plateau is a popular **bike route**, and on any given day you will be assailed by squadrons of helmet-clad cyclists. Enterprising cycle tour operators in Iraklio and Agios Nikolaos ferry bikes and cyclists to the plateau but you can also get bikes locally.

From Iraklio there are daily buses to Tzermiado (€3.50, two hours), Agios Georgios (€4.70, two hours) and Psyhro (€4.70, 2¼ hours). There are also buses to the villages from Agios Nikolaos (p186).

TZERMIADO ΤΖΕΡΜΙΆΔΟ
pop 762

Tzermiado (dzer-mee-*ah*-do) is a sleepy town with dusty little streets lined with houses overgrown with vines and hanging plants. It's the largest and most important town on the Lasithi Plateau and has a fair amount of visitors from the tour buses going to the Dikteon Cave. A number of shops sell rugs and embroideries, although they're not of a particularly high quality. Of better quality are Lasithi's superior potatoes, which are celebrated in a three-day festival at the end of August in Tzermiado.

There is only one main road running through town that takes you past the town square, with a couple of ATMs and a post office.

South just outside Tzermiado is the **Kronios Cave** (Trapeza), for which you need a torch (and preferably a guide – they tend to hang out waiting) to explore. From the signposted turnoff, you can drive to the end of the dirt path, from where you go up about 150 steps to the cave.

North of Tzermiado, perched on a dramatic rocky hill, is the Minoan settlement of **Karfi**, a crude refuge for Minoans fleeing the Dorians. You can drive the bulk of the way and walk for about 40 minutes up to the site. Otherwise it takes about two hours to do the 6km climb. Take plenty of water. Follow the signs to the Timios Stavros church (where you need to leave the car) to the well-marked path up to the ruins.

Argoulias (☎ 28440 22754; www.argoulias.gr; d incl breakfast €60-80) is a delightful small complex of 11 stone spacious apartments built into the hillside in the abandoned part of the village, with panoramic views of the plateau. The rooms are well-equipped and traditionally decorated, and breakfast is made from fresh local produce.

Some of the best Cretan cuisine around is served at **Kourites** (☎ 28440 22054; mains €7-8; www.kourites.eu), including vegetarian delights such as artichokes. Try some of the dishes cooked in the wood oven – the suckling pig with baked potatoes is delicious. There are simple room above the taverna with small balconies (single/double including breakfast €25/35) and you can have free use of the bicycles.

AGIOS GEORGIOS ΑΓΙΟΣ ΓΕΩΡΓΙΟΣ
pop 541

Agios Georgios (*agh*-ios ye-*or*-gios) is a tiny village on the southern side of the Lasithi

LASITHI

Plateau and the most pleasant to stay in. If you have your own bicycle, you can base yourself here and explore the plateau at your leisure.

The village also boasts an excellent **folklore museum** (☎ 28440 31462; admission €3; ⏲ 10am-4pm Apr-Oct) housed in the original home belonging to the Katsapakis family. Exhibits are spread over five rooms and include some intriguing personal photos of writer Nikos Kazantzakis.

You cannot miss the signs in the region directing you to the massive **Lasinthos Eco Park** (☎ 28440 89100; www.lasinthos.gr; admission €2.50; ⏲ 9am-6pm), just past Agios Georgios. This new complex, including the barn of a taverna, craft displays and a massive souvenir store, caters to tour buses. The workshops of traditional crafts are contrived and the 'farm' is rather light on.

On the northern side of the village, **Hotel Maria** (☎ 28440 31774; s/d €20-35) has spacious rooms, nicely decorated with weaving and traditional furnishings (although larger people should note that the beds are very narrow). Maria does the cooking at **Taverna Rea** (☎ 28440 31209; mains €4.50-6.50) on the main street, which rustles up excellent grilled local meats (her husband is the butcher) and good-value Cretan staples. They also rent out studios above the taverna (€30).

PSYHRO ΨΥΧΡΟ
pop 208

Psyhro (psi-*hro*) is the closest village to the Dikteon Cave. It has one main street with a few tavernas, and plenty of souvenir shops selling 'authentic' rugs and mats of largely non-Cretan origin. It is prettier than Tzermiado and makes for a better rest stop. Buses to Psyhro drop you at the end of the town where it's about a kilometre's walk uphill to the cave (the bus may take you all the way if lots of passengers are going there).

If you do need to stay the night, the rather featureless **Zeus Hotel** (☎ 28440 31284; s/d €25/30) is near the start of the Dikteon Cave road. You can find the owners at the Halavro taverna near the cave entrance.

With its neat folksy interior and streetside tables, **Stavros** (☎ 28440 31453; grills €5-8) serves a good range of traditional homestyle Cretan dishes. Most of the meat and produce is from the family farm.

Former cave guardian Petros Zarvakis has opened **Petros Taverna** (☎ 28440 31600; grills

€6) opposite the entrance to Dikteon Cave, serving Cretan food and grills. He also organises regular hikes up to Mt Dikti, camping out under the stars.

DIKTEON CAVE ΔΙΚΤΑΙΟΝ ΑΝΤΡΟΝ

Lasithi's major sight is the **Dikteon Cave** (adult/child €4/2; ⏲ 8am-6pm Jun-Oct, 8am-2.30pm Nov-May), just outside the village of Psyhro. Here, according to legend, Rhea hid the newborn Zeus from Cronos, his offspring-gobbling father.

The cave, also known as the Psyhro Cave, covers 2200 sq metres and features both stalactites and stalagmites. It was excavated in 1900 by the British archaeologist David Hogarth, who found numerous votives indicating it was a place of cult worship. These finds are housed in the Archaeological Museum (p149) in Iraklio.

The cave began to be used for cult worship in the Middle Minoan period and continued, though less intensely, up to the 1st century AD. An altar for offerings and sacrifices was in the upper section. Stone tablets inscribed with Linear A script were found here, along with religious bronze and clay figurines.

The upper cave is large and generally devoid of stalactites or stalagmites. A steep downward path brings you to the more interesting lower cave. In the back on the left is a smaller chamber where legend has it that Zeus was born. There is a larger hall on the right, which has small stone basins filled with water that Zeus allegedly drank from in one section and a spectacular stalagmite that came to be known as the Mantle of Zeus in the other. The entire cave is illuminated, although not particularly well, so watch your step.

It is a steep 15-minute (800m) walk up to the cave entrance. You can take the fairly rough but shaded track on the right with great views over the plateau or the unshaded paved trail on the left of the car park next to the Halavro taverna. You can also let a donkey do the hard work (€10 or €15 return).

NORTHEAST COAST

GOURNIA ΓΟΥΡΝΙΑ

The important Late Minoan site of **Gournia** (☎ 28410 24943; admission €2; ⏲ 8.30am-3pm Tue-Sun) pronounced goor-*nyah*, lies just off the coast road, 19km southeast of Agios Nikolaos.

The ruins, which date from 1550 to 1450 BC, are made up of a town overlooked by a small palace. Gournia's palace was far less ostentatious than the ones at Knossos and Phaestos as it was the residence of an overlord rather than a king. The town is a network of streets and stairways flanked by houses with walls up to 2m high. Domestic, agricultural and trade implements found on the site indicate that Gournia was a thriving little community.

South of the palace is a large rectangular **court**, which was connected to a network of paved stone streets. South of the palace is a large **stone slab** used for sacrificing bulls. The room to the west has a stone **kernos** (large earthen dish) ringed with 32 depressions and probably used for cult activity. North of the palace was a **Shrine of the Minoan Snake Goddess**, which proved to be a rich trove of objects from the Postpalatial Period. Notice the storage rooms, workrooms and dwellings to the north and east of the site. The buildings were two-storey structures with the storage and workrooms in the basement and the living quarters on the 1st floors.

Near the site is **Gournia Moon Camping** (☎ /fax 28420 93243; www.gourniamoon.com; sites per person/tent €5.70/5.70; ☒), the closest camp site to Agios Nikolaos. The shaded and well-organised site has a taverna, swimming pool, snack bar and mini-market.

Sitia and Ierapetra buses from Agios Nikolaos can drop you at the site.

MOHLOS ΜΟΧΛΟΣ
pop 87

Mohlos (*moh-*los) is a pretty fishing village reached by a 5km winding road from the Sitia-Agios Nikolaos highway. In antiquity, it was joined to the homonymous island that now sits 200m offshore and was once a thriving Early Minoan community dating from the period 3000–2000 BC. Excavations still continue sporadically on both Mohlos Island and at Mohlos village. An information board overlooking the harbour explains the archaeology of the area.

Mohlos is a chill-out place with a small pebble-and-grey-sand beach, simple accommodation, plenty of good walks and interesting villages to explore nearby. Beware of strong currents further out in the small strait between the island and the village.

Mohlos attracts mainly French and German independent travellers, while the tavernas enjoy a good reputation for fresh local fish and seafood and are packed with locals on weekends.

When we last visited, an ominous construction frenzy nearby did not bode well for peaceful Mohlos.

There's a mini-market and a couple of gift shops. **Barbarossa Tours** (☎ 28430 94723; barbarasso@otenet.gr) can arrange rooms, excursions, boat and air tickets and car hire. Yiannis Petrakis and his Belgian botanist wife Ann Lebrun run nature walks and guided jeep and bike **tours** (☎ /fax 28430 94725; annelebrun@caramail.com; walks €12-20, mountain bike/motorcycle tours €35/75).

Sleeping & Eating
Kyma (☎ 28430 94177; soik@in.gr; studio €30) Fairly well signposted on the village's western side near a supermarket, the self-contained studios are spotless and good value.

Hotel Sofia (☎ /fax 28430 94554; r €35-45; ☒) The rooms above the Sofia taverna have been spruced up with new furniture and bedding, and all have TV and fridge, but some are rather cramped. The front rooms have balconies with sea views. The family also has spacious apartments 200m east of the harbour, for families and longer stays. Try the home cooking at the taverna.

Mohlos Mare (☎ /fax 28430 94005; d €45; ☒) Just outside the village along the coast road, these well-maintained spacious, well-appointed apartments are bright and airy and the top rooms have great views from the big balconies. There's a vineyard and garden out the front with hundreds of roses, and a communal outdoor kitchen and barbecue.

To Bogazi (☎ 28430 94200; mezedes €2.50-6.50) Serves more than 30 mezedes, including many vegetarian-friendly dishes and a range of seafood and Cretan specials.

Ta Kochilia (☎ 28430 94432; mains €4.50-6.50) This excellent place enjoys a lovely setting and is known for its fresh fish and simple, good food. Seafood lovers should try the sea-urchin salad – dip your bread in it – or the braised cuttlefish in black ink.

Getting There & Away
There is no public transport to Mohlos. Buses between Sitia and Agios Nikolaos will drop you off at the Mohlos turn-off.

LASITHI

You'll need to hitch or walk the 6km to the village.

SITIA ΣΗΤΕΙΑ

pop 8754

Sitia (si-*tee*-a) is an attractive mid-sized coastal town with a pretty harbour-side promenade lined with tavernas and cafés that makes for a pleasant evening stroll. It has fortunately managed to escape the tourist frenzy that grips most of the north coast in summer. While the town is traveller-friendly, it exists for the locals, who rely on agriculture and commerce rather than tourism.

In the bustling streets of the old town that wind their way uphill from the harbour, you'll find the occasional example of old Venetian architecture mixed in with the new. A sandy beach skirts a wide bay to the east of town. Sitia attracts lots of French and Greek tourists, but even at the height of the season the town has a relatively laid-back feel that is refreshing compared with the commercialism further west.

It also makes a good jumping-off point for the Dodecanese islands.

History

Archaeological excavations indicate that there were Neolithic settlements around Sitia and an important Minoan settlement at nearby Petras. The original settlement was destroyed and eventually abandoned after an earthquake in 1700 BC.

In the Greco-Roman era there was a town called Iteia in or around modern Sitia although its exact site has not yet been located. In Byzantine times Sitia became a bishopric, which was then eliminated by the Saracens in the 9th century. Under the Venetians, Sitia became the most important port in eastern Crete. The town was hit by a disastrous earthquake in 1508 – a blow from which it never really recovered – and the Turkish blockade of Sitia in 1648 marked its death knell. The remaining inhabitants fled and the town was destroyed. It was not until the late-19th century when the Turks decided to make Sitia an administrative centre that the town gradually came back to life. Crete's most famous poet, Vitsentzos Kornaros, was born in Sitia in 1614.

Orientation & Information

The town's main square is Plateia Iroon Polytehniou – recognisable by its palm trees and statue of a dying soldier. There are lots of ATMs and places to change money. The bus station is inland near the museum. Ferries dock about 500m north of Plateia Agnostou.

Akasti Travel (☎ 28430 29444; www.akasti.gr; Kornarou & Metaxaki 4) Good source of information.

Java Internet Café (☎ 28430 22263; Kornarou 113; ☾ 9am-late; internet per hr €2)

National Bank of Greece (Papanastasiou & Katapoti) Has a 24-hour exchange machine.

Post office (Dimokritou; ☾ 7.30am-3pm)

Tourist office (☎ 28430 28300; Karamanli; ☾ 9.30am-2.30pm & 5-8.30pm Mon-Fri, 9.30am-2.30pm Sat) On the promenade.

Tourist police (☎ 28430 24200; Therisou 31) At the main police station.

Sights & Activities

The excellent **Archaeological Museum** (☎ 28430 23917; Piskokefalou; admission €2; ☾ 8.30am-3pm Tue-Sun) houses a well-displayed and important collection of local finds spanning Neolithic to Roman times, with emphasis on the Minoan civilization. One of the most significant exhibits is the *Palekastro Kouros* – a figure pieced together from fragments made of hippopotamus tusks and adorned with gold (see the boxed text, p198). Finds from the palace at Zakros include a wine press, a bronze saw, jars, cult objects and pots that are clearly scorched from the great fire that destroyed the palace. Among the most valuable objects are the Linear A tablets, which reflect the palace's administrative function.

Towering over the town is the **kazarma** (fort; admission free; ☾ 8.30am-3pm) (from 'casa di arma'), which was a garrison under the Venetians. The only remains of the wall that once protected the town, the site is now used as an open-air venue.

The **folklore museum** (☎ 28430 28300; Kapetan Sifinos 28; admission €2; ☾ 10am-1pm Mon-Fri) displays a fine collection of local weaving and other exhibits of folk life.

The **Union of Agricultural Cooperatives of Sitia** (☎ 28430 29354; admission & tour €2; ☾ 8am-3pm), about 1km before town, showcases the area's wines, oil and raki. Tours include a video and wine tasting. The charge is often waived if you make a purchase.

About 2km southeast of town is the interesting Minoan archaeological site of **Petras** on a low hill overlooking the sea. You can see the remains of the settlement, including two houses from the New Palace period. The site is open to the public.

Universal Diver (☎ /fax 28430 23489; pavlossimos@yahoo .gr; Kornarou 140) is a PADI dive centre offering all levels of scuba diving.

Festivals & Events

Sitia produces superior sultanas and the town holds a **Sultana Festival** in honour of the grape in the last week of August.

The **Kornaria Festival** runs from mid-July to the end of August, with concerts, folk dancing and theatre productions staged in the *kazarma* and other venues. Posters around town announce the events, some of which are free.

Sleeping

Hotel Arhontiko (☎ 28430 28172; Kondylaki 16; d/studio €30/33) This guesthouse, in a beautifully main-tained neoclassical building uphill from the port, has a real old-world feel. It's spotless, with shared bathrooms and a lovely shady garden in the front and the top rooms have sea views.

Apostolis (☎ 28430 28172; Kazantzaki 27; d/tr €37/47) These domatia have ceiling fans, and relatively modern bathrooms with handy touches such as shower curtains. There's a communal balcony and fridge.

El Greco Hotel (☎ 28430 23133; elgreco@sit.forth-net.gr; G Arkadiou 13; s/d incl breakfast €35/50;) The quaint and friendly old-style El Greco has very clean and presentable rooms, and all have a fridge, phone and extras such as hairdryers. Some sleep up to four.

Hotel Flisvos (☎ 28430 27135; www.flisvos-sitia .com; Karamanli 4; s/d/tr from €40/50/60;) Along the

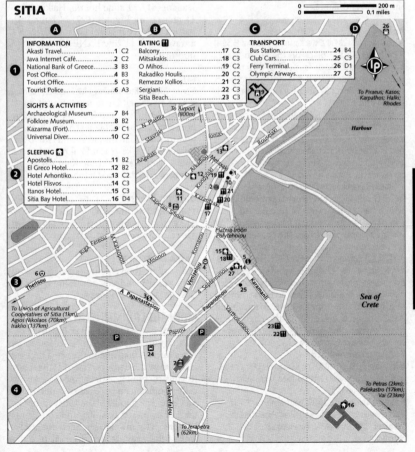

SITIA

INFORMATION	
Akasti Travel	1 C2
Java Internet Café	2 C2
National Bank of Greece	3 B3
Post Office	4 B3
Tourist Office	5 C2
Tourist Police	6 A3

SIGHTS & ACTIVITIES	
Archaeological Museum	7 B4
Folklore Museum	8 B2
Kazarma (Fort)	9 C1
Universal Diver	10 C2

SLEEPING	
Apostolis	11 B2
El Greco Hotel	12 B2
Hotel Arhontiko	13 C2
Hotel Flisvos	14 C3
Itanos Hotel	15 C3
Sitia Bay Hotel	16 D4

EATING	
Balcony	17 C2
Mitsakakis	18 C3
O Mihos	19 C3
Rakadiko Houlis	20 C3
Remezzo Kollios	21 C3
Sergiani	22 C3
Sitia Beach	23 C3

TRANSPORT	
Bus Station	24 B4
Club Cars	25 C3
Ferry Terminal	26 D1
Olympic Airways	27 C3

To Piraeus; Kasos;
Karpathos; Halki;
Rhodes

Harbour

To Airport
(800m)

Plateia Iroön
Polytehniou

To Union of Agricultural
Cooperatives of Sitia (1km);
Agios Nikolaos (70km);
Iraklio (137km)

Sea of
Crete

To Petras (2km);
Palekastro (17km);
Vai (23km)

To Ierapetra
(62km)

LASITHI

southern waterfront, Flisvos is a decent modern hotel. Rooms are neat and have air-con, TV, fridge, phone and balconies and there is a recently renovated back wing with more spacious rooms and a lift.

Itanos Hotel (☎ 28430 22900; www.itanoshotel.com; Karamanli 4; sea view s/d incl breakfast €42/56; ✿ 🖳) You could also try this place on the waterfront. There's a rooftop terrace restaurant and internet access downstairs.

Sitia Bay Hotel (☎ 28430 24800 www.sitiabay.com; Paraliaki Leoforos 8; apt/ste from €110/160; ✿) It looks like another modern hotel but the service is as personal and friendly as it gets, with homemade bread, marmalade and cakes brought to your room daily. Most of the comfortable and tasteful one- and two-room apartments have sea views, and there's a pool, hydrospa, mini-gym and sauna.

Eating

Sitia Beach (☎ 28430 22104; Karamanli 28; mains €5.50-8) This unassuming place on the beach makes a decent pizza but it is more highly recommended for home-style cooking that appears daily on the specials board. Try the pork with lemon and rice.

O Mihos (☎ 28430 22416; Kornarou 117; mixed grill for 2 €20) This *psistaria* in a traditional stone house one block back from the waterfront has excellent charcoal-grilled meats as well as Cretan cooking. There are also tables on a terrace nearby on the beach.

Houlis Rakadiko (☎ 28430 28298; Venizelou 57) For a more classic local experience try this old place, which has a wide range of fine mezedes accompanied by good raki. It has no signage, but it's the second place from the corner; by day it's packed with men playing backgammon.

our pick **Balcony** (☎ 28430 25084; Foundalidou 19; mains €10.60-18.80) The finest dining in Sitia is on the 1st floor of this charmingly decorated neoclassical building. It has an eclectic menu of fusion cuisine, from Cretan to Mexican and Asian-inspired dishes from the charmingly feisty owner-chef (and ex-singer) Tonya's travels. Service can be patchy.

Also recommended:

Mitsakakis (☎ 28430 22377; Karamanli 5) For a sweet treat, the *galaktoboureko* (custard-filled pastry with syrup) is highly recommended.

Remezzo Kollios (☎ 28430 28607; Venizelou 167 12; seafood dishes €5-18) On the waterfront. Popular but pricey.

Sergiani (☎ 28430 24092; Karamanli 38) On the waterfront.

Getting There & Away

AIR

Sitia's **airport** (☎ 28430 24666) has an expanded international-size runway but international flights had yet to operate in 2007.

Olympic Airlines (☎ 28430 22270; www.olympicair lines.com; 4 Septemvriou 3) has four weekly flights to Athens (€71, one hour), Alexandroupolis (€8, two hours) and three flights per week to Preveza (€80, two hours and 20 minutes). There are also daily flights (€47) with three stops to Kassos (20 minutes), Karpathos (1 hour) and Rhodes (2 hours).

BOAT

LANE Lines (☎ 28430 25555; www.lane.gr) has weekly ferries from Sitia to Rhodes via Kasos (€19.50, six hours), Karpathos (€19.50, eight hours), Diafani (€17.90, nine hours), Halki (€18.20, 11 hours) and Rhodes (€27, 14 hours). Departure times change annually, so check with a travel agent or ring LANE Lines for latest information.

BUS

From Sitia's **Bus Station** (☎ 28430 22272) there are six buses per day to Ierapetra (€5.40, 1½ hours), seven buses to Iraklio (€13.10, three hours) via Agios Nikolaos (€6.90, 1½ hours), four to Vai (€3, 30 minutes), and two to Kato Zakros via Palekastro and Zakros (€4.50, one hour). The buses to Vai and Kato Zakros only run between May and October.

Getting Around

TO/FROM THE AIRPORT

The airport (signposted) is 1.5km out of town. There is no airport bus; a taxi costs about €5.

CAR & MOTORCYCLE

Car- and motorcycle-hire outlets are mostly found on Papandreou and Itanou. Try **Club Cars** (☎ 28430 25104; Papandreou 4).

MONI TOPLOU ΜΟΝΗ ΤΟΠΛΟΥ

East of Sitia, the imposing **Moni Toplou** (☎ 28430 61226; admission €2.50; ⏱ 9am-6pm Apr-Oct) looks more like a fortress than a monastery – a necessity imposed by the dangers it faced at the time of its construction. It is one of the most historically significant and progressive monasteries on Crete. The middle of the 15th century was marked by piracy, banditry and constant rebellions. The monks defended themselves with all the means at their disposal, including a heavy gate, cannons (the name Toplou is Turkish for 'with a cannon') and small holes for pouring boiling oil onto the heads of their attackers. Nevertheless, it was sacked by pirates in 1498, looted by the Knights of Malta in 1530, pillaged by the Turks in 1646 and captured by the Turks in 1821.

Moni Toplou had always been active in the cause for Cretan independence and paid a price for it. Under the Turkish occupation, a secret school operated in the monastery, while its reputation for hiding rebels led to severe reprisals. During WWII, Abbot Silingakis was executed after sheltering resistance leaders operating an underground radio transmitter.

The monastery's star attraction is undoubtedly the icon *Lord Thou Art Great* by celebrated Cretan artist Ioannis Kornaros. Each of the 61 small scenes painted on the icon is beautifully worked out and inspired by a phrase from the Orthodox prayer that begins 'Lord, Thou Art Great'. The icon is in the northern aisle of the church, along with 14th-century frescoes and an icon stand from 1770.

An excellent **museum** tells the monastery's history and has a fine collection of icons, engravings and books, as well as weapons and military souvenirs from the resistance.

The abbot, Filotheos Spanoudakis, is one of the most dynamic on Crete, promoting organic farming through the local agricultural cooperative and cultivating the monastery's large landholdings. He built an olive oil and wine bottling plant on the monastery grounds for the local community. Controversial plans for a massive tourism development on monastery land on the remote northern tip of the island have sparked major protests from environmentalists.

The well-stocked shop sells the monastery's award-winning organic olive oil and wine.

The monastery is a 3km walk from the Sitia-Palekastro road. Buses can drop you off at the junction.

EAST COAST

VAI ΒΑΪ

The beach at Vai, on Crete's east coast 24km from Sitia, is famous for its unique palm forest. There are many stories about the origin of these palms, including the theory that they sprouted from date pits spread by Roman legionaries relaxing on their way back from conquering Egypt. While these palms are closely related to the date, they are a separate species found only on Crete.

In July and August, you'll need to arrive early to appreciate the setting, because the place is packed and the beach is covered in sun-beds and umbrellas (€6).

It's possible to escape the worst of the ballyhoo – jet skis and all – by clambering over a rocky outcrop behind the taverna to a stunning secluded beach. Alternatively, you can go over the hill in the other direction to a series of quiet coves frequented by nudists.

The **Restaurant-Cafeteria Vai** (☎ 28430 61129; mains €4-6) is dependable and welcome after a hard day on the beach.

There are buses to Vai from Sitia (€2.50, one hour, five daily). The car park charges €3.

ITANOS ΙΤΑΝΟΣ

If you're after more secluded beaches, head north for another 3km to the ancient Minoan site of Itanos. Although inhabited from about 1500 BC, Itanos was clearly prosperous by the 7th century BC since it was an important trading post for exports to the Near East and Middle East. Its archrival was Praisos, near Ierapetra, and in 260 BC Itanos hosted a garrison of Egyptians to fortify its position against Praisos.

When Ierapetra destroyed Praisos in 155 BC, Itanos fought with Ierapetra as well and again received foreign help from Magnesia, a Roman city. The town was destroyed somewhere towards the end of the Byzantine era and may have been re-inhabited by the Venetians. It's difficult to discern any recognisable building in Itanos, but there are remains of two early Christian basilicas and a Hellenistic wall. The site is well marked and next to swimming coves shaded by pine trees.

PALEKASTRO ΠΑΛΑΪΚΑΣΤΡΟ
pop 1084
Palekastro (pah-*leh*-kas-tro) is a modern farming town that is more of a stopover or useful base for exploring eastern Crete than as a destination in itself. It's situated in the midst of a rocky, barren landscape, but is within easy striking distance of the lovely Kouremenos Beach, Vai Beach and Moni Toplou.

About 1km from town, towards Hiona beach, is the archaeological site of Roussolakkos, where archaeologists believe a major

LASITHI

Minoan Palace is buried (see boxed text, below). This is where the *Palekastro kouros* – now residing in the Archaeological Museum in Sitia (p194) – was found.

Tucked in a back street and badly sign-posted is the well-presented **Folk Museum of Palekastro** (☎ 28430 61123; admission €2; ⏱ 10am-1pm & 5-8pm Mon-Sat), housed in a traditional old manor house with displays also in the old stables and bakery.

Palekastro's economy is built on fishing and agriculture, with tourism limited to July and August. It's best to have your own transport.

Orientation & Information

The main street runs through the town and forks in the town centre. The **tourist office** (☎ 28430 61546; www.palaikastro.com ⏱ 9am-10pm May-Oct) changes money and has information on rooms and transport. There's an ATM next door and a postal agent near Itanos rooms. Check email at **Hellas Internet Café** (⏱ 10am-11.30pm). The bus stop is in the centre of town.

Sleeping & Eating

Hotel Hellas (☎ 28430 61240; hellas _h@otenet.gr; s/d €30-45; ✖) This place offers simple rooms with air-con, TV, telephone and fridge, updated bathrooms and double-glazed windows. Downstairs at the taverna, Marika cooks up reputedly the best lunch in town, with hearty home-style cooking (dishes €4-6.90). The *stifado* (stew) and aubergine *imam* (Turkish vegetable stew) are recommended.

Hiona Holiday Hotel (☎ 28430 29623; s/d €50/60) If you want modern, this new hotel has a glitzy exterior and more of a city hotel feel, but the rooms are tastefully decorated and have decent facilities.

To Finistrini (☎ 28430 61117; mezedes €2-6) About 200m along the Vai road, this neat little *ouzerie*-cum-*mezedopoleio* (mezes restaurant) dishes up tasty mezedes that go down well with a shot or 10 of raki.

Mythos (☎ 28430 61243; mains €4.80-5.90) Opposite Hellas, this pleasant and popular taverna has a big vegetarian mezes selection and traditional *mayirefta*, fish and grills.

Getting There & Away

There are five buses per day from Sitia that stop at Palekastro on the way to Vai. There are also two buses daily from Sitia to Palekastro (€2.20, 45 minutes) that continue to Kato Zakros (€4.50, 1 hour).

AROUND PALEKASTRO

Kouremenos, north of Palekastro, is a nearly deserted pebble beach with good shallow-water swimming and excellent windsurfing. You can hire boards from **Freak Surf Station** (☎ 28430 61116; www.freak-surf.com, board hire per week €190, courses from €45) on the beach.

Hiona Beach is another quiet choice to the east, with some great fish tavernas on the beach. **I Hiona** (☎ 28430 61228) is considered the best of the three, with super-fresh fish, but Kakavia, which is renowned for its fish soup, is also recommended.

BURIED PALACE

About a kilometre from Palekastro town, there's a significant Minoan archaeological site believed to be part of a yet-to-be unearthed Minoan palace complex that is the second-largest Minoan city after Knossos. The **Roussolakos** site, next to Hiona beach, is being excavated by the British School of Archaeology.

Excavations have so far produced important finds such as the **Palekastro Kouros**, on display in the Sitia Archaeological Museum (p194), along with mostly Bronze Age Kamares pottery, amphorae, soapstone serpentine lamps and *pithoi* (large storage jars). The Kouros, made of gold and ivory, is believed to be the first image of a Minoan god. Archaeologists believe this site is one of two major temples on Crete referred to by Greek philosophers.

Although the site was excavated in the early 1900s, the 1960s and several times since 1988, those digs did not get to the heart of the site. With new technology used in oil exploration, archaeologists have confirmed that there is a huge structure under the olive groves nearby but it will be years before there is funding for such a massive dig and a museum would have to be built on site for the finds.

The site is open to visitors and makes for a pleasant walk. You can see the layout of the streets and there are signs indicating what was underneath the sections that were covered.

Casa di Mare (☎ 28430 25304; www.casadimare.com; studio €40-60; 🅿 🖳), opposite Kouremenos Beach, has six spacious, comfortable studios with stone floors and rustic-style décor that sleep up to four. There's a small pool among the olive groves.

Apartments Grandes (☎ 28430 61496; www.grandes .gr; q studio €65; 🅿) is a pretty place on Kouremenos Beach surrounded by a flower garden and trees. It's well-equipped, decorated with style and has a beachfront taverna.

ZAKROS & KATO ZAKROS
ΖΑΚΡΟΣ ΚΑΙ ΚΑΤΩ ΖΑΚΡΟΣ

pop 753 & 15

The village of Zakros (*zah*-kros), 45km southeast of Sitia, an important agricultural centre, is the nearest permanent settlement to the east-coast Minoan site of Zakros, 7km away. While there is little incentive to linger in the village (there is only one hotel), it's a lively place where the *kafeneia* and *ouzeries* are always animated and there is rarely a tourist in sight. Zakros is the starting point for the trail through the Zakros Gorge, known as the **Valley of the Dead**. It takes its moniker from the fact that ancient burial sites are located in the numerous caves dotting the canyon walls, rather than from hapless hikers who failed to make it (see the boxed text, p200).

Kato Zakros (*kah*-to *zah*-kros) is just about the most tranquil place to stay on Crete's southeastern coast. It's little more than a long stretch of pebbly beach shaded by pine trees and bordered by a string of tavernas. The settlement is unlikely ever to expand, thanks to restrictions imposed by the archaeological service. Once you've done the gorge and poked around the palace site, there is little to do but relax on the beach, snorkel, fish, sleep and deliberate on what to have for dinner.

Sleeping

The domatia in Kato Zakros fill up fast in the high season, so it is best to book. If there are no rooms available you can camp at the southern end of the beach.

Stella's Apartments (☎ /fax 28430 23739; www.ste lapts.com; studio €40-75) These charming studios are in a lovely verdant, pine-tinged setting 800m along the old road to Zakros. Decorated with wooden furniture made by Elias, the handyman (and hiker), they have barbecues, external kitchen with an honour-system for supplies, and hammocks under the trees. They are perfect for longer stays.

Kato Zakros Palace (☎ /fax 28430 29550; www .palaikastro.com/katozakrospalace; r/studio/apt €45-75) Up on the hill as you approach, this is a bit of an eyesore but does have superb views and spacious new accommodation.

Four good accommodation places in Zakros are under the same **management** (☎ 28430 26893; www.katozakros.cret efamilyhotels.com).

Athena & Coral Rooms (d €30-50; 🅿) Behind the Akrogiali taverna. Athena has pleasant rooms with heavy stone walls, while Coral has excellent, small but spotless rooms equipped with a fridge and great veranda with sea views.

Katerina Apartments (apt €40-60) Four excellent stone-built studios and maisonettes opposite Stellas, which can sleep up to four and enjoy a superb setting.

Poseidon Rooms (d €20-40) Budget rooms in a great spot right on the beach, (some with shared bathrooms) and there's a communal fridge.

Eating

The rivalry can be fierce among the tavernas on the beach.

Akrogiali Taverna (☎ 28430 26893, mains €5-9) Relaxed seaside dining and excellent service from the inimitable owner Nikos Perakis. The speciality is grilled swordfish steak (€9) and the raki is excellent.

Restaurant Nikos Platanakis (☎ 28430 26887; mains €5-7.50) This well-regarded restaurant has a wide range of Greek staples such as rabbit stew, excellent *hortopitakia* (pittas with spinach and greens) and grilled meat and fish. Most of the produce is from the massive vegetable garden out the back.

Getting There & Away

There are buses to Zakros from Sitia via Palekastro (€4.50, one hour, two daily). From June to August, the buses continue to Kato Zakros.

ZAKROS PALACE

Although **Zakros Palace** (☎ 28430 26897; Kato Zakros; admission €3; 🕑 8am-7.30pm Jul-Oct, 8.30am-3pm Nov-Jun) was the last Minoan palace to have been discovered (1962), the excavations proved remarkably fruitful.

The exquisite rock-crystal vase and stone bull's head now in Iraklio's Archaeological Museum (see p149) were found at Zakros, along with a treasure trove of Minoan antiquities. Ancient Zakros, the smallest of Crete's four palatial complexes, was a major port in Minoan times, trading with Egypt, Syria,

LASITHI

WALKS AROUND ZAKROS

A walk through the spectacular Valley of the Dead to Kato Zakros is a must, but there are many other interesting and well-marked but little-traversed trails in the area. Not as lush and dramatic as Crete's west, the barren landscape around Zakros is nonetheless spectacular, with the aroma of wild oregano and thyme wafting from underfoot. Apart from the gorge, all the walks are un-shaded but they are relatively level and much easier than the west for less-fit or older walkers. Always take food and water and wear sturdy footwear.

Most of the walking trails around Zakros have been cleared and signposted with handmade wooden signs by hiking fanatic Elias Pagianidis (find him at Stella's Apartments, p199). He is happy to pass on his knowledge of the area and update Anavasi's Zakros hiking map (which he has posted on a board at the start of the gorge). Elias' suggested walks are listed here. If you have wheels you can also drive to the start of the Hohlakies Gorge and do the one-hour walk to the lovely isolated Karoumes beach.

Zakros Gorge

The walk starts from just below Zakros village and winds it way through a narrow and (at times) soaring canyon with a riot of vegetation and wild herbs. About 3km from Zakros is an alternative starting point, but this way you miss a significant section of the gorge. The trail emerges close to the Zakros Palace, 200m from the beach (two hours).

Kato Zakros to Traostalos

About 10m from the southern mouth of the gorge is a well-marked path up to Mt Traostalos (turn right after 25 minutes at the fork in the path), which offers superb views from the rise at Skopeli (1½ hours). You can walk back the same way or continue to the Pelekita cave, taking the coastal walk back (four hours round trip).

Kato Zakros–Azokeramos–Zakros Gorge

Taking the same path towards Traostalos, this time you take the left fork towards Azokeramos. Rather than go all the way to Azokeramos, at the marked junction near Skafi, veer left towards Vahlias and follow the dry Xeropotamos riverbed south, which meets the Zakros gorge at Lenika, taking you back to the beach (three hours round trip).

Northern coastal walk: Zakros–Pelekita–Karoumes Beach

This is a spectacular route above the sea past an ancient quarry and cave at Pelekita (2½ hours).

Southern coastal walk: Zakros–Xerokambos–Katsounaki Beach

A walk along the east coast (1¾ hours).

Anatolia and Cyprus. The ruins are not well preserved and water levels have risen over the years so that some parts of the palace complex are submerged (and home to many turtles).

If you enter the palace complex on the southern side you will first come to the **workshops** for the palace. The **King's apartment** and **Queen's apartment** are to the right of the entrance. Next to the King's apartment is the **Cistern Hall**, which once had a cistern in the centre surrounded by a colonnaded balustrade. Seven steps descended to the floor of the cistern, which may have been a swimming pool, an aquarium or a pool for a sacred boat. Nearby, the **Central Court**

was the focal point of the whole palace. Notice the altar base in the northwestern corner of the court; there was also a **well** in the southeast corner of the court at the bottom of eight steps. When the site was excavated the well contained the preserved remains of olives that may have been offered to the deities.

Adjacent to the central court is the **Hall of Ceremonies** in which two rhytons were found. To the south is the **Banquet Hall**, so named for the quantity of wine vases found there. To the north of the central court is the **kitchen**. The column bases probably supported the dining room above. To the west of the central court is another **light well** and to the left of the banquet hall is the **Lustral Basin**, which once contained a magnificent marble amphora. The Lustral Basin served as a washroom for those entering the nearby **Central Shrine**. You can still see a ledge and a niche in the south wall for the ceremonial idols.

Below the Lustral Basin is the **Treasury**, which yielded nearly a hundred jars and rhytons. Next to the treasury is the **Archive Room** that once contained Linear A record tablets. Northeast of the archives room is the **bathroom** with a cesspit.

XEROKAMBOS ΞΕΡΟΚΑΜΠΟΣ
pop 28

Xerokambos (kse-*ro*-kam-bos) is a quiet and spread-out agricultural settlement on the far southeastern flank of Crete. Its isolation means that tourism is pretty much low key and most certainly of the unpackaged kind. Its appeal lies in that very isolation. There are a couple of splendid beaches, a few scattered tavernas and studio accommodation.

Ambelos Beach, north of the rocky headland that splits Xerokambos in two, is a small, intimate beach and enjoys some shade. **Mazidas Beach**, on the south, is larger but has no shade. Most accommodation and tavernas are near Ambelos. There is a well-stocked mini-market on the north side of Mazidas Beach.

Sleeping & Eating
Ambelos Beach Studios (☎ /fax 28430 26759; studio €30-40) These cosy studios have basic

ZAKROS PALACE

Archive Room	1	A3
Banquet Hall	2	B3
Bathroom	3	C3
Central Shrine	4	A3
Cistern Hall	5	C4
Hall of Ceremonies	6	B3
King's Apartment	7	B3
Kitchen & Dining Room	..8	B3
Light Well	9	A3
Lustral Basin	10	A3
Main Gate	11	C3
Queen's Apartment	12	B3
Storeroom Block	13	B3
Storerooms	14	B3
Treasury	15	A3
Well	16	B4
Workshops	17	B4

0 — 50 m

Central Court

North East Court

South Entrance

LASITHI

kitchenettes, fridges and flyscreens. There is a barbecue and outdoor wood oven for guests, and a tree-shaded garden courtyard that makes it well-suited to families. It's just across from the beach.

Akti Apartments (☎ 28430 26780; studio €35-45; 🞨) With balconies overlooking the beach, these comfortable studios are perfect for couples. They are light and nicely decorated and have kitchenettes. There are also family apartments (€65-80).

Villa Petrino (☎ 28430 26702; www.xerokampos.eu; d €40; 🞨) These attractive, large, fully equipped apartments are suitable for families. Overlooking the garden, they have built-in beds, marble floors and the top rooms have beach views.

Kostas Taverna (☎ 28430 26702; mains €3-6) Next to Villa Petrino, this friendly and well-regarded taverna has a shady veranda with views out to sea. The multilingual owner, Nikos, is happy to show you the day's offering in the trays and pots in the kitchen. Try the rabbit *rismarato* with rosemary and vinegar served with hand-cut fried potatoes.

Akrogiali Taverna (☎ 28430 26777; mains €4.50-8) Near Ambelos Beach Studios, this is the only real beachside taverna in Xerokambos. Under new management, it does a range of mezedes, grills and home-style specials such as rabbit (in busy periods).

Getting There & Away

There are no buses to Xerokambos. From Zakros there's a signposted turnoff to Xerokambos, via an 8km winding dirt road that is rough but drivable in a conventional vehicle (it was slowly being asphalted when we were there). Otherwise there is a good paved road from Ziros.

SOUTH COAST

IERAPETRA ΙΕΡΑΠΕΤΡΑ
pop 11,877

Ierapetra (yeh-*rah*-pet-rah) is Europe's most southerly major town that services the surrounding farming region. Ierapetra's main business continues to be agriculture rather than tourism, as the greenhouses that line the landscape along the coast will attest. Despite being one of the wealthiest cities in Greece, it is a largely unremarkable place

and it attracts relatively few tourists. There are tavernas and cafés along the waterfront, a small Venetian fort on the harbour and the odd remnant of a Turkish quarter. The town beach and surrounding beaches are good, the nightlife busy enough and the scene is still Cretan enough to give you a less touristy experience of the island.

Ierapetra was an important city for the Dorians and the last city to fall to the Romans, who made it a major port of call in their conquest of Egypt. The city languished under the Venetians, but they did build the small fortress at the western end of the harbour.

From Ierapetra you can visit the offshore, low-lying, sandy island of Gaidouronisi (also known as Hrysi).

Every Saturday there is a street **market** on Psilinaki St from 7am to 2pm.

Orientation & Information

The bus station is on the eastern side of town and there are ATMs around the main square. Find town information at www.ierap etra.net.

City Netcafé (☎ 28420 23164; Kothri 6; per hr €2.50; 🕙 9am-late) Check email here.

Post office (☎ 28420 22271; Kornarou 7; 🕙 7.30am-2pm)

Sights

Ierapetra's one-room **archaeological museum** (☎ 28420 28721; Adrianou (Dimokratias) 2; admission €2; 🕙 8.30am-3pm Tue-Sun) is perfect for those with a short concentration span. It does have a good collection of headless classical statuary and a superb statue of the goddess Persephone that dates from the 2nd century AD. Also notable is a *larnax* (clay coffin), dated around 1300 BC, decorated with 12 painted panels showing hunting scenes, an octopus and a chariot procession. The 1899 building was a school during Ottoman times.

South along the waterfront is the **medieval fortress** (admission free; 🕙 8.30am-3pm Tue-Sun), built in the early years of Venetian rule and strengthened by Francesco Morosini in 1626. It was in a pretty fragile state and closed for restoration at the time of research.

Inland from here is the labyrinthine **old quarter**, where you will see a **Turkish fountain**, the restored **mosque** with its minaret, and the old churches of **Agios Ioannis** and **Agios Georgios**. **Napoleon's house** is where the man

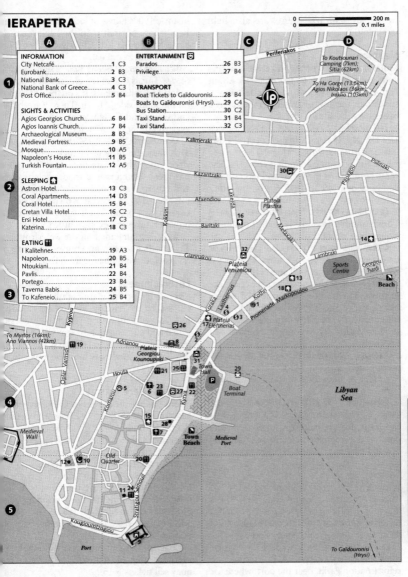

IERAPETRA

INFORMATION		
City Netcafé	1	C3
Eurobank	2	B3
National Bank	3	C3
National Bank of Greece	4	C3
Post Office	5	B4
SIGHTS & ACTIVITIES		
Agios Georgios Church	6	B4
Agios Ioannis Church	7	B4
Archaeological Museum	8	B3
Medieval Fortress	9	B5
Mosque	10	A5
Napoleon's House	11	B5
Turkish Fountain	12	A5
SLEEPING		
Astron Hotel	13	C3
Coral Apartments	14	D3
Coral Hotel	15	B4
Cretan Villa Hotel	16	C2
Ersi Hotel	17	C3
Katerina	18	C3
EATING		
I Kalitehnes	19	A3
Napoleon	20	B5
Ntoukiani	21	B4
Pavlis	22	B4
Portego	23	B4
Taverna Babis	24	B5
To Kafeneio	25	B4

ENTERTAINMENT		
Parados	26	B3
Privilege	27	B4
TRANSPORT		
Boat Tickets to Gaïdouronisi	28	B4
Boats to Gaïdouronisi (Hrysi)	29	C4
Bus Station	30	C2
Taxi Stand	31	B4
Taxi Stand	32	C3

himself is said to have stayed incognito with a local family when his ship anchored in Crete for one night in 1798 on the way to Egypt. He apparently left a note revealing his identity.

The main **town beach** is near the harbour, while a second **beach** stretches east from the bottom of Patriarhou Metaxaki. Both have coarse, grey sand, but the main beach offers better shade.

Festivals & Events

Ierapetra's annual **Kyrvia Festival** runs from July to August and features a wide range of concerts, plays and art exhibitions. Brochures are available in hotels and at the town hall. Cultural events are also held in spring.

Sleeping

Koutsounari Camping (☎ 28420 61213; www.camping-koutsounari.epimlas.gr; per tent/adult €4/6) About 7km east at Koutsounari, it has a restaurant, snack bar and mini-market. Ierapetra-Sitia buses pass the site.

Ersi Hotel (☎ 28420 23208; Plateia Eleftherias 19; d €30; ✗) This refurbished central hotel has neat rooms with a fridge, TV and sea views, though some are rather compact. The same family runs the Coral and larger fully-equipped apartments (€45-60) on the other side of town.

Coral Hotel (☎ 28420 22846; Katzonovatsi 12; d €30) This is another reasonable budget option in a quiet pocket of the old town.

Cretan Villa Hotel (☎ /fax 28420 28522; www.cretan-villa.com; Lakerda 16; s/d with aircon €40/50, without aircon €35/44; ✗) This well-maintained 18th-century house is the most atmospheric place in town. The traditionally furnished rooms have a fridge and TV, and there is a peaceful courtyard. It's a five-minute walk from the bus station. The rooms without air-con are cheaper.

Katerina (☎ 28420 28345; fax 28420 28591; Markopoulou 95; r €45; ✗) The sea views are the saving grace of these dreary rooms with basic bathrooms.

Astron Hotel (☎ 28420 25114; htastron@otenet.gr; Kothri 56; s/d incl breakfast €50/75; ✗) The town's top hotel, it's a block from the beach. The comfortable rooms here come with satellite TV and telephone; some have sea views.

Eating

Ierapetra has an excellent tradition of *rakadika*, relaxed evening hang-outs where a carafe of raki or wine comes with half a dozen or more tasty tid-bits, making it a good value slow dining experience. You could try **To Kafeneio** opposite the town hall, the popular **Ntoukiani** (Ethnikis Antistaseos 19) or the modern reincarnation **Pavlis**, near the port, where for €3 per carafe you get six or seven plates of excellent mezes.

ourpick **Portego** (☎ 28420 27733; Foniadaki 8; mezedes €3-5, wood-oven specials €5-9) This delightful restaurant serves excellent Cretan and Greek cuisine and has dishes cooked in the wood-fired oven (as is their bread). Try the lamb in a clay pot with yogurt. It is housed in the historic 1900s house of local character Anna Bey, whose portrait is in the back room. I has a good wine list, a lovely courtyard for summer and a cool bar.

Napoleon (☎ 28420 22410; Stratigou Samouil 26; main €4.50-9) This is one of the oldest and most respected establishments. It's on the waterfront on the south side of town. There is fresh fish and Greek and Cretan specialties, but whatever you order is of a high quality.

I Kalitehnes (☎ 28420 28547; Kyprou 26; mains €4-7) This colourful little place tucked in a back street among hardware stores and tyre shop has great-value organic food, such as okra and potatoes and spicier falafel and kebab introduced by the Egyptian owner, as well as its own tasty bread. The Turkish squat toilet, however, takes the exotic a little too far.

Also recommended on the waterfront are Taverna Babis, with an enormous range of mezedes, or Gorgona for fresh fish.

Entertainment

Kyrva is Ierapetra's main nightlife strip, with clubs such as Privilege and others catering to locals with non-stop Greek club music. You'll find more nightclubs around the corner on Foniadaki. Portego is a classy place for a drink, while Parados, behind the museum, is known for jazz.

Getting There & Away

There are nine buses per day from Ierapetra's **bus station** (☎ 28420 28237; Lasthenous) to Iraklio (€8.60, 2½ hours), via Agios Nikolaos (€3.30, one hour) and Gournia; seven to Sitia (€5, 1½ hours) via Koutsounari (for camp sites); and seven to Myrtos (€1.60, 30 minutes).

Taxis (☎ 28420 26600) can take you anywhere for a fixed fare. Fares are posted outside the town hall rank for destinations including Iraklio (€74), Agios Nikolaos (€33), Sitia (€50) and Myrtos (€14). There is another rank at Plateia Venizelou.

Boats for Gaidouronisi leave from the quay every morning. Most travel agents around the quay sell tickets (€15).

GAIDOURONISI (HRYSI ISLAND)
ΓΑΙΔΑΡΟΥΝΗΣΙ/ΧΡΥΣΙ

Just off the coast of Ierapetra, you will find greater tranquillity at Gaidouronisi (Donkey Island) – universally marketed in Ierapetra as Hrysi or Hrissi (Golden Island) – where there are good sandy beaches, a taverna (alarmingly rumoured to be taken over by a chain snack store), and a stand of Lebanon cedars, the only one in Europe. It can get very crowded when the tour boats are in, but you can always find a quiet spot.

In summer, **excursion boats** (€15) leave from the Ierapetra quay every morning and return in the afternoon.

HA GORGE ΦΑΡΑΓΓΙ ΧΑ

Some 13.5km north of Ierapetra is the wild and beautiful **Ha Gorge**, perhaps the most challenging gorge to traverse in all of Europe. More of an extreme climbing experience than a hike – most of the time you need ropes or must swim – the Ha Gorge is a narrow rent in the imposing mountains with water running its entire length – including 27 waterfalls. The first intrepid climbers to successfully cross it (1987) took seven days to tackle the 1800m gorge. It was secured in recent times and an experienced team of climbers can do the gutwrenching and occasionally dangerous hike in three to six hours (see p74).

EAST OF IERAPETRA

The good beaches to the east of Ierapetra tend to be crowded in peak season and you really need a car to explore the area. About 13km east is the lovely beach of **Agias Fotias**, although it's no longer the isolated beach that was popular with campers.

Much of this coastline has been dotted by plastic-covered greenhouses and haphazard unattractive tourism development. There's little on the drive through to make you want to stop but there are some appealing tucked-away places. You would be excused for driving straight through **Koutsouras**, but just off the main road **Rovinsona's** (☎ 28430 51026; mezes €4-7; ◷ 3pm till late) is a delightful surprise, overlooking the beach under giant tamarisk trees,

with superb food and excellent music. It has a refreshing yogurt dip with purslane, but the highlight is the wood-oven pies – share the goat-and-cheese pie with fennel (€8).

Kalliotzina (☎ 28430 51207) next door is a highly regarded taverna, with tables overlooking the beach and standard taverna fare. Signposted off the beach road, **Big Blue** (☎ 28430 52100; d €40; ⊠) has a range of bright studios and apartments right on the pebble beach with a pleasant beach bar.

The fine white sandy beach at the eastern end of **Makrigialos,** 24km from Ierapetra, is one of the best on the southeastern coast, but the town has been swamped by the giant Sunwing resort and other development that obscures the beachfront promenade and the pleasant port.

On the road to Sitia, you can take a detour to the abandoned medieval village of **Voila**, on a hill 1km above the village of Handras (well signposted). A relatively well-preserved tower and arches on the dwellings reveal a mix of architectural styles. There is also a flowing Venetian fountain nearby.

About 7km east of Makrigialos, on the scenic drive along the rocky coastline, is **Moni Kapsa** (☎ 28430 51638; ◷ 8.30am-12.30pm & 3.30-8pm), built into the craggy cliffs. It has a colourful history, flourishing under small-time crook and self-proclaimed miracle worker Gerontogiannis (after a timely vision from god) who used his ill-gotten fame and fortune to extend the monastery. There are some fine icons and ornate wooden temples in the chapels. The monastery is built at the mouth of the **Perivolakia Gorge** (Kapsa), a 3.5km walk from the village Perivolakia, which emerges at a decent small beach.

At the half-way point to Kapsa from Makrigialos, it is worth a detour up the hill to the signposted **Spilia Tou Drakou** (Cave of the Dragon;

LASITHI

MUSICAL SURPRISES

What's Pavarotti's old Bosendorfer grand piano doing in the southern resort of Makrigialos? It was one way Norwegian-born businessman Gunnar Stromsholm showed he was serious about hosting a world-class music festival in Crete. Since the first concert was held in the courtyard of his villa, Case dei Mezzo, in 2004, the **Casa dei Mezzo music festival** (☎ 28430 29183; www .casadeimezzo-festival.com; tickets €10) has become an annual event, held in June, with leading pianist and conductor Bryan Stanborough as patron and artistic director. Among the eclectic 2007 lineup was Japan's foremost soprano Ranko Kurano performing *Madame Butterfly*. Performances are held at several venues, including the original de Mezzo tower and **Epavli** – the nearby ruins of a stunning Venetian mansion in the abandoned medieval village of Etia.

LASITHI

ROUGHING IT

The primitive 300-year-old stone cottages at **Aspros Potamos** (☎ 28430 51694; www.asprospotamos .com; r €32-60) were traditionally used by farmers from the hillside village of Pefki during the winter. Aspros Potamos is just above Makrigialos on the road to Pefki. Twenty years ago, Aleka Halkia bought the abandoned ruins of the settlement and has slowly restored them in original style as guesthouses for people wanting to go back to nature and simple living. An award-winning eco-friendly photovoltaic system is used to heat water and power the bathroom light and fridge. The 11 cottages are lit with oil lamps and candles, and have stone floors, traditional furnishings and most have fireplaces for the winter. One has a bedroom built right into the rock face. Aleka lives there year-round and runs them with her daughter Myrto, who has now moved to town for some mod cons. It's a few kilometres along the turn-off north to Pefki. It can be a little tricky to find, so call ahead and they'll meet you.

Just above Aspros Potamos you will come across the **Stausa Workshop** (☎ 28430 51410) of artisans Maria Palumbo and Makis Ladas, who live in their isolated stone cottage year-round creating unique pieces from driftwood and other recycled natural materials. It is a pleasant walk from Makrigialos or the road is signposted on the western side of the bridge.

☎ 28430 51494). The cave is actually named after the guy who runs the taverna below, which has stunning sea views from the terrace and excellent food. Try the grilled lamb cutlets (€8.50) or the local speciality *nerati*, a *myzithra*-and-fennel pie.

MYRTOS ΜΥΡΤΟΣ
pop 425

One of the few places on this stretch of coast that retains an element of authenticity and vil-

lage ambience is Myrtos (*myr*-tos), 14km west of Ierapetra. It is popular with more mature travellers, many of whom have been coming back for years. Myrtos has no big hotels, there's a reasonable patch of beach, some decently priced places to stay and eat and some interesting excursions in the area.

There is no post office or bank. Internet access is available at **Prima Travel** (☎ 28420 51035; www.sunbudget.net; per hr €3.50), which serves as the town's quasi-tourist office and leads guided walks around the area.

DETOUR: THE HINTERLAND

There is some great off-road exploring to be done in the mountains above Ierapetra and the lesser-known misty Omalos Plateau if you have the right vehicle. But even in a conventional vehicle (or on foot) you can see some relatively untrodden parts of Crete. There are several routes to explore. Taking the scenic road northeast from Ierapetra, you pass the **Bramiana Dam**, a manmade dam that has become a significant wetland for migratory birds. From above, you can see the scale of the plastic greenhouses but then you enter a dramatic ever-changing mountain landscapes, from barren rocky precipices to verdant forests. From the peak of the picturesque village of **Kalamafka,** one of the narrowest and highest points on the island, you can see both the north coast and the Libyan sea to the south.

South of Kalamafka is the heritage-protected, virtually abandoned village of **Anatoli**, which is being restored thanks to EU funds. It has a remarkably preserved main street with original shopfronts, and at the time of research a couple of guesthouses were opening in anticipation of the village's revival.

Just outside Males is the tiny **Agia Paraskevi chapel** built into the rock face near a running waterfall and café. The old-style taverna on the road below the chapel is run by an elderly couple who just cook a bit extra for occasional passing guests, so there are only a few options (we had the local speciality *gardoumia* – stomach wrapped in intestines).

At the foot of the superb **Selekano forest,** part of the E4 trail, is the tiny village of Selekano, which was one of the last places in Crete to get power – in 2006. Until then the quaint **Stella's kafeneio** used to run on a wood oven and gas. Her shady vine canopy is a good place for a break. There is a scenic drive back to Myrtos via Mythi.

Myrtos' small **museum** (☎ 28420 51065; admission
ee; ⊙ 9am-1pm Mon-Fri) houses the private col-
ection of a former teacher who sparked the
rchaeological digs in the area after finding
Minoan artefacts on field trips with students.
The collection includes Vasiliki pottery from
he nearby Minoan sites of **Fournou-Korifi** and
Pyrgos as well as an impressive model of the
Fournou-Korifi site exactly as it was found,
with all the pots and items in situ.

The consensus on the waterfront tavernas seems to be Taverna Akti for the daily
pecials, Manos at the eastern end for grilled
meats and Beach on the west side for fresh
fish and mezes.

Big Blue (☎ 28420 51094; www.big-blue.gr; d/studio/
pt €35/60/75; 🔲) On the western edge of town,
his is one of the best places to stay and is
andy for the beach. You have a choice of
more expensive, large airy studios with sea
iews, or cheaper, cosy ground-floor rooms.
All have cooking facilities.

Cretan Rooms (☎ 28420 51427; d €35) These
cosy, excellent traditional-styled rooms with
balconies, fridges and shared kitchens are
popular with independent travellers. Owner
Maria Daskalaki keeps them neat and clean.
They are prominently signposted from the
main street.

Hotel Myrtos (☎ 28420 51227; www.myrtoshotel
.com; s/d/triple incl breakfast €30/35/40; 🔲) This
superior C-class place in the middle of
the main street has large, well-kept rooms
with TV, phone, mini-bar and balconies.
Its taverna (mains €4 to €7) is popular with
both locals and tourists for its wide range of
mezedes and *mayirefta*, which include many
vegetarian dishes.

Platanos (☎ 28420 51363; mains €4.50-8) This
seems to be the heartbeat of the town for foreigners. It's a cosy place for a drink or dinner
under a giant plane tree.

There are seven buses daily from Ierapetra
to Myrtos (€1.60, 30 minutes).

LASITHI

Directory

CONTENTS

PRACTICALITIES

- Use the metric system for weights and measures (see inside front cover for conversion formulas).

- Plug your electrical appliances into a two-pin electrical adaptor before plugging into the electricity supply (220V AC, 50Hz).

- The main English-language newspapers in Greece are the weekly *Athens News* and the eight-page English-language section of the Greek daily *Kathimerini*, published with the *International Herald Tribune*.

- The English and German newspaper *Cretasummer* is published monthly during the summer in Rethymno. The monthly magazine *Kreta* is on sale in a variety of languages. *Frappe* is published in Hania in German and English. Crete's e-zine *Stigmes* (www.stigmes.gr) is also worth a look. *Crete Gazette* is a free monthly newsletter distributed at various outlets and is also available online (www.cretegazette.com).

- You can often pick up CNN and the BBC on free-to-air TV, and cable is available at many hotels.

- Greece uses the PAL video system, which is incompatible with the North American and Japanese NTSC system.

ACCOMMODATION

Crete has a wide range of places to stay to suit every taste and budget, from cheap, ultra-basic rooms and well-equipped self-catering studios to traditional village houses and super-luxury resorts. Crete still offers good value accommodation compared to other islands, with the south and the inland villages being significantly cheaper than the north coast. Outside July and August you can pretty much turn up and find accommodation, but booking is advisable at the peak of summer.

The industry is subject to strict price controls. By law, a notice must be displayed in every room (usually behind the door) stating the category and the maximum price they can charge that season. Generally the prices quoted in this book are these official high-season rates (or the higher end of what you are likely to pay, as many places never charge the official rates), but outside the peak July and August period there is often plenty of room for negotiation, especially for longer stays. Spring and autumn are good times to test your bargaining skills.

A mandatory charge of 20% extra is levied if an extra bed is put into a room.

Some domatia owners charge extra for air-conditioning. This is only permissible if the total price is not higher than the advertised maximum (which should include air-con).

Rip-offs do occasionally occur so, if you suspect you've been exploited, report it to either the tourist police or regular police.

Many accommodation proprietors will want to keep your passport during your stay. However, this is not a compulsory requirement – they only need it to take down the details.

Camping

There are only about a dozen or so camping grounds in Crete. Most are privately run, very few are open outside the summer high season, and the quality is patchy. Most have an attached taverna and some more upmarket complexes have pools and their own caravans and tents for hire.

The **Panhellenic Camping Association** (☎ /fax 21036 21560; www.panhellenic-camping-union.gr; Solonos 102, Athens) website has lists of their member camp sites and facilities. A free booklet on Camping in Greece is also published annually by the Greek national tourist office, Ellinikos Organismos Tourismou (EOT) – known abroad as the Greek National Tourism Organisation (GNTO).

Camping fees are highest from mid-June to the end of August. Most camping grounds charge from €4 to €6 per adult. Children under 12 are normally charged half price and students get a discount. There's no charge for children aged under four. Tent sites cost from €3 to €6 per night, depending on size. Caravan sites start at around €8.

Between May and mid-September it is warm enough to sleep out under the stars, although you will still need a lightweight sleeping bag to counter the pre-dawn chill. It's a good idea to have a foam pad to lie on and a waterproof cover to protect your sleeping bag.

Free (wild) camping is illegal, but the law is not always strictly enforced and some areas are more tolerant and renowned for it, especially along the south coast. It is wise to ask around.

Domatia

Domatia are the Greek equivalent of the British B&B, minus the breakfast. Once upon a time domatia (also called *pensions*) comprised little more than spare rooms in the family home that were rented out to travellers, which made for very cheap holidays. Nowadays most are purpose built, and simple (and cheap) older-style basic lodgings are becoming rarer as many have been upgraded into 'studios' and come complete with well-equipped kitchenettes, TVs and air-con. They remain a popular option for budget travellers and are often far more appealing (and sometimes better equipped) than many bland, impersonal midrange hotels.

Domatia are rated under a 'key' system, which determines what owners can charge. Standards of cleanliness are generally high. The décor runs the gamut from cool grey marble floors, coordinated pine furniture, pretty lace curtains and tasteful pictures on the walls, to outright spartan.

Expect to pay from €20 to €30 for a single, and €30 to €50 for a double, depending on facilities, the season and how long you plan to stay.

Some domatia have solar-heated water, which means hot water is not guaranteed, though this is rarely a problem. Most operate only between April and October.

Hostels

There are official youth hostels in Rethymno, Plakias and Iraklio, as well as a few hotels operating as unofficial hostels. The Rethymno and Plakias hostels are well-run and sociable places, with decent facilities.

Hostel rates vary from €7 to €15 and you don't have to be a member to stay in any of them.

Hotels & Resorts

Crete has some of the best resort hotels in Greece, including some elite spa-hotel developments, but standards vary dramatically. While most of the top hotels are world class and have all the expected amenities, some midrange hotels are little better than domatia. There are some smart boutique-style hotels in the major cities, while Hania and Rethymno have many atmospheric guesthouses in superbly restored Venetian mansions or historic buildings.

The official classification system in Greece has changed from the old letter grading (A–E, plus L for deluxe categories) to a more international star-rating system with much higher standards. What might have qualified as an

A-class hotel under the old system is probably three-star under the new guidelines. Hotels built since 2002 meet the new criteria, but most existing hotels were automatically switched over to the star-rating (L – five stars, A – four stars, B – three stars, C – two stars, D and E – one star). Greek hotels are now in a transitional stage as the slow process of inspecting all hotels to ensure they comply with their classification is still under way.

Overall, quality of hotels and service in Crete varies dramatically and often irrespective of price. Expect to pay about €60 – 70 for a double in a two-star hotel in Iraklio and about €80 – 120 per double in a three-star. There has been a shift towards all-inclusive holiday packages in many of the hotels, which are booked by tour operators and not very appealing to independent travellers. Many hotels offer significant internet discounts.

Mountain Refuges

Mountain refuges are not plentiful on Crete but there are some lodges scattered around the Lefka Ori, Mt Psiloritis and Mt Ditki run by the mountaineering clubs in the region. A bunk bed will cost around €13 for non members. Further information can be obtained from the mountaineering clubs (p74) and are listed in www.crete.tournet .gr/outdoor/shelters-en.jsp.

Studios & Apartments

Self-catering studios or apartments are a popular option for travellers on longer stays, or families. Studios are usually two-person affairs, while apartments can normally accommodate two to five people. Facilities usually include a kitchenette, fridge and TV, and many include air-conditioning, heating for winter, a separate lounge area, separate bedrooms and occasionally washing facilities and microwave ovens. Costs for a studio in high season range from €35 to €60 while an apartment for four people in high season will cost between €50 and €80.

Traditional Houses, Eco-Lodges & Villas

Many historic houses and lovely stone cottages across Crete have been restored and converted into fine accommodation, from rustic studios to upmarket villas with private pools. EU funding for restoration of old villages with buildings of architectural merit has spawned many new rural developments, though most

have gone for the mid- to higher-end market. There are also places where you can stay on farms or rural estates.

Some of the more established examples are at Vamos (p119) and the eco-lodges at Milia (p115) and near Markigialos in the south (p206). Traditional features such as fireplaces, stone kitchens and traditional rustic furnishings provide an atmospheric experience. A traditional house for two to four people in Vamos will cost around €75 to €120, while a small stone cottage for two in Milia will cost around €65 to €70.

Check out www.agrotravel.gr for a list of villas and traditional-style homes.

In recent years there has been a proliferation of new villa developments and restored historic houses across Crete for people wanting to rent an idyllic private place for a week or more. Most of these are in the high end of the market and are rented through foreign companies.

ACTIVITIES

Crete's adventurous terrain lends itself to a host of activities for the more active traveller. For the full lowdown see the Crete Outdoors chapter (p70).

BUSINESS HOURS

Banks are open from 8am to 2.30pm Monday to Thursday, and 8am to 2pm Friday.

Post offices are open 7.30am to 2pm Monday to Friday. In the major cities the main post office stays open until 8pm, and opens from 8am to 2pm on Saturday.

In summer, shops are open 9am to 2pm and 5.30pm to 8.30pm Tuesday, Thursday and Friday, and 8am to 3pm Monday, Wednesday and Saturday. They open 30 minutes later in winter, although these times are not always strictly adhered to. Many shops in tourist areas are open seven days a week until 11pm. *Periptera* (street kiosks) open

---

BOOK ACCOMMODATION ONLINE

For more accommodation reviews and recommendations by Lonely Planet authors, check out the online booking service at www.lonelyplanet.com. You'll find the true, insider lowdown on the best places to stay. Reviews are thorough and independent. Best of all, you can book online.

from early morning until late at night and sell everything from bus tickets and cigarettes to condoms. Supermarkets are generally open until 8pm.

Opening times of museums and archaeological sites vary, depending on when extra staff are hired to cover afternoon shifts. Check if you plan to visit after 3pm. Most sites are closed on Monday.

CHILDREN

Crete is a safe and relatively easy place to travel with children, especially easy if you're staying by the beach or at a resort hotel. Greeks love kids, to the point of spoiling them, so they are normally welcome everywhere. Greek children join their parents at tavernas or play happily outside in the squares or streets at night in keeping with the local late routine.

There is a shortage of decent playgrounds and recreational facilities across the island. However, there are air-conditioned indoor children's play centres for children in most major cities if you want a respite from the heat.

Don't be afraid to take children to ancient sites. Many parents are surprised by how much children enjoy them.

Hotels and restaurants are usually very accommodating when it comes to meeting the needs of children, although highchairs are a rarity outside resorts. The service in tavernas is normally very quick, which is great when you've got hungry kids on your hands.

Fresh milk is readily available in large towns and tourist areas, but harder to find in small villages. Formula is available everywhere.

Mobility is an issue for parents with very small children. Strollers (pushchairs) aren't much use in Crete unless you're going to spend all your time in one of the few flat spots. They're hopeless on rough stone paths and up steps, and a curse when getting on and off buses and ferries. Backpacks or front pouches are best.

Children under four travel free on ferries and buses. They pay half fare up to the age of 10 (ferries) and 12 (buses); the full fare applies otherwise. On domestic flights, you'll pay 10% of the fare to have a child under two sitting on your knee. Kids aged two to 12 pay half fare.

The Greek publisher Malliaris-Paedia produces a good series of books on Greek myths, retold in English for young readers by Aristides Kesopoulos. *The Moon Over Crete,* by Jyotsna Sreenivasen and Sim Gellman, is a modern-day story based in Crete, written for young girls but with a mature message.

CLIMATE CHART

Crete has a typically Mediterranean climate with hot, dry summers and milder winters. You can comfortably swim off the island's southern coast from mid-April to November.

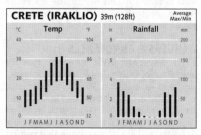

COURSES

The **University of Crete** (☎ 28310 77278; www.philology .uoc.gr) in Rethymno runs four-week summer courses in Modern Greek for foreigners during July. Classes are in the mornings and cater for beginners to advanced level. Contact the university for full details.

UK-based **YOGA Plus** (☎ +44 1273-276175; www .yogaplus.co.uk) runs Astanga Vinyasa yoga workshops for one week or longer at its retreat in Agios Pavlos. The courses include accommodation, other activities and wholesome food. The nearby **Triopetra Yoga Centre** (www .astanga.gr) also runs courses from beginners to advanced levels.

Workshops in Cretan cuisine are offered in around Crete (see p63 for details).

UK-based **World Spirit** (www.worldspirit.org .uk) organises a writing and poetry course in the southern village of Loutro in June and September.

CUSTOMS

There are no longer duty-free restrictions or sales within the EU. Random and cursory customs searches are still made for drugs.

You can bring an unlimited amount of foreign currency into Greece but you can only leave with US$2500 cash (or equivalent). Any more must be in a bank cheque or money order. Exporting antiquities (anything over 100 years old) is strictly forbidden without a permit. It is an offence to remove even the smallest article from an archaeological site.

Non-EU residents can bring 200 cigarettes or 50 cigars; 1L of spirits or 2L of wine; 50g of perfume; 250mL of eau de Cologne and gifts with a value of up to €175.

Importation of works of art and antiquities is free, but they must be declared on entry, so you can take them with you.

Importing codeine-based medication is illegal without a doctor's certificate and it is wise to have a doctor's certificate if you are taking any medication. Dogs and cats must have a vet's certificate.

DANGERS & ANNOYANCES

Crime, especially theft, is low in Crete but keep track of your valuables on public transport and in markets. Do not leave luggage unattended in cars. The vast majority of thefts from tourists are still committed by other tourists; the biggest danger of theft is probably in hostels and at camping grounds. If you are staying in a hotel room, and the windows and door do not lock securely, ask for your valuables to be locked in the hotel safe.

DISCOUNT CARDS
Senior Cards
Card-carrying EU pensioners can claim a range of benefits such as reduced admission charges at museums and ancient sites and discounts on trains.

Student & Youth Cards
The most widely recognised form of student ID is the **International Student Identity Card** (ISIC; www.isic.org). These cards are widely available from budget travel agencies (take along proof that you are a student). Holders qualify for half-price admission to some museums and ancient sites. There are no travel agencies authorised to issue ISICs in Crete, so arrange for one before leaving home or get one in Athens from the **International Student & Youth Travel Service** (ISYTS; ☎ 210 323 3767; 2nd fl, Nikis 11, Athens).

Some travel agencies in Greece offer student discounts on organised tours. Olympic Airways gives a 25% student discount on domestic flights that are part of an international flight.

If you are under 26 years of age but not a student, the **Federation of International Youth Travel Organisation** (FIYTO; www.fiyto.org) card gives similar discounts. Many budget travel agencies issue FIYTO cards.

EMBASSIES & CONSULATES

Remember that you are bound by Greek laws. Your embassy will not be sympathetic if you end up in jail after committing a crime locally, even if such actions are legal in your own country.

In genuine emergencies you might get some assistance, but only if other channels have been exhausted. If you need to get home urgently, a free ticket is highly unlikely – the embassy would expect you to have insurance. If you have all your money and documents stolen, it will assist with getting a new passport.

Greek Embassies & Consulates
Some Greek diplomatic missions abroad:

Australia (☎ 02-6273 3011; greekemb@greekembassy-au.org; 9 Turrana St, Yarralumla, ACT 2600)

Canada (☎ 613-238-6271; www.greekembassy.ca; 76-80 Maclaren St, Ottawa, Ontario K2P 0K6)

Japan (☎ 03-3403 0871/2; www.greekemb.jp; 3-16-30 Nishi Azabu, Minato-ku, Tokyo 304-5853)

New Zealand (☎ 04-473 7775; info@greece.org.nz; 5-7 Willeston St, Wellington)

South Africa (☎ 12-430 7351; embgrsaf@global.co.za; 1003 Church St, Hatfield, Pretoria 0028)

UK (☎ 020-7229 3850; www.greekembassy.org.uk; 1A Holland Park, London W11 3TP)

USA (☎ 202-939-1300; www.greekembassy.org; 2221 Massachusetts Ave NW, Washington, DC 20008)

Embassies & Consulates in Greece
The **UK embassy** (☎ 2810 224 012; Papalexandrou 16) in Iraklio is the only foreign embassy in Crete. The rest are in Athens and its suburbs.

Australia (☎ 210 870 4000; Kifisias 1, Ambelokipi)

Canada (☎ 210 727 3400; Genadiou 4, Evangelismos)

Cyprus (☎ 210 723 7883; Irodotou 16, 10675)

Ireland (☎ 210 723 2771; Leoforos Vasileos Konstantinou 7, 10674)

Japan (☎ 210 670 9900; Ethnikis Antistaseos 46, Halandri)

Netherlands (☎ 210 723 9701; Vasileos Konstantinou 5-7, 10674)

COPIES

All important documents (passport data page and visa page, credit cards, travel insurance policy, air/bus/train tickets, driving licence etc) should be photocopied before you leave home. Leave one copy with someone at home and keep another with you, separate from the originals.

New Zealand (☎ 210 692 4136; Kifisias 76, Ambelokipi)
South Africa (☎ 210 680 6645; Kifisias 60, Marousi, 15125)
USA (☎ 210 721 2951; Vasilissis Sofias 91, Ambelokipi)

FESTIVALS & EVENTS

The Greek year is a succession of festivals and events, some of which are religious, some cultural, others an excuse for a good feast, and most a combination of all three. The following is by no means an exhaustive list, but it covers the most important events, both national and regional. If you're in the right place at the right time, you'll certainly be welcome to join the revelry.

In summer, cultural festivals are staged across Crete. The most significant include the annual **Renaissance Festival** in Rethymno (p126), which features art exhibitions, plus dance, drama and films, and the **Kyrvia Festival** in Ierapetra (p203), which includes a range of musical, theatrical and artistic presentations.

Iraklio's **Summer Arts Festival** (p154) runs from July to September and attracts international artists as well as local singers and dancers, while the **Lato Cultural Festival** in Agios Nikolaos (p183) features traditional and modern works performed by local and international orchestras and dance troupes. Sitia's **Kornaria Festival** (p195) presents music, theatre, art exhibits and a beach volleyball competition.

January

Feast of Agios Vasilios (St Basil) The year kicks off with the New Year's Day festival. A church ceremony is followed by the exchanging of gifts, singing, dancing and feasting; the *vasilopita* (New Year pie) is cut and the person who gets the slice containing a coin will supposedly have a lucky year.

Epiphany (the Blessing of the Waters) On 6 January, Christ's baptism by St John is celebrated throughout Greece. Seas, lakes and rivers are blessed and crosses are thrown into the water. The brave soul who retrieves the cross is blessed for the year.

February/March

Shrove Monday (Clean Monday) On the first day of Lent, people take to the hills throughout Greece to have picnics and fly kites.

March

Independence Day The anniversary of the hoisting of the Greek flag at Moni Agias Lavras in the Peloponnese is celebrated on 25 March with parades and dancing. It marked the start of the War of Independence. Independence Day coincides with the Feast of the Annunciation, so it is also a religious festival.

March/April

Easter The most important religious holiday in Greece is Easter (which most years fall at a different time to non-Orthodox Easter because the date is calculated using a different formula and calendar). On Palm Sunday (the Sunday before Easter), worshippers return from church services with a cross woven of palm and myrtle. If you are in Crete at Easter you should endeavour to attend some of the Easter services, which include a candle-lit procession through the streets on Good Friday evening and fireworks at midnight on Easter Saturday.

Feast of Agios Yiorgos (St George) The feast day of St George, patron saint of Crete and of shepherds, takes place on 23 April or the Tuesday following Easter (whichever comes first). The most elaborate celebration is in Asi Gonia, where thousands of goats and sheep are gathered at the town church for shearing, milking and blessing. Fresh milk accompanies the ensuing feast.

Hohliovradia (Snail Night) Vamos celebrates the popular Cretan delicacy with a festival of cooked snails, washed down with wine and *tsikoudia* (a grape distilled spirit).

May

May Day On the first day of May there is a mass exodus from towns to the country. During picnics, wildflowers are gathered and made into wreaths to decorate houses.

Battle of Crete During the last week of May, the island commemorates the Battle of Crete with athletic competitions, folk dancing and ceremonial events in Hania, Rethymno, Iraklio and key battle memorials at Souda Bay, Stavronas and Preveli monastery. Representatives of Commonwealth countries attend the ceremonies each year.

June

Navy Week Celebrated during the last week in June in even-numbered years, it commemorates Crete's relationship with the sea. In Crete's harbour cities there is music and dancing on land and swimming and sailing competitions on the water.

Feast of St John the Baptist This feast day on 24 June is widely celebrated. Wreaths made on May Day are kept until this day, when they are burned on bonfires.

Casa dei Mezzo Music Festival Classical, Cretan and world music in Makrigialos.

July

Feast of Agia Marina (St Marina) Celebrated on 17 July in many parts of the island, this feast day is a particularly important event in Agia Marina, outside Hania.

Feast of Profitis Ilias Celebrated on 20 July at hill-top churches and monasteries dedicated to the prophet.

Wine Festival This Rethymno festival is held in the municipal park with wine tastings and local cuisine.

Yakinthia Festival The mountain village of Anogia stages an annual week-long cultural and musical extravaganza in the last week of July. There are poetry recitals, talks, exhibitions and outdoor concerts featuring Cretan music.

Renaissance Festival Rethymno's main festival is held during July to September, and features performances by Greece's leading theatre companies, as well as dance, music and acts from around Europe.

Summer Arts Festival International guest orchestras and dance troupes as well as local talent appear in Iraklio from July to September, with the main events held in an immense open-air theatre.

July/August

Kornaria Festival In Sitia, this festival runs from mid-July to the end of August, with concerts, folk dancing and theatre productions staged in the *kazarma* (fort) and other venues.

Lato Cultural Festival Agios Nikolaos hosts this festival, which includes concerts by local and international musicians, Cretan music played on traditional instruments, folk dancing, *mandinades* (improvised rhyming couplets) contests, theatre, art exhibitions and swimming competitions.

Kyrvia Festival Ierapetra's main festival includes concerts, plays and art exhibitions.

August

Wine Festival In Arhanes, 15 August is the merry conclusion of a five-day festival celebrating the excellent local wine.

Assumption Day Greeks celebrate Assumption Day (15 August) with family reunions. This prompts the big annual summer exodus, so it's wise to avoid public transport in the days before and after.

Traditional Cretan Wedding In late August, the village of Kritsa puts on a traditional Cretan wedding complete with songs, dancing, traditional food (and a happy couple).

Sultana Festival Sitia celebrates its superior sultana raisins with wine, music and dancing in the last week of the month.

Potato Festival Lasithi produces superior potatoes, a product which is celebrated in a three-day festival at the end of August in Tzermiado.

September

Genisis tis Panagias (the Virgin's Birthday) Celebrated on 8 September throughout Greece with various religious services and feasting.

October

Chestnut Festival The village of Elos stages a chestnut festival on the third Sunday of the month, when every-

one is offered roasted chestnuts, chestnut sweets and *tsikoudia*.

Ohi (No) Day Metaxas' refusal to allow Mussolini's troops free passage through Crete during WWII is commemorated on 28 October with a number of remembrance services, military parades, folk dancing and feasting.

November

Anniversary of the Explosion at Moni Arkadiou
This is one of the most important holidays in Crete, commemorated at the monastery from 7 to 9 November.

December

Christmas Day Although not as important as Easter, Christmas is still celebrated with religious services and feasting. Nowadays much Western influence is apparent, including Christmas trees, decorations and presents.

FOOD

For information on Greek and Cretan cuisine, see p55. For large cities and towns, restaurant listings in this book are divided into budget (under €15), midrange (€15 to €24) and top end (over €24) for two courses. Note that the separate 'cover' charge that used to be added to the bill for each person no longer applies, though some places still charge for bread.

GAY & LESBIAN TRAVELLERS

While there is no legislation against homosexual activity in Greece, it is wise to be discreet and to avoid public displays of togetherness.

Unlike islands such as gay-friendly Mykonos, Crete does not have a thriving gay scene. Homosexuality is generally frowned upon and there is no overtly gay nightlife.

A number of venues in Iraklio are quietly gay-friendly, as are relaxed resorts such as Paleohora and most nude beaches.

The *Spartacus International Gay Guide* (Bruno Gmunder, Berlin) is widely regarded as the leading authority on the gay travel scene and has a wealth of information on gay venues around the Greek Islands. There's some information on Crete on www.gaygreece.gr, as well as limited English sections on www.gay.gr and www.lesbian.gr.

HOLIDAYS

All banks and shops and most museums and ancient sites close on public holidays.

Greek national public holidays observed in Crete:

New Year's Day 1 January
Epiphany 6 January

First Sunday in Lent February
Greek Independence Day 25 March
Good Friday March/April
(Orthodox) Easter Sunday March/April
Spring Festival/Labour Day 1 May
Feast of the Assumption 15 August
Ohi Day 28 October
Christmas Day 25 December
St Stephen's Day 26 December

INSURANCE

It's wise to have travel insurance to cover theft, loss and medical problems. Be aware that some policies specifically exclude dangerous activities such as scuba diving, motorcycling, even trekking. Check that the policy covers ambulances or an emergency flight home.

You may prefer a policy that pays doctors or hospitals directly rather than you having to pay on the spot and claim later. If you have to claim later, ensure you keep all documentation.

INTERNET ACCESS

Crete has a reasonable number of internet cafés in major towns and tourist resorts and, apart from more remote areas, most are gradually using broadband. Access costs range from €2 to €4 per hour. Many larger hotels also offer high-speed internet access, while some towns such as Agios Nikolaos have free wireless hot spots downtown (Sitia and Ierapetra were about to follow suit at the time of writing). Travellers with their own laptops or personal organisers can arrange internet roaming with their local ISP. You can also buy prepaid internet cards from *periptera* (kiosks) from €3 to €20.

If you need to access a specific account, rather than web-based email such as Yahoo or Hotmail, you'll need to know your incoming (POP or IMAP) mail server name. You should then be able to access your email from anywhere in the world.

Travellers from the UK must have an adaptor for the modem line as the phone jack in Greece is different.

LEGAL MATTERS

Greek drug laws are the strictest in Europe. Greek courts make no distinction between possession and pushing. Possession of even a small amount of marijuana is likely to land you in jail.

MAPS

Mapping is an important feature of this guide. Unless you are going to trek or drive, you probably won't need additional maps. Do not rely on the free maps handed out by tourist offices, which are often out of date and not particularly accurate. The maps below are widely available in bookshops and tourist shops in Crete.

Excellent up-to-date road and hiking maps published by **Anavasi** (☎ 210 321 8104; www.anavasi.gr) are GPS compatible. Anavasi has three separate road maps covering Crete – *Hania, Rethymno and Iraklio*, and *Lasithi* – at a scale of 1:100,000 (€7.50). It has also produced the most accurate walking maps at a scale of 1:25,000 for the *Lefka Ori* (Sfakia and Pahnes), *Samaria/Sougia*, *Mt Psiloritis* and *Zakros-Vai*.

Road Editions (☎ 210 364 0723; www.road.gr) produces the comprehensive 1:200,000 blue-covered *Crete* map (€6), which has handy maps of the major cities. There are also dedicated 1:100,000 *Eastern Crete* and *Western Crete* maps (€8).

Iraklio-based trekker Giorgos Petrakis of **Petrakis Editions** (☎ 2810 282630; €5) has produced trekking and road maps for each of the four prefectures at a scale of 1:100,000. They include the E4 trail and all the mountainous routes of Crete, and are widely available on the island.

The German-published **Harms Verlag** (☎ 07275 8201; www.harms-ic-verlag.de) 1:100,000 *Kreta Touristikkarte* maps cover the east *(Der Osten)* and the west *(Der Westen)* of Crete.

MONEY

The unit of currency in Greece is the euro (€). Coins come in denominations of one, two, five, 10, 20, and 50 cents. Banknotes come in €5, €10, €20, €50, €100 and €500.

ATMs

There are ATMs in almost every town large enough to support a bank – and certainly in all the tourist areas. If you've got MasterCard or Visa/Access, there are plenty of places to withdraw money. Cirrus, Plus and Maestro users can make withdrawals in all major towns and tourist areas.

AFEMs (Automatic Foreign Exchange Machines) are common in major tourist areas. They take all the major European currencies, Australian and US dollars and Japanese yen.

DIRECTORY

Cash

Nothing beats cash for convenience, but if you lose any it's gone for good, and very few travel insurers will come to your rescue. Those who do normally limit the amount to about $300. It's best to carry no more cash than you need for the next few days. It's also a good idea to set aside a small amount of cash as an emergency stash.

Credit Cards

The main credit cards – MasterCard and Visa – are widely accepted in Crete. American Express and Diners Club charge cards are accepted in tourist areas, but unheard of elsewhere.

Big hotels and some midrange places accept credit cards, but budget hotels and domatia do not. Likewise, upmarket shops and restaurants accept plastic but village tavernas and small shops don't.

Moneychangers

Banks will exchange all major currencies in either cash, travellers cheques or Euro-cheques. A passport is required to change travellers cheques, but not always for cash.

Commission charged on the exchange of banknotes is less than for travellers cheques (some banks charge €2 per cheque, regardless of the amount). Post offices can exchange banknotes – but not travellers cheques – and charge less commission than banks. Travel agencies and hotels often change money and travellers cheques at bank rates, but commission charges are higher.

Tipping

In restaurants the service charge is included in the bill, but it is customary to leave a small tip or at least round off the bill. Likewise for taxis – a small amount is expected and appreciated.

Bargaining is not widespread in shops in Crete, though it can be effective in souvenir shops and markets – walking away often gets results.

It is worth haggling over the price of accommodation, especially if you intend to stay a few days. You may get short shrift in peak season, but prices can drop dramatically at other times

Travellers Cheques

Travellers cheques are losing popularity as more and more people opt to withdraw cash from ATMs as they go along. American Express, Visa and Thomas Cook cheques are all widely accepted and have efficient replacement policies. Maintaining a record of the cheque numbers and recording when you use them is vital for replacing lost cheques. Keep this record separate from the cheques themselves.

PHOTOGRAPHY & VIDEO
Film & Equipment

Most major brands and types of film are widely available, and many stores in main towns and tourist areas do digital printing or can burn photos to CD or transfer to USB drive. Most places charge from €0.15 to €0.19 per digital print and around €8.50 for a 36-print film roll. Greece uses the PAL video system, which is incompatible with the North American and Japanese NTSC and the French Secam, unless you have a multisystem machine.

Restrictions

Never photograph a military installation or anything else that has a sign forbidding photography. The plight of the jailed British plane spotters in 2001 should come as a warning that Greek authorities take these matters seriously. Flash photography is not allowed inside churches, and it's considered taboo to photograph the main altar. Cretans usually love having their photos taken, but always ask permission first. The same goes for video cameras.

POST

Tahydromia (post offices) are easily identifiable by the blue and yellow signs outside. Normal post boxes are also yellow, with red boxes for express mail.

Postal Rates

The postal rate for postcards and airmail letters to destinations within the EU is €0.65 for up to 20g and €1 for up to 50g. To other destinations the rate is €0.65 for up to 20g and €1.60 for up to 100g. Post within Europe takes four to five days; to the USA, Australia and New Zealand takes five to eight days. Some tourist shops also sell stamps, but with a 10% surcharge.

Express mail costs €2.85 and should ensure delivery in three days within the EU – use the special red post boxes. Valuables should be sent by registered post, which costs an extra €1.

Receiving Mail

You can receive mail poste restante (general delivery) at any main post office. The service is free, but you must have your passport. Ask senders to write your family name in capital letters on the envelope and underline it, and to mark the envelope 'poste restante'. If letters you are expecting cannot be located, ask the post office clerk to check under your first name as well.

After one month, uncollected mail is returned to the sender. If you are about to leave a town and expected mail hasn't arrived, ask the post office to forward it to your next destination, c/o poste restante.

Parcels are not delivered; they must be collected from the post office.

Sending Mail

It is usually advisable not to wrap a parcel before you post it – the post office may (but not always) wish to inspect the contents. In Iraklio, take your parcel to the central post office on Plateia Daskalogianni; elsewhere, take it to the parcel counter of any post office. Post offices usually only have small boxes for sale, so if you need a large box to ship stuff home supermarkets are your best bet (go early or ask them to keep some for you).

SHOPPING

Crete has a long tradition of artisanship. Ceramics, handmade leather goods, woven rugs, icons, embroidered linen and finely wrought silver and gold jewellery fill shops in all the tourist centres. In addition to crafted objects there are also Cretan wild herbs, olive oil, wine, sweet fruit preserves, cheeses, olives and other edible souvenirs. Do check if you're allowed to take these food items into the next country you're travelling to.

Most of the products available in the ubiquitous souvenir shops are mass-produced. Although they can still offer good value, it's worthwhile to seek out special shops that offer authentic Cretan goods.

Of all the large towns, you'll find the best selection of crafts at Hania where, in the streets behind the harbour, inspired artisans produce Crete's most artful leather, jewellery, ceramics and rugs.

Rethymno has a few good craft places, while Iraklio has more high-end designer and mainstream shops for clothing and other goods.

Several villages in the interior are known for their crafts. Theoretically, you can get good buys on linen and embroidery in Anogia and Kritsa. However, take note – these days many of the items on sale are mass-produced in Hong Kong or Indonesia. Check the origin of the item carefully before buying. Weaving shops in Hania or lace stores in Gavalohori (p120) can usually be relied upon to provide the genuine article.

Antiques

It is illegal to buy, sell, possess or export any antiquity in Crete (see Customs, p211). However, there are antiques and 'antiques'; a lot of items only a century or two old are regarded as junk, rather than part of the national heritage. These items include handmade furniture and odds and ends from rural areas, ecclesiastical ornaments from churches and items brought back from farflung lands. Do check with the dealer you're buying from.

Ceramics

You will see ceramic objects of every shape and size – functional and ornamental – for sale throughout Crete.

The main pottery centres are in Margarites (p134), which has its distinctive designs and motifs, and in Thrapsano (p165), famous for its giant *pitharia* (urns). Some more contemporary artisans use ancient Greek firing and glazing techniques (see Carmela, p88) to create unique designs.

The most commonly found Cretan ceramics are distinguishable for the shiny dark-blue glaze, which should be hard enough not to be scratch by the blade of a knife; a glazed bottom is the best sign of machine-made pottery.

Jewellery

Greek designers produce exquisite jewellery sold in select stores throughout Crete. Some local artisans can be seen in their studios, especially in Hania. You'll find more original and unusual pieces in silver than gold. For more traditional designs, look for replicas of Minoan objects such as the Phaestos disk, which are well crafted and available only in Crete.

Knives

Cretans are rightly proud of their distinctive, hand-crafted knives with rams-horn handles and heat-forged, razor-sharp blades. You'll see them on sale in many tourist centres, but few of them are made the old-fashioned way and, while they may look good, they don't always cut the mustard.

DIRECTORY

Leather Work

Most of the leather is hard rather than supple, but it's fairly priced nonetheless. Durable bags, wallets, shoes and boots are best bought on 'leather lane' in Hania (p87). In Rethymno you will find several shops that sell excellent leather goods, including the Silverhorse (p129).

Weaving

You will see many woven rugs and wall hangings for sale all over Crete. While these may look good and even be of a reasonable quality, much of the product on sale is machine-made in Crete or, worse still, in Asia. For really genuine articles that you can see being woven, look in Hania's Old Town (see p87).

SOLO TRAVELLERS

Crete is generally a safe, friendly and hospitable place and you will have no problem travelling alone. It is common to see solo travellers backpacking through the island and you will no doubt hook up with others if you are staying at hostels, which is the best option for solo travellers. Most hotels or domatia will knock 20% off the double room rate.

In general, use common sense when travelling. Avoid dark streets and parks at night, particularly in the major cities, and ensure your valuables are safely stored.

TELEPHONE

The Greek telephone service is maintained by the partly privatised public corporation known as OTE (pronounced o-tay; Organismos Tilepikinonion Elladas). The system is modern and efficient. Public telephones take phonecards, which cost €3 for 100 units, and are widely available at *peripteria*, corner shops and tourist shops; cards for higher amounts can be bought at OTE offices.

All phones take international calls. The 'i' button brings up the operating instructions in English. Don't remove your card before you are told to do so or you could wipe out the remaining credit. Local calls cost one unit per minute.

You can also buy a range of prepaid international calling cards (*hronokarta*).

Villages and remote islands almost always have at least one metered phone for international and long distance calls – usually in a shop, *kafeneio* (coffee house) or taverna.

For reverse-charge (collect) calls, dial the operator (domestic ☎ 129; international ☎ 139) to get the number in the country you wish to call.

To call overseas direct, dial the access code (☎ 00), followed by the appropriate country code.

Mobile Phones

Greece uses the same GSM system as most EU countries, Asia and Australia. You must activate global roaming through your provider before you leave, although the charges can be hefty.

Greece's three mobile phone service providers – Vodafone, Cosmote and Wind – offer prepaid local SIM cards with your own Greek mobile number. These automatically revert to global roaming when you leave Greece and can be used to send and receive SMS messages.

Cosmote tends to have the best coverage in the more remote areas, so try re-tuning your phone to Cosmote if you find coverage patchy.

American and Canadian mobile (cell) phone users will not be able to use their handsets in Greece unless they are dual- or tri-band.

TIME

Greece is two hours ahead of GMT/UTC and three hours ahead on daylight-saving time, which begins on the last Sunday in March when clocks are put forward one hour. Daylight saving ends on the last Sunday in September.

TOILETS

One peculiarity of the Greek plumbing system is that it can't handle toilet paper – apparently the pipes are too narrow, or at least most places are paranoid about blockages. Toilet paper etc should be placed in the small bin provided.

Very occasionally outside the big towns you might come across Asian-style squat toilets in older houses, *kafeneia* (coffee houses) and public toilets.

Public toilets are rare, except at airports and bus and train stations. Cafés are the best option if you get caught short, but you may be expected to buy something for the privilege.

USEFUL PHONE NUMBERS

Directory inquiries	☎ 11888
from a mobile phone	☎ 11831
Greece country code	☎ 30
International access code	☎ 00
International directory inquiries/reverse charges	☎ 139

Toll-Free 24-Hour Emergency Numbers

Ambulance	☎ 166
Fire Brigade	☎ 199
Forestry Fire Service	☎ 191
Police	☎ 100
Roadside Assistance (ELPA)	☎ 10400
Tourist Police	☎ 171

TOURIST INFORMATION

The Greek National Tourism Organisation (EOT in Greek) office in Iraklio has a range of brochures and some maps but is the least helpful of the island's tourist information offices. The municipal tourist offices in major towns have handy maps, brochures, museum and transport information and some help with accommodation lists.

TOURIST POLICE

The **tourist police** (☎ 171) work in cooperation with the regular police and EOT. There's always at least one member of staff who speaks English. Hotels, restaurants, travel agencies, tourist shops, tourist guides, waiters, taxi drivers and bus drivers all come under their jurisdiction. If you think that you've been ripped off, report it to the tourist police. If you need to report a theft or loss of a passport, the tourist police will act as interpreters between you and the regular police. Some tourist police also dispense maps, brochures and transport information.

TOURS

The vast majority (80%) of visitors to Crete opt for a package holiday. Flight and accommodation packages from Europe can be a remarkably good deal, costing far less than booking separately. Charter flights alone can be hard to get, leading many regular visitors to book a cheap package but only stay at the hotel the first night (or not at all) and make their own arrangements. The best-value deals can often pop up at the last minute as opera-

tors struggle to fill charter flights and block-booked hotel rooms. Most of the offerings are for large resorts along the northern coast. For a less industrialised holiday experience, try one of the following companies:

Diktynna Travel (☎ 28210 41458; www.diktynna-travel.gr; Arhontaki 6, Hania, Greece)

Pure Crete (☎ 020-8760 0879; www.pure-crete.com; 79 George Street, Croydon, Surrey CR0 1LD, UK)

Simply Crete (☎ 020-8541 2201; www.simplytravel.com; Kings Place, Wood St, Kingston upon Thames, Surrey KT1 1SG, UK)

VISAS

Countries whose citizens can stay in Greece for up to three months without a visa include Australia, Canada, all EU countries, Iceland, Israel, Japan, New Zealand, Norway, Switzerland and the USA. Others include Cyprus, Malta, the European principalities of Monaco and San Marino, and most South American countries. The list changes, so contact Greek embassies for the latest information. Those not on the list can expect to pay about €20 for a three-month visa (see www.greekembassy.org for more details).

Visa Extensions

To stay in Greece for longer than three months, apply at a consulate abroad or at least 20 days in advance to the **Aliens Bureau** (☎ 210 510 2831; Leoforos Alexandras 173, Athens; ☒ 8am-1pm Mon-Fri). Take your passport and four passport photographs along. You may be asked for proof that you can support yourself financially (bank statement, exchange slips).

In Crete, apply to the main prefecture in Iraklio. You will be given a permit that will authorise you to stay in Greece for a period of up to six months. Most travellers get around this by visiting Bulgaria or Turkey briefly and then re-entering Greece.

TRAVELLERS WITH DISABILITIES

If mobility is a problem, visiting Crete will present some serious challenges. Most hotels, ferries, museums and sites are not accessible to people in wheelchairs and the terrain of many areas is not suitable (although new hotels are required to be disability-friendly).

If you are determined, then take heart in the knowledge that wheelchair-users do go to Crete for holidays. The **Eria Resort** (☎ 28210 62790; www.eria-resort.gr) in Maleme, western Crete is one of the few in Greece designed for travellers with disabilities. It caters for special needs and equipment and offers medical support and appropriate excursions and activities.

There is some useful English-language information on travelling in Greece on www .disabled.gr. Plan carefully before you travel.

WOMEN TRAVELLERS

Many women travel alone in Crete. The crime rate remains relatively low, and solo travel is probably safer than in most European countries. This does not mean that you should be lulled into complacency; bag snatching and rapes do occur, although violent offences are very rare.

The biggest annoyance to foreign women travelling alone are the guys the Greeks have nicknamed *kamaki*, although they appear to be a dying breed. The word means 'fishing trident' and refers to their favourite pastime, 'fishing' for foreign women. Once they were found everywhere there were lots of tourists, but they are the exception these days, more of a nuisance than a threat. The majority of Greek men treat foreign women with respect, and are genuinely helpful.

WORK
Permits

EU nationals don't need a work permit, but they need a residency permit if they intend to stay longer than three months. Nationals of other countries should in theory have a work permit.

Bar & Hostel Work

The best bar and hotel jobs can pay quite well – so well that they are usually taken by young Greeks from the mainland or seasonal workers from Eastern Europe working through agencies. You can try your luck at the bigger resorts or more remote places in the south. Resorts such as Hersonisos and Malia that cater to British travellers are the best bet for Brits looking for bar work.

Holiday Representatives

Crete provides terrific opportunities for working as a representative for a package tour company. British-based companies begin looking for personnel around February for the summer season. The pay is low but you can make tips and some outfits allow reps to earn a percentage of the packages they sell.

Summer Harvest

Seasonal harvest work seems to be monopolised by migrant workers from Albania and Eastern Europe, and is no longer a viable option for travellers.

Volunteer Work

The **Sea Turtle Protection Society of Greece** (☎ / fax 210 523 1342; www.archelon.gr; Solomou 57, Athens 10432) welcomes volunteers for its monitoring programmes on Crete. See p69 for more information.

If you're keen to do some horse riding around Iraklio, make sure you ask around about the quality of treatment of the animals and the validity of any volunteering programs. Not all places hold to the same standards.

Other Work

Jobs are often advertised in the classifieds of the English-language newspapers (see p208), or you can place an advertisement yourself.

Transport

CONTENTS

GETTING THERE & AWAY

For many visitors, getting to Crete means first getting to mainland Greece, usually Athens. However, it is also possible to fly directly to Crete from all over Europe on scheduled and charter flights.

Flights, tours and rail tickets can be booked online at www.lonelyplanet.com/travel _services.

ENTERING THE COUNTRY

Visitors to Greece with EU passports are rarely given more than a cursory glance, though customs may be interested in what you are carrying. EU nationals may also enter Greece with a national ID card but some non-EU passport holders may require a visa. Check with consular authorities or travel agents. Passports or ID cards must be produced when you register in a hotel or pension in Crete.

THINGS CHANGE...

The information in this chapter is particularly vulnerable to change. Check directly with the airline or a travel agent to make sure you understand how a fare works and be aware of the security requirements for international travel. The details given in this chapter should be regarded as pointers and are not a substitute for your own careful, up-to-date research.

AIR

Most travellers arrive in Crete by air. There are regular flights from Athens, where most international flights arrive. In summer, there are direct charter flights from the UK and many European cities to Iraklio and Hania, but very few direct international scheduled flights; most change at Athens or Thessaloniki.

Airports & Airlines

Most scheduled international flights arrive in Athens (or possibly Thessaloniki).

Athens International Airport (Eleftherios Venizelos) (code ATH; ☎ 210 353 0000; www.aia.gr) is 27km east of Athens.

Iraklio's **Nikos Kazantzakis International Airport** (code HER; ☎ 2810 228 401) is Crete's biggest and main airport. Built many years ago when tourism was just taking off in Crete, it is adequate, but can be strained at times with the massive influx of arrivals during the summer. There are plans for a new airport near Kastelli, 40km from Iraklio.

Hania airport (code CHQ; ☎ 28210 83800) is 14km from Hania's town centre. It is convenient for travellers heading to the west of Crete.

Sitia airport (code JSH; ☎ 28430 24666) opened a long runway but international flights had yet to start operating in 2007.

See p223 for frequency and approximate costs of flights from mainland Greece to Crete.

AIRLINES FLYING TO & FROM GREECE

Aegean Airlines (A3; ☎ 801 11 20000; www.aegean air.com)
Air Canada (AC; ☎ 210 617 5321; www.aircanada.ca)
Air France (AF; ☎ 210 960 1100; www.airfrance.com)
British Airways (BA; ☎ 210 890 6666; www.britishair ways.com)
Cyprus Airways (CY; ☎ 210 372 2722; www.cyprusair .com.cy)
Delta Air Lines (DL; ☎ 210 331 1660; www.delta.com)
easyJet (U2; ☎ 210 353 0300; www.easyjet.com)
Emirates (EK; ☎ 210 933 3400; www.emirates.com)
KLM (KL; ☎ 210 911 0000; www.klm.com)
Lufthansa (LH; ☎ 210 617 5200; www.lufthansa.com)
Olympic Airlines (OA; ☎ 210 966 6666; 801 11 44444; www.olympicairlines.com)

TRANSPORT

Singapore Airlines (SQ; ☎ 210 372 8000; www
.singaporeair.com)
Thai Airways (TG; ☎ 210 969 2010; www.thaiair.com)
Transavia (HV; ☎ 281 030 0878; www.transavia.nl)
United Airlines (UA; ☎ 210 924 2645; www.ual.com)
Virgin Express (TV; ☎ 210 949 0777; www.virgin-
express.com)

DOMESTIC AIRLINES
Olympic Airlines, Greece's national carrier,
handles the vast majority of domestic flights.
Olympic offers a 25% student discount as well
as special youth fares for 18- to 24-year-olds
on domestic flights, but only if the flight is
part of an international journey.

Aegean Airlines flies between Athens,
Hania and Iraklio on modern aircraft with
generally excellent service. Aegean accepts internet bookings, issues e-tickets and has heavily discounted fares if you book early. There
also are flights from Crete to Thessaloniki
and connections via Athens or Thessaloniki
to Frankfurt, Düsseldorf, Munich, Stuttgart,
Paris, Milan and Rome.

Sky Express (☎ 2810 223 500; www.skyexpress.gr)
is a new airline running flights from Hania
to Rhodes and from Iraklio to Rhodes, Santorini, Mytilini, Kos, Samos and Ikaria on
its 18-seater planes (baggage is restricted
to 12.5kg).

It is advisable to book early as flights can
be packed in the high season. See individual
destination chapters for details of flights to
specific destinations.

The information throughout this book
is for flights during high season (from
mid-June to late September). Outside these
months, the number of flights to the islands
drops considerably.

CHARTER FLIGHTS
Cheap charter flights to Crete operate from
all over Europe between April and October
but these can be increasingly difficult to find
unless you also book a package holiday as they
have been block-booked by tour operators.
Tickets are cheap but flights are often at un-
godly hours and conditions may apply, such
as 'compulsory' accommodation vouchers (although in practice this requirement may be
overlooked nowadays). Some regular visitors
find it is cheaper to book a charter package to
get to Crete and then go to other accommodation they have booked independently.

Charter flight tickets are valid for up to
four weeks, and usually have a minimum-
stay requirement of at least three days. The
tickets can be so cheap that it might be worth
buying a charter return even if you plan to
stay for longer.

CLIMATE CHANGE & TRAVEL

Climate change is a serious threat to the ecosystems that humans rely upon, and air travel is the
fastest-growing contributor to the problem. Lonely Planet regards travel, overall, as a global ben-
efit, but believes we all have a responsibility to limit our personal impact on global warming.

Flying & Climate Change

Pretty much every form of motorised travel generates CO2 (the main cause of human-induced
climate change) but planes are far and away the worst offenders, not just because of the sheer
distances they allow us to travel, but because they release greenhouse gases high into the atmosphere. The statistics are frightening: two people taking a return flight between Europe and
the US will contribute as much to climate change as an average household's gas and electricity
consumption over a whole year.

Carbon Offset Schemes

Climatecare.org and other websites use 'carbon calculators' that allow travellers to offset the
level of greenhouse gases they are responsible for with financial contributions to sustainable
travel schemes that reduce global warming – including projects in India, Honduras, Kazakhstan
and Uganda.

Lonely Planet, together with Rough Guides and other concerned partners in the travel industry, support the carbon offset scheme run by climatecare.org. Lonely Planet offsets all of its
staff and author travel.

For more information check out our website: www.lonelyplanet.com.

FLIGHTS FROM MAINLAND GREECE TO CRETE

The following table will give you an idea of the high-season frequency and approximate costs of one-way flights between mainland Greece and Crete.

Origin	Destination	Frequency	Fare (€)*
Athens	Hania	5 daily	85-125
Athens	Iraklio	12 daily	85-125
Athens	Sitia	4 weekly	71
Thessaloniki	Hania	4 daily	106-135
Thessaloniki	Iraklio	3 daily	106-135
Rhodes	Iraklio	2 daily	89-98
Alexandroupoli	Sitia	3 weekly	92

*One way, including tax

Look for cheap charter deals in the travel section of major newspapers or on the internet.

Australia

Thai Airways and Singapore Airlines have convenient connections to Athens two to three times a week. Emirates has daily flights between Melbourne and Athens via Dubai.

Canada

Olympic Airlines has flights from Toronto to Athens via Montreal. From Vancouver, there are connecting flights via Toronto, Amsterdam, Frankfurt and London on Air Canada, KLM, Lufthansa and British Airways. British Airways flies from Montreal to Athens via London.

Europe

Athens is linked to every major city in Europe by either Olympic Airlines, Aegean Airlines or the flag carrier of each country.

CYPRUS

Cyprus Airways has four flights weekly direct from Larnaca to Iraklio and five to six flights daily to Athens. Olympic Airlines has a daily flight from Larnaca to Iraklio and several daily to Athens.

GERMANY

Aegean Airlines has several flights from Iraklio connecting to Stuttgart, Düsseldorf, Munich and Frankfurt. Iraklio is linked by Lufthansa to Frankfurt, while several airlines rush scheduled flights to Iraklio from cities across Germany in summer.

NETHERLANDS

KLM-associate Transavia has direct flights between Amsterdam and Iraklio.

UK

Daily flights between London and Athens are operated by British Airways, Olympic Airlines and easyJet. Olympic also runs five direct London–Thessaloniki flights a week from Heathrow.

There are numerous charter flights to Crete from London, Birmingham, Bristol, Cardiff, Edinburgh, Glasgow, Luton, Manchester and Newcastle. Try www.charterflights.co.uk or www.justthef light.co.uk.

New Zealand

There are no direct flights from New Zealand to Athens. However, there are connecting flights via Sydney, Melbourne, Bangkok and Singapore on Olympic Airlines, United Airlines, Thai Airways and Singapore Airlines.

USA

Flight options to Europe from the North Atlantic are bewilderingly extensive. For online bookings try www.cheaptickets.com, www.expedia.com and www.orb itz.com.

New York has the widest range of options to Athens. Both Olympic Airlines and Delta Airlines have direct flights but there are numerous other connecting flights.

There are no direct flights to Athens from the west coast. There are, however, connecting flights to Athens from many US cities, either linking with Olympic Airlines in New York or flying with one of the European national airlines to their home country, and then on to Athens.

LAND

Travellers arriving in Greece overland from Western Europe normally drive to the Italian ports such as Venice, Ancona, Bari or Brindisi and ship vehicles across to Igoumenitsa or Patra. To get to Crete, you would have to drive to Piraeus to take a ferry. Passports are rarely required when crossing western European borders, the exception being the borders with Switzerland.

TRANSPORT

ISLAND HOPPING TO CRETE

From Piraeus there are only two options for hopping off at other islands along the way to Crete. ANEN Lines' F/B *Myrtidiotissa* does a long 'milk run' via Gythio and the islands of Kythira and Antikythira, while LANE Lines makes a stop in Milos and Santorini in the western Cyclades on its thrice-weekly run to eastern Crete ports, continuing to Rhodes via Karpathos and other islands. From Thessaloniki, you have a choice of stopping off at Skiathos, Skopelos, Tinos, Paros, Naxos, Ios or Santorini on GA Ferries F/B *Milena* on its haul from one end of the Aegean to the other. Alternatively, you can head to any of these intermediate islands from Piraeus or elsewhere and pick up the Iraklio connection at your leisure. From Rhodes you have a choice of four ports to hop off at: Halki, Diafani, Karpathos and Kasos, using LANE Lines' connections from the Dodecanese (twice weekly).

There are no bus services to Greece from western or northern Europe, but there are buses from Albania and Bulgaria.

Car & Motorcycle

Crossing from Italy to Greece no longer requires border formalities and is preferred by the great majority of drivers and riders heading to Greece. There are four main Italian ports serving Greece: Bari, Brindisi, Ancona and Trieste.

It is still possible to travel to Greece via Slovenia, Croatia, Bulgaria and the Former Yugoslav Republic of Macedonia, but the savings are not huge and are far outweighed by the distance involved and the necessity to cross five borders.

It is feasible on weekends in summer to arrive in Patra by ferry in the morning and be on a high-speed ferry to Crete by lunchtime, arriving in Iraklio late the same day. Otherwise, you can just as easily take an overnight ferry to Crete on the same day you arrive in Greece.

Train

Unless you have an **InterRail** (www.interrail.net) or **Eurail** (www.eurail.com) pass or are aged under 26 or over 60 and eligible for a discounted fare, travelling to Greece by train is prohibitively expensive. To get to Crete, you can take a train to Brindisi in Italy and use your rail pass for a free passage to Patra. From Patra you can take a train to Kiato, then change to the suburban rail (included in your pass) which goes directly to Piraeus harbour for your ferry connection to Crete.

SEA

Crete is well served by ferries in the summer, with mainland connections from Piraeus, Thessaloniki, Rhodes, Kalamata and Gythio, plus a smattering of Cyclades islands and Kythira. From November to April, however, services are considerably curtailed. Ferries are generally large car ferries and range in quality from 'comfortable' to luxurious. See www.ferries.gr or www.gtp.gr for routes and timetables.

Routes

Greece's ferry hub is Piraeus, the sprawling port of Athens. Ferries to Crete depart from the western end of the port. The departure points are slightly more convenient for the suburban rail train station in Piraeus, but involve a 10-minute hike from the metro station. From central Piraeus allow a good 15 to 20 minutes' walking to reach the Crete quays. Ferries leave here for Iraklio, Rethymno, Hania, Agios Nikolaos and Kissamos-Kastelli. Check the destination board at the stern of the ferry.

Schedules

Ferry timetables change from season to season, and ferries are subject to delays and cancellations at short notice due to bad weather, strikes or mechanical problems. No timetable is infallible, but a comprehensive weekly list of departures from Piraeus is put out by the EOT (Ellinikos Organismos Tourismou, Greece's main tourist office) in Athens. The main ferry schedules are also published in the English-language edition of *Kathimerini* (included in the *International Herald Tribune)* or check the websites www.gtp.gr and www.open seas.gr.

Throughout the year there is at least one ferry daily from Piraeus to the major ports in Crete, with three or four per day in summer.

Travelling time can vary considerably, depending on the ship and the route it takes.

Hania's fast catamaran can do the trip in 4½ hours, whereas Iraklio takes eight hours.

Costs & Classes

Prices are fixed by the government, and are determined by the distance travelled rather than by the facilities of a particular boat. There can be big differences in the size, comfort and facilities of boats offering rival services, but the fares will be the same. You may find that differences in prices at ticket agencies are the result of some agents sacrificing part of the commission to qualify as a 'discount service'. The discount is seldom more than €1.

The large ferries nominally have two classes (first and second) but the demarcation lines between them are often blurred. You pay instead for either the quality of the cabin, or the choice between aircraft-type seats or deck passage.

Deck class remains a cheap way to travel, while a 1st-class ticket can cost almost as much as flying on some routes. Children under the age of four travel free, while children between four and 10 pay half fare. Full fares apply for children over 10 years of age. Unless you state otherwise when purchasing a ticket, you will automatically be given deck class, though you can usually upgrade on board if you can't find a comfortable spot. See boxed text (below) for some sample fares.

Cabins range from double-berth outside cabins (1st class) to four-berth inside cabins (2nd class). Aircraft-type seats can be very comfortable (the new high-speed catamarans) to bearable (most older boats). Deck class is hard and uncompromising and not usually custom-designed for deck-class sleepers. Modern ferry boats tend to have bare, exposed deck sections, but there are always wind-protected areas where you can set up temporary camp and several places inside where you can roll out your sleeping bag if you get in early. Many people nab a spot in the café area or lounges but these are invariably smoky. The self-service restaurants on board are decent value.

Tickets

Ferries can be prone to delays and cancellations in bad weather, so it's best not to buy a ticket until it has been confirmed that the ferry is operating (unless you want a cabin or it's the August peak season). If you need

TRANSPORT

FERRY TRAVEL TO CRETE

It wasn't too long ago that ferry travel in Greece was a true ordeal. Deregulation of the formerly closed domestic ferry market, a gradual upgrade of fleets and the aftershock of the F/B *Express Samina* sinking in September 2000 have significantly improved the domestic and international ferry scene.

Ferry services to and from Crete still differ in quality and service. The high-speed boats of Minoan Lines linking Piraeus and Iraklio, and Hellenic Seaways catamaran services to Hania, are by far the most comfortable. NEL Lines also runs a high-speed catamaran service to Rethymno in peak season (five hours).

Minoan's services make the run between Iraklio and Piraeus in a flat eight hours on modern, monster ferries – notably the F/B *Festos Palace* and the almost identical F/B *Knossos Palace*. Minoan's competitor ANEK is a comfortable option, although it still uses older, smaller boats. ANEK's F/B *Preveli* makes the overnight run between Rethymno and Piraeus. Larger ANEK boats also link the western port of Souda, which serves Hania.

The one-boat ANEN Lines of western Crete runs a small ferry linking Piraeus and Gythio in the Peloponnese with Kissamos-Kastelli via Kythira and Antikythira. To the east, LANE Lines links Piraeus with Agios Nikolaos and Sitia with a stop in Milos and Santorini. Its two boats F/B *Vitsentzos Kornaros* and F/B *Ierapetra* are fairly old, but comfortable enough.

Origin	Destination	Frequency	Duration	Fare (one way, €)
Piraeus	Agios Nikolaos	2 weekly	14hr	34
Piraeus	Hania (Souda)	2 daily	6-9hr	30-51.50
Piraeus	Iraklio	2 daily	8hr	37
Piraeus	Rethymno	2 daily	9hr	24
Gythio	Kissamos-Kastelli	1 weekly	7hr	29-57
Thessaloniki	Iraklio	4 weekly	31hr	46.50

TRANSPORT

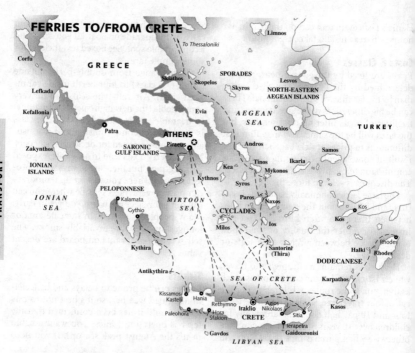

FERRIES TO/FROM CRETE

to reserve a car space, you may need to pay in advance. If the service is cancelled, you can transfer your ticket to the next available service with that company.

Agencies selling tickets line the waterfront of most ports, but there's rarely one that sells tickets for every boat, and often an agency is reluctant to give information about a boat it doesn't sell tickets for. This means you will have to check the timetables displayed outside each agency to find out which ferry is next to depart – or ask the port police. Ticket booths open up beside a ferry about an hour before departure.

Yacht

Yachting is probably *the* way to see the Greek Islands, but Crete is a long way from other islands and does not have a huge yachting industry. There are companies that offer sailing trips around Crete, especially along the south coast and from Agios Nikolaos (see p76).

The sailing season lasts from April until October. In July and September, the *meltemi* winds in the Aegean can ground you regularly.

GETTING AROUND

BICYCLE

Cycling is becoming more common on Crete, but the often-hilly terrain means you need strong leg muscles and endurance. You can hire bikes in most tourist areas. Prices range from €8 to €20 per day. Bicycles are carried free on ferries. See the Crete Outdoors chapter (p70) or www.cycling.gr for information on mountain-biking tours and equipment hire.

BOAT
Ferry

Smaller boats link the towns along Crete's south coast, some of which are only accessible by sea.

In summer there are daily boats from Paleohora to Hora Sfakion, via Agia Roumeli, Sougia and Loutro. Schedules change from year to year, but there are usually two to three boats a day between Hora Sfakion and Agia Roumeli and one boat a day from Hora Sfakion to Paleohora. Boats to Gavdos Island leave from Hora Sfakion and Paleohora (though these were going via Hora Sfakion in 2007, making it a five-hour trip).

Tourist boats run excursions to offshore islands, including Ierapetra to Gaidouronisi (Hrysi) Island, Agios Nikolaos to Spinalonga, and Kissamos-Kastelli to the Gramvousa Peninsula.

Taxi Boat

Most southern port cities have taxi boats – small speedboats – transporting people to places that are difficult to get to by land. Some owners charge a set price for each person, and others charge a flat rate for the boat, with the cost divided by the number of passengers. Either way, prices are quite high.

BUS

Crete's comprehensive public bus service makes it relatively easy to travel around the island. Frequent buses link the major towns along the north coast highway from Kissamos-Kastelli to Sitia. Less-frequent buses operate between the north-coast towns and the south coast, via the interior villages. Fares are fixed by the government, and are very reasonable by European standards.

Buses are operated by regional collectives known as **KTEL** (www.ktel.org). Every prefecture has its own KTEL. Their website has schedules for all the island's buses, or try www.crete-buses.gr (Iraklio–Lasithi) and www.bus-service-crete-ktel.com (Rethymno–Hania). Alternatively, you can pick up a handy leaflet with Crete's bus schedules at major KTEL bus stops.

Larger towns usually have a central, covered bus station with waiting rooms, toilets and a snack bar. In small towns and villages the 'bus station' may be no more than a bus stop outside a *kafeneio* (coffee house) or taverna, which doubles as a booking office. Most timetables are in both Greek and English.

The buses running along the north coast are generally in good shape and air-conditioned. They do not have toilets on board or refreshments, so make sure you are prepared on both counts. Smoking is prohibited on all buses; only the chain-smoking drivers occasionally dare to ignore the 'no smoking' signs.

Most buses use the northern highway, but at least one or two buses each day use the scenic but slower old roads so ask before you buy your ticket. In major towns it's best to buy your ticket at the station to ensure you get a seat, but if you board at a stop along the way you can buy your ticket on the bus. Bus stations in major towns keep long opening hours and are a good source of information. See the destination chapters for timetable information.

CAR & MOTORCYCLE

Having your own vehicle is the best way to explore Crete if you can brave the roads and drivers. There are plenty of places to hire cars and motorcycles and roads have improved enormously in recent years, but in the more remote areas (particularly the south) you'll still find unpaved roads that are only suitable for 4WDs.

Beyond the main highways, prepare to spend a lot of time poring over maps, as country roads are generally badly signposted. Road signs, when they exist, are usually marked in Greek and English (the English phonetic sign follows a few metres after the Greek) except in remote areas. Even when written in Latin letters, the spelling of place names can vary wildly from the names on your map or in this book. Invest in a good map, but even the best maps don't cover all the side roads.

Don't expect reassuring signs along the way telling you you're on track or the remaining distance to your destination. The rule of thumb is just to keep going until told otherwise and keep in mind you generally won't get much warning before a turn-off.

The E75 highway that runs along the north coast from Sitia to Hania is continually being upgraded and is better in some parts than others.

But the danger in Crete lies in the driving culture rather than the state of the highway. Slower drivers are expected to straddle the narrow service lane and let the traffic pass. The laid-back Cretans are manic drivers and inexplicably immediately in a hurry once they get behind the wheel so expect to be tailgated, honked and overtaken if you move too slowly. Overtaking on bends and ignoring double lines is prevalent. Road rules are routinely ignored and there is barely any police presence (see Road Rules, p229).

Inland and to the south, narrow and windy mountain roads can be hazardous.

TRANSPORT

It is best to avoid driving at night, especially as late-night revellers are plentiful and drink-driving laws are barely policed.

Motorcycles are great for short-haul trips but bear in mind Crete is a massive island and the distances can make it hard work for bikers.

Automobile Associations

The Greek automobile association **ELPA** (☎ 210 606 8800; www.elpa.gr; Leoforos Mesogion 395, Agia Paraskevi, Athens) offers reciprocal services to members of national automobile associations with a valid membership card. If your vehicle breaks down, dial ☎ 10400.

Bringing Your Own Vehicle

EU-registered vehicles are allowed free entry into Greece but may only stay six months without road taxes being due. Only a green card (international third-party insurance) is required. The only proof of the date of your entry – if requested by the police – is your ferry ticket if you arrive from Italy, or your passport entry stamp if entering from elsewhere. Vehicles with non-EU registration may be logged in your passport.

Crete is well served by car ferries, but they are fairly expensive. The price for a car from Piraeus to Crete is about €86. Small motorbikes are normally free, but larger bikes cost from €16 to €32.

Driving Licences

Crete recognises all national driving licences, provided they have been held for at least one year. International Driving Permits can be obtained before you leave home, but is not normally necessary. If you are hiring a motorcycle, a European driver's licence allowing you to drive a bike under 50cc is accepted, but travellers from other countries or those hiring bigger bikes will need the appropriate motorcycle licence. A growing number of vehicle-hire agencies require them – and, in any case, you are not insured if you don't have one.

Fuel & Spare Parts

Some service stations close on Sunday and public holidays, especially in Iraklio prefecture. Self-service pumps are not the norm in Greece, nor are credit-card pumps, and out-of-the-way stations don't take plastic at all, so it is always advisable to keep the tank topped up. Unleaded petrol – available everywhere – averages around €1 per litre. Diesel is cheaper.

Spare parts can be tricky to find, especially if you are in the remoter parts of the island. Spare-parts dealers do deliver to all over Crete, including two specialist companies based in Moires, in central Iraklio. If you are stuck try **O Germanos** (☎ 28920 29122; www.o-germanos.com) or **Eltrak** (☎ 2810 311 903; www.eltrak.gr).

Hire

CAR

Crete has cheaper car hire than many islands due to the level of competition. Major international companies have offices in most towns and airports, but you'll usually get a much better deal if you hire from a local company and negotiate. If you choose a company with offices across Crete, you can arrange to pick up the car at one end of the island and drop it off at the other.

High-season daily rates with unlimited mileage and insurance start at about €35 for the smallest models, dropping to €20 to 25 in low season. Check what insurance is included: it is wise to insist on full insurance that covers the hire car if an accident is your fault (third party only covers the other vehicle) or if the car is damaged by an unknown third party.

Most companies will only let you hire a car if you have a credit card.

The minimum driving age is 18 years, but most firms require you to be at least 23 years old. Many will accept drivers under 21 as long as they have had their licence for more than a year.

Most hire cars are manual, so book ahead if you need an automatic car as they are rare and usually more expensive.

See the Getting Around sections of relevant cities for details of car-hire outlets.

MOTORCYCLE

Mopeds and motorcycles are widely available for hire but Crete is not the best place to initiate yourself into the world of motorcycling: many tourists have accidents every year. Caution should be exercised as roads change without warning from smooth and paved to cracked and pothole-ridden.

Experienced motorcyclists will find that a lightweight Enduro motorcycle between 400cc and 600cc is ideal for negotiating

ROAD DISTANCES (KM)

	Agia Galini	Agios Nikolaos	Anogia	Elafonisi	Hania	Hora Sfakion	Ierapetra	Iraklio	Kissamos-Kastelli	Kolymbari	Malia	Matala	Omalos	Paleohora	Plakias	Rethymno	Sitia	Spili	Tzermiado	Zakros
Agia Galini	---																			
Agios Nikolaos	144	---																		
Anogia	118	104	---																	
Elafonisi	224	314	218	---																
Hania	119	209	113	105	---															
Hora Sfakion	45	215	119	70	70	---														
Ierapetra	137	36	140	352	247	182	---													
Iraklio	75	69	35	247	142	148	105	---												
Kissamos-Kastelli	173	263	167	51	54	124	291	196	---											
Kolymbari	144	234	138	65	25	95	261	167	14	---										
Malia	112	32	72	284	179	185	68	37	233	204	---									
Matala	29	138	104	253	148	123	131	69	265	173	106	---								
Omalos	163	253	157	149	44	114	291	186	98	69	223	255	---							
Paleohora	206	296	200	64	87	157	335	229	51	65	266	298	131	---						
Plakias	50	198	94	200	95	44	187	123	149	120	161	79	139	183	---					
Rethymno	62	152	56	162	57	63	190	85	111	62	122	91	101	144	39	---				
Sitia	199	73	177	387	282	290	62	142	336	307	105	211	326	369	265	227	---			
Spili	26	182	86	192	87	68	163	215	141	112	252	55	131	174	24	30	257	---		
Tzermiado	130	49	90	302	197	202	85	55	251	222	44	124	241	284	178	139	122	270	---	
Zakros	235	106	211	421	316	322	98	176	370	341	138	229	360	405	285	259	36	289	155	---

TRANSPORT

Crete's roads. In many cases maintenance is minimal, so check the machine thoroughly before you hire it – especially the brakes: you'll need them! When you hire a moped, tell the agent where you'll be going to ensure that your vehicle has enough power to get you up Crete's steep hills.

Motorbike-hire rates start from €20 per day for a moped or 50cc motorbike to €50 for a top enduro bike. Out-of-season prices drop considerably. Third-party insurance is usually included in the price, but this will not include medical expenses so check that your travel insurance covers you for motorbike injuries – many don't. Motorcyclists riding bikes of 50cc or more must wear helmets.

Road Rules

Greece has one of the highest road-fatality rates in Europe and will test your defensive driving skills. Overtaking is the biggest cause of accidents. Slow-driving tourists in hire cars can be a hazard, provoking impatient and dangerous overtaking manoeuvres from others.

Driving in the major cities and small towns is a nightmare of erratic one-way streets, double parking and irregularly enforced parking rules. Cars are not towed away but fines can be expensive. Designated parking for disabled drivers is a rarity.

In Greece, as throughout Continental Europe, you drive on the right and overtake on the left. Major highways have four lanes, although some are still two-lane highways with large hard shoulders. These hard shoulders are used for driving in, especially when being overtaken. Be prepared to move over if someone wants to pass you.

Seatbelts must be worn in the front and back seats, and you must in theory travel with a first-aid kit, fire extinguisher and warning triangle. Carrying cans of petrol is banned. Outside built-up areas, traffic on a main road has right of way at intersections. In towns, vehicles coming from the right have right of way. Hefty fines are levied for speeding and other traffic and parking offences. Speed limits for cars are 120km/h on highways, 90km/h on other major roads and 50km/h in built-up areas. Speed limits for motorcycles are 70km/h (up to 100cc) and 90km/h (above 100cc).

The blood-alcohol limit is 0.05%; anything over 0.08% is a criminal offence.

Traffic fines are not paid on the spot – you will be told where to pay. Reciprocal legal agreements between EU countries may well mean that an ignored parking fine will turn up in your mailbox at home a few weeks later. If you are involved in an accident and no-one is hurt, the police will not be required to write a report, but it is advisable to go to a nearby police station and explain what happened. A police report is required for insurance purposes. If an accident involves injury, a driver who does not stop and does not inform the police may face a prison sentence.

HITCHING

Hitching is never entirely safe in any country, and we don't recommend it. People who do choose to hitch will be safer if they travel in pairs and should let someone know where they are planning to go. Greece has a reputation for being a relatively safe place for women to hitch, but it is still unwise to do it alone and it's better to have a male companion. In Crete you don't hitch with your thumb up as in northern Europe, but with an outstretched hand, palm down to the road.

Getting out of major cities tends to be hard work; hitching is much easier in remote areas. On country roads, it is not unknown for someone to stop and ask if you want a lift even if you haven't asked for one (or to hail you for a ride).

LOCAL TRANSPORT
Bus

Local city buses operating from Iraklio, Rethymno and Hania largely service the suburbs and are not practical for getting around (most routes they serve are walkable anyway). Tickets are normally bought at *periptera* (kiosks) or on board the bus.

Taxi

Taxis are widely available except in remote villages, and are relatively cheap by European standards. Large towns have taxi stands that post a list of prices to outlying destinations, which removes any anxiety about overcharging. Otherwise you pay what's on the meter. Flag fall is €1 followed by €0.34 per km (€0.64 per km outside town or between midnight and 5am). There's a €2.15 surcharge from the airport and a €0.86 surcharge from a bus station or port. Each piece of luggage weighing more than 10kg carries a surcharge of €0.32, and there's a surcharge of €1.60 for radio taxis. Rural taxis often do not have meters, so you should always settle on a price before you get in.

Taxi drivers in Crete are, on the whole, friendly, helpful and honest. If you have a complaint, take the cab number and report it to the tourist police.

Health

CONTENTS

BEFORE YOU GO

Prevention is key to staying healthy while abroad. A little planning before departure, particularly for pre-existing illnesses, will save trouble later on. Bring medications in their original, clearly labelled, containers. A signed and dated letter from your physician describing your medical conditions and medications, including generic names, is a good idea (also see Warning, below). If carrying syringes or needles, be sure to have a physician's letter stating their medical necessity. If you're planning a long trip, make sure your teeth are OK and take your optical prescription with you.

INSURANCE

If you're an EU citizen, the European Health Insurance Card (which replaced the E111 form in 2006) covers you for most medical care but not for non-emergencies or for emergency repatriation. You can apply for one online in many EU countries via your government health department's website. Citizens from other countries should find out if there is a reciprocal arrangement for free medical care between their country and Greece. If you do need health insurance, make sure you get a policy that covers you for the worst possible scenario, such as an accident requiring an emergency flight home. Find out in advance if your insurance plan will make payments directly to providers or reimburse you later for overseas health expenditure.

RECOMMENDED VACCINATIONS

No jabs are required to travel to Greece, but a yellow-fever vaccination certificate is required if you are coming from an infected area. The World Health Organization (WHO) recommends that all travellers be covered for diphtheria, tetanus, measles, mumps, rubella and polio.

ONLINE RESOURCES

The WHO publication *International Travel and Health* is revised annually and is available online at www.who.int/ith. Other useful websites include www.mdtravelhealth.com (travel health recommendations for every country; updated daily), www.fitfortravel .scot.nhs.uk (general travel advice for the layperson), www.ageconcern.org.uk (advice on travel for the elderly) and www.mariest opes.org.uk (information on women's health and contraception).

WARNING

Codeine, which is commonly found in headache preparations, is banned in Greece; check labels carefully, or risk prosecution. There are strict regulations applying to the importation of medicines into Greece, so obtain a certificate from your doctor that outlines any medication you may have to carry into the country with you.

IN TRANSIT

DEEP VEIN THROMBOSIS (DVT)

Blood clots may form in the legs during plane flights, chiefly because of prolonged immobility (the longer the flight, the greater the risk). The chief symptom of DVT is swelling or pain of the foot, ankle, or calf, usually but not always on just one side. When a blood clot travels to the lungs, it

HEALTH

may cause chest pain and breathing difficulties. Travellers with any of these symptoms should immediately seek medical attention. To prevent the development of DVT on long flights you should walk about the cabin, contract the leg muscles while sitting, drink plenty of fluids and avoid alcohol, tobacco and caffeine. Compression socks are also being recommended for people at risk of DVT.

JET LAG

To avoid jet lag drink plenty of nonalcoholic fluids and eat light meals. Upon arrival, get exposure to natural sunlight and readjust your schedule (for meals, sleep, etc) as soon as possible.

IN CRETE

AVAILABILITY & COST OF HEALTH CARE

If you need an ambulance in Crete call ☎ 166. Crete's major cities of Iraklio, Hania and Rethymno have modern, well-equipped hospitals. Pharmacies can dispense medicines that are available only on prescription in most European countries, so you can consult a pharmacist for minor ailments.

All this sounds fine but, although medical training is of a high standard in Greece, the health service is badly under funded. Hospitals can be overcrowded, hygiene is not always what it should be and relatives are expected to bring in food for the patient – which could be a problem for a tourist. Conditions and treatment are better in private hospitals, which are expensive. All this means that a good health-insurance policy is essential.

TRAVELLER'S DIARRHOEA

If you develop diarrhoea, be sure to drink plenty of fluids, preferably in the form of an oral rehydration solution such as dioralyte. If diarrhoea is bloody, persists for more than 72 hours or is accompanied by fever, shaking, chills or severe abdominal pain you should seek medical attention.

ENVIRONMENTAL HAZARDS
Bites, Stings & Insect-Borne Diseases

Watch out for sea urchins around rocky beaches; if you get some of their needles embedded in your skin, olive oil will help to loosen them. If they are not removed they will become infected. Be wary also of jelly-fish, particularly during the months of September and October. Although they are not lethal in Greece, their stings can be painful. Dousing in vinegar will deactivate any stingers that have not 'fired'. Calamine lotion, antihistamines and analgesics may reduce the reaction and relieve the pain. Much more painful than either of these, but thankfully much rarer, is an encounter with the weever fish. It buries itself in the sand of the tidal zone with only its spines protruding, and injects a painful and powerful toxin if trodden on. Soaking your foot in very hot water (which breaks down the poison) should solve the problem. It can cause permanent local paralysis in the worst cases.

Greece's only dangerous snake is the adder. To minimize the possibilities of being bitten, always wear boots, socks and long trousers when walking through undergrowth where snakes may be present. Don't put your hands into holes and crevices, and be careful when collecting firewood. Snake bites do not cause instantaneous death and an antivenin is widely available. Keep the victim calm and still, wrap the bitten limb tightly, as you would for a sprained ankle, and attach a splint to immobilize it. Seek medical help, if possible taking the dead snake (or preferably a photo) with you for identification. Don't attempt to catch the snake if there is a possibility of being bitten again. Tourniquets and sucking out the poison are now comprehensively discredited.

Always check all over your body if you have been walking through a potentially tick-infested area as ticks can cause skin infections and other more serious diseases such as Lyme disease and typhus. If a tick is attached, press down around its head with tweezers, grab the head and gently pull upwards. Avoid pulling the rear of the body as this may squeeze the tick's gut contents into the skin, increasing the risk of infection and disease. Lyme disease begins with the spreading of a rash at the site of the bite, accompanied by fever, headache, extreme fatigue, aching joints and muscles and severe neck stiffness. If untreated, symptoms usually disappear but disorders of the nervous system, heart and joints can develop later. Treatment works best early in the illness – medical help should be sought. Typhus begins with a fever, chills, headache

nd muscle pains, followed a few days later
>y a body rash. There is often a large painful
ore at the site of the bite and nearby lymph
10des are swollen and painful. There is no
vaccine available.

Rabies is still found in Greece but only in
solated areas. Any bite, scratch or even lick
rom a warm-blooded, furry animal should
>e scrubbed with soap and running water
immediately and then cleaned with an alcohol
olution. If there is any possibility that the ani-
1al is infected medical help should be sought
immediately. Even if the animal is not rabid,
ill bites should be treated seriously as they can
>ecome infected or can result in tetanus.

Heatstroke

Heatstroke occurs following excessive fluid
oss and inadequate replacement of fluids and
alt. Symptoms include headache, dizziness
ind tiredness. Dehydration is already hap-
>ening by the time you feel thirsty – aim to
lrink sufficient water to produce pale, diluted
irine. To treat heatstroke drink water and/or
ruit juice, and cool the body with cold water
ind fans.

Hypothermia

Hypothermia occurs when the body loses
1eat faster than it can produce it. As ever,
>roper preparation will reduce the risks of
getting it. Even on a hot day in the moun-
1ains, the weather can change rapidly so
arry waterproof garments, warm layers
ind a hat, and inform other people of your
oute. Hypothermia starts with shivering,
loss of judgment and clumsiness. Unless
re-warming occurs, the sufferer deteriorates
into apathy, confusion and coma. Prevent
any further heat loss by seeking shelter,
putting on warm dry clothing, drinking
something hot and sweet, and sharing
body warmth.

TRAVELLING WITH CHILDREN

Make sure children are up to date with
routine vaccinations and discuss possible
travel vaccines well before departure as
some vaccines are not suitable for children
under a year old. Lonely Planet's *Travel with
Children* includes travel health advice for
younger children.

WOMEN'S HEALTH

Emotional stress, exhaustion and travelling
through different time zones can all contribute to an upset in the menstrual pattern.

If using oral contraceptives, remember
some antibiotics, diarrhoea and vomiting
can stop the pill from working. Time zones,
gastrointestinal upsets and antibiotics do not
affect injectable contraception.

Travelling during pregnancy is usually possible but always consult your doctor before
planning your trip. The most risky times for
travel are during the first 12 weeks of pregnancy and after 30 weeks.

SEXUAL HEALTH

Condoms are readily available but emergency
contraception may not be, so take the necessary precautions.

HEALTH

Language

CONTENTS

The Greek language is probably the oldest European language, with an oral tradition of 4000 years and a written tradition of approximately 3000 years. Its evolution over the four millennia was characterised by its strength during the golden age of Athens and the Democracy (mid-5th century BC); its use as a lingua franca throughout the Middle Eastern world, spread by Alexander the Great and his successors as far as India during the Hellenistic period (330 BC to AD 100); its adaptation as the language of the new religion, Christianity; its use as the official language of the Eastern Roman Empire; and its proclamation as the language of the Byzantine Empire (380–1453).

Greek maintained its status and prestige during the rise of the European Renaissance and was employed as the linguistic perspective for all contemporary sciences and terminologies during the period of Enlightenment. Today, Greek constitutes a large part of the vocabulary of any Indo-European language, and much of the lexicon of any scientific repertoire.

The modern Greek language is a southern Greek dialect which is now used by most Greek speakers both in Greece and abroad. It is the result of an intralinguistic influence and synthesis of the ancient vocabulary combined with words from Greek regional dialects, namely Cretan, Cypriot and Macedonian.

Greek is spoken throughout Greece by a population of around 10 million, and by some five million Greeks who live abroad.

PRONOUNCIATION

All Greek words of two or more syllable have an acute accent which indicates where the stress falls. For instance, άγαλμα (statue) is pronounced *aghalma*, and αγάπη (love) is pronounced *aghapi*. In the following transliterations, italic lettering indicate where stress falls. Note also that **dh** is pronounced as 'th' in 'then' and **gh** is a softer slightly guttural version of 'g'.

ACCOMMODATION

I'm looking for ...

psa·hno yi·a ...	Ψάχνω για ...
a room	
e·na dho·*ma*·ti·o	ένα δωμάτιο
a hotel	
e·na kse·no·dho·*chi*·o	ένα ξενοδοχείο
a youth hostel	
e·nan kse·*no*·na	έναν ξενώνα
ne·o·ti·tas	νεότητας

Where's a cheap hotel?
pou *i*·ne e·na fti·*no* xe·no·do·*hi*·o
Πού είναι ένα φτηνό ξενοδοχείο;
What's the address?
pya *i*·ne i dhi·*ef*·thin·si
Ποια είναι η διεύθυνση;
Could you write the address, please?
pa·ra·ka·*lo* bo·*ri*·te na *ghra*·pse·te ti· dhi·*ef*·thin·si
Παρακαλώ, μπορείτε να γράψετε τη διεύθυνση;
Are there any rooms available?
i·*par*·chun e·*lef*·the·ra dho·*ma*·ti·a
Υπάρχουν ελεύθερα δωμάτια;

I'd like to book ...

tha *i*·the·la na *kli*·so ...	Θα ήθελα να κλείσω ...
a bed	
e·na kre·*va*·ti	ένα κρεββάτι
a single room	
e·na mo·*no*·kli·o·no	ένα μονόκλινο
dho·*ma*·ti·o	δωμάτιο
a double room	
e·na *dhi*·kli·no	ένα δίκλινο
dho·*ma*·ti·o	δωμάτιο

LANGUAGE

THE GREEK ALPHABET & PRONUNCIATION

Greek	Pronunciation Guide		Example		
A α	a	as in 'father'	αγάπη	a-gha-pi	love
B β	v	as in 'vine'	βήμα	vi-ma	step
Γ γ	gh	like a rough 'g'	γάτα	gha-ta	cat
	y	as in 'yes'	για	ya	for
Δ δ	dh	as in 'there'	δέμα	dhe-ma	parcel
E ε	e	as in 'egg'	ένας	e-nas	one (m)
Z ζ	z	as in 'zoo'	ζώο	zo-o	animal
H η	i	as in 'feet'	ήταν	i-tan	was
Θ θ	th	as in 'throw'	θέμα	the-ma	theme
I ι	i	as in 'feet'	ίδιος	i-dhyos	same
K κ	k	as in 'kite'	καλά	ka-la	well
Λ λ	l	as in 'leg'	λάθος	la-thos	mistake
M μ	m	as in 'man'	μαμά	ma-ma	mother
N ν	n	as in 'net'	νερό	ne-ro	water
Ξ ξ	x	as in 'ox'	ξύδι	ksi-dhi	vinegar
O o	o	as in 'hot'	όλα	o-la	all
Π π	p	as in 'pup'	πάω	pa-o	I go
P ρ	r	as in 'road'	ρέμα	re-ma	stream
		a slightly trilled 'r'	ρόδα	ro-dha	tyre
Σ σ, ς	s	as in 'sand'	σημάδι	si-ma-dhi	mark
T τ	t	as in 'tap'	τόπι	to-pi	ball
Y υ	i	as in 'feet'	ύστερα	is-tera	after
Φ φ	f	as in 'find'	φύλλο	fi-lo	leaf
X χ	kh	as the 'ch' in Scottish 'loch', or like a rough 'h'	χάνω	kha-no	I lose
			χέρι	he-ri	hand
Ψ ψ	ps	as in 'lapse'	ψωμί	pso-mi	bread
Ω ω	o	as in 'hot'	ώρα	o-ra	time

Combinations of Letters
The combinations of letters shown here are pronounced as follows:

Greek	Pronunciation Guide		Example		
ει	i	as in 'feet'	είδα	i-dha	I saw
οι	i	as in 'feet'	οικόπεδο	i-ko-pe-dho	land
αι	e	as in 'bet'	αίμα	e-ma	blood
ου	u	as in 'mood'	πού	pou	who/what
μπ	b	as in 'beer'	μπάλα	ba-la	ball
	mb	as in 'amber'	κάμπος	kam-bos	forest
ντ	d	as in 'dot'	ντουλάπα	dou-la-pa	wardrobe
	nd	as in 'bend'	πέντε	pen-de	five
γκ	g	as in 'God'	γκάζι	ga-zi	gas
γγ	ng	as in 'angle'	αγγελία	an-ge-li̱a	announcement
γξ	ks	as in 'minks'	σφιγξ	sfinks	sphynx
τζ	dz	as in 'hands'	τζάκι	dza-ki	fireplace

The pairs of vowels shown above are pronounced separately if the first has an acute accent, or the second a dieresis, as in the examples below:

γαϊδουράκι	gai-dhou-ra-ki	little donkey
Κάιρο	kai-ro	Cairo

Some Greek consonant sounds have no English equivalent. The υ of the groups αυ, ευ and ηυ is generally pronounced 'v'. The Greek question mark is represented with the English equivalent of a semicolon ';'.

a room with a double bed

e·na dho·*ma*·ti·o me	ένα δωμάτιο με
dhi·plo kre·*va*·ti	διπλο κρεβάτι

a room with a bathroom

e·na dho·*ma*·ti·o me	ένα δωμάτιο με
ba·ni·o	μπάνιο

I'd like to share a dorm.

tha *i*·the·la na mi·ra·*sto* e·na ki·*no* dho·*ma*·ti·o me *al*·la *a*·to·ma

Θα ήθελα να μοιραστώ ένα κοινό δωμάτιο με άλλα άτομα

How much is it ...? *po·so ka*·ni ...	Πόσο κάνει ...;
per night ti ·vra·*dhya*	τη βραδυά
per person to *a*·to·mo	το άτομο

May I see it?

bo·*ro* na to dho	Μπορώ να το δω;

Where's the bathroom?

pou *i*·ne to·*ba*·ni·o	Πού είναι το μπάνιο;

I'm/We're leaving today.

fev·gho/*fev*·ghou·me	Φεύγω/φεύγουμε
si·me·ra	σήμερα

CONVERSATION & ESSENTIALS
Hello.

ya·sas (pol)	Γειά σας.
ya·su (inf)	Γειά σου.

Good morning.

ka·*li* me·ra	Καλή μέρα.

Good afternoon/evening.

ka·*li* spe·ra	Καλή σπέρα.

Good night.

ka·*li nikh*·ta	Καλή νύχτα.

Goodbye.

an·*di*·o	Αντίο.

Yes.

ne	Ναι.

No.

o·hi	Όχι.

Please.

pa·ra·ka·*lo*	Παρακαλώ.

Thank you.

ef·ha·ri·*sto*	Ευχαριστώ.

That's fine/You're welcome.

pa·ra·ka·*lo*	Παρακαλώ.

Sorry. (excuse me, forgive me)

sigh·*no*·mi	Συγγνώμη.

What's your name?

pos sas *le*·ne	Πώς σας λένε;

My name is ...

me *le*·ne ...	Με λένε ...

Where are you from?

a·*po* pou *i*·ste	Από πού είστε;

I'm from ...

i·me a·*po* ...	Είμαι από ...

I (don't) like ...

(dhen) ma·*re*·si ...	(Δεν) μ' αρέσει ...

Just a minute.

mi·*so* lep·*to*	Μισό λεπτό.

DIRECTIONS
Where is ...?

pou *i*·ne ...	Πού είναι...;

Straight ahead.

o·lo ef·*thi*·a	Ολο ευθεία.

Turn left.

strips·te a·ri·ste·*ra*	Στρίψτε αριστερά

Turn right.

strips·te dhe·ksi·*a*	Στρίψτε δεξιά

at the next corner

stin *e*po·me·ni gho·*ni*·a	στην επόμενη γωνία

at the traffic lights

sta *fo*·ta	στα φώτα

SIGNS

ΕΙΣΟΔΟΣ	Entry
ΕΞΟΔΟΣ	Exit
ΠΛΗΡΟΦΟΡΙΕΣ	Information
ΑΝΟΙΧΤΟ	Open
ΚΛΕΙΣΤΟ	Closed
ΑΠΑΓΟΡΕΥΕΤΑΙ	Prohibited
ΑΣΤΥΝΟΜΙΑ	Police
ΑΣΤΥΝΟΜΙΚΟΣ ΣΤΑΘΜΟΣ	Police Station
ΓΥΝΑΙΚΩΝ	Toilets (women)
ΑΝΔΡΩΝ	Toilets (men)

---

behind	*pi*·so	πίσω
in front of	bro·*sta*	μπροστά
far	ma·kri·*a*	μακριά
near (to)	kon·*da*	κοντά
opposite	a·*pe*·nan·di	απέναντι

acropolis	a·*kro*·po·li	ακρόπολη
beach	pa·ra·*li*·a	παραλία
bridge	*ye*fira	γέφυρα
castle	*ka*·stro	κάστρο
island	ni·*si*	νησί
main square	ken·*dri·ki*· pla·*ti*·a	κεντρική πλατεία
market	a·*gho*·ra	αγορά
museum	mu·*si*·o	μουσείο
old quarter	pa·li·*a* po·li	παλιά πόλη
ruins	ar·*he*·a	αρχαία
sea	tha·las·sa	θάλασσα
square	pla·*ti*·a	πλατεία
temple	na·os	ναός

TRANSLITERATION & VARIANT SPELLINGS: AN EXPLANATION

The issue of correctly transliterating Greek into the Latin alphabet is a vexed one, fraught with inconsistencies and pitfalls. The Greeks themselves are not very consistent in this respect, though things are gradually improving. The word 'Piraeus', for example, has been variously represented by the following transliterations: *Pireas*, *Piraievs* and *Pireefs*; and when appearing as a street name (eg Piraeus St) you will also find *Pireos*!

This has been compounded by the linguistic minefield of diglossy, or the two forms of the Greek language. The purist form is called *Katharevousa* and the popular form is *Dimotiki* (Demotic). The Katharevousa form was never more than an artificiality and Dimotiki has always been spoken as the mainstream language, but this linguistic schizophrenia means there are often two Greek words for each English word. Thus, the word for 'baker' in everyday language is *fournos*, but the shop sign will more often than not say *artopoieion*. The baker's product will be known in the street as *psomi*, but in church as *artos*.

A further complication is the issue of anglicised vs hellenised forms of place names: Athina vs Athens, Patra vs Patras, Thiva vs Thebes, Evia vs Euboia – the list goes on and on! Toponymic diglossy (the existence of both an official and everyday name for a place) is responsible for Kerkyra/Corfu, Zante/Zakynthos, and Santorini/Thira. In this guide we usually provide modern Greek equivalents for town names, with one well known exception, Athens. For ancient sites, settlements or people from antiquity, we have tried to stick to the more familiar classical names; so we have Thucydides instead of Thoukididis, Mycenae instead of Mykines.

Problems in transliteration have particular implications for vowels, especially given that Greek has six ways of rendering the vowel sound 'ee', two ways of rendering the 'o' sound and two ways of rendering the 'e' sound. In most instances in this book, **y** has been used for the 'ee' sound when a Greek *upsilon* (υ, Υ) has been used, and **i** for Greek *ita* (η, Η) and *iota* (ι, Ι). In the case of the Greek vowel combinations that make the 'ee' sound, that is οι, ει and υι, an **i** has been used. For the two Greek 'e' sounds αι and ε, an **e** has been employed.

As far as consonants are concerned, the Greek letter *gamma* (γ, Γ) appears as **g** rather than **y** throughout this book. This means that *agios* (Greek for male saint) is used rather than *ayios*, and *agia* (female saint) rather than *ayia*. The letter *fi* (φ, Φ) can be transliterated as either **f** or **ph**. Here, a general rule of thumb is that classical names are spelt with a **ph** and modern names with an **f**. So Phaistos is used rather than Festos, and Folegandros is used rather than Pholegandros. The Greek *chi* (χ, Χ) has usually been represented as **h** in order to approximate the Greek pronunciation as closely as possible. Thus, we have Haralambos instead of Charalambos and Polytehniou instead of Polytechniou. Bear in mind that the **h** is to be pronounced as an aspirated 'h', much like the 'ch' in 'loch'. The letter *kapa* (κ, Κ) has been used to represent that sound, except where well known names from antiquity have adopted by convention the letter **c**, eg Polycrates, Acropolis.

Wherever reference to a street name is made, we have omitted the Greek word *odos*, but words for avenue (*leoforos*, abbreviated *leof*) and square (*plateia*) have been included.

HEALTH

I'm ill.	*i·*me *a·*ro·stos	Είμαι άρρωστος.
It hurts here.	po·*nai·* e·*dho*	Πονάει εδώ.

I have ... / e·ho ... / Εχω ...

asthma / *asth·*ma / άσθμα

diabetes / za·ha·ro·dhi·a·*vi·*ti / ζαχαροδιαβήτη

diarrhoea / dhi·*a·*ri·a / διάρροια

epilepsy / e·pi·lip·*si·*a / επιληψία

I'm allergic to ... / *i·*me a·ler·yi·*kos*/ a·ler·yi·*ki* ... (m/f) / Είμαι αλλεργικός/ αλλεργική ...

antibiotics / sta an·di·vi·o·ti·*ka* / στα αντιβιωτικά

aspirin / stin a·spi·*ri·*ni / στην ασπιρίνη

penicillin / stin pe·ni·ki·*li·*ni / στην πενικιλλίνη

bees / stis *me·*li·ses / στις μέλισσες

nuts / sta fi·*sti·*ki·a / στα φυστίκια

condoms	pro·fi·la·kti·*ka* (ka·*po*·tez)	προφυλακτικά (κάποτες)
contraceptive medicine	pro·fi·lak·ti·*ko* *farm*·a·ko	προφυλακτικό φάρμακο
sunblock cream	*kre*·ma i·*li*·u	κρέμα ηλίου
tampons	tam·*bon*	ταμπόν

LANGUAGE DIFFICULTIES

Do you speak English?
mi·*la*·te an·gli·*ka*   Μιλάτε Αγγλικά;
Does anyone speak English?
mi·*lai* ka·*nis* an·gli·*ka*   Μιλάει κανείς αγγλικά;
How do you say ... in Greek?
ps *le*·ghe·te ... sta   Πώς λέγεται ... στα
el·li·ni·*ka*   ελληνικά;
I understand.
ka·ta·la·*ve*·no   Καταλαβαίνω.
I don't understand.
dhen ka·ta·la·*ve*·no   Δεν καταλαβαίνω.
Please write it down.
ghrap·ste to pa·ra·ka·*lo*   Γράψτε το, παρακαλώ.
Can you show me on the map?
bo·*ri*·te na mo·u to   Μπορείτε να μου το
dhi·xe·te sto *har*·ti   δείξετε στο χάρτη;

NUMBERS

0	mi·*dhen*	μηδέν
1	*e*·nas	ένας (m)
	mi·a	μία (f)
	e·na	ένα (n)
2	*dhi*·o	δύο
3	tris	τρεις (m&f)
	tri·a	τρία (n)
4	*te*·se·ris	τέσσερεις (m&f)
	te·se·ra	τέσσερα (n)
5	*pen*·de	πέντε
6	*e*·xi	έξη
7	ep·*ta*	επτά
8	oh·*to*	οχτώ
9	*e*·*ne*·a	εννέα
10	*dhe*·ka	δέκα
20	*ik*·o·si	είκοσι
30	tri·*an*·da	τριάντα
40	sa·*ran*·da	σαράντα
50	pe·*nin*·da	πενήντα
60	*exin*·da	εξήντα
70	ev·dho·*min*·da	εβδομήντα
80	oh·*dhon*·da	ογδόντα
90	*eneninda*	ενενήντα
100	e·ka·*to*	εκατό
1000	*hi*·li·i	χίλιοι (m)
	hi·li·ez	χίλιες (f)
	hi·li·a	χίλια (n)
2000	*dhi*·o chi·*li*·a·dhez	δυό χιλιάδες

EMERGENCIES

Help!
vo·*i*·thya   Βοήθεια!
There's been an accident.
ey·i·ne a·*ti*·hi·ma   Έγινε ατύχημα.
Go away!
fi·ye   Φύγε!

Call ...!   fo·*nak*·ste ...   Φωνάξτε ...!
   a doctor   *e*·na yi·a·*tro*   ένα γιατρό
   the police   tin a·sti·no·*mi*·a   την αστυνομία

PAPERWORK

name
o·no·ma·te·*po*·ni·mo   ονοματεπώνυμο
nationality
i·pi·ko·o·*ti*·ta   υπηκοότητα
date of birth
i·me·ro·mi·*ni*·a   ημερομηνία
yen·*ni*·se·os   γεννήσεως

place of birth
to·pos yen·*ni*·se·os   τόπος γεννήσεως
sex (gender)
fil·lon   φύλον
passport
dhia·va·*ti*·ri·o   διαβατήριο
visa
vi·za   βίζα

QUESTION WORDS

Who/Which?
pi·*os*/pi·*a*/pi·*o* (sg m/f/n)   Ποιος/Ποια/Ποιο;
pi·*i*/pi·*es*/pi·*a* (pl m/f/n)   Ποιοι/Ποιες/Ποια;
Who's there?
pi·*os* i·ne e·*ki*   Ποιος είναι εκεί;
Which street is this?
pi·*a* o·*dhos* i·ne af·*ti*   Ποια οδός είναι αυτή;
What?
ti   Τι;
What's this?
ti i·ne af·*to*   Τι είναι αυτό;
Where?
pu   Πού;
When?
po·te   Πότε;
Why?
yi·a·*ti*   Γιατί;
How?
pos   Πώς;
How much?
po·so   Πόσο;
How much does it cost?
po·so ka·*ni*   Πόσο κάνει;

HOPPING & SERVICES

d like to buy ...		
the·lo n'a·gho·ra·so ...	Θέλω ν' αγοράσω ...	
ow much is it?		
po·so ka·ni	Πόσο κάνει;	
don't like it		
dhen mu a·re·si	Δεν μου αρέσει.	
Aay I see it?		
bo·ro na to dho	Μπορώ να το δω;	
m just looking.		
ap·los ki·ta·zo	Απλώς κοιτάζω.	
t's cheap.		
i·ne fti·no	Είναι φτηνό	
t's too expensive.		
i·ne po·li a·kri·vo	Είναι πολύ ακριβό.	
ll take it.		
tha to pa·ro	Θα το πάρω	

o you accept ...?	dhe·che·ste ...	Δέχεστε ...;
credit cards	pi·sto·ti·ki kar·ta	πιστωτική κάρτα
travellers	tak·si·dhi·o·ti·kes	ταξιδιωτικές
cheques	e·pi·ta·ghes	επιταγές

nore	pe·ri·so·te·ro	περισσότερο
ess	li·gho·te·ro	λιγότερο
maller	mi·kro·te·ro	μικρότερο
igger	me·gha·li·te·ro	μεγαλύτερο

'm looking for ...	psach·no ya ...	Ψάχνω για ...
a bank	mya tra·pe·za	μια τράπεζα
the church	tin ek·kli·si·a	την εκκλησία
the city centre	to ken·dro tis po·lis	το κέντρο της πόλης
the ... embassy	tin ... pres·vi·a	την ... πρεσβεία
the market	ti· lai·ki· a·gho·ra	τη λαϊκή αγορά
the museum	to mu·si·o	το μουσείο
the post office	to ta·chi·dhro·mi·o	το ταχυδρομείο
a public toilet	mya dhi·mo·sia tu·a·let·ta	μια δημόσια τουαλέτα
the telephone centre	to ti·le·fo·n·i·ko ken·dro	το τηλεφωνικό κέντρο
the tourist office	to tu·ri·st·iko ghra·fi·o	το τουριστικό γραφείο

TIME & DATES

What time is it?	ti o·ra i·ne	Τι ώρα είναι;
It's (2 o'clock).	i·ne (dhi·o i· o·ra)	είναι (δύο η ώρα).
in the morning	to pro·i	το πρωί
in the afternoon	to a·po·yev·ma	το απόγευμα
in the evening	to vra·dhi	το βράδυ
When?	po·te	Πότε;
today	si·me·ra	σήμερα
tomorrow	av·ri·o	αύριο
yesterday	hthes	χθες

Monday	dhef·te·ra	Δευτέρα
Tuesday	tri·ti	Τρίτη
Wednesday	te·tar·ti	Τετάρτη
Thursday	pemp·ti	Πέμπτη
Friday	pa·ras·ke·vi	Παρασκευή
Saturday	sa·va·to	Σάββατο
Sunday	kyri·a·ki	Κυριακή

January	ia·nou·ar·i·os	Ιανουάριος
February	fev·rou·ar·i·os	Φεβρουάριος
March	mar·ti·os	Μάρτιος
April	a·pri·li·os	Απρίλιος
May	mai·os	Μάιος
June	i·ou·ni·os	Ιούνιος
July	i·ou·li·os	Ιούλιος
August	av·ghous·tos	Αύγουστος
September	sep·tem·vri·os	Σεπτέμβριος
October	ok·to·vri·os	Οκτώβριος
November	no·em·vri·os	Νοέμβριος
December	dhe·kem·vri·os	Δεκέμβριος

TRANSPORT
Public Transport

What time does the ... leave/ arrive?	ti o·ra fev·yi/ fta·ni to ...	Τι ώρα φεύγει/ φτάνει το ...;
boat	pli·o	πλοίο
(city) bus	a·sti·ko	αστικό
(intercity) bus	le·o·fo·ri·o	λεωφορείο
plane	ae·ro·pla·no	αεροπλάνο
train	tre·no	τραίνο

I'd like a (a) ...	tha i·the·la (e·na) ...	Θα ήθελα (ένα) ...
one way ticket	a·plo isi·ti·ri·o	απλό εισιτήριο
return ticket	i·si·ti·ri·o me e·pi·stro·fi	εισιτήριο με επιστροφή
1st class	pro·ti· the·si	πρώτη θέση
2nd class	def·te·ri the·si	δεύτερη θέση

I want to go to ...
the·lo na pao sto/sti...
Θέλω να πάω στο/στη ...
The train has been cancelled/delayed.
to tre·no a·ki·rothi·ke/ka·thi·ste·ri·se
Το τραίνο ακυρώθηκε/καθυστέρησε

the first		
to pro·to	το πρώτο	
the last		
to te·lef·te·o	το τελευταίο	
platform number		
a·rithmos a·po·va·thras	αριθμός αποβάθρας	
ticket office		
ek·dho·ti·ri·o i·si·ti·ri·on	εκδοτήριο εισιτηρίων	

LANGUAGE

timetable

dhro·mo·*lo*·gio   δρομολόγιο

train station

si·dhi·ro·dhro·mi·*kos*   σιδηροδρομικός
stath·*mos*   σταθμός

Private Transport

I'd like to hire a ...	tha *i*·the·la na ni·ki·*a*·so ...	Θα ήθελα να νοικιάσω ...
car	e·na af·ti·*ki*·ni·to	ένα αυτοκίνητο
4WD	e·na tes·se·ra e·pi tes·se·ra	ένα τέσσερα επί τέσσερα
(a jeep)	(e·na tzip)	(ένα τζιπ)
motorbike	mya mo·to·si·*klet*·ta	μια μοτοσυ·κλέττα
bicycle	e·na po·*dhi*·la·to	ένα ποδήλατο

Is this the road to ...?

af·*tos* i·ne o *dhro*·mos ya ...
Αυτός είναι ο δρόμος για ...

Where's the next service station?

pu *i*·ne to e·*po*·me·no ven·zi·*na*·dhi·ko
Πού είναι το επόμενο βενζινάδικο;

Please fill it up.

ye·*mi*·ste to pa·ra·ka·*lo*
Γεμίστε το, παρακαλώ.

I'd like (30) euros worth.

tha *i*·the·la (30) ev·ro
Θα ήθελα (30) ευρώ.

diesel	pet·*re*·le·o *ki*·ni·sis	πετρέλαιο κίνησης
leaded petrol	su·per	σούπερ
unleaded petrol	a·*mo*·liv·dhi	αμόλυβδη

Can I park here?

bo·*ro* na par·*ka*·ro e·*dho*
Μπορώ να παρκάρω εδώ;

Where do I pay?

pu pli·*ro*·no
Πού πληρώνω;

Lonely planet phrasebooks

Greek

with 3500-word two-way dictionary

Also available from Lonely Planet:
Greek Phrasebook

ROAD SIGNS	
ΠΑΡΑΚΑΜΨΗ	Detour
ΑΠΑΓΟΡΕΥΕΤΕΑΙ Η ΕΙΣΟΔΟΣ	No Entry
ΑΠΑΓΟΡΕΥΕΤΑΙ Η ΠΡΟΣΠΕΡΑΣΗ	No Overtaking
ΑΠΑΓΟΡΕΥΕΤΑΙ ΗΣΤΑΘΜΕΥΣΗ	No Parking
ΕΙΣΟΔΟΣ	Entrance
ΜΗΝ ΠΑΡΚΑΡΕΤΕ ΕΔΩ	Keep Clear
ΔΙΟΔΙΑ	Toll
ΚΙΝΔΥΝΟΣ	Danger
ΑΡΓΑ	Slow Down
ΕΞΟΔΟΣ	Exit

The car/motorbike has broken down (at ...)

to af·to·*ki*·ni·to/mo·to·si·*klet*·ta cha·la·se sto ...
Το αυτοκίνητο/η μοτοσυκλέττα χάλασε στο ...

The car/motorbike won't start.

to af·to·*ki*·ni·to/mo·to·si·*klet*·ta dhen *per*·ni· bros
Το αυτοκίνητο/η μοτοσυκλέττα δεν παίρνει μπρος.

I have a flat tyre.

e·pa·tha *la*·sti·cho
Επαθα λάστιχο.

I've run out of petrol.

e·mi·na a·*po* ven·*zi*·ni
Εμεινα από βενζίνη.

I've had an accident.

e·pa·tha a·*ti*·chi·ma
Επαθα ατύχημα.

TRAVEL WITH CHILDREN

Is there a/an ...?	i·*par*·chi ...	Υπάρχει ...;
I need a/an ...	chri·a·zo·me ...	Χρειάζομαι ...
baby change room	me·ros nal·*lak*·so to mo·*ro*	μέρος ν'αλλάξω το μωρό
car baby seat	ka·this·ma ya mo·*ro*	κάθισμα για μωρό
child-minding service	ba·bi sit·ter	μπέιμπι σίττερ
children's menu	me·*nu* ya pe·dhya	μενού για παιδία
(disposable) nappies/diapers	pan·nez Pam·pers	πάννες Pampers
(English-speaking) babysitter	ba·bi sit·ter pu mi·*la* an·ghl·ika	μπέιμπι σίττερ που μιλά αγγλικά
highchair	pe·dhi·*ki* ka·*rek*·la	παιδική καρέκλα
potty	yo·yo	γιογιό
stroller	ka·rot·*sa*·ki	καροτσάκι

Do you mind if I breastfeed here?

bo·*ro* na thi·*la*·so e·*dho*
Μπορώ να θηλάσω εδώ;

Are children allowed?

e·pi·*tre*·pon·de ta pe·dhya
Επιρέπονται τα παιδιά;

LANGUAGE

Glossary

Achaean civilisation – see *Mycenaean civilisation*

acropolis – highest point of an ancient city

agia (f), agios (m), agii (pl) – saint(s)

agora – commercial area of an ancient city; shopping precinct in modern Greece

amphora – large two-handled vase in which wine or oil was kept

architrave – part of the *entablature* that rests on the columns of a temple

arhontika – 17th- and 18th-century-AD mansions that belonged to arhons, the leading citizens of a town

baglama – miniature *bouzouki* with a tinny sound

basilica – early Christian church

bouleuterion – council house

bouzouki – stringed lute-like instrument associated with *rembetika* music

bouzoukia – any nightclub where the *bouzouki* is played and low-grade folk songs are sung; see also *skyladika*

Byzantine Empire – characterised by the merging of Hellenistic culture and Christianity and named after Byzantium, the city on the Bosphorus that became the capital of the Roman Empire in AD 324; when the Roman Empire was formally divided in AD 395, Rome went into decline and the eastern capital, renamed Constantinople after Emperor Constantine I, flourished; the Byzantine Empire dissolved after the fall of Constantinople to the Turks in 1453

caïque – small, sturdy fishing boat

capital – top of a column

cella – room in a temple where the cult statue stood

choregos – wealthy citizen who financed choral and dramatic performances

classical Greece – period in which the Greek city-states reached the height of their wealth and power after the defeat of the Persians in the 5th century BC; ended with the decline of the city-states as a result of the Peloponnesian Wars, and the expansionist aspirations of Philip II, King of Macedon (r 359–336 BC) and his son, Alexander the Great (r 336–323 BC)

Corinthian – order of Greek architecture recognisable by columns with bell-shaped capitals with sculpted elaborate ornaments based on acanthus leaves

cornice – the upper part of the *entablature*, extending beyond the *frieze*

cyclopes – mythical one-eyed giants

dark age (1200–800 BC) – period in which Greece was under the rule of the *Dorians*

delfini – dolphin; common name for hydrofoil

dimarhio – town hall

Dimotiki – Demotic Greek language; the official spoken language of Greece

domatio (s), domatia (pl) – room; a cheap form of accommodation in most tourist areas

Dorians – Hellenic warriors who invaded Greece around 1200 BC, demolishing the city-states and destroying the Mycenaean civilisation; heralded Greece's *dark age*, when the artistic and cultural advancements of the Mycenaeans and Minoans were abandoned; the Dorians later developed into land-holding aristocrats, encouraging the resurgence of independent city-states led by wealthy aristocrats

Doric – order of Greek architecture characterised by a column that has no base, a fluted shaft and a relatively plain capital, when compared with the flourishes evident on *Ionic* and *Corinthian* capitals

ELPA – Elliniki Leshi Periigiseon & Aftokinitou; Greek motoring and touring club

ELTA – Ellinika Tahydromia; Greek post office

entablature – part of a temple between the tops of the columns and the roof

EOS – Ellinikos Orivatikos Syllogos; the association of Greek Mountaineering Clubs

EOT – Ellinikos Organismos Tourismou; Greek National Tourism Organisation

Epitaphios – structure depicting Christ on his bier, decorated for the Easter procession

estiatorio – restaurant

faïence – an ancient glazing technique that uses quartz instead of glass

Filiki Eteria – friendly society; a group of Greeks in exile; formed during Ottoman rule to organise an uprising against the Turks

fluted – of a column having vertical indentations on the shaft

FPA – foros prostithemenis axias; Value Added Tax, or VAT

frieze – part of the *entablature*, which is above the architrave

galaktopoleio (s), galaktopoleia (pl) – a shop that sells dairy products

Geometric period (1200–800 BC) – the period characterised by pottery decorated with geometric designs; sometimes referred to as Greece's *dark age*

Hellas, Ellas or Ellada – the Greek name for Greece

Hellenistic period – prosperous, influential period

of Greek civilisation ushered in by Alexander the Great's empire-building and lasting until the Roman sacking of Corinth in 146 BC

hora – main town, usually on an island

iconostasis – altar screen embellished with icons

ikonostasia – miniature chapels

Ionic – order of Greek architecture characterised by a column with truncated flutes and capitals with ornaments resembling scrolls

kafeneio (s), kafeneia (pl) – traditionally a male-only coffee house where cards and backgammon are played

kalderimi – cobbled footpath

kastro – caste, fortress, bastion

katholikon – principal church of a monastic complex

kefi – an indefinable feeling of good spirit, without which no Greek can have a good time

kilimia – flat-woven rugs that were traditional dowry gifts

Koine – Greek language used in pre-Byzantine times; the language of the church liturgy

kore – female statue of the Archaic period; see also *kouros*

kouros – male statue of the Archaic period, characterised by a stiff body posture and enigmatic smile

kri-kri – endemic Cretan animal similar to a goat

KTEL – Kino Tamio Eispraxeon Leoforion; national bus cooperative, which runs all long-distance bus services

labrys – double-axe symbol of Minoan civilization

lammergeier – bearded vulture

leoforos – avenue

libation – in ancient Greece, wine or food that was offered to the gods

Linear A – Minoan script; so far undeciphered

Linear B – Mycenaean script; has been deciphered

lyra – small violin-like instrument, played on the knee; common in Cretan and Pontian music

malaka – literally 'wanker'; used as a familiar term of address, or as an insult, depending on context

manga – 'wide boy' or 'dude'; originally a person of the underworld, now any streetwise person

mandinada (s), mandinades (pl) – traditional Cretan rhyming song/s, often with improvised lyrics

mayirefta – pre-made casseroles and bakes served at *tavernas* and other eateries

megaron – central room of a Mycenaean palace

meltemi – northeasterly wind that blows throughout much of Greece in the summer

metope – sculpted section of a Doric *frieze*

mezedopoleio – *mezes* restaurant

mezes (s), mezedes (pl) – appetiser/s

Minoan civilisation (3000–1200 BC) – Bronze Age culture of Crete named after the mythical King Minos

and characterised by pottery and metalwork of great beauty and artisanship; it has three periods: Protopalatial (3400–2100 BC), Neopalatial (2100–1580 BC) and Postpalatial (1580–1200 BC)

mitata – round stone shepherd's huts

moni – monastery or convent

Mycenaean civilisation (1900–1100 BC) – first great civilisation of the Greek mainland, characterised by powerful independent city-states ruled by kings; also known as the *Achaean civilisation*

narthex – porch of a church

Nea Dimokratia – New Democracy; conservative political party

necropolis – literally 'city of the dead'; ancient cemetery

nomarhia – prefecture building

nomos – prefectures into which the regions and island groups of Greece are divided

nymphaeum – in ancient Greece, building containing a fountain and often dedicated to nymphs

odeion – ancient Greek indoor theatre

odos – street

OTE – Organismos Tilepikinonion Elladas; national telephone carrier

oud – a bulbous, stringed instrument with a sharply raked-back head

ouzeri – place that serves ouzo and light snacks

Panagia – Mother of God; name frequently used for churches

Pandokrator – painting or mosaic of Christ in the centre of the dome of a Byzantine church

pandopoleio – general store

paralia – waterfront

parapente – paragliding

pediment – triangular section, often filled with sculpture above the columns, found at the front and back of a classical Greek temple

periptero (s), periptera (pl) – street kiosk

peristyle – columns surrounding a building, usually a temple or courtyard

pinakothiki – picture gallery

pithos (s), pithoi (pl) – large Minoan storage jar

plateia – square

propylon (s), propylaia (pl) – elaborately built main entrance to an ancient city or sanctuary; a propylon had one gateway and a propylaia more than one

prytaneion – the administrative centre of the city-state

raki – Crete's fiery spirit, distilled from grapes

rembetika – blues songs commonly associated with the underworld of the 1920s

rhyton – another name for a *libation* vessel

rizitika – traditional, patriotic songs of western Crete

santouri – hammered dulcimer from Asia Minor

skyladika – literally 'dog songs' (and the venues they're sung in); popular, but not lyrically challenging, often sung in *bouzoukia* nightclubs

spileo – cave

stele (s), stelae (pl) – gravestone that stands upright

stoa – long colonnaded building, usually in an *agora*; used as a meeting place and shelter in ancient Greece

tahydromio (s), tahydromia (pl) – post office

taverna – traditional restaurant that serves food and wine

temblon – votive screen

tholos – Mycenaean tomb shaped like a beehive

toumberleki – small lap drum played with the fingers

triglyph – sections of a Doric *frieze* between the *metopes*

trireme – ancient Greek galley with three rows of oars on each side

tsikoudia – also called raki, the Cretan distilled spirit from grapes

volta – promenade; evening stroll, outing or excursion

volute – spiral decoration on *Ionic* capitals

Behind the Scenes

THIS BOOK

This guidebook was commissioned in Lonely Planet's London office. The 1st edition was written in 2000 by Jeanne Oliver. Paul Hellander wrote the 2nd edition in 2002 and Victoria Kyriakopoulos wrote the 3rd edition in 2005. This 4th edition was produced by the following:

Commissioning Editor Sally Schafer
Coordinating Editor Shawn Low
Coordinating Cartographer Anthony Phelan
Coordinating Layout Designer Jacqui Saunders
Managing Editor Melanie Dankel
Managing Layout Designer Celia Wood
Managing Cartographer Mark Griffiths
Assisting Editors Janice Bird, Michael Day, Margged Helioz, Rowan McKinnon, Susan Paterson
Cover Designer Travis Drever
Project Manager Sarah Sloane

Language Content Coordinator Quentin Frayne
Thanks to David Burnett, Mark Germanchis, Michala Green, Lisa Knights, Adam McCrow

THANKS
VICTORIA KYRIAKOPOULOS

This book is dedicated to the memory of Leon Zingiris.

My heartfelt thanks to the many people who welcomed and steered me throughout Crete. Their advice, tips, assistance and generous hospitality are greatly appreciated. Special thanks to Sonia Panagiotidou, Lefteris Karatarakis, Dimitris Skoutelis and Maya, Dimitris Kornaros in Iraklio; Yiannis Genetzakis in Arhanes; the Patramani family in Episkopi; Manolis Klironomakis in Paleohora; Vasilis Karamanlis in Makriyialos; Giannis Labouskos and Iakovos Sourgoutsidis in Hania (where the late Tony

---

LONELY PLANET: TRAVEL WIDELY, TREAD LIGHTLY, GIVE SUSTAINABLY

The Lonely Planet Story

The story begins with a classic travel adventure: Tony and Maureen Wheeler's 1972 journey across Europe and Asia to Australia. There was no useful information about the overland trail then, so Tony and Maureen published the first Lonely Planet guidebook to meet a growing need.

From a kitchen table, Lonely Planet has grown to become the largest independent travel publisher in the world, with offices in Melbourne (Australia), Oakland (USA) and London (UK). Today Lonely Planet guidebooks cover the globe. There is an ever-growing list of books and information in a variety of media. Some things haven't changed. The main aim is still to make it possible for adventurous individuals to get out there – to explore and better understand the world.

The Lonely Planet Foundation

The Lonely Planet Foundation proudly supports nimble nonprofit institutions working for change in the world. Each year the foundation donates 5% of Lonely Planet company profits to projects selected by staff and authors. Our partners range from Kabissa, which provides small nonprofits across Africa with access to technology, to the Foundation for Developing Cambodian Orphans, which supports girls at risk of falling victim to sex traffickers.

Our nonprofit partners are linked by a grass-roots approach to the areas of health, education or sustainable tourism. Many projects we support – such as one with BaAka (Pygmy) children in the forested areas of Central African Republic – choose to focus on women and children as one of the most effective ways to support the whole community.

Sometimes foundation assistance is as simple as helping to preserve a local ruin like the Minaret of Jam in Afghanistan; this incredible monument now draws intrepid tourists to the area and its restoration has greatly improved options for local people.

Just as travel is often about learning to see with new eyes, so many of the groups we work with aim to change the way people see themselves and the future for their children and communities.

Fennymore was sorely missed); Giorgos Niotakis and Sifis Papadakis in Agios Nikolaos; Pavlos and Renata Myssor in Sitia; Nikos Perakis and Elias Pagianidis in Zakros and Manolis Tambakos in Ierapetra. Special thanks for their expertise to Alexander MacGillivray and Nikki Rose in Crete and Yiorgos Xylouris in Athens.

I am especially grateful for the support of Eleni Bertes, Antonis Bekiaris, and all the crew at Vox in Athens. In Melbourne, thanks to John and Suzie Rerakis, Bill Kyriakopoulos and Chris, Sam and Nikolas Anastassiades.

OUR READERS

Many thanks to the travellers who used the last edition and wrote to us with helpful hints, useful advice and interesting anecdotes:

Gillian Anderson, Antonio Asenjo, Ludo Beckers, Jim Beffa, Magnus Birkhorst, Ray Burston, Brynn Canfield, Carolyn Devine, Alexander Douglas, John Douglas, John. A Dougles, Guy Fearon, Stratos Giannikos, Nikos Grivakis, Jörg Kahl, Peter Lauf, Sarah Lawson, Gregory Mantell, Robert Nylén, Joerg Oehlenschlaeger, Marie Pritchard, Sheila Reynolds, Jo Richards, Andrew Thompson, Roger Tully, Roman Virdi, Nichola Walker, Nadia Wechsler

ACKNOWLEDGMENTS

Many thanks to the following for the use of their content:

Globe on title page ©Mountain High Maps 1993 Digital Wisdom, Inc.

Internal photographs: p5 Juergen Richter/LOOK Die Bildagentur der Fotografen GmbH/Alamy; p8 (#6) IML Image Group Ltd/Alamy; p10 (#1) Jochem Wijnands/Picture Contact/Alamy; p11 (#7) Victoria Kyriakopoulos; p12 IML Image Group Ltd/Alamy. All other photographs by Lonely Planet Images, and p6, (#1, #2) Neil Setchfield; p7 (#3) John Elk III; p7 (#5) Neil Setchfield; p8 (#7) Linda Musick; p9 (#4), p11 (#6), Jon Davison; p9 (#1) Chris Christo; p10 (#4) Diana Mayfield.

All images are the copyright of the photographers unless otherwise indicated. Many of the images in this guide are available for licensing from Lonely Planet Images: www.lonelyplanetimages.com.

SEND US YOUR FEEDBACK

We love to hear from travellers – your comments keep us on our toes and help make our books better. Our well-travelled team reads every word on what you loved or loathed about this book. Although we cannot reply individually to postal submissions, we always guarantee that your feedback goes straight to the appropriate authors, in time for the next edition. Each person who sends us information is thanked in the next edition – and the most useful submissions are rewarded with a free book.

To send us your updates – and find out about Lonely Planet events, newsletters and travel news – visit our award-winning website: **www.lonelyplanet.com/contact**.

Note: we may edit, reproduce and incorporate your comments in Lonely Planet products such as guidebooks, websites and digital products, so let us know if you don't want your comments reproduced or your name acknowledged. For a copy of our privacy policy visit www.lonelyplanet.com/privacy.

Index

INDEX

000 Map pages
000 Photograph pages

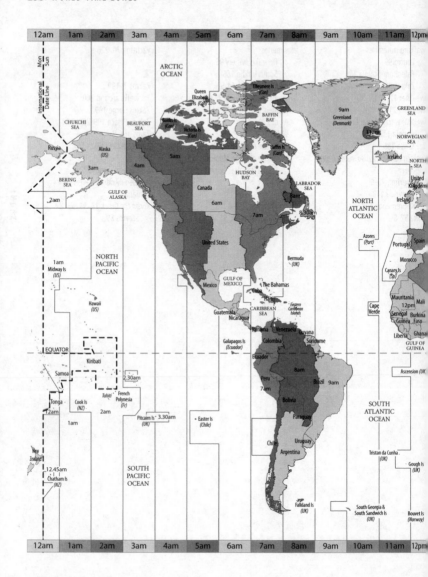

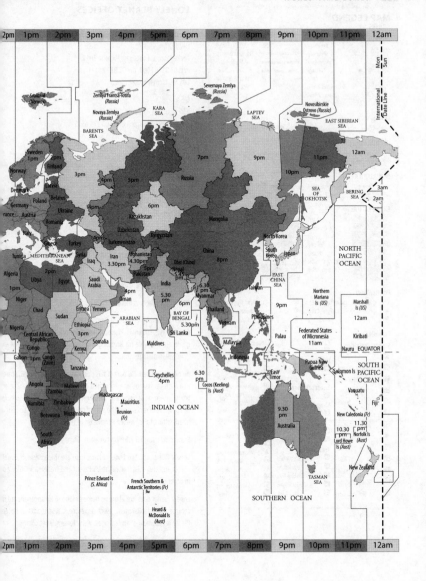

BIBLIO RPL Life

6 - JUIN 2008

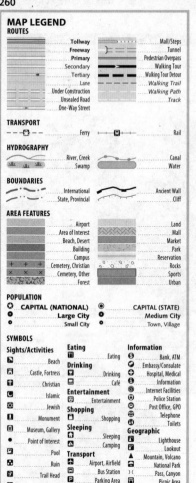

MAP LEGEND
ROUTES

	Tollway		Mall/Steps
	Freeway		Tunnel
	Primary		Pedestrian Overpass
	Secondary		Walking Tour
	Tertiary		Walking Tour Detour
	Lane		Walking Trail
	Under Construction		Walking Path
	Unsealed Road		Track
	One-Way Street		

TRANSPORT

	Ferry		Rail

HYDROGRAPHY

	River, Creek		Canal
	Swamp		Water

BOUNDARIES

	International		Ancient Wall
	State, Provincial		Cliff

AREA FEATURES

	Airport		Land
	Area of Interest		Mall
	Beach, Desert		Market
	Building		Park
	Campus		Reservation
	Cemetery, Christian		Rocks
	Cemetery, Other		Sports
	Forest		Urban

POPULATION

◎	CAPITAL (NATIONAL)	◉	CAPITAL (STATE)
●	Large City	●	Medium City
●	Small City	○	Town, Village

SYMBOLS

Sights/Activities
- Beach
- Castle, Fortress
- Christian
- Islamic
- Jewish
- Monument
- Museum, Gallery
- Point of Interest
- Pool
- Ruin
- Trail Head
- Winery, Vineyard
- Zoo, Bird Sanctuary

Eating
- Eating

Drinking
- Drinking
- Café

Entertainment
- Entertainment

Shopping
- Shopping

Sleeping
- Sleeping
- Camping

Transport
- Airport, Airfield
- Bus Station
- Parking Area
- Petrol Station
- Taxi Rank

Information
- Bank, ATM
- Embassy/Consulate
- Hospital, Medical
- Information
- Internet Facilities
- Police Station
- Post Office, GPO
- Telephone
- Toilets

Geographic
- Lighthouse
- Lookout
- Mountain, Volcano
- National Park
- Pass, Canyon
- Picnic Area
- Shelter, Hut
- Waterfall

LONELY PLANET OFFICES

Australia
Head Office
Locked Bag 1, Footscray, Victoria 3011
☎ 03 8379 8000, fax 03 8379 8111
talk2us@lonelyplanet.com.au

USA
150 Linden St, Oakland, CA 94607
☎ 510 893 8555, toll free 800 275 8555
fax 510 893 8572
info@lonelyplanet.com

UK
2nd Floor, 186 City Road,
London, EC1V 2NT
☎ 020 7106 2100, fax 020 7841 9001
go@lonelyplanet.co.uk

Published by Lonely Planet Publications Pty Ltd
ABN 36 005 607 983

© Lonely Planet Publications Pty Ltd 2008

© photographers as indicated 2008

Cover photograph: Road shrine in Lefka Ori (White Mountains
Diana Mayfield/Lonely Planet Images. Many of the images in th
guide are available for licensing from Lonely Planet Images: ww
.lonelyplanetimages.com.

All rights reserved. No part of this publication may be copied, store
in a retrieval system, or transmitted in any form by any means, elec
tronic, mechanical, recording or otherwise, except brief extracts fc
the purpose of review, and no part of this publication may be sold c
hired, without the written permission of the publisher.

Printed by Hang Tai Printing Company, China

Lonely Planet and the Lonely Planet logo are trademarks of Lonel
Planet and are registered in the US Patent and Trademark Office an
in other countries.

Lonely Planet does not allow its name or logo to be appropriated b
commercial establishments, such as retailers, restaurants or hotels
Please let us know of any misuses: www.lonelyplanet.com/ip.

BIBLIO RPL Ltée

G - JUIN 2008

Although the authors and Lonely Planet have taken
all reasonable care in preparing this book, we make
no warranty about the accuracy or completeness of
its content and, to the maximum extent permitted,
disclaim all liability arising from its use.